PRAISE FOR THE MARATHON DON'T STOP

"Rob Kenner was part of the original editorial team who brought my vision for *Vibe* to reality, and during his seventeen years at the magazine he always did outstanding work. Since then, we've both been on a mission to document hip-hop culture with nothing but love and respect. Rob is MY dude, and *The Marathon Don't Stop* is a beautiful tribute to a legendary artist. Keep on keepin' on my brother. We need your work!"

—Quincy Jones

"The assassination of Nipsey Husssle was, in many ways, the death of modern classical hip-hop. In death, Nipsey's star has risen to the heavens. Rob Kenner illuminates the artist's mortal side while artfully unpacking his humble beginnings and momentous victories. You see his flowers in bloom, in Technicolor, then and now. Behold."

—Sacha Jenkins, filmmaker

"With *The Marathon Don't Stop: The Life and Times of Nipsey Hussle*, Rob Kenner has given us the book the world—and hip-hop and pop culture—has been waiting for. It is a powerfully written and reported biography of a life gone too soon, yes. But it is also history, sociology, psychology, and a case study of what is humanly possible, even for those of us born with very little. This is one of the finest pieces of literature about a real life I've ever read, and one that should be celebrated alongside the best biographies ever about iconic figures we have loved—and lost."

—Kevin Powell, author of *When We Free the World*

"What made Rob one of my favorite editors and my primary long-form collaborator was his insightful eye, his innate sense of story, and his ability to appreciate the importance of minutiae as they relate to a larger narrative. He brings all of those skills to the forefront with this incredible book. Not only do you walk way appreciating Nipsey's work, love for his community, and yes, hustle, but Rob also paints a sensitive portrait of Ermias the man. God rose inside of this man, and Rob captures every moment."

—Cheo Hodari Coker, author of *Unbelievable: The Life, Death, and Afterlife of The Notorious B.I.G.*

"An extraordinary accomplishment: a book about a rapper, a neighborhood, business and ownership, racism, immigration, friendship, family, art, and love . . . from the Pacific Ocean to the Red Sea. A masterclass in music journalism's higher calling, *The Marathon Don't Stop* is a book not only for Nipsey Hussle fans, but for anyone who wants to understand the brutal and beautiful truths of the country called America. Rob Kenner has been to the mountaintop, and brought the word back down for the rest of us."

—Peter Relic, coauthor of *For Whom the Cowbell Tolls: 25 Years of Paul's Boutique*

"From the cradle to the grave, *The Marathon Don't Stop: The Life and Times of Nipsey Hussle* is a deep dive into the man, music, and motivation of one of the most gifted rappers to emerge from the West in decades. More than a hustler, Nipsey Hustle was both a businessman and teacher who was equally inspired by family, the streets, and the motherland. With an eye for the real, writer Rob Kenner has composed a biography that is journalistically solid, cinematically vivid, as gritty as the streets of Crenshaw, and beautiful as a rose growing through concrete."

—Michael A. Gonzales, coauthor of *Bring the Noise: A Guide to Rap Music and Hip-Hop Culture*

"A rigorously reported, gripping account of how Ermias Joseph Asghedom hustled his way into the hearts and minds of millions. Veteran journalist Rob Kenner takes us on a harrowing journey, from the embattled streets of South L.A. to the ancient shores of East Africa to tell the story of a conflicted gang member, gifted hip-hop artist, and crafty businessman who devoted his life to transforming himself and his community by any means necessary."

—Carter Harris, screenwriter, producer, and former editor at *The Source* and *VIBE* magazines

THE MARATHON DON'T STOP

The Life and Times of Nipsey Hussle

ROB KENNER

ATRIA BOOKS

New York · London · Toronto · Sydney · New Delhi

ATRIA
BOOKS

An Imprint of Simon & Schuster, Inc.
1230 Avenue of the Americas
New York, NY 10020

First Atria Books hardcover edition March 2021

ATRIA BOOKS and colophon are trademarks of Simon & Schuster, Inc.

For information about special discounts for bulk purchases, please contact Simon &
Schuster Special Sales at 1-866-506-1949 or business@simonandschuster.com.

The Simon & Schuster Speakers Bureau can bring authors to your live event. For more
information or to book an event, contact the Simon & Schuster Speakers Bureau at
1-866-248-3049 or visit our website at www.simonspeakers.com.

Interior design by Timothy Shaner, NightandDayDesign.biz

Manufactured in the United States of America

10 9 8 7 6 5 4 3 2 1

Library of Congress Cataloging-in-Publication Data has been applied for.

ISBN 978-1-9821-4029-8
ISBN 978-1-9821-4031-1 (ebook)

For Hugh Kenner, my first and best teacher.

"Time is now fleeting, the moments are passing,
passing from you and from me."

"The main thing you got to remember is that everything in the world is a hustle."

—Freddie in *The Autobiography of Malcolm X* (1964)

———————

2PAC OF MY GENERATION
BLUE PILL IN THE FUCKIN' MATRIX
RED ROSE IN THE GRAY PAVEMENT
YOUNG BLACK NIGGA TRAPPED AND HE CAN'T CHANGE IT
KNOW HE A GENIUS, HE JUST CAN'T CLAIM IT
'CAUSE THEY LEFT HIM NO PLATFORMS TO EXPLAIN IT

—Nipsey Hussle, "Dedication," *Victory Lap* (2018)

CONTENTS

TOP OF THE TOP

WHEN IT'S ALL OVER ALL THAT COUNTS IS HOW THE STORY'S TOLD
SO WRITE MY NAME DOWN, WRITE MY AIM DOWN
TO DO THIS MY WAY AND CARVE MY OWN LANE OUT

—Nipsey Hussle, "Outro," *The Marathon Continues* (2011)

Lauren London walked gracefully to the podium inside the Staples Center, wearing a long white dress and dark glasses. This building held many fond memories for her and Nipsey Hussle. They loved sitting together courtside at Lakers games. Only two months earlier she'd come here with him for the sixty-first annual Grammy Awards when his official debut, *Victory Lap*, was nominated for Best Rap Album. Lauren had worn white that night too; Nipsey was regal in his black tux and velvet loafers with gold tassels. A red carpet correspondent said the couple looked like they were on top of a wedding cake. "Wow, okay, we'll take that," Nip replied.[1] Boog just smiled. He called her Boog, short for L-Boogie. Eventually she would go by a new name. "Forever and even after," she declared, "call me Lady Hussle."[2]

The vibe was different as she crossed the stage on April 11, 2019. Had she ever heard the place so quiet?

On this occasion Lauren was accompanied by Samantha Smith, Hussle's younger sister. Nip's close friend, "shadow," and longtime bodyguard J Roc towered behind them in a black suit and matching cap, his golden All Money In medallion glinting over his black tie. Nip's little homie BH stood by silently, a blue rag tied around his braids. At the center of the stage, Lauren's beloved lay in a casket like a fallen king, surrounded by a profusion of blue, white, and purple flowers beneath an oversize AMI logo. "Never was I prepared for anything like this," she began. "So bear with me, y'all."[3]

Unseen voices cried out, offering support from all over the cavernous arena. *Take your time, Lauren!*

On a large screen above her appeared a portrait of Hussle and Boog glowing together on the set of his "Double Up" video, in which he played a hustler on the rise and she played the girlfriend who tries to learn the game but folds under pressure—a far cry from the strength she was showing now. On either side of that image was Awol Erizku's full-length portrait of Nipsey from "California Love," the magical photo spread about "the people's champ of West Coast hip-hop and New New from *ATL*" that appeared in *GQ* magazine soon after the Grammys. The piece was a rare public celebration of this intensely private power couple. "Our Grandchildren will frame this," Lauren wrote when she shared an image from the story on Instagram. There she sat, resplendent on a white horse in the streets of the Crenshaw District, her man by her side like some valiant knight from a storybook, Nip Hussle the Great. Their life seemed very much like a fairy tale at that precise moment. And then on March 31, everything changed.

With their three beautiful children, generations of extended family, and another twenty thousand or so mourners hanging on every word, Lauren somehow made it through her eulogy without breaking down. A million and one emotions flashed across her face as she spoke. "I know everyone's hurting," she said, "but I'd like to say something to my city, Los Angeles. Y'all from L.A., stand up."

Without hesitation, twenty thousand people moved as one, rising and cheering for her, for Hussle, for themselves. "Because this pain is really ours," she said. "We know what Nip meant to us. We lost an incredible soul, we lost someone very rare to us, and we lost a real one. And we won't ever be the same."

Lauren's voice grew just a little bit stronger as she began channeling Hussle's words: "He used to always say this," she said with a confident flourish. "The game is gonna test you. Never fold. Stay ten toes down. It's not on you; it's *in* you. And what's in you they can't take away. And he's in *all* of us."

Sparked by the spirit, the Staples Center erupted in applause once more. Lauren let the sound die down before continuing, in a softer voice now. Hand on heart, she directed her closing remarks to her man. "And to Ermias, the love of my life, you know what it is," she said. "Grief is the final act of love. My heart hears you. I feel you everywhere. I'm so grateful that I had you. I love you beyond this earth, and until we meet again, the Marathon continues!"

CIRCLE GOT SMALLER, EVERYBODY CAN'T GO

—Nipsey Hussle, "Victory Lap," *Victory Lap* (2018)

Hussle's three-word rallying cry and the #TMC hashtag have become a universally recognized inspirational mantra. At this point "the Marathon" is much more than the title of a mixtape

series or the name of the successful business that Hussle and his
brother Blacc Sam built brick by brick in the heart of a community where so many others had given up. "While most folks look
at the Crenshaw neighborhood where he grew up and see only
gangs, bullets, and despair," Barack Obama wrote in his tribute
to Hussle, "Nipsey saw potential."[4]

The final musical performance at the Celebration of Life was
"Real Big," one of the first songs Hussle recorded for his debut
album, *Victory Lap*. Standing at the foot of the casket, Marsha
Ambrosius summoned all her strength and sang cascades of color-
atura through a black veil as Hussle's mother danced with the
ancestors, *Ase! Ase!* Her son's voice floated in through the Staples
Center sound system, blending with Marsha's voice almost like
they did on the album, which had seen a 2,776 percent spike in
sales since Hussle's murder.[5] "I knew one day I would do it real
big," Nipsey Hussle *sang*. "Real shit, real shit, I know all my real
niggas feel this."

It was all too much for Ralo Stylez. "I got up out of there,"
says Hussle's high school classmate, who became one of his earliest musical collaborators. "That song made me cry, bro. I couldn't
listen to it after he died. That song is our story. He really summed
up the whole feeling of what it's like to be from over here." As the
coproducer of standout *Victory Lap* tracks "Dedication" and "Young
Niggas," Ralo benefits financially from the explosion of interest in
Hussle's music, but he's not content with the money. "I'm embit-
tered by it," he says. "If I get a check, I'll be happy, then I'll cry, and
then I'll spend the money real fast. It's a destructive energy on my
life," he says with a mirthless laugh. "Just because of the connotation of what's involved and how this all went down. Like 'Damn,
why didn't they give him this respect while he was alive?'"[6]

The Marathon is the ultimate test of endurance in every
sense: mentally, physically, emotionally, spiritually, economically.

It represents competing in the race of life and being in it to win it, against all odds, for the duration—much longer than 26.2 miles. "That's why we call it a Marathon," Hussle explained. "Cause we ran a lot of laps."[7] It was a race Nipsey Hussle was determined to win by all means necessary, and he wanted to see his whole community in the winner's circle with him. Still, the Marathon is not a team sport. You can get support from your crew and train together, but nobody else can run those laps for you. Even in a crowded field, the long-distance runner goes it alone, testing their character and spirit as much as their physical limits, pushing for a personal best, competing against themselves and the clock. *Tick-tick-tick.*

Before Hussle rebranded the ultimate Olympic event, the concept of the marathon had a long history rooted in sacrifice and struggle. According to legend, the footrace was inspired by Pheidippides, a young messenger who was dispatched from a bloodstained battlefield in the ancient city of Marathon, where vastly outnumbered Greek troops miraculously defeated invading forces sent by the mighty Persian empire in 490 BC. After running all the way to Athens—a distance of some 150 miles, nearly six modern-day marathons—the exhausted messenger announced the glorious victory, then collapsed and died on the spot. The tragic story inspired paintings and poetry, and eventually the race was created as a way to honor Pheidippides's heroism.[8]

Going the distance meant summoning the courage to confront one's fears. "It stands for stayin' down," Hussle said. "Not quittin', acceptin' the ups and downs of whatever game you commit yourself to and ridin' it out, you feel me? Because that's the reality of success or greatness, that it comes with a roller coaster ride."[9]

Nobody saw Nipsey Hussle coming. Not just in the sense of his being a "slept-on rapper," although he was that too—especially outside of Los Angeles. The whole world slept on Nipsey. The rap game slept. The media slept. Even his own neighborhood slept on that man. He deserved more support than he got. More airplay. More respect. Less police harassment. Less hate—and more life. Most of all he deserved more life.

Few recognized the audacity of his vision until it began to unfold. Blinded by low expectations, many mistook this tatted-up Slauson Boy, who repped East Africa as hard as he did the Rollin' 60s Neighborhood Crips, for your average aspirational street entrepreneur. They overlooked his discipline, underestimated his focus, miscalculated his capacity to hustle and motivate, to study and model self-empowerment and "get it straight up out the mud." Even though it was written right there on his face: PROLIFIC. And just below that, by his right temple: GOD WILL RISE.

That the man born Ermias Asghedom possessed the resilience to overcome the post-traumatic stress of urban warfare and build a positive, productive life is a blessing. That he would go on to disrupt not just music industry business models but long-standing cycles of racial and economic oppression—and share his process step by step so that others might replicate it—is truly remarkable. That anyone could do all of that without turning his back on his neighborhood, or his set, would seem pretty much impossible, until Nipsey Hussle showed and proved that it could be done.

There's really no other rapper, dead or alive, who accomplished the things that he did. When Nipsey decided to sell physical copies of his *Crenshaw* mixtape for $100 each, people said he was crazy. Impressed by the brilliance and the arrogance of this move, Jay-Z bought 100 copies for a total of $10,000 and instructed his Life&Times blog to report on the purchase. "When Jay tapped into the wave, everybody became a believer,"

Nipsey told me with a smile. The two had their first conversation not long after that. "He told me 'I just bought a streaming company,'" Nipsey recalled. "And that became Tidal."[10]

It made sense that Jay would be one of the first to recognize Nipsey's business acumen. Like Jay before him, Nipsey was a student of the rap game—not just how to make powerful music but how to extract wealth from a system that was designed to exploit content creators. He'd soaked up the case studies of other hip-hop executives who built independent empires from the streets—James Prince's Rap-A-Lot, E-40's Sick Wid It, Master P's No Limit, and yes, Jay-Z and Dame Dash's Roc-A-Fella. He'd drawn inspiration from Puffy's entrepreneurial achievements beyond music and watched Dr. Dre diversify his business portfolio with the billion-dollar Beats by Dre play. He'd followed the astute investments of artists like 50 Cent, whose Vitamin Water deal made him tens of millions overnight, and Chamillionaire, who's now a full-time venture capitalist. But even as he borrowed pages from all of their playbooks, Nipsey did something nobody had done before. True to his slogan "All Money In," he became the first hip-hop entrepreneur to reinvest 100 percent of his business interests back into the streets that raised him. He was unrepentantly gangster, all about his paper, and utterly committed to his hood.

More than a rapper, more than a businessman, Hussle was a cultural activist, a philanthropist, a role model and leader for young Black men seeking to overcome a troubled past and achieve greatness.

Applying lessons learned from the corner of South Crenshaw Boulevard and West Slauson Avenue, from his family in Eritrea, and from a lifetime of voracious reading and information gathering, Nip set up a comprehensive strategy, developing an infrastructure to build generational wealth for himself, his family, and eventually the whole Crenshaw District. The all-too-familiar rap-star narrative of pursuing new business ventures while turning your back on the streets that raised you did not apply to Nipsey. His was a vision that went way beyond handing out turkeys on Thanksgiving.

"He said he was the people's champ," Blacc Sam told me. "The people in the area were the first people who supported him, so he was very prideful and he just wanted to always be around and inspire. As a youngster he never respected people that made it and left . . . It was much bigger for him. It wasn't, 'I'ma get some money and leave.' It was, 'I'ma achieve my goals and bring things that's bigger than music. I'm gonna be at the forefront of a movement.'"[11]

The businesses and organizations Hussle and his partners established changed countless lives, providing jobs and opportunities for many residents of South L.A., including people with criminal records who would have found it hard to secure employment elsewhere. Through his support of the Our Opportunity economic stimulus program, he opened a state-of-the-art coworking space that included a business incubator and classes in science, technology, engineering, and mathematics (STEM), giving bright kids in the area a chance to develop their talents that he never had. Hussle also supported social justice initiatives like Time Done, a program to assist ex-convicts rebuilding their lives, as well as civic programs such as the public art installation and cultural awareness project Destination Crenshaw. In short, Hussle put on for his city like few other rappers in history.

"You can divide hip-hop entrepreneurship into a bunch of different categories," says Dan Charnas, author of *The Big Payback: The History of the Business of Hip-Hop*. "You have the home-grown capitalists like Master P and J. Prince, who start with a record store and then fold it into a personal company and then broaden horizontally. You have the super-capitalists like Jay-Z, Puffy, and 50, who do all their deals upward. They're trying to do joint ventures with the capitalistic cloud, and they stay in those clouds. What's interesting about Nipsey Hussle is that his capitalism was activism. He was doing redevelopment, and that's very, very different from a Jay-Z on the one hand and a Master P on the other. Nipsey was an interesting combination of capitalist and activist on a scale that I don't think hip-hop has ever produced before. But you shine too bright, you see what they do to you."[12]

Much of the world wouldn't catch on until it was too late. Then they all lined up to light a candle, lay a rose at the altar, or post a photo with a checkered-flag emoji.

✅

SHIT CAN CHANGE YOUR LIFE, MY NIGGA
TAKE YOU A LONG WAY

—Nipsey Hussle, "Rap Music," *Bullets Ain't Got No Name Vol. 3* (2009)

The first time I met Nipsey Hussle, in the Wall Street offices of *Vibe* magazine in late 2009, it was clear there was something special about him. His aura lit up the conference room. His braids were flawless. His Jordans were crisp. His *Bullets Ain't Got No Name* mixtapes were as hard as anything out of L.A. since the rise of Death Row.

I was old enough to appreciate his rap name, a sly reference to Nipsey Russell—the Black actor and comedian who worked his way up from serving burgers at the Atlanta drive-in restaurant The Varsity, to Vaudeville and late-night TV. Russell became a fixture on 1970s game shows and celebrity roasts, cracking jokes with the likes of Dean Martin and Don Rickles. Famous for reciting humorous and political poems on TV, Russell went on to play the Tin Man opposite Michael Jackson and Diana Ross in *The Wiz*.

All that stuff was before Nipsey's time, of course. He was blessed with his rap name by Baby Gooch, one of the elder homies from the set who was impressed with the young man's mind as well as his grind—both on the streets and as an aspiring artist. Back then a write-up in the pages of *Vibe* might have seemed like a dream, but Hussle made it a goal, set his mind to it, and took steps to realize that goal. "Nipsey used to submit for new rapper of the month in *Vibe*," one of his early mentors, Dexter Browne, told me years later. "He got his music and his little picture and he sent it in. He was like 'Man, I'm hoping.'"[13]

I was a founding editor of Quincy Jones's monthly magazine *Vibe*, established in 1992 when Ermias Asghedom was seven years old. Although I was completely unaware of Hussle's submissions to our Next section, being slept on did not deter him in the least. Nip's persistence was undeniable, unconquerable. Somehow he'd hustled his way into a major label deal and made it all the way to *Vibe*'s New York City offices in person. Now that I was in his presence, the intensity of his focus was palpable. I could tell dude was on a mission, but I didn't know the half.

As with the ancient parable of the blind men and the elephant, most of us in the hip-hop media were unable to comprehend the fullness of Nipsey Hussle at first. The picture he was painting was bigger than any canvas, any wall. Outside the frame of fame, beyond the box of beats and bars, his vision was grander than most could even imagine. "Gangsta rapper," they called him. "Street entrepreneur," they said. "Six-Owe Crip." Meanwhile Hussle kept on running laps, flying under the radar, handling his business day after day with minimal external validation.

Like Dan Freeman, the revolutionary hero of one of his favorite books, Sam Greenlee's *The Spook Who Sat by the Door*,

Nipsey Hussle understood that the system would underestimate him. He was cool with that—made peace with it early on, used it to his advantage. Flying under the radar suited him. Fame never really interested him anyway. His was a higher calling. Tangible results—ownership, freedom, justice—those were the things he valued.

The lanky twenty-four-year-old's energy was electric from the moment he introduced himself, making sure to mention both the Rollin' 60s Neighborhood Crips and the notorious Los Angeles intersection where he'd made his name: Crenshaw and Slauson. The beat to Snoop Dogg's classic "Gin & Juice" was soon thundering through the conference room speakers as track 13 on *Bullets Ain't Got No Name Vol. 1*, "Dre Jackin' for Beats," sent me and *Vibe*'s whole editorial staff on a ride down G-funk memory lane.

Having edited Snoop's first *Vibe* cover back in 1993, I felt an overwhelming sense of déjà vu. And in the year of "Stanky Legg" and "Swag Surfin'," Nipsey's hard-hitting West Coast sound was more than a little refreshing. I was not the first nor would I be the last to note the resemblance between Hussle and Snoop in spirit, appearance, and gang affiliation. Moreover, on this particular record he was channeling the Doggfather's flow. "With so much drama in the RSC," Nip rapped (substituting the Rollin' 60s Crips initials for Snoop's Long Beach shout-out), "most of these niggas in L.A. ain't got the heart to beef."

A lesser MC might have hesitated to revisit such a timeless track, but Nip laid down his lyrics with cool bravado, making the song his own and leaving no question that he was willing and able to stand behind every word.

The young man could spit. His bars were loaded with internal rhymes, clever metaphors, and visual detail. Plus, the young hoodsta's "tiny loc" mindset was tempered with knowledge of self and a hard-earned mistrust for the LAPD, one of the most notoriously corrupt, abusive, and racist police forces in America. Blessed with natural charisma, Hussle spoke with the confidence that comes from knowing that you're a rising star in your city and that you're backed by one of L.A.'s most powerful street organizations.

Nipsey and I had a brief conversation before he and his team left for their next appointment. Laughing off the Snoop comparison, he mentioned that he'd recently collaborated with the Cali rap legend. I gave him a pound and told him I looked forward to hearing more music from him in the future. Hussle's persistence paid off; he did finally get his write-up in the magazine. We ran a one-page profile on Hussle shortly before *Vibe* folded, falling victim to outmoded business models and a reluctance to embrace new technologies that were transforming the media landscape. Meanwhile, Hussle had foreseen the digital revolution and was already exploiting it to maximum benefit.

BEFORE YOU RUN YOUR RACE YOU GOTTA FIND A PACE
JUST MAKE SURE YOU CROSS THE LINE AND FUCK THE TIME IT TAKES
—Nipsey Hussle, *"Perfect Timing"* (2018)

The last time I spoke with Nip was February 22, 2018, not quite a week after the debut of *Victory Lap*. After a good deal of back-and-forth with my editorial colleagues at *Mass Appeal*, I was able to convince the powers that be to book Hussle for an on-camera interview. Everybody had their own social media strategies and concepts, but I was certain Hussle would come through and drop gems if given the chance. He did not disappoint.

While I already knew the man was about his grind, I was

slightly taken aback when Atlantic Records publicity manager
Brittany Bell set up a 9:30 a.m. call time for our interview. I have
been a hip-hop journalist since 1992, and never in my career had
I interviewed any artist before 10 a.m., unless they were calling
in from another time zone. This was my first clue that Nipsey
was moving on a whole different modus operandi. The early call
time made sense. Hussle had been looking forward to dropping
his official debut for a very long time. Now that it was finally
happening, he was going to make sure to roll it out *properly*. He'd
even given up smoking weed for the past several months and
stopped drinking soda. The man was focused.

After showing up five minutes early, Hussle settled on the
studio couch with a mug of green tea. He was dressed in a simple
gray sweatsuit with no visible jewelry, though I could hear his
links clinking when he sipped his tea. I remarked that he'd grown
quite a beard since the last time I saw him.

I congratulated Nip on what was looking like a strong debut
for *Victory Lap*. "We ain't really get the numbers back yet," he
said, "but it's lookin' good, lookin' good. We in that Top Ten
most likely. I ain't really been focusing on the charts after the first
couple days, like the iTunes chart." Last time that he checked,
Victory Lap was hanging tough in the Top 3. "We'll see what
happens," he said. "Tomorrow gon' make a week."[14]

The album would officially debut at number 4 on *Billboard*,
racking up 53,000 album equivalent units in its opening week.
I remarked that the journey to this moment had not been a
short one.

"Nah, it's been a Marathon," he replied. "Most definitely."

As I pointed out, he was used to Marathon mode. "Considering the amount of work that you've given us," I said, "it's crazy
to think that this is your debut album." He explained that he
wanted his official debut album—the first one he'd ever mixed

and mastered and gone to retail with—to be called *Victory Lap*. For him the name symbolized the completion of the *Marathon* mixtape trilogy, the waving of the checkered flag. It also marked the end of the completely independent doing-it-on-our-own mode. "I wanted *Victory Lap* to represent successfully establishing a new partnership that was in our favor this time," he said. "More in the direction of what we came in trying to establish, to be a label ourself." He said that he first began talking about *Victory Lap* around 2012, and that some of the songs on the album had been in the works almost that long.

One of those early songs was "Dedication," the fifth track on *Victory Lap*. That was the one where he referred to himself as the "2Pac of my generation," a big statement, to say the least. Descended from members of the Black Panther Party, Tupac Shakur was one of the most compelling, complex, and controversial artists hip-hop has ever seen, a powerful and iconic figure who belonged on any rap fan's Mount Rushmore. I asked Nipsey what he meant by the comparison.

"I know that was a big statement," he replied calmly. "I was speaking on his intentions. Pac was like a Trojan horse for the streets." Now used to describe innocent-looking computer programs that contain malware or a virus, the original Trojan Horse was a clever strategy described in Virgil's *Aeneid* whereby ancient Greek warriors hid inside a giant wooden horse that was presented to Troy as a gift. The Trojans lowered their defenses and accepted the gift, allowing the Greeks to conquer them. "Pac was highly intelligent," Nipsey explained, "but in our culture—street culture, especially in this generation—intelligence was viewed as a form of weakness. *Oh he's smart*—that's almost the opposite of strong. It's less of that now, but it still exists. There's still a taboo against speaking intelligent, representing intelligence."

His Trojan horse metaphor got me thinking about Hussle's

public image when he first entered the rap game. The first thing most people heard about him was that he was a "gangsta rapper" from L.A. who was down with the Rollin' 60s. And while breathless reports that he was really "about that life" were not untrue, there was much more to his story. Few people were aware that Hussle's first rap name was Concept, or that as a teenager he was an overtly "conscious" MC known for thought-provoking songs like "Nigga Nonfiction."

"Before any success, before any notoriety, before Epic Records, before Atlantic Records, before the gang, he was already doing some rap shit," says Ralo, who flew to Atlanta with Hussle in 2002 at Afeni Shakur's invitation. "We was already out of town on the airplane. We was already taking trips. You hear me?" The purpose of that particular trip was to perform at the release party for Tupac Shakur's posthumous album *Better Days*. "That really should be the highlight when you tell the story about Nip," says Ralo. "In the formative years of his artistry, Afeni and Mtulu Shakur gravitated to him in a supernatural manner." Ralo laughs that mirthless laugh again. "I feel like I'm lying and I know I ain't. It feels like fairy tale shit."[15]

When I heard the news of Nipsey Hussle's murder on March 31, 2019, amid the shock and sadness, my mind flashed back to our final conversation. Some have suggested that Nipsey calling himself the "2Pac of my generation" was some sort of eerie premonition, but Hussle had too much to live for to focus on an untimely death. "Obviously they'll both go down as legends," says E.D.I. Mean, Tupac's childhood friend. A member of the groups Dramacydal and Outlaw Immortalz, E.D.I. Mean collaborated on "Hit 'em Up," one of Pac's most incendiary diss tracks. "But for the most part I think they're two very different individuals who left this planet at two very different points in their life. Pac's transition was super early and Nip really had a chance to impact the world, and L.A. more specifically, because obviously he was here longer."[16]

When people talk about Tupac's accomplishments, they speak about his potential, sometimes referencing Detroit Red's transition into Malcolm X. But Nipsey didn't just rap about changing the world or talk about it in interviews. He was patiently taking steps to make it happen, in ways no other rapper, dead or alive, had ever done before. Hussle's commitment to channel the power of hip-hop back into the community that created it hearkens back to the culture's origins in the South Bronx, when groups of Black and brown youth channeled their frustration away from gang violence and toward creative expression. In this respect Hussle's lifelong work may represent the ultimate fulfillment of hip-hop's true purpose.

It's clear that the Marathon Nipsey started will continue. The phenomenal outpouring of love and grief in the wake of his senseless murder—an atrocity that was captured on video and beamed around the world like the Rodney King beating or the murder of George Floyd—sparked similarly profound reactions.

Hussle's powerful music and the vision that informed it have gone on to inspire millions, and its fulfillment will be his enduring legacy—a legacy that continues to unnerve the powers that be while motivating those excluded from power. As America experiences a great reckoning over its own legacy of racism and oppression, Hussle has emerged as an iconic figure comparable to Pac, Bob Marley, or Malcolm X. During nationwide marches and protests, his music, particularly "FDT," the protest anthem he recorded with YG back when the possibility of Trump being elected seemed like a bad joke, has become the soundtrack for a new resistance movement.

Despite ongoing attempts to throw dirt on his name, at this point it hardly seems worth debating whether or not Hussle is a hip-hop legend. "I'm not saying I'm gonna rule the world or I'm gonna change the world," Tupac Shakur said in a 1994 interview with MTV, broadcast when Ermias Asghedom was nine years old. "But I guarantee you that I will spark the brain that will change the world."[17] Pac would not live to see his twenty-sixth birthday, but looking back on his statement with the benefit of 20/20 hindsight, Hussle may well have been the person Pac had in mind. When it comes to his legacy, the Marathon will never stop.

Chapter 1

TRUE STORY

IT WAS ALL A DREAM . . .

—The Notorious B.I.G., "Juicy," released in 1994, when Ermias Asghedom was nine

Nipsey Hussle stood tall in the blazing Los Angeles sunshine wearing an immaculate white T-shirt, blue snapback cap turned to the back, and a few kilos of 14-karat gold Cuban links draped around his neck. Just behind him in the doorway to The Marathon Clothing smart store stood his big brother, Blacc Sam; his godbrother Adam Andebrhan; their business partner Fatts; and longtime head of security J Roc. They were surrounded by hundreds of friends, family, and honored guests, including NBA star Russell Westbrook, Atlanta rapper 21 Savage, and Emory "Vegas" Jones of Roc Nation—not to mention the love of Hussle's life, actress Lauren London. Slauson Avenue was shut down for two blocks west of Crenshaw Boulevard. The police were outside. But on June 17, 2017, the parking lot was full of love.

"This was always one of our dreams, to be able to come inside," explained Nipsey, who once described the shopping plaza at Slauson and Crenshaw to *Forbes* magazine as "a hub for local entrepreneurs."[1] Neighborhood Nip perfected his hustle on this stretch of asphalt, progressing from a young G's perspective to become an inspirational figure in the community. Illicit transactions gave way to poppin' the trunk of his car and pumping his own self-produced CDs with Magic Marker lettering. "Just out of bein' there for so long, we realized that it would make sense to be owners or have businesses," he said. "It was an important intersection, a lot of commerce goin' on. And it made sense. If we can actually get in here, we'll be able to really elevate what we tryin' to do."

"Nip coulda taken his money and opened up a store anywhere," said L.A. radio personality Big Boy, standing next to Hussle for the ribbon-cutting ceremony that kicked off the store's grand opening. "But of course you know real recognize real and he chose to stay at the crib."[2] Billed as "the world's first smart store," The Marathon Clothing was like nothing else in Hyde Park, a close-knit but economically disenfranchised area on South L.A.'s west side. The new business represented a quantum leap forward from their previous business, Slauson Tees, formerly a hole-in-the-wall beauty supply shop with rotting carpet that Blacc Sam and Fatts took over and renovated in the mid-2000s. Beyond the hardwood floors, crown molding, and a curated retail experience befitting a boutique on Melrose, what truly set the new space apart was the technology.

"We need to make this the Apple Store of the hood," said Iddris Sandu, the twenty-year-old coding prodigy who designed the TMC app, which allowed customers to unlock exclusive audio and video content linked to designated hot spots within the store and on TMC merchandise, an interactive experience known as augmented reality. Born in Accra and raised in Compton, Sandu has worked with Elon Musk and Kanye West and received a letter of commendation from President Obama. Hussle spotted the slim software engineer in Starbucks one day while he was fine-tuning the technology behind Uber's first self-driving car and politely struck up a conversation. Nipsey soon hired Sandu as chief technical officer of the family business, All Money In.[3]

"A month after we went live, the NBA announced that they got smart jerseys," Nip would note during an appearance on L.A.'s own *Home Grown Radio*.[4] "He was introducing shit that regular people didn't even know about," exclaimed cohost Chuck Dizzle, who championed Nip and many other rising local rappers. "So imagine some kid from the hood walkin' in and seein' that! 'Oh, you can scan this T-shirt and play the music.' That just sparks something completely different other than, 'Oh, I can be a rapper . . . Oh, I can play in the NBA. *Damn*, I can be an engineer! I can program this.' It just gives them possibilities." There can never be too many ways to try to rise above.[5]

"I wanna thank everybody for coming out and bearing witness to this," Big Boy told the crowd at the ribbon-cutting. "Usually when they turn the cameras on us, it's for all the wrong reasons." Nipsey nodded, holding a giant pair of scissors in his hand, ready to slice through the wide red ribbon stretched across the store's entrance. "And it's hot as hell," Big Boy added. "They say we act crazy when it's hot, but we ain't actin' crazy, man."[6]

Despite his humble demeanor, Nipsey had every right to feel proud. The Marathon Clothing grand opening was like a carnival on Crenshaw and Slauson. There were food trucks, inflatable bouncy castles for the kids, games, giveaways, and homies rollin' up and down the block on motorbikes and ATVs. "If it wasn't for Nipsey we wouldn't have nothin' around here for real," said one lady in attendance that day. "All we need is Black people that really stick together and make things happen out here in the community . . . Nip really for the hood and for the family."[7]

Big Boy passed the microphone to Marqueece Harris-Dawson, a lifelong Hyde Park resident who represents District 8 in the L.A. City Council. On behalf of the City of Los Angeles, he pronounced the event "the biggest grand opening of any business anywhere in Southern California today."[8] In a private moment with Sam and the family, the councilman observed that there are a lot of CEOs who get paid millions of dollars who wouldn't even attempt what this family business had accomplished.

"Nip need to be recognized by the city, man," his big brother said. "'Cause he doin' something that a lot of people cannot do. And that's rehabilitate an area, give felons jobs, and make motherfuckers be productive. There's a lot of corporations that can't even do this."[9]

The crowd cheered as the councilmember passed the mic to "the one and only Nipsey Hussle." He waited for them to quiet down before speaking. "Y'all know how many years and damn near decades this has been in the makin'," Hussle said, gesturing with the oversize scissors in his hand. "We started out in this parking lot as teenagers, when all this was abandoned . . . When it was all type of things goin' down on this corner that don't go down on this corner no more. Because some people from over here changed the intention of what this corner was about. And y'all was a part of that."

As the crowd inched forward and Nipsey continued following his train of thought, doing his best to explain all of his big ideas with his usual sense of urgency, the scissors were getting uncomfortably close to the heads of people standing in the front row. Big Boy reached up as discreetly as possible and took the enormous shears out of Nip's hand. "I had a tight grip on them scissors," Nip said as the crowd laughed. "Don't even worry."[10]

Big Boy cracked a smile. He wasn't worried, but he wanted this moment to be perfect for Nipsey, who'd been a frequent guest on his radio program over the years. Hussle's final appearance on *Big Boy's Neighborhood* would come not quite two years later. By that time Hussle and his brother had partnered with a young

Black real estate investor named David A. Gross to purchase the entire shopping plaza for $2.5 million. Big Boy congratulated Hussle on his latest power move, noting that the neighborhood was "starting to slip away from us" due to the forces of gentrification. "I think people that know you know why you stayed," Big Boy told him that day. "I think there is such a shield of protection that would be around any venture you do."[11]

NOW, EVERYBODY KEEP YOUR EYES ON THE PRIZE 'CAUSE THE RIDE GET TRICKY

—2Pac, "Heartz of Men," *All Eyez on Me*, released in 1996, when Ermias Asghedom was eleven

There was so much to be shielded from—stickups, gang-related violence, racist cops who could be as dangerous as any street crew. So even after all the fistfights, the gunshots, the police harassment, why stay? Nipsey was asked this question a lot. He always made it clear that his decision was based on more than self-interest. "It was a higher purpose I believe for what we doin' over here," he said. "It wasn't to get in trouble with the police. It wasn't to be a menace to the area. It wasn't to continue a tradition of self-destruction. It was to build. So all the obstacles and everything we've been through of being misjudged and misunderstood, it didn't stop us. You know, it wasn't a brick wall; it was a speed bump. And I embrace it as, you know, the resistance, the gravity, of trying to do something great."[12]

"I feel like my area put me on," Nipsey told the crowd, thanking the people assembled in the parking lot for their support of his come-up, for buying his five-dollar mixtapes, for coming to those first shows even when there were just thirty people in attendance,

for "makin' us look like we was doin' something." Along the way
Hussle upgraded from his first car, a blue '85 Cutlass, to the black
Maybach that was parked nearby. "Thanks, everybody," he said.
"It's been a long time comin'. This is for y'all. This is for us. And
it's just a first example of what we all can do over here. We don't
need to go take nobody else money. We don't need to go let them
take ownership from us. We can do this shit ourselves."[13] And
with that, Nipsey cut the ribbon. The Marathon Clothing flagship smart store was open for business, the first step of what was
supposed to be a nationwide rollout—TMC smart stores in major
cities across America. The cameras flashed. The crowd cheered.
It was all good.

To look back on the grand opening ceremony is to remember a perfect moment, pregnant with possibility and unlimited
potential. If only it were possible to turn back time and somehow bypass the pain of March 31, 2019. "We launched that store
together," says Sandu. "For him to pass away in that very same
spot . . . *Right* in front. It wasn't in the store. For him to pass
away right on that same pavement that we cut the ribbon on . . .
it was very . . ." He trails off, at a loss for words. "These are all
signs that the universe gives us."[14]

"I can't talk about our last day together, and I still have to be
strong for my children," London told *GQ* magazine eight months
after his death. "I have a three-year-old that's still asking, 'Where
is Daddy?' He doesn't understand the concept of death. I haven't
gotten to digest the fullness of it, because it's overwhelming and
I'm in the process of healing myself and my family. But I absolutely feel the love of the city."[15]

"It's a blow for—not just the hip-hop community," says Big
Boy. "I think it's a blow for all of us, just for human beings. For
us being on earth. This is somethin' that's extremely horrible to
happen to one of the best people, man."[16]

"It's just sickening and disgusting," says Councilmember Harris-Dawson. "Every time I think about it I get so angry that I don't have words."[17]

"He represented redemption and hope," said Los Angeles mayor Eric Garcetti, calling Hussle's murder "a devastating shock." Although Mayor Garcetti noted that Hussle "had come from the world of gangs and gotten out," the Los Angeles City Attorney's Office and the LAPD apparently had a different view of things. After years of trying to evict the businesses that Nipsey Hussle and his brother operated, and attempting to block the opening of The Marathon Clothing smart store in 2017, city authorities had been shocked when the Asghedom brothers partnered with Gross to purchase the shopping plaza in February 2019.[18] Hussle's work goes on, despite ongoing resistance—not to mention the utter absurdity of his death.

"I mean, shit, Nipsey Hussle got murdered in front of his store," says Chuck Dizzle. "To even think about how crazy that is—and that's why people are so taken aback by it, because it wasn't supposed to happen. But this is the identity of Los Angeles. And of course that happens in different cities, but it's just a different tone in L.A., where the street politics really rule everything. It's *way* bigger than music. And that's what Los Angeles is all about."[19]

※※※

WE HUSTLE OUT OF A SENSE OF HOPELESSNESS,
SORT OF A DESPERATION...

—Jay-Z, "Can I Live," *Reasonable Doubt*, released in 1996 when
Ermias Asghedom was eleven

At the end of *Crenshaw*, Nipsey Hussle's game-changing 2013 mixtape, there's a plaintive three-part opus called "Crenshaw &

Slauson (True Story)." Although the project received more attention for its innovative business model—selling a limited-edition CD for $100 even while the album was available for free download—the music has stood up well over time, particularly the closing track. Like all of Hussle's best work, the narrative is autobiographical, both painfully honest and fiercely guarded at the same time. "The demonstrations speak loud so I ain't sayin' much," he raps. "No details till the statute of limitations up."

Nevertheless, the twelve-minute song reveals a musical mosaic pieced together from hard-edged fragments of fact, speaking of Hussle's journey through the streets and the rap game, the automatic pistol under his pillow, the MAC-11s stashed in a safe in the floor, the surveillance cameras around the house he shared with Sam, and the double-pane bulletproof glass on their car for "pushin' past the haters" with relative peace of mind. Nipsey raps from the perspective of a man surrounded by threats from every angle—rivalry, jealousy, incarceration. Surviving all of that by sheer will, and by God's grace, prepared him for the perils of the music industry, reinforcing Hussle's refusal to be treated like a slave by record labels. Through it all, he seemed to realize he was destined to fulfill a singular mission. "I'm not a rapper or a poet, I'm a poem, nigga," he said. "Ain't it amazing how I'm standing on my own, nigga?"

Back in 2006, a fresh-faced twenty-one-year-old Nipsey Hussle, who released his first "official" mixtape, *Slauson Boy Vol. 1*, the year prior, attended the Hip-Hop Summit Action Network's "Get Your Money Right" summit at the USC campus. After participating in a panel discussion he stopped to chat with legendary Bay Area broadcaster Davey D.

Although Nip was sporting a thick gold chain and a small princess-cut diamond stud in each earlobe, his look struck Davey as understated, at least for an up-and-coming rapper of the day. "How come you not blingin' and havin' all kind of crazy diamonds and all that?" he asked the young man. "I guess you here to get your money right, huh?"

"All the time," young Hussle replied. "You know, all that is cool for the image and all that, but all them is liabilities, you feel me? I'd rather invest in some real estate."

"Wait, wait," Davey replied, visibly surprised at the young man's acumen. "Can you repeat that?"

"I said *invest* in some *assets*," Hussle said, louder this time. "As opposed to trick off my money on some liabilities like diamonds, you know what I'm sayin'? Cars that lose value as soon as you drive 'em off the lot."

"So you trying' to get land?" Davey asked Nip, who at the time was still more than a decade away from purchasing the shopping plaza at West Slauson Avenue and South Crenshaw Boulevard, turning the slogan "Buy Back the Block" into a legitimate plan of action.

"Exactly, homie," Hussle said. "A real asset to take care of my peoples." Jewelry might look good, he reasoned, "but at the end of the day, it's losin' value. It ain't appreciatin'—it's depreciatin'." Although the young rapper was an invited guest at the financial literacy conference, he sounded more like a seasoned investment adviser giving out game to anyone prepared to soak it up.[20]

Reflecting back on one of his earliest on-camera interviews, Nipsey realized that he'd been wise beyond his years. "We was a little mature just from what we went through before rap," he said. "We had experienced a little bit of life to where we kinda like had dealt with reality and had to mature and to think as a man kinda early." His father had come to the United States in his late teens as a political refugee from the East African nation of Eritrea. He and his brother grew up in their grandmother's two-bedroom house in South Central, sharing a bed with their mom. "I just didn't have nobody that was established in my family," he recalled. "And so bein' a young boy, and not seein' no business you can go into when you get outta high school or no college graduates in your family, what really motivated us to get out here was just settin' something up. Bein' established. Bein' a first-generation boy that was gonna turn into a man."[21]

Around 2006, Nipsey founded his own record label, calling it All Money In, No Money Out. Much more than a pithy name for Hussle and his team, All Money In was a mission statement—a formula for self-empowerment based on the principle of keeping every dollar earned circulating in the community, with the larger aim of building generational wealth. Growing up in South Central, a once-thriving Black neighborhood blighted by decades of divestment and a policy known as redlining that amounted to real estate apartheid, Hussle took these goals to heart, and spread these ideas as much as humanly possible.

All Money In was a mantra of self-discipline that saw Nipsey and his associates through countless setbacks and incessant police harassment, prompting them to invest in the human capital of their community, pay their bills and taxes on time, open ancillary businesses, and still have enough left over to turn the AMI logo into gold medallions for the whole team. All Money In was a way of life that kept them focused on the long game, a mindset Hussle came to call the Marathon. Their commitment to the independent grind allowed the upstart label to resist any temptation to sign away their rights for a quick check, giving them patience to build enough leverage to negotiate a partnership with Atlantic Records—clearing the way for the 2018 release of *Victory Lap*, Hussle's long-awaited Grammy-nominated debut album. Adhering to the credo All Money In, No Money Out was ultimately what allowed Nipsey Hussle to proclaim, on the album's first single, "I ain't nothin' like you fuckin' rap niggas."

One day before *Victory Lap*'s release, Hussle and Gross opened the doors of Vector90, a 4,700-square-foot "coworking space, cultural hub, and incubator" located in a former Wonder Bread factory five minutes away from the Marathon Clothing store. The top floor of the sleek space had a WeWork vibe, offering reasonable rates to paying members, while downstairs was a mixed-use area that served multiple community functions, including STEM classes to help prepare residents of the Crenshaw District for science and technology jobs. Lyrics from "Bigger Than Life," the hidden final track of Hussle's 2010 mixtape *The Marathon*, were painted in bold white capital letters on the steps connecting the two levels: "So life is what you make it. I hope you make a movement. Hope your opportunity survives the opportunist."

"In our culture, there's a narrative that says, 'Follow the athletes, follow the entertainers,'" Hussle told the *Los Angeles Times* on Vector90's opening day. "And that's cool, but there should be something that says, 'Follow Elon Musk, follow [Mark] Zuckerberg.' I think that with me being influential as an artist and young and coming from the inner city, it makes sense for me to be one of the people that's waving that flag."[22]

For Gross, who grew up in South Central until age ten and went on to become a successful investment banker in New York City, the vision for Vector90 became a passion project, his way of giving back to a community that had not progressed much during the twenty years he'd been away. "I knew I'd need a partner from the neighborhood," he said. "Someone that was closely connected to it, that was authentic, that the community would embrace and trust." Gross and Hussle finally met in 2016 at a Lakers game, getting to know each other over tequila shots. "Literally the next day he came to my office," Gross recalls. "I showed him the deck for Vector90, and he said, 'I'm all in.'"[23]

While some celebrities turn out to be different from their public persona when you meet them, Hussle was even more genuine than Gross expected. Not only did he help fund the project, he also began spending time at Vector90, working on his own projects, meeting with Gross every Wednesday. "His commitment to this, and to his people, and to making a radical change was such that he actually did a launch party for *Victory Lap* at a coworking space in the heart of the hood, when typically someone would do it at some fancy spot," Gross recalled. "He took away from his moment . . . from that energy, which was the perfect All-Star Weekend in L.A., his debut album finally coming. He came and spent half the day here. That's one of those things that kind of defines who he was."[24]

On the *Victory Lap* track "Dedication," Nipsey Hussle poses a poignant question: "How long should I stay dedicated? How long till opportunity meets preparation?" The line was inspired by a quote attributed to the Roman philosopher Seneca: "Luck is what happens when opportunity meets preparation." Malcolm Gladwell wrote about the importance of preparation in his book *Outliers*, formulating the famous ten-thousand-hour rule, calculating the commitment and diligence that Gladwell considers a prerequisite for success in any given field. A voracious reader, Hussle studied all of Gladwell's work. But he knew full well that all the preparation in the world will not help if opportunity never knocks at your door.

The ultimate aim of Vector90 is to maximize opportunity by all means necessary, providing educational programs, networking, mentorship, resources, and platforms, as well as direct investment. In aeronautics, "vector" is a verb meaning to guide an object, such as a plane or a missile, toward a particular destination. When used in physics and mathematics, "vector" refers to a quantity that has both direction and magnitude. A 90-degree vector points straight up.

"You need a home base," Hussle explained with evident pride soon after the space opened. "You need a space to work and take your meetings in and have Wi-Fi and have a trademark lawyer in the building. And have a synergy that you can bounce off each other."[25] As he explained near the top of track 7 on *Victory Lap*, "It's all I'm tryna do: hustle and motivate."

Among the budding entrepreneurs who began working in the space early on was Hussle's younger sister, Samantha Smith, who was developing her own business, a therapeutic spa service called Glo. "Vector90 is a place where you know you can come and there's like-minded people," she says. "There's people on a similar path as you. And there's people that can help catapult your career or whatever it is you wanna do for yourself." Smith believes that Vector90 made a major difference in her community. "When it comes to minorities, we don't have anything like this," she says. "We often get slipped through the cracks."[26]

Hussle and Gross planned to expand the Vector90 network from Crenshaw all across the United States. Both were motivated by the idea of what such a place might have meant to them when they were just getting started. "I wanted to impact someone who was a younger version of me," Gross said in a conversation with prominent podcaster Van Lathan. "It took a really stark transition for me to move from South Central Los Angeles to a really small town in Texas, where some of the issues around poverty and money were the same for me, but just the chaos of being in a large inner city in the eighties, it wasn't there. And so that forced kind of calm that I went into, it let me learn things about myself."[27]

Having grown up knee-deep in the madness that prevailed in Rollin' 60s territory, and all across South Los Angeles, in the years following the Rodney King verdict and the L.A. uprising, Hussle would sometimes reflect on how things might have been different had he been able to make other choices. Five years before he opened Vector90, he was asked what he'd be doing if he weren't in the music industry. The twenty-eight-year-old rattled off a list of options, none of them involving criminal activity: "Something with technology, something with the arts . . . I was always fascinated with space. I'm not sure, but something fun and creative."[28]

A few weeks after Vector90 opened, Hussle told me that having access to a resource like that would have changed his life. "My trajectory I'm sure would've been different," he said. "I can't be specific on what, but I know I was curious and passionate early about just creativity and being productive. And out of frustration, I fell into the streets. But if I'd have been able to catch a few of these opportunities early, for sure it would've had a different effect."[29]

Hussle and Gross would collaborate on other ventures as well. In 2018, Hussle, DJ Khaled, and Luol Deng invested in Gross's bid to purchase the Viceroy hotel in Santa Monica, along with self-made Black billionaire Don Peebles, who serves on Vector90's board. Although the Viceroy deal didn't work out, Gross was able to help Hussle and his brother literally "buy back the block" in January 2019, partnering with them to purchase the shopping plaza at Slauson and Crenshaw where the Marathon Clothing store is located—and where Hussle first came up hustling. Their moment of triumph turned to tragedy on March 31, but Hussle's passing has only strengthened Gross's resolve to carry on their mission.

Hardly a day goes by when Gross doesn't reflect on how irreplaceable his business partner was. "The range of his reach is what's unique about him," Gross says. "He could be at the Roc Nation Brunch with Jay and Puff and relate to them and be respected as a peer. And then he could be on Slauson and Crenshaw and be embraced over here as someone still accessible and someone relatable. That's a very unique thing. He made a lot of people want to be entrepreneurs, want to be bosses, want to start businesses—and do it with their own people."[30]

The tragic events of March 31, 2019, destroyed countless hopes and dreams and deferred others. At the time of Hussle's murder, he and Gross were in the process of raising a massive real estate fund focused on inner-city investment and redevelopment. "We were headed to DC to speak before the Ways and Means Committee," Gross says. "We were going as a coalition—myself, Nipsey, and T.I.—for this broad agreement that we were working on called Our Opportunity." They hoped to build it into a bulwark against gentrification—"the economic version of Black Lives Matter," as Gross once described it.[31]

One of the lesser-known details tucked into Donald Trump's 2017 tax overhaul provided lucrative tax incentives for investing in so-called Opportunity Zones. Touted as a way to develop underprivileged neighborhoods, the benefits were only accessbile to people who pay capital gains tax and can afford to make new investments. The resulting influx of funds was directed toward areas that were handpicked by state governors in a behind-closed-doors process that led to some questionable choices. Trump called Opportunity Zones the "hottest thing going"—but predictably enough, members of his own inner circle, including son-in-law Jared Kushner's family, were first in line to reap the benefits, building luxury developments that would provide few jobs and accelerate the rate of gentrification, potentially displacing longtime residents. Inspired by Hussle's spirit of community engagement, David Gross launched a program to leverage Opportunity Zones and encourage residents of South Los Angeles to "own our own." He called the new program Our Opportunity, but the basic concept was just a variation on Hussle's profoundly simple strategy—keep all the money in, and let none of it out.

PERFECTION IS PERFECTED
SO I'MA LET 'EM UNDERSTAND . . .

—Dr. Dre ft. Snoop Dogg, "Nuthin' but a 'G' Thang," released in 1992, when
Ermias Asghedom was seven

Although Hussle did not win the Best Rap Album Grammy in 2019 for *Victory Lap*, his first-attempt nomination was a major milestone on his Marathon. The next morning he was up early to shoot the "Racks in the Middle" video. Lurking around the edges of that video shoot were members of the All Money In team, a small circle of day-ones and handpicked talents from the community where he grew up. Before he dropped his first *Bullets Ain't Got No Name* mixtape, Hussle was developing the Slauson Boyz, a crew that included homies from Nipsey's section: Cuzzy Capone aka Yung Cuz, Cobby Supreme aka G-Bob, H60dsta Rob aka H&R, Rimpau the Rebel, Infant J Stone, Wee-Dogg, Tiny Boss Hogg, and Tiny Drawz.

All Money In evolved from a mindset into an official business that Hussle developed with Blacc Sam, as well as founding part-ners Adam Andebrhan and Stephen "Fatts" Donelson. According to research by hood historian Kev Mac, "All Money In, No Money Out" was a slogan made famous by an old-school player affiliated with the Rollin' 30s. Hussle adapted the phrase from street slang and turned it into a successful company.[32] His concept was all about ownership and the empowerment of young Black men with no industry support taking control of their destinies and building an empire straight off the curb. After being released from his deal with Epic Records in 2010, Hussle started *The Marathon* mixtape series and his independent movement began in earnest. Always a planner, he conceived *Victory Lap* as the conclusion of the musical Marathon. He did not foresee that it would become the final project released during his lifetime.

When two of Hussle's post–*Victory Lap* releases won Grammy Awards in 2020, the victory was bittersweet, to say the least. Hussle did not live to celebrate with DJ Khaled and John Legend when "Higher" won the award for Best Rap/Sung Performance or when "Racks in the Middle," featuring Roddy Ricch and Hit-Boy, won the award for Best Rap Performance. The latter song reflects Nip's determination to carry on despite the tragic murder of his partner Fatts—just as their team was preparing to announce their hard-won partnership with Atlantic Records. Friends and fans did their best to draw strength from words Hussle wrote to keep himself going: "Live your life and grow . . . Finish what we started, reach them heights, you know?"

It was the family's first time at the Staples Center since Hussle's heartbreaking memorial service. Lauren arrived at the ceremony all in black, from her dress to her hair. Around her neck was a locket containing a photo of Nipsey in his tux snapped on the red carpet at the previous year's Grammy ceremony. When the time came, Lauren accepted the award "on behalf of our family and in honor of Nip, who was a phenomenal vessel." His grandmother and his sister stood at her side for yet another public ceremony in Hussle's honor. "Nip did it not just for the awards, but for the people," Lauren added. "And God allowed him to use this music to speak his truth, give us wisdom, and something that we will forever be able to live with."[33]

After the ceremony, Atlantic Records publicist Brittany Bell had flashbacks of fond memories. "I'm emotionally all over the place this morning," she wrote on her IG. "Nip, the last big meeting we had you pushed 'Racks in the Middle' so hard, you knew it was THAT RECORD and stood by it. You dropped the artwork on socials the night of the Grammy Awards as we were walking out and now we're here!"[34]

The man who said "Fuck the Grammys until we get one"[35] never did get the chance to bring one home for his neighborhood, much less to apply all the lessons he learned from the process of making his major label debut to all the future projects he had in mind. Nipsey felt he was just getting started, and after focusing on building his businesses for so long, felt he'd been making music with a "handicap." He was looking forward to taking the frequency of his music higher on his next two albums, which he was thinking of calling *Exit Strategy* and *The Spook Who Sat by the Door*, tantalizing titles, both rich with Trojan Horse implications.

While he wasn't planning to exit when he did, Hussle always prepared for every eventuality. Although he left no last will and testament, the proud father did set up seven-figure trust funds for his daughter, Emani, and his son, Kross, to provide for them when his own earthly Marathon came to an end.[36] In fact, when NFL star Reggie Bush started a crowdfunding campaign to support Hussle's kids, the Asghedom family declined the donations because the children were well provided for.[37] Always a devoted dad, Hussle harbored no illusions about whether money could take the place of his loving presence. Years later on "Picture Me Rollin'," he mused on the grief of losing a father, rapping: "It's never enough to console her / Telling 'Your daddy's a soldier' / She needs you right now in this moment / Not dead on your back pushin' roses."

Chapter 2

SLAUSON BOY

I'M SLAUSON AVE AND EVERYTHING ON THAT STREET
USED TO CARVE OUR NAMES IN THE WET CONCRETE

—Nipsey Hussle, "Blacc Ice," *Bullets Ain't Got No Name Vol. 2* (2008)

The summer before he entered fifth grade, Ermias Asghedom's mother gave him forty dollars to go back-to-school shopping. *This isn't gonna really cut it*, he said to himself.[1] But it was all she had, and he didn't want his mother to feel bad, so he went to the local Ross "Dress for Less" store and did the best he could. Instead of pressuring her, he made up his mind that he'd earn some money of his own so he would never have to go back to school unprepared.

Ermias went all over the neighborhood, seeking employment, but everybody thought the skinny eleven-year-old was too young to hire. "I went to Taco Bell on Sixtieth and Crenshaw and asked for a job like ten different times," he would later recall. "I couldn't really understand why it was so hard. Of course, I have no employment history, bro!"[2]

By the time he walked into Chambers Shoe Shine Parlor on Slauson Ave, he was determined not to take no for an answer.

"I wanna work, man!" he declared. "I'll come every day. I'll show up early. I need a job." Paul and Stefan Chambers agreed to give the kid a shot and Ermias finally had his first job.[3]

First, strip your shoe with a little paint thinner—boom! Buss it down. Clean it with the stripper. Buss it down again . . .[4]

Besides becoming a master shoe shiner, Ermias took full advantage of the opportunity to learn advanced hustle-nomics. He would earn $2.50 for every pair of shoes he serviced, plus the profits from selling candy bars on the side. "Go to the ninety-nine-cent store," he reasoned, "you get three for a dollar and triple up!"[5] His bosses laughed at the young man's hustling spirit, but his profits were no joke. Working six days a week, he would come home dizzy from the fumes but with almost $600 in his pocket.

"I learned about saving money, stacking and flipping early on," he said. "I bought my whole sixth and seventh grade wardrobe offa that."[6] When it was time to go back-to-school shopping again, he asked a friend's parents to drive him to the outlet stores, where he used his earnings to cop the latest Polo and Hilfiger gear. Years later he was still proud of the yearbook photo he took in his Tommy Jeans jacket. "I was fresh!"[7]

His mother, Angelique Smith, who worked long hours to support her sons, didn't consider "fresh" clothes as much of a priority as getting an education. "She never told me no about a book," Hussle recalled in later years. "We might not go to Toys 'R' Us and get what I want every time, but if I be like, 'Take me to the bookstore,' she'll stop what she was doing and take me."[8] Though young Ermias learned a lot from his love of books, the streets of Crenshaw taught him many important lessons as well.

Named after George Lafayette Crenshaw, a California banker and real estate mogul, Crenshaw Boulevard runs for twenty-three miles from the historic movie star mansions of Hancock Park in central L.A. all the way to the dramatic ocean views of Palos Verdes. As the city's growing Black population coalesced in the area that came to be known as South Central—their movements restricted by legal trickery, economic pressure, and threats of violence—Crenshaw became the main drag of Black Los Angeles, affectionately known as "the Shaw."

Storied nightclubs like Maverick's Flat, which took over the title "Apollo of the West" when the Lincoln Theatre on Central Avenue closed its doors, would book top Black musicians from Marvin Gaye to Funkadelic, with celebrities like Muhammad Ali and Marlon Brando in the audience. Every Sunday evening, lowriders would cruise up and down the Shaw, flaunting L.A.'s vibrant car culture. Ermias Asghedom was six years old when John Singleton's Oscar-nominated film *Boyz N the Hood* brought Crenshaw to the big screen in 1991. As a kid he loved to watch the Chevy Impalas, El Caminos, and Monte Carlos—even the occasional Cadillac Eldorado—riding slow and low, lovingly customized to the last detail, booming funk, soul, and hip-hop from their systems while bouncing on hydraulics. "Before we could drive," Hussle remembered years later, "a bunch of us kids would be chasing lowriders down the street, yelling out, 'Hit a switch! Hit a switch!'"[9]

"My whole life took place on these four corners," said Nipsey Hussle, recalling his teenage years in the plaza at 3420 West Slauson Avenue. Before he could afford his own car, Ermias would ride his bike to check out the action up and down Slauson. "I mean, this really was my whole foundation," he said. "Everything." He even met Tanisha Foster, the mother of his firstborn child, right here in that same parking lot.[10]

Like Crenshaw Boulevard, Slauson Avenue was named for a wealthy white man—New York attorney Jonathan Sayre Slauson, who moved out west and opened a bank, ran for mayor, built churches and orphanages, and planted vast orange and lemon groves. The busy thoroughfare named in his honor runs over twenty miles east from Culver City, the home of MGM Studios. Culver City was one of many areas of Los Angeles known as a "sundown town," meaning that any nonwhite visitors were warned to get out of town before nightfall.

Just over a century ago, developer Harry Culver offered 250 residential lots for sale with "proper restrictions" to ensure that Culver City became "a model little white city," as it was advertised. Harry Culver would go on to spread his segregation strategies as president of the Los Angeles Realty Board, which issued an official recommendation in 1927 that "Realtors should not sell property to other than Caucasians in territories occupied by them."[11]

The systematic segregation of Black families is all the more outrageous in light of California's rich Black history. The state was named for Calafia, a Black warrior queen made famous in a sixteenth-century Spanish novel.[12] Free of slavery since becoming America's thirty-first state in 1850, California was once seen as a beacon of hope for African Americans leaving the South in search of a better life. "Los Angeles is wonderful," wrote the author and activist W. E. B. DuBois. "Nowhere in the United States is the Negro so well and beautifully housed."[13] Founded long before California became part of the U.S., the Mexican city known as El Pueblo de Nuestra Señora la Reina de los Ángeles de Porciúnculá ("Town of Our Lady the Queen of Angels") was settled by forty-four people, many of African descent. Mexico's first Black president, Vincent Guerrero, abolished slavery back in 1829, decades before U.S. president Abraham Lincoln. Three years later Alta California had a Black governor named Pío Pico. A self-made mogul of mixed African descent, Pico was the wealthiest rancher in California for decades, owned half a million acres of land, built the most luxurious hotel in Los Angeles, Pico House, and inspired the name of Pico Boulevard.[14]

Today L.A. is one of the most racially and culturally diverse cities in the world, home to over ten million people who trace their heritage to more than 140 countries.[15] It's also the most diverse city in America, and the next four most diverse—Long Beach, San Diego, Anaheim, and Sacramento—are all in California.[16] Because non-Hispanic whites are outnumbered by other ethnic groups, L.A. is sometimes referred to as a "minority majority" city—but this racially loaded term belies painful truths that Hussle's music sought to expose. Who makes up terms like "minority" anyway, and for what purpose? "It's a war goin' on outside, no man is safe from," Hussle rapped on "Payback," echoing the Mobb Deep classic "Survival of the Fittest," then adding his own insight: "But since it's just niggas killing niggas, you just turn prison to a business."

L.A.'s long history of racial segregation led to disinvestment, economic inequality, and an adversarial relationship between Black people and police. As the African American population grew, the early optimism expressed by DuBois was undercut by "restrictive covenants," legal language in property deeds designed to prevent nonwhite people from buying or renting in certain neighborhoods. Meanwhile Black folks were moving west in record numbers. During World War II some 10,000 African American families came to Los Angeles seeking work in factories producing military supplies. This kicked off the "Great Migration" that saw L.A.'s Black population swell by over 1,000 percent in thirty years—from 60,000 to 700,000—including Hussle's forebears.[17]

By the 1940s Hussle's maternal grandmother and grandfather had bought property in the area along Central Avenue.[18] On his song "Dedication" Hussle rapped about "Fifty-Ninth and Fifth

Ave, Granny's house with vanilla wafers." Her home, where he spent so much of his life, was half a block below Slauson. Hussle explained that, even before the days of gangbanging, the avenue was a dividing line in L.A. "You couldn't live north of Slauson," Hussle said. "Like if you was a Black person in Los Angeles a real estate agent wouldn't sell you a house. They wouldn't approve your loan . . . And that's why they say South Central L.A."[19]

Even as a young man Hussle understood how city planners deliberately concentrated Black families south of Slauson. And just like in the Jim Crow South, segregation in California was enforced by violence. Starting in the 1940s, racist gangs like the "Spook Hunters" terrorized Black people who dared to enter white neighborhoods. When the first Black family moved to the northeast Los Angeles community of Eagle Rock in 1948, a uniformed police officer joined a mob that burned a twelve-foot cross outside their home.[20] Black families reported racially motivated bombings and vandalism to no avail. Walking to and from school, Black students risked ambush. The Spook Hunters wore jackets with an image of a person being lynched on the back.[21] Young Black people began forming neighborhood protection groups with names like the Slausons, the Businessmen, the Farmers, and the Gladiators. Their purpose was simply to defend their own.[22]

"What you see emerging are Black youth fighting back against attacks by white gangs," says historian and urban theorist Mike Davis in Cle Sloan and Antoine Fuqua's documentary *Bastards of the Party*, "and beginning to create what they didn't call gangs at the time." The film examines the roots of L.A.'s gangs and how community defense groups evolved into the Black Power movement, long before the Crips and Bloods. Ongoing conflict with groups like the Spook Hunters—twentieth-century forerunners of today's Proud Boys and Boogaloo Bois—who operated with the full support of the LAPD[23] shaped the neighborhood groups into a force for resistance. "The whites were predominant in the area," says Bird, a founding member of the Slausons. "So we banded together at Slauson Park."[24]

While they took their name from a specific location, the Slausons were all about freedom of movement, defying those who sought to prevent them from roaming throughout the city. "We couldn't go here, we couldn't go there," says Chinaman, another founder of the Slausons. "We're not gangs. We are the pioneers that opened up Los Angeles."[25] Other groups like the Businessmen operated in a similar fashion, bringing them into conflict with police as well as groups from different neighborhoods. Police from South Central's Seventy-Seventh Street Station had a reputation for picking up members of one group and dropping them in rival territory.

The murder of Malcolm X on February 21, 1965, followed by the nationally televised tear-gassing and beating of peaceful marchers in Selma, Alabama, trying to exercise their right to vote, helped set the stage for the Watts Rebellion later that year. On August 11, 1965, California Highway Patrol Officer Lee Minimus pulled over twenty-one-year-old Marquette Frye near 116th Place and Avalon Boulevard. Frye was driving in his mother's 1955 Buick with his brother. Frye had been drinking and the officer placed him under arrest, refusing to let his brother drive the car home, which was just two blocks away. As a crowd gathered, Frye's brother walked home and brought his mother to the scene.[26]

Exactly what transpired in those days before cell phone video is difficult to pin down, but a scuffle led to the crowd throwing rocks, which led to six days of fire and mayhem. L.A.'s notoriously racist chief of police William H. Parker did not help matters when he described Black protesters as "monkeys in a zoo."[27]

Chief Parker called in the National Guard, who had begun joint training exercises with the FBI and LAPD the previous year. Some 14,000 troops were deployed, including commandoes airlifted in to occupy a forty-mile war zone. When the smoke cleared 34 people were dead, more than 1,000 injured, and 4,000 arrested, and there had been an estimated $40 million in damages.[28]

While President Lyndon B. Johnson would later declare that "looting, murder, and arson have nothing to do with civil rights," many people of Watts considered the rebellion a victory because it drew attention to issues affecting their community.[29] "It was an absolutely transforming event," said Mike Davis, "youth on the streets coming together and uniting with each other to drive the LAPD out." Rivalries among local groups were set aside.[30] Grassroots activism and the Black Arts Movement, including organizations like the Watts Towers Arts Center—where young Ermias Asghedom would take music classes years later—helped to heal the community by creating new creative opportunities and by raising awareness of the issues underlying the conflict.[31] In the aftermath of the Watts Rebellion, community organizations for Black people flourished all over Los Angeles. Meanwhile local street clubs and neighborhood groups stepped up their cooperation to protect area residents from abusive police. Among these was The Black Panther Party for Self Defense, founded by Huey Newton and Bobby Seale in Oakland in 1966.

Among L.A.'s neighborhood organizations, the Slausons emerged as a unified force to be reckoned with. "The Slausons was an idea," said Louis Tackwood, a member of a rival organization called the Dartanians. "They didn't wear no jackets. They just considered themselves Slausons and that was it. Slausons were sharp dressers and their ladies were good-looking too. We were trying to kill an idea, just couldn't do it. Everybody was a Slauson. They had Little Slausons, Baby Slausons, and Slausonettes."[32]

The leader of the Slausons was Alprentice "Bunchy" Carter, a charismatic young man known for driving a red-and-black MGB convertible.[33] "According to Bunchy he was so pretty that it brought tears of envy from other men's eyes when they saw him," recalled former Panther leader Eldridge Cleaver, the author of *Soul on Ice*.[34] While serving time for bank robbery in California's Soledad prison, Bunchy got to know Cleaver, who encouraged him to open a Los Angeles chapter of the Black Panther Party, which had already spread to Chicago and New York. Bunchy began recruiting at house parties and inspired many former gang members to join the movement, giving them a new sense of purpose. "His mannerisms were street, but his mind had been developed," said Slauson-turned-Panther Ronald Freeman of Bunchy's transition from gangster to activist. "He became political. We called him 'the mayor of the ghetto.'"[35]

The Panthers thrived under Bunchy's leadership. New branches opened from San Diego to Santa Monica, but the headquarters remained at Forty-First Place and Central Avenue in Watts. Their Free Breakfast for Children program served vital needs in the community, attracting support from celebrities and scrutiny from FBI director J. Edgar Hoover, who declared the Panthers to be "the greatest threat to the internal security of the country."[36] Hoover's secret Counter Intelligence Program, known by the acronym COINTELPRO, targeted the Panthers as well as Dr. Martin Luther King Jr. and other civil rights leaders using undercover agents, smear campaigns, and anonymous threats with the aim of stirring up dissent in any way possible. For many years the FBI's secret program was only a rumor, until a group of private citizens—including a cab driver, two professors, and a child care worker—broke into an

FBI office in Pennsylvania and stole reams of classified documents, which they leaked to newspapers. In an internal memo, Hoover had described COINTELPRO as an effort "to expose, disrupt, misdirect, discredit, or otherwise neutralize the activities of black nationalist hate-type organizations and groupings, their leadership, spokesmen, membership, and supporters, and to counter their propensity for violence and civil disorder."[37]

Rather than countering violence, COINTELPRO's activities appeared to have the opposite effect. On April 4, 1968, Dr. King was assassinated in Memphis. On January 17, 1969, shots rang out during a meeting of UCLA's Black Student Union, where Bunchy Carter and fellow Panther John Huggins were killed by members of a rival group called the US Organization. Carter's death at age twenty-six was a crippling blow to the Panthers. Whether COINTELPRO agents were behind the shooting is still a matter of debate, but there is no doubt that the FBI stoked the rivalry between the two groups.[38]

That same day, in New York, twenty-one Panthers were arrested in an alleged bomb plot, including Afeni Shakur, who served time in jail and stood trial while pregnant with the son she would name Tupac. She and her codefendants were eventually acquitted.[39] When Hussle called himself the "Tupac of my generation," he was tapping into a revolutionary as well as a musical legacy.

Early in the morning of December 4, 1969, Chicago police working with the FBI raided the apartment of Fred Hampton, state chairman of the Illinois Black Panther Party. They executed Hampton with a barrage of more than forty bullets while he slept. Fellow Panther Mark Clark, who had dozed off while guarding the door with a shotgun in his lap, was also killed. Hampton's pregnant wife heard cops fire the last two shots into his head. "He's good and dead now," a policeman's voice said.[40]

Four days later another early-morning raid went down at the Southern California Black Panther headquarters established by the late Bunchy Carter. Hundreds of LAPD officers, including a SWAT team and a helicopter dropping explosives, converged at Forty-First and Central, where a handful of Panthers trained by the decorated U.S. Army veteran Geronimo Pratt held them off for four hours. After the smoke cleared, all of these raids dealt a crippling blow to the movement.

Something had to fill the void left behind in the aftermath of the Panthers' "neutralization." Around 1969 a high school student named Raymond Washington organized a group known as the Baby Cribs. Washington was born in Texas and grew up in Los Angeles around Seventy-Sixth and Wadsworth, just west of Central Avenue. Short and muscular, Washington was renowned for his hand-to-hand fighting skills and his disdain for guns. By the early 1970s, he joined forces with a teenage crew formed by Stanley "Tookie" Williams, uniting the East and West Sides of South Central to form what would eventually become known as the Crips. According to Tookie's memoir *Blue Rage, Black Redemption*, the Crips were mostly high-school-age boys who came together to protect themselves from outside threats.

The group's rapid expansion throughout L.A. led to tension and conflict with certain neighborhoods. Youths from Piru Street, Harvard Park, Arlington Heights, and Athens Park came together to form an alliance of independent sets like the LA Brims and the Black P Stones known as the Original Blood Family. Some early members had once been children nourished by the Panthers' dismantled breakfast program. Conceived in opposition to the Crips, the Bloods feuded with them from the outset.

Although they had a different leadership structure than the Panthers, the Crips did their best to build on the party's work early on, forming a Consolidated Crip Organization, or CCO. "We come from a neighborhood of the leader of the Black Panther Party which was a neighborhood called the Slausons," said pioneering Crips member Danifu Bey. "Our neighborhood was the neighborhood where Bunchy Carter came from . . . We were taught that we had the power to develop our own destiny." Danifu Bey helped draft the Crip Constitution, which set out the Crips' objectives and turned their name into an acronym for Community Revolutionary Inter Party Service. There would be several variations on this acronym/mission statement over time. Nipsey Hussle preferred to use "Community Reprogression in Process."[41]

All of this context was lost on most Americans, who first heard about gang culture through movies like *Colors* and in lurid nightly news reports highlighting the groups' most negative aspects. "If gangs are pathological they're also heroic in a way," says historian Mike Davis, citing values of loyalty and self-sacrifice. "Gangs carried on the [Panthers'] residue of unity and pride, but it was now narrowly focused. It wasn't the whole community anymore. It was a particular street."[42]

"Anybody who thinks that gangs aren't doing anything positive or are fundamentally criminal has never been around gangs," says Dr. Melina Abdullah, a professor of Pan-African Studies at California State University who cofounded the L.A. branch of Black Lives Matter. "On their face gangs are really pseudo-familial constructions," she says. "Crime and the existence of gangs are two separate things. We've been duped by mass media in particular, but also a police state and a white supremacist structure that seeks to criminalize what could be our greatest strength."[43]

"It's a difference between what [Tookie and Raymond Washington] was doin' and what eventually morphed into what it is today," said Eugene "Big U" Henley, who would eventually become Hussle's business partner. "They the original Crips and where the name came from. What we ended up doin' after '79 was what we call gangbangin'. And that was where everything had changed."

The way Big U tells it, some of his homies asked permission to start their own Crip faction in the early 1970s, which became the Rollin' 60s, one of the oldest and largest African American gangs in Los Angeles. "We always were known as the so-called 'wealthy Crips,'" Big U said. "In our area we live in houses. Certain parts of Watts and Compton and all that, they in tenements and projects. So in our area, which is called the 60s, it's different. It's generational. You'll have people who've been going to school or knew each other since age five years old because they mothers own these houses. And they have ownership instead of living in apartments . . . transitioning in and out. Ours is different. We lived on the block."[44]

Although he's often identified as an OG, or even as the leader of the 60s, Big U is more focused on gang prevention these days. His nonprofit organization, Developing Options, has been changing lives since 2004 and is supported by the Los Angeles mayor's GRYD (Gang Reduction & Youth Development) Foundation. Developing Options also supports the Crenshaw Rams in the Snoop Youth Football League.

"The ultimate goal is to be for young African-American kids what the YMCA and these other places could've and should've been," he told *Vibe* magazine. "I always hear them talk about the YMCA and the Boys' Club. In the Crenshaw area we don't have one. I wanted to be the pioneer, the first to do it. Because most neighborhoods in California are infested with gangs."[45]

In fact, Big U insists he never officially joined the 60s. "I'm one of them guys who's just here," he says, quoting a line Nipsey often repeated, words that were spoken at his memorial service. When you live a certain life and you're from a certain area, "it ain't on you sometimes, it's in you."[46]

**MY GRANNY CAME FROM DOWN SOUTH WHEN THEY FREED THE SLAVES
WITH AN AIM TO MAKE A BETTER LIFE THAN YESTERDAY**

—Nipsey Hussle, "Cali," *Slauson Boy Vol. 1* (2005)

"She was real big on keeping a tight family," Hussle said of his grandmother, Margaret Boutte, "and big on love."[47] Margaret's family came from Louisiana, and she moved to California during the Great Migration. Raised Roman Catholic, she suffered eleven miscarriages before the birth of her second child, Angelique. After being bedridden for most of that pregnancy, she saw the girl as a blessing and called her Angel. "Imagine if I would have gave up on my tenth miscarriage, my ninth miscarriage," Hussle's grandmother would tell him.[48]

Dawit Asghedom emigrated to America from Eritrea in the 1970s before his twentieth birthday, seeking asylum from the war raging in his East African homeland. Situated between Ethiopia and the Red Sea, Eritrea was an Italian colony from the late nineteenth century until the end of World War II. After the territory was annexed by Ethiopia around 1960, Eritrean rebels began a thirty-year battle for independence.[49] "If you think about the Eritrean struggle," Hussle would say years later during an interview on Eritrean television, "there's so many metaphors that you can take from that. If you stand for principle and you stand for what you believe in, and you're willing to live and die for what you believe is right, you can do the impossible."[50]

A black-and-white photo on Hussle's Instagram shows Dawit marching in the streets of L.A. with a group of young Eritrean men. He's rocking bellbottoms and an Afro, and carrying a sign that reads DOWN WITH APARTHEID AND IMPERIALISM. In one corner of the sign are the initials EFLNA, standing for Eritreans for Liberation in North America. Hussle captioned the photo "I see u Pops ✊." It's not hard to imagine where Ermias got his revolutionary spirit.

Hussle was inspired to shed light on his parents' courtship in "Higher," his Grammy-winning collaboration with DJ Khaled and John Legend, which ended up being the first song released after his death. "Pops turned sixty, he proud what we done," Hussle rapped. "In one generation he came from Africa young / He said he met my moms at the Century Club."

Dawit and Angelique welcomed their first son, Samiel Ghebrehet Asghedom, on March 4, 1982. As the young parents adjusted to the excitement of taking on such a big new responsibility, larger forces were shaping the world their son would grow up in. On October 14 of that year, the Hollywood actor turned California governor turned U.S. president Ronald Reagan gave a speech calling for a "War on Drugs." Reviving former president Richard Nixon's rhetoric, Reagan declared illicit drugs to be a threat to U.S. national security. The policies that Reagan implemented following this speech—combined with rising unemployment and cuts to vital social programs—set the stage for a boom in mass incarceration and the militarization of urban police departments, nowhere more notably than in L.A.

Samiel Asghedom was born during a time when LAPD tactics were becoming more extreme, especially toward people of color. The same year, 1982, Los Angeles police chief Daryl Gates was forced to ban dangerous choke holds that he had authorized officers to use. Also known as the "bar arm hold" and the "carotid control hold," these moves blocked the flow of oxygen to the brain, causing the deaths of fifteen people, twelve of them Black, over a seven-year period. (The lethal police practice continues several decades later, as confirmed by the deaths of Eric Garner and George Floyd.) At first, Chief Gates tried to shift blame away from the police, citing a "hunch" that the deaths might have resulted from some sort of physical abnormality related to the victims' race. Gates asked his staff to look into the theory: "We may be finding that in some blacks when [the chokehold] is applied, the veins or arteries do not open as fast as they do in normal people."[51]

Did it cross his mind that his officers might be applying the choke hold more often or with greater force against Black suspects? It's hard to say. But Chief Gates did call Dr. Richard Allen Williams, a black cardiologist on the UCLA faculty, saying he wanted to discuss a "very delicate medical matter." Dr. Williams, author of *The Textbook of Black-Related Diseases*, recalled Gates asking if he could verify that "African-Americans were very susceptible to chokeholds because they had an anatomical defect in their necks." The doctor's response was unequivocal: "No, Chief Gates, I don't agree with that."[52] Although his remarks prompted outrage, Chief Gates refused to apologize.

"I will admit, we were a very aggressive police department," he said later, looking back over his career with something like pride. "We went after crime before it occurred . . . Our people went out every single night trying to stop crime before it happened, trying to take people off the street that we believed were involved in crime. That made us a very aggressive, proactive police department."[53] Such self-justifications perpetuated an ongoing conflict between the LAPD and the city's Black community that would profoundly impact the lives of young men like Samiel Asghedom and his younger brother, Ermias.

During the early 1980s, South Central Los Angeles would become ground zero for the introduction of crack cocaine to America, which combined with President Reagan's War on Drugs to set the stage for an explosion of arrests and killings nationwide. Texas-born cocaine kingpin Freeway Ricky Ross (aka "the real Rick Ross") usually gets the blame for spreading crack all over L.A., creating a booming illicit economy that spread addiction, murder, and Crip- and Blood-affiliated entrepreneurs across the United States.

In 1996 investigative journalist Gary Webb shed new light on another key player in the crack boom: Oscar Danilo Blandón, the Nicaraguan trafficker who supplied Ross with tons of cocaine. Accord to Webb, Blandón had ties to the CIA and some of his profits went to buy weapons for the right-wing Contras accused of murder, rape, and torture—whom President Reagan hailed as "freedom fighters"—to support their guerrilla war against the socialist Sandinista regime. Although it sparked federal hearings, Webb's reporting was criticized by several major newspapers, ruining his career. He died eight years later of an apparent suicide.[54]

Years later, when Nipsey Hussle rapped about how "Reagan sold coke, Obama sold hope," this is exactly what he was talking about. So was the crack epidemic a CIA conspiracy after all? Declassified evidence confirms that the U.S. government's National Security Council and the CIA organized an elaborate international scheme to purchase Iranian weapons with money from the sale of drugs shipped to the U.S. from Central America.[55] According to Washington lawyer Jack Blum, the former chief counsel for the U.S. Senate Foreign Relations Committee, cocaine trafficking in the 1980s transformed into a "mass-production huge vertically integrated business." Among the gangs bringing a flood of drugs into Los Angeles was the one working with the Contras. "There were clandestine airstrips," Blum confirmed. "There were airplanes that were flying in and out to supply the Contras. These guys know they can come and go and nobody is gonna ask any questions."[56] Not only did these secret government plans add to the scourges of addiction, violence, and incarceration in communities of color in the U.S., they also led to the birth of Central American street gangs like MS13, now considered one of the world's most dangerous criminal organizations, in the U.S.[57]

Blum ran a Senate investigation into the allegations raised by Gary Webb's reporting. "There's no question that they [employees of the federal government] looked the other way," he said. "We put that all out on the table publicly. Nobody paid any attention to it." Meanwhile the flood of drugs, money, and weapons was turning the streets of cities like Los Angeles and Miami into a war zone.[58]

"When cocaine actually hit was like '83," Big U recalled. "Two things happened major—the influx of a different kind of guns, and when the cocaine hit it made it so we had more money than we ever had." The drugs and money brought another serious downside: "The conflict with the homies started coming," he said. "The inside conflict, the mistrust kicked in."[59]

That mistrust led to an epidemic of violence, murder, and misery. Between 1984 and 1994, the homicide rate for Black males between the ages of fourteen and twenty-four doubled as incarceration rates soared.[60] Starting in 1986 federal law stipulated mandatory minimum sentences punishing crack possession one hundred times more severely than powder cocaine possession, exacerbating the racial disparity in America's prison population.[61]

For those whose knowledge of L.A. is primarily based on movies, TV shows, and rap videos, this would be a good time to clear up a few common misconceptions. Los Angeles is not just a city; it's also a county—the most populous county in America, to be precise.[62] With more than 10 million residents, Los Angeles County has more people than all but nine of the states in the U.S.[63] As such, it's policed by the world's largest sheriff's agency, a sprawling bureaucracy with a budget in excess of $3 billion.[64]

Along with policing the county's "unincorporated areas," the Los Angeles County Sheriff's Department is contracted to patrol dozens of cities throughout the county, from West Hollywood to Compton. The Sheriff's Department also operates the county jail system. Dozens of other city police forces also patrol various parts of Los Angeles County, including the LAPD, which has around ten thousand officers (only slightly more than the Sheriff's Department).[65]

Starting in 1979, the LAPD deployed a special anti-gang unit known as CRASH (an acronym for Community Resources Against Street Hoodlums). Its original name, TRASH (an abbreviation for Total Resources . . .), was a more accurate reflection of the unit's mindset. "We tried calling it TRASH . . . as a way of demeaning gang activity," said Chief Daryl Gates. "But some activists in the community objected. It was unseemly, they said, to call our units TRASH because we were dealing with human beings out there."[66] Most of the young Black human beings "out there" in South Los Angeles were all too familiar with the intricacies of these law enforcement agencies, as the Asghedom brothers would eventually learn for themselves.

One year before Ermias Asghedom's birth, the 1984 Summer Olympics took place in L.A. The 1984 Olympics were not a great time for South Central. The police presence there has been aptly compared to a military occupation. Young Black men were being jailed en masse, and complaints of police brutality rose by 33 percent for the next five years. The district attorney rarely prosecuted accused officers; instead the force was commended for "keeping the peace" during the Olympics.[67] One of their most notorious peacekeeping methods would be immortalized in an underground L.A. rap song. The same year Ermias Asghedom was born, Compton MC Toddy Tee released a 12-inch single called "Batterram." The song's humorous lyrics were inspired by a deadly serious weapon in the LAPD's War on Drugs. The V-100 was a Vietnam-era military surplus armored vehicle that police SWAT teams fitted with a 14-foot steel battering ram that was used to bash down the doors—and sometimes the walls— of suspected drug dealers' homes.[68] Ice-T also mentioned the Batterram on his breakout 1986 hit "6 in the Mornin'," the first West Coast record to get spins in New York, where few listeners had any clue what he was talking about. The NYPD lagged far behind the LAPD when it came to the militarization of law enforcement. "At first they called it the tank," said an official of the L.A. Police Museum. "They also looked at giving it an artillery piece, so they could just fire into a structure with a certain type of explosive device."[69] Facing such over-the-top aggression by the LAPD, the Black community's most effective countermeasure was to rally support using the power of community organizations—whether in the church or in the streets—and the power of hip-hop.

TRYIN' TO STAY FOCUSED, KINDA LIKE MOSES
LIKE SOMEBODY CHOSE US

—Nipsey Hussle, "Picture Me Rollin'," *Slauson Boy 2* (2016)

If it's true that a person's name shapes their destiny, then Ermias Joseph Asghedom was marked for excellence since his birth on August 15, 1985. In the Tigrinya language of Eritrea, the name Ermias means "God will rise." The name was chosen by his father, who would later say that his son "was sent by God to give some love to bring us together."

"When Ermias was born I was in the delivery room," said Dawit Asghedom. "And I saw him struggling because his umbilical cord was around his neck. We thought we were gonna lose him, but he made it. So I knew that he was very strong. He's a fighter."

Like many young parents raising kids under economic pressure, Dawit and Angelique felt the strain on their relationship. Although the marriage ended in divorce when the boys were very small, Dawit did his best to remain a presence in their lives. "It happens to a lot of families and it happened to us," said Dawit. "The kids are the ones who suffer. It was very devastating to become a weekend father. But still, whenever we meet, we had fun."[70]

Ermias used to cry when his father dropped him off at his grandmother's house. "We never lived in the same house," he recalled. "As far as I can remember my mom and him was separated, but I always had a high respect and a genuine love for my pops, 'cause he put the best foot forward." Dawit and his sons loved watching movies together. He would take them to the cinema or the bowling alley, or stay home and cook the boys traditional Eritrean food. "My pops was always energetic, always had a positive aura, always had a good vibe," Ermias remembered. "Always smiling, always lit up a room when he walked in."[71]

Just three years apart, Ermias and his big brother were very close, sharing a bedroom growing up. "When my mom came in the room and he was cryin', I got whupped," Sam recalled at his brother's memorial service. "That was my little bro, man. And I just did as much as I could to lead a good example and make sure he was good."[72] In his 2008 song "Reality," Hussle raps that "It was just me and my brother. Look, my brother's my nigga."

They were lucky to have each other because the neighborhood outside their home was going through some very tough times. "The mid-1980s represented the nadir of South Central's already tumultuous history," wrote California State University, Northridge, professor Josh Sides, in his history of Black Los

Angeles, *L.A. City Limits.* "Fueled primarily by the wave of plant closures, black unemployment and poverty rates rose throughout the decade."[73]

Growing up on South Central's West Side, in the neighborhood of Hyde Park, the Asghedom brothers were raised within the jurisdiction of the LAPD's Seventy-Seventh Street Division, remembered by one area resident as "the last bastion of white supremacy."[74] Among the officers stationed there was Detective Mark Fuhrman, who would gain notoriety for his role in the O. J. Simpson murder trial. Starting in 1985, the year of Ermias Asghedom's birth, Fuhrman began giving a series of interviews to an aspiring screenwriter. His remarkably candid statements, which he never expected to be attributed to him by name, offer a peek behind the "blue wall of silence" and inside the Seventy-Seventh. "They knew damn well I did it," Fuhrman said of an incident where he "basically tortured" Black suspects, then lied to Internal Affairs about the incident. "But there was nothing they could do about it. Most of the guys worked Seventy-Seventh together. We were tight. I mean, we could have murdered people and got away with it. We all knew what to say."[75]

Exactly one week before Ermias turned three years old, N.W.A solidified West Coast rap's nationwide respect level with *Straight Outta Compton.* 1988 was a landmark year in hip-hop, with classic albums dropping left and right. Contrasted with the Black empowerment of Public Enemy's *It Takes a Nation of Millions to Hold Us Back* or the playful narrative bravado of Slick Rick's *Great Adventures*, N.W.A struck a decidedly more somber note starting with the intro to their LP's title track: "When somethin' happens in South Central, Los Angeles, nothin' happens. It's just another nigga dead."

Although South Central has since been rebranded South L.A., N.W.A's harsh observation rings painfully true more than three decades later in the Black Lives Matter era. Eazy-E, Dr. Dre, Ice Cube, MC Ren, The D.O.C., and DJ Yella gave voice to their own frustration and that of an entire community with songs like "Fuck tha Police," which was banned from radio airwaves and public libraries and drew attacks from police unions and the FBI. Also known as "The World's Most Dangerous Group," N.W.A had a distinctive sound thanks to the production genius of Andre "Dr. Dre" Young and a mindset that matched the name of their record label: Ruthless. Although they were not the first to rap about street life, N.W.A brought what would come to be called "gangsta rap" to worldwide attention. Efforts to ban "Fuck tha Police" made N.W.A First Amendment heroes and the song became a protest anthem that still gets play to this day.

Two years later, "gangsta rap" achieved another cultural milestone when Crip OG Michael Concepcion assembled a group he called the West Coast Rap All-Stars to record a seven-minute posse cut titled "We're All in the Same Gang." Produced by Dr. Dre and featuring verses by N.W.A members Eazy-E and MC Ren, the song included the voices of nationally famous L.A. rappers Ice-T and Tone Lōc, rising Oakland stars MC Hammer and Digital Underground, and a few other fresh talents—all sending a clear antiviolence message and promoting unity at a time when gang-related killings were on the rise.

"I wanted to stop these kids from making the same bad mistakes I did," said Concepcion, who was paralyzed from the waist down by gunshot wounds. The single topped *Billboard*'s newly established chart devoted to Hot Rap Singles, broke into the pop Top 40, and earned a Grammy nomination. The song was getting play but its message fell on deaf ears. Violence in the streets continued to escalate through the early '90s.

Despite all the madness going on outside, Ermias and Samiel Asghedom grew up surrounded by love. "I have so many good memories," Sam recalls. "We went to school, rode bikes, went to summer camps, church."[76] In one family video Sam directs his younger brother, who seems barely able to contain his energy. "Introducing the rockin' brothers," Sam says off-camera, "Ermias Asghedom and Samiel Asghedom!" Ermias suddenly bursts into the living room to show off his dance moves in pajamas and socked feet, soon to be joined by his big brother.[77]

"First things first," Nipsey wrote in a 2018 essay for the Players Tribune. "If you want to know about Crenshaw, you gotta get to know my granny. My granny is a G. Bro, in a neighborhood with actual gangsters, my granny's more of a G than all of 'em. Her preferred weapon was a type of love and calm that was so big, it could consume the toughest O.G." He remembered her house smelling like coffee and cinnamon, with the TV tuned to *The Price Is Right*, her favorite game show. "There was so much peace in that house." There was also a basketball court at the elementary school across the street. What more could two kids who loved hoopin' ask for?

"We played 24/7," Nipsey recalled. "It'd be me and my brother Sam, and we'd meet up with a couple of our homies: Tiffany, Chris, Bryan, Jermaine, and any one of our neighbors that live down the street from us. We banged blocks, so we challenged kids from other blocks to play us. We were the 60th Street crew."[78]

On hot days in the summer the best way to cool off was in the local swimming pool,[79] which charged one dollar for admission. "That used to be a mission to get a dollar, to put it together," Hussle remembers. "We'd ask the lady to let us help her take her groceries in, to give us a quarter or whatever."

From an early age, Sam noticed that his brother had a knack for getting money by applying his intelligence. While Sam and his friends would get busy washing cars, watering lawns, and shoveling up neighbors' dog poop, Nip found other ways to make a buck. "He always had a scheme," Sam recalled. "We'd work hard all day and it seemed Nip would just put in ten minutes and come back with two, three hundred. We couldn't believe it!"[80]

Every day their mom would get up early—awakened by a rooster in a neighbor's yard—and travel to work at Kaiser Permanente West Los Angeles Medical Center.[81] Ermias attended the Open School, an alternative elementary program with a diverse student body that was near her work. He showed a talent for creative writing. At age seven Ermias wrote a short story called "The Snow Monster" about four brave friends, one of whom had the same name as his big brother.[82]

> On a steep, scary mountain lived a monster. He ate meat and grilled it with his breath. Everybody was afraid of him, except four boys, Jack, Johnathan, Sam, and me." The boys' decision to chase the monster away comes back to haunt them years later when the monster's family turns the tables.

The story's themes of courage, friendship, adventure, and consequences would continue to resonate through Ermias's school writings. The following year he wrote a funny story about a boy with an unpronounceable name beginning with *E*—but the similarities end there. "Once there was a kid named Ejksrl," the tale begins, unfolding on a "hot, dripping Sunday morning." E and his friend Coyote learn life lessons the hard way—jumping off cliffs, landing in wet cement, munching on cactus sandwiches. The trouble is that Ejksrl does not listen.

By age ten Ermias had transitioned to poetry. His free verse "Clouds in the Desert" is filled with emotion and haunting imagery:

YOU ARE BURNING THROUGH THE DAY
AS I RUN YOU FOLLOW ME.
YOU ARE ALL OVER.
AS I CRY OUT FOR HELP,
I AM STRUCK BY THE LIGHT.
NOT A SOUL RESPONDS TO MY CRY.

David, the classmate who shared these student writings on social media, remembered Ermias as "just a nice sweet smart kid I used to know."[83]

Unfortunately, schoolteachers didn't always recognize his intelligence in the classroom. "In third grade, I had a homie that was Korean, super smart. I got another homie who was Jewish. They used to copy off my work," Ermias recalled in an interview years later. While those same classmates were tested to see if they could join a special program for gifted students, Ermias was not given a chance to take the test. When Ermias asked, his teacher said students had to be selected for the special curriculum.

His mother soon paid the teacher a visit. "Y'all better test my son," she insisted. Sure enough, Ermias tested off the charts. "That was an introduction to how the world was for me," he later reflected. "People gonna doubt you and that don't mean that they right. It just mean they don't understand."[84]

CAN'T EVEN SEE THE STARS BUT WE STILL WISH
REAL SHIT, REAL SHIT
WHO WOULD EVER THOUGHT THAT WE WOULD BUILD THIS?

—Nipsey Hussle, "Real Big," *Victory Lap* (2018)

Ermias was six years old in February 1992 when the teenage rap duo Kris Kross dropped "Jump," topping the pop charts for eight weeks straight. Like the rest of America's youth, he was soon *Totally Krossed Out*, drawing serious inspiration from the pint-size Atlanta rap stars born Chris Smith and Chris Kelly, but better known as Daddy Mac and Mac Daddy.

"I thought I was gonna be like Kris Kross," Ermias later confessed on the *Rap Radar* podcast. He began formulating his own raps with a clear objective in mind. "My goal was by the time I was twelve, thirteen I would be signed and crackin' as a little kid," he said. "I got frustrated when I didn't get turned into Bow Wow."[85]

For a bright kid who was underestimated at school, the rap game promised a more level playing field where a young Black man could be recognized for his talents. But just as Ermias's visions of stardom were taking shape, the reality outside his family's home was getting crazier. On April 29, 1992—just one day after the grassroots Community Self-Determination Institute established a fragile truce among rival gangs in Watts—two dramatic events shook the neighborhood to its core.[86]

First, four members of a set known as the Du-Roc Crips were arrested for the execution-style murder of Keith Cardell Thomas, better known as Stone, a respected leader within the Rollin' 60s. Stone was honored by many of his peers for maintaining a code of ethics and even reaching out to rival sets. By choosing unity over self-destruction, Stone hearkened back to the Crips' original mission—before the crack epidemic turned brother against brother. For him and an associate from the neighborhood to be killed in what appeared to be a drug deal gone bad was a tragedy on many levels.[87]

That same day a mostly white jury failed to convict four LAPD officers whose savage beating of unarmed Black motorist Rodney King fractured his skull and damaged his brain. Such outrages were not unprecedented, but in this case the cops' excessive use of force had been captured on video and broadcast on the nightly news for months on end, burning the sickening images into the national psyche. Within hours of the verdict's announcement the streets of L.A. erupted in outrage that police were powerless to contain. Five days of burning, looting, and assaults on white- and light-skinned motorists ended with more than 60 people dead—at least 10 of them shot by LAPD and National Guard troops—over 2,000 injured, almost 6,000 arrested, and approximately $1 billion worth of property damaged. The moral, social, and psychological toll remains incalculable. "By year's end, Los Angeles had 1,096 homicides, a record," the *Los Angeles Times* reported. "Almost two decades later 1992 remains L.A.'s deadliest year."[88]

Ermias was six years old when the riots kicked off; his brother was ten. Dawit Asghedom was an avid CNN viewer, so his sons were always exposed to current events. "We talked about it," said Hussle's friend and musical collaborator, Baby Gooch, who was older than Hussle and related some of his firsthand experiences in the street. "He understood what was up, 'cause he was sharp. Everybody was lookin' at the police brutality and all of that."[89]

The flashpoint of the uprising was the intersection of Florence and Normandie Avenues, just a short drive from Crenshaw and Slauson. "We were right in the middle of everything," recalls hip-hop artist Hoodsta Rob, who grew up in the 60s and would later collaborate with Nipsey as a member of the Slauson Boyz. "We was goin' crazy because we didn't receive justice. But at the same time it made us look bad 'cause we was tearin' our own stuff up. But in reality we didn't own none of this stuff."[90]

According to Gooch, not all of the destruction was as random as media reports indicated. "After a while, the second or third day, you had idiots just settin' shit on fire that was drinkin'," he says. "But in the beginning the stuff people was burnin' was places they already had a grievance with. Like one of the first places they burned was the store where they shot Latasha Harlins," the fifteen-year-old Black girl who was killed by a Korean store owner over a bottle of orange juice.[91]

"It was just like, 'Don't mess with us,'" says Hoodsta Rob. "At the end of the day what needed to happen was for us to receive the right justice so we wouldn't have to take it into our own hands."[92]

Whether you prefer to call them the L.A. Riots, the L.A. Uprising, or *las quemazónes*—the great burning—the events that began on April 29, 1992, could not have come as a complete surprise to anybody who was paying attention. Many of the injustices that gave rise to the 1965 Watts Rebellion had yet to be corrected decades later, so the aftershock was only a matter of time. Those who had no other clue could always follow the advice of A Tribe Called Quest and "Check the Rhime." As Chuck D of Public Enemy famously remarked, "Rap is Black America's TV station."[93]

While songs like "Batterram" and "Fuck tha Police" foretold the frustration that set Los Angeles ablaze, those smoldering embers sparked the blunt of Dr. Dre's solo debut *The Chronic*, which set new sales benchmarks and made Death Row Records the hottest rap label in the world. Recorded while the city was still burning and released just eight months after the smoke cleared, *The Chronic* became an American pop culture milestone. Snoop later admitted in Allen Hughes's documentary *The Defiant Ones* that he "went out lootin' and stole all kinds of shit and brought it back to the studio" while making the album.[94]

Dre and Snoop's magnum opus would become the soundtrack to Ermias Asghedom's life. "You didn't have to spend $16 at the

Wherehouse to hear the new Death Row record," he wrote. "You didn't choose Pac or Snoop or Dre. It came to you, outta every car and every house on the block. It became part of you and part of everything you did. It was with you on the boom box next to the court, it was with you at parties and it was with you in the car. I started listening to Pac and Dre, and Nate Dogg and Warren G, and it led me to Biggie and Jay-Z. Death Row was the bridge."

As commercially successful as it was raw, *The Chronic* brought all the pain and fury of the L.A. uprising to the pop charts, solidifying Dre as a multiplatinum hitmaker, ushering in Snoop as a charismatic new superstar, and setting off the meteoric rise of Death Row. Run by NFL defensive lineman turned bodyguard turned music entrepreneur Marion "Suge" Knight, Death Row gave new resonance to the term "gangsta rap." Suge grew up in Compton with close ties to the Mob Piru Blood set (Tupac would later align himself with the Mob as well), while Snoop and Daz of Tha Dogg Pound were affiliated with the Rollin' 20s Crips of Long Beach. Tha Dogg Pound's other half, Philadelphia-born MC Kurupt, was managed for a time by Big U and repped the Rollin' 60s.

According to Big U, who was incarcerated during the L.A. Uprising, the unrest "unified the Crips and the Bloods to a certain degree." He believes that the success of Death Row was made possible by "the unity from the riots and dudes not trippin' on the gangs and each other." The idea of a label run by a man with a fondness for wearing red suits, and featuring talent with a clear preference for blue, was something new in L.A. rap. "That was something, of course, the overseers couldn't have happen," Big U observed, "but it was good for a moment for the people to see that they could get together."[95]

Snoop's success changed the rap game forever, sending "gangsta rap" into heavy rotation on MTV and making Los Angeles the capital of the rap game. "The East Coast had it for a *long* fuckin' time," Snoop told me. "*This is what the fuck we do. This is our shit. Woo woo woo* . . . And they treated everybody different until you earned your respect, which was the rules and regulations which made you have to be great in hip-hop . . . We understood the dialect of structure, how they put the shit together, how you must be great, you must have a stage show . . . So that's what the clash was—we had took something that they created. And nobody was used to shit being taken back then."[96]

Artists like Nipsey Hussle and Kendrick Lamar represented a new generation of West Coast rappers who bridged the gap between L.A. and NYC. "Now you can't spell New York without Los Angeles," Snoop says. "We're all together now. There's so much brotherhood, from gang culture to rap culture. We got Bloods and Crips all over my city and all over New York. They all connect with each other . . . You got brothers from the same walk of life, the same mind state."[97] If Death Row started that process of reconciliation, it was artists like Nipsey Hussle and YG who brought it to fulfillment. Although there were more than a few bumps along the way.

A year after *The Chronic* was released, Snoop appeared at the 1993 MTV Video Music Awards to present the Moonman trophy for Best R&B Video—along with two big homies of funk, Dr. Dre and George Clinton. En Vogue's "Free Your Mind" beat out Prince, Boyz II Men, and Mary J. Blige that year, while "Nuthin' but a 'G' Thang" was nominated for the Best Rap Video award, along with Naughty By Nature's "Hip Hop Hooray" and "Rebirth of Slick (Cool Like Dat)" by Digable Planets—all three of which lost out to the squeaky clean Sly Stone update "People Everyday" by Arrested Development.

Immediately after the ceremony, Snoop turned himself in to police investigating him in connection with a gang-related homicide.[98] The twenty-two-year-old star would go on to stand trial, beat the charges against him with representation by Death Row Records in-house counsel David Kenner, and flip the whole experience into the short film *Murder Was the Case*, complete with a chart-topping certified double-platinum soundtrack album. While he was still out on bail, Snoop had the audacity to perform his hit single "Murder Was the Case" at the following year's MTV Video Music Awards.[99]

Listening keenly every step of the way was young Ermias Asghedom. Snoop was more than influential; he was ubiquitous. "You didn't have to buy Snoop albums in L.A.," Hussle often said. "You'd go outside and hear every song . . . That shit was everywhere."[100] Ermias would emulate Snoop's flows, sometimes substituting his own words. "It's like this and like that and like *this* and uh . . ."

Ermias first experienced the thrill of hearing his voice over a beat while messing around with his homeboy Jermaine Jenkins, who lived nearby on Sixtieth Street. Jermaine's mom used to drive Ermias to elementary school, and the Jenkins family even had a computer in the house. "Back then that was big shit to have a computer!" Nip recalled years later. Through ingenuity and sheer force of will the boys figured out how to plug a rudimentary mic into the machine, and before long Ermy was rapping over Snoop instrumentals, fitting his own lyrics into Doggy Dogg's flows from *Tha Doggfather*.[101]

Playing around with the computer was cool, but what Ermias wanted more than anything was to record in a real studio. He and Jermaine would go in the backyard and pretend to make their own. "We'd just be clearing the dirt," he recalled. "Sweepin' the backyard up, like, 'We gonna build it right here.'" But in reality studio equipment was expensive. "We gonna have to get money to do this," he realized. "We can't just wing it on a dream."[102]

"Stereotypes of a Black male misunderstood," The Notorious B.I.G. rapped on his breakout hit "Juicy"—"and it's still all good." The year was 1994, and for Ermias it was *not* all good. "I took a lot of losses," he reflected later in life. "Getting your bike stolen out the backyard a loss. That was heartbreaking as a kid. That's like your car. You can't even do *nothin'* no more. You stuck."[103]

But a bike could be replaced. Nine-year-old Ermias had bigger goals than moving around his neighborhood. Blessed with ability, ambition, and a sensitive heart, he felt a sense of frustration. "Growing up as a kid, I was looking for somebody," he reflected later. "Not to give me anything, but somebody that cared. Someone that was creating the potential for change and that had an agenda outside of their own self-interest."[104]

His mother had his best interests at heart, but she also had her hands full. "I was living as a single mother with the boys," Angelique Smith recalled. "I just thought that I didn't need a man, 'cause I could make my own money."[105] Staying with her mother while saving up to buy a house, she kept her kids on a strict budget. "We lived with Granny for the first seven years of my life," Hussle recalled. "She had a two-bedroom house. It was me, moms, and bro in the other bedroom in the bed together."[106]

By the time he was eleven, Ermias had a new favorite rapper. Raised by members of the Black Panther Party, Tupac Shakur was a poet, actor, and charismatic leader with a rebellious spirit who never backed down from a challenge and didn't hesitate to escalate. Since Suge Knight bailed him out of prison to sign with Death Row in October 1995, Pac had collaborated with Snoop and released the classic double album *All Eyez on Me* in February of the following year. Then he proceeded to heat up the summer of 1996 with "Hit 'em Up," featuring his crew the Outlaw Immortalz. The scathing diss track inflamed Death Row's musical war with East Coast rival Bad Boy Records to meltdown levels.

"I remember bein' a kid and my homie mama pickin' us up, like 'Pac just dissed Biggie, listen!'" Nipsey said. "She popped on 'Hit 'em Up,' the cussin' version, 'That's why I fucked your bitch, you fat motherfucker!' And went crazy! We was little eleven-year-old kids. That's how much of an event that was."[107]

A few months later, on September 7, 1996, Suge was driving Pac through Las Vegas in his black BMW when a white Cadillac pulled up alongside them at a red light. Earlier that evening, following Mike Tyson's first-round knockout of Bruce Seldon at the MGM Grand, they had brawled with some Southside Crips in the casino lobby. When the Cadillac window rolled down, somebody squeezed off shots from a Glock, striking Shakur four times. "I thought that Tupac was gonna live forever," says L.A. rapper Yo-Yo, one of the few people who were allowed to visit him in the hospital. "I swear I thought he was gonna survive. I just knew that Pac had nine lives."[108] Six days after the shooting, he died at age twenty-five.

Already a superstar, Tupac Shakur became a mythic figure in death. His final masterpiece was released under a new name, Makaveli. *The Don Killuminati: The 7 Day Theory* cast an ominous spell over listeners as Pac spit some of the realest shit he ever wrote in an atmosphere heavy with fear and loathing, overlaid with grief. Young Ermias couldn't get enough.

During a trip to the Wherehouse in late 1996, Ermias asked his father to buy him a copy of the Makaveli album. "I told him, 'No, why do you want this?'" Dawit Asghedom recalled. "At the same time, deep in my head, I thought maybe it will teach him something. There was always music at my house—R&B

mostly—and books. So I changed my mind and told him, 'I'll buy you this one.'"[109]

"L.A. rap taught me what a complete artist was," Nipsey would reflect years later. "Them dudes weren't just rappers. They was autobiographers, with a full array of emotional subject matter. They was telling deep stories in their music. Stories about being human, about being a man. Stories about *me*."[110] The words he heard from the prematurely deceased artist made a powerful impression on Ermias. When he grew up to fulfill his ambitions as a rapper, he shouted Pac out in many of his raps, and even released a track titled "Picture Me Rollin'" twenty years after Shakur's song of the same name. Surrounded by haters, Pac's song asked, "Will God forgive me for all the dirt a nigga did to feed kids?" Hussle's version seemed more at peace: "Feeling connected to God, tryna get closer."

As a student at Edwin Markham Middle School, home of the Soaring Eagles, Ermias did most of his rollin' on public transportation. If his mom didn't drop him off, he would catch the L.A. Metro's Blue Line to and from Watts, where his favorite teacher was Merelean Wilson. Born in Compton, Ms. Wilson worked at NASA before devoting herself to education, and like all great teachers, she had a way of bringing out the best in her students. "It is important that our youths realize that the difference between the impossible and the possible lies in their determination," she wrote in an essay for the Los Angeles NAACP Youth Council. "To succeed—do the best you can, where you are, with what you have."[111]

"I'm going to be a rapper," Ermias used to tell her while tapping out a beat with two pencils, but he was serious about his schoolwork.

Ms. Wilson remembered him as a straight-A student who ate lunch with her just to make sure he understood his assignments. Writing in wobbly cursive script, twelve-year-old Ermias left a touching inscription in her 1997 yearbook. "To: Ms. M. Wilson, Over all the hard times and long days I will always love you." His handwriting in her 1999 yearbook was a bit looser and the sentiment more upbeat. "To: Miss Wilson," wrote fourteen-year-old Ermias, "You were my favorite teacher and friend at Markham. Please don't ever stop teaching because everyone at Markham needs a little bit of you in their life. Love Always, Ermias Asghedom." Next to his signature he added "Class of '99' Whop!! Whop!!" drawing the year in big bubble letters.[112]

Watts was a long way from his home, but Ermias was making new friends in the neighborhood, like Killa Twan. "We first connected in the streets," recalls Twan, who grew up in the Nickerson Gardens projects. Though he loved school, he didn't go to Markham because he was kicked out of the district in sixth grade, allegedly for an incident involving a gun. "The older dudes used to come from high school from projects we didn't get along with," Twan remembers. Many of the students at nearby Locke High School were Crip-affiliated, but Twan's projects was the home of the Bounty Hunter Bloods. "They'd come fuck us up at the school and I wasn't havin' that shit."[113]

Even though Ermias came from Crenshaw, he got nothing but love in Watts. "Just his whole stature, you could tell he was one hundred percent solid," Twan recalls. "He was raised to carry himself like a man at a young age. His whole demeanor was cool as fuck." Twan described himself and Ermias as "regular street dudes gettin' it by any means," and says they spent most of their time "hustling." Their musical connection would come a few years later.[114]

Twan was friendly with O.F.T.B. (Operation From The Bottom), a trio of older rappers from Nickerson Gardens whose break-out single, "Slangin' Dope," landed them an album deal with Big Beat Records. The independent New York label was founded by Craig Kallman, a DJ turned record executive who went on to become president of Atlantic Records, where he would eventually partner with All Money In. O.F.T.B.'s success inspired Twan to dream big. "I was always into the music from up under them," says Twan. "I used to be out here just rappin', sayin' shit to people."[115]

Meanwhile Ermias continued to nurture his own passion for music, pursuing the goal of teenage stardom. His mother couldn't afford to pay for studio time, but she did find him a free music class. On Saturdays she would drop him off at the Watts Towers Arts Center to study with a classically trained composer. "He taught us how to use the MPC, which is the beat machine, a sixteen-track recorder," Nipsey recalled. "That was my first exposure to production." By tapping on the MPC's four rows of rubber pads, Ermias could trigger an infinite variety of drum sounds and samples. But every beat started with the sound of a metronome counting out the time. *Tick-tick-tick.*[116]

"My moms would always see me writing raps and all that, listening to CDs and buyin' *The Source* magazines," Hussle said later. "She was just like, 'I know you're on your music real heavy. If you want, I'll start droppin' you off.'"[117]

When he was twelve his stepfather's dad bought the family a home computer, which somehow broke down and had to be thrown away. It was a tragic setback, but Ermias refused to quit, studying the computer magazines his grandfather had given them along with the discarded machine. One day he came home from school with a backpack full of computer parts. Sam, who liked to keep their room tidy, was not happy with all the creative clutter and asked his brother to get rid of the mess.[118]

"Nah," Ermias told him. "I'm gonna build a computer."

"There's no way," Sam replied. "Get this shit outta here!"

Undeterred, Ermias kept coming home day after day with more computer parts. "Took him about a week, maybe two weeks," Sam recalled. "We just had loose parts on the floor." Then Ermias purchased a case and power supply at a computer auction and it was finally ready.

"He turned it on," Sam remembered during his eulogy at the memorial service. "I could not believe this. He had built the computer and it was workin'!" At that moment the entire Staples Center burst into thunderous applause. "I was just amazed. I really was mind-boggled. I was proud of him. My mom, everybody—we couldn't believe it." Astonished family members visited to get a glimpse of Ermias's homemade computer, impressed at both the machine itself and the remarkable young man who built it from scratch.

Building his own computer was only one step on the musical journey that Ermias would later come to call his Marathon. "He ended up gettin' software and being able to record music on that computer," Sam continued. "I remember hearin' something that he recorded at a young age and I couldn't believe it." The composition was so complex, so accomplished. Sam had to pull him to the side: *Bro, did you write this?*

The next day Sam decided to try his own luck at making music—just in case the talent ran in the family. "If bro did it," he said to himself, "let me see." Within two weeks, he'd given up on the idea. "It skipped me," he said with a smile. From that day on Sam knew for sure his little brother was special.

"Whatever you can do," Sam told him, "we believe."[119]

Chapter 3

ON HOOD

POPS WAS GONE, MOMS WAS NEVER HOME
BUT THE STREETS WAS RIGHT THERE
SO THEY TOOK YOU AS THEY OWN

—Nipsey Hussle, "Blue Laces," *The Marathon* (2010)

Ermias was starting to wonder when opportunity would meet preparation. He'd been preparing for as long as he could remember, but opportunities were hard to come by. By the age of thirteen, he hadn't gained much traction toward reaching his goal of blowing up in the rap game, and with each passing day it was like he heard a clock ticking inside his head. *Tick-tick-tick*.

That ticking sounded even louder when you grew up in an area immersed in gang culture. Riding his bike around the neighborhood, it wasn't unusual for him to hear gunshots, and everybody knew somebody who got locked up or died before their time. At the mall, the basketball court, on the way to school—anything could go down at any moment. Years down the line Hussle would speak on these feelings in "Real Big" (originally titled "Rescue Me"): "Tryin' to walk to school, get your jaw socked / Tryin' to pump your gas, get your car shot."

As with all his best raps, the song's subject matter was rigorously factual. "That just show you being a kid trying to get to school, what you had to navigate through," he said during the *Victory Lap* promo run. "You get jacked for your Jordans. That was a thing. Nigga ask you what size shoe you wear on your way to the bus stop, seven in the morning. Like, it been goin' on for years. It's been the reality since we was kids."[1] *Tick-tick-tick.*

Realizing that tomorrow wasn't promised, Ermias lived with a sense of urgency. He already felt he was reaching a crossroads in life. He had a strong sense of purpose for his age. An inner voice was telling him to follow his love of music, just like his mother's older brother, who was a hustler and a musician.

But instead of following in his uncle's footsteps, he was sticking with his studies—mostly out of respect for his mother's wishes. She had long since remarried and Samiel and Ermias now had a half sister, Samantha. She used to sneak into Ermy's room and read his prized lyric notebooks. Ermias would spend hours filling the pages with rhymes and drawing on the covers. He wanted them to look like a piece of art, inside and out. "I had no idea what it even meant," Samantha admitted, but something told her the books were important.[2]

Having graduated from Markham Middle School, Ermias started attending Alexander Hamilton High. Located in the more affluent neighborhood of South Robertson, Hamilton was a magnet school that boasted a diverse student body and a strong arts program. Hamilton's alumni include renowned jazz musician Kamasi Washington, pop stars Fiona Apple and Omarion, and Hollywood heartthrob Shia LaBeouf.

Most kids from the neighborhood went to Crenshaw High, the alma mater of Darryl Strawberry, Ice-T, and ScHoolboy Q. It certainly would have been much more convenient, but Ermias's mother placed a high priority on getting the best possible education. Making his way to and from Hamilton every day was a journey requiring multiple bus transfers. Ermias would ride with his friend Jermaine, whose parents had also made the effort to apply to Hamilton. One day Jermaine introduced him to a kid from the neighborhood named Evan. People called him Rimpau after the street he lived on.

"I remember the first time I heard Nip rap," Rimpau recalled in a Kev Mac video interview. They were heading home from school on the crosstown number 3 bus and Ermias spit a verse that deeply impressed his friend. "I was like, '*That shit is hard,*'" Rimpau recalls. "I knew at that point cuz was gonna be something." Rimpau became a true believer in himself too. From that day forward he started taking rap more seriously.[3]

Despite his passion for music, Ermias was committed to academic achievement. "He was always deep, even him being younger than me," remembers Jaire Lewis, another Hamilton hip-hop head who was three years ahead of the kid they called Ermy. "He was really quiet at first, but he's a major thinker. The type that just soaks things up." They used to gather with other aspiring rappers on the quad at school, and freestyle rhymes back and forth. As they got to know each other, Ermias opened up and showed his sense of humor. Lewis admired his rap skills and his vocabulary. "At school I always thought I was smart, but he was an *anomaly*," Lewis recalls. "It was like, 'What the fuck did you just say?' Always ahead of his time, beyond his years—that's just who he is."[4]

When Ermias heard that Lewis had studio equipment at his house, he promptly invited himself over to work. "Him and Rimpau ended up being regular guests at the house," recalls Lewis, who came from a musical family with deep roots in South Los Angeles. His mother was the principal of Fifty-Fourth Street Elementary School in Crenshaw, and fully supported her son's musical aspirations. He went by the name EQ at the time, but would later be known as Ralo Stylez.

They spent hours listening to all sorts of music. Ermy's musical tastes were extremely diverse. "I was influenced by anybody that was great," he said, everything from Bob Marley to Marvin Gaye to Jimi Hendrix.[5] When it came to hip-hop he was similarly open-minded, unlimited by regional bias or bicoastal rivalries.

Ever since Biggie was shot dead in L.A. on March 9, 1997—just six months after Pac's murder in Vegas—Ermias had been getting into the latest lyrical genius to arise from the streets of Brooklyn, a cat named Jay-Z who started his own label, Roc-A-Fella Records, when the industry fronted on his talent. Jay's intricate bars were studded with jewels to enrich the mind. "I ain't no rapper," he stated on the intro to his 1998 album, *In My Lifetime Vol. 1*. "I'm a hustler. It just so happens that I know how to rap." The following track, "A Million and One Questions," had answers for anyone seeking to overstand the economics of the rap game: "What's the position you hold?" Jay asked. "Can you really match a triple-platinum artist buck by buck but only a single goin' gold?"

Ermias loved the way DJ Premier's beat switched up in the middle of the record—classic hip-hop shit. Jay-Z was nice on the mic, and his hustler's spirit completed the package. Hussle was also a fan of Bay Area legends like Too $hort and E-40. As much as he felt their music, he admired their independent grind, selling cassettes straight out of the trunks of their cars and keeping 100 percent of the profits.

Staying up on the latest rap releases soon became more than a passion for Ermias. He turned it into a hustle. Using their computer knowledge, he, Rimpau, and Ralo would burn their own mix CDs and flip them at school for five dollars apiece. "Before we had our own music," Rimpau recalls, "we was selling

bootlegs at Hamilton. That was my first real hustle, just fuckin'
with Nip." Ermias also introduced his big brother to the CD
game. Applying his relentlessly disciplined grind, Sam took the
idea and ran with it.[6]

"I was hella nonchalant in school," Rimpau remembers. "I
would go to class and go to sleep." Ermias, on the other hand,
was a diligent student—at first. "Nip was real focused in excel-
ling. We was ditchers, though. We would jump the gates and
leave, go to the mall and shit . . . Fun shit."[7] Rimpau called
Ermias "the flyest young nigga at Hamilton," and they both used
to search for the latest drops from cool streetwear brands of the
day like Akademiks, Ecko, and Enyce.[8]

School was cool, but by this point there were many things
competing for Ermias's attention. He joined the Hamilton High
basketball team, and even though he could dunk he eventually
quit. "I wasn't with gettin' yelled at," he told Big Boy.[9]

Sometimes he worked the counter at his stepfather's seafood
restaurant in Inglewood, but every spare moment away from
school was spent working on music. Ermias told Rimpau about
the Watts Towers center and invited him to come practice beat-
making with him. They'd catch the 108 bus together and ride
the L.A. Metro Blue Line train for the chance to make as many
beats as they could in an hour. The journey could be challenging,
especially walking through the Blood neighborhood between the
108 bus stop and the Metro station. "Niggas had some issues
gettin' on that Blue Line sometimes," Rimpau recalls.[10]

Rare S and Daddy O Cocaine, aspiring artists from Watts
who they met in the program, invited them to hang out around
Jordan Downs projects in Grape Street Crip territory. They went
along, knowing it was risky. "You was brave bro," Rimpau posted
on Instagram after Nipsey's death. "You wasn't scared of nothing
and if you was you never showed it."[11]

Slowly but surely, music was taking on more importance in their lives than school. When they weren't studying production in Watts they were spending time with Ralo. "They was already a package deal," Ralo remembers of Ermias and Rimpau. "I was with this other crew. We called ourselves the Knuckleheads."[12]

Around this time Rimpau's parents pulled him out of Hamilton and he started homeschooling. Ermias would come over and chill instead of going to class. They hung posters of their favorite rappers on the walls. "That's when we started smoking weed and shit, and just being bad," he recalls. "We wanted to be rappers. That was really our dream."[13] Evan aka Rimpau went by EMC and sometimes Eve D (not to be confused with New York rapper Heavy D) while Ermias aka Concept started wearing Africa medallions and cut his hair in a flat-top like Brooklyn rapper Special Ed. For a while they were part of a group called Stranded Minds along with Kid Ink (then known as B Side) and another L.A. artist named Ed Wriott. Around the year 2000 they performed together at the Malcolm X Day Festival in Leimert Park. "For sure we was conscious rappers," Rimpau recalls. "We used to all study that shit. Trying to really elevate our minds."[14]

Ermias could keep creating music on his own, but to really make it pop he needed studio time. That cost money, and he wasn't the type to ask for a handout. "I was a man even when I was thirteen, homie," he once said, trying to explain his mindset at the time. "Don't do me no favors. Let me run mine. You feel me?"[15]

Sometimes Ermias would ride his bike to Slauson and Crenshaw, over by the shopping plaza that he and his brother would purchase one day. "The reason why this lot is special to us, we started in this parkin' lot," Sam explained in a 2017 documentary about the shopping plaza directed by Chucky Millions. "This Shell gas station behind us used to be owned by a Black man. When we was younger we used to catch the bus goin' to school there and we used to always wanna own something. And we used to walk this way goin' home. Across the street at this Louisiana Fried Chicken we used to hustle in that parkin' lot."[16]

Even before opening his first store, Sam had a gift for the business of retail, and when his school days were done, he focused on his grind. Having lived in the neighborhood all his life, he understood the lives of people in the Crenshaw District, people who ate at Hungry Harold's, shopped at the Slauson Swap Meet. He knew what they wanted and he found a way to get paid by meeting their demands. Each morning he would link up with family friend Stephen Donelson, a heavyset, hardworking dude affectionately known as Fatts. Sam would pick Fatts up at six in the morning and they'd set up a table in the Louisiana Fried Chicken parking lot, selling socks, T-shirts, CDs, and DVDs. "Gettin' it," Sam would say, "every day."[17]

Ermias had been on his own get-money missions. Sometimes he'd skip school to hustle at the Shell station or the ARCO station on the other side of Crenshaw Blvd. "Probably like six or seven of us would meet up and sell our little trees, make our little swerves every morning," he recalled. "It became our little hangout. Girls from Culver City and West L.A. would pull up, get their little weed, CDs, DVDs, whatnot, couple other things people would tap in for. Basically bein' young and hustlin', that was our area that we controlled."[18]

When his mom questioned the choices he was making, Ermias told her not to worry—he was going to be a rap star. Though she'd always felt spiritually connected to her youngest son, any mom would be skeptical. "I started to understand the difference between the truth and what your parents are supposed to tell you," Ermias said. "There's a difference."[19]

Angelique Smith knew her son was gifted. All she wanted was the best for him. And she wouldn't tolerate him smoking weed and hanging out all day. "She couldn't see herself workin' so hard, sacrificing everything for me to be a fuckup under her roof," Ermias said. "Basically, you gotta man up and do your own thing if you feel like you've got it like that."[20] While his mom wasn't thrilled that her boy felt he was "too cool for school," his grandmother and father were more understanding. He started spending more time at his childhood home, eventually moving into Granny's place at 59th and 5th Ave. He still had every intention of becoming a successful rapper, he just couldn't say exactly when.

Sensing he had reached a crossroads in life, Ermias searched for signs that he was on the right path. "It was two times where someone came and prophesied to him," says Ralo. In two different songs he rapped about a "crazy lady" who spoke in tongues and told him to "lead the way" and everything was going to work out. "Another time a guy told him he was gonna deal with three people—two of them would betray him but one would do right by him. He said two of them would be in suits and one would be in street clothes." Ermias couldn't be sure who was on which team, but he knew exactly what game he wanted to play.[21]

All kinds of traffic runs along Slauson Avenue, from classic American automobiles to European luxury sedans to city buses, all passing through the heart of South Los Angeles. Slauson connects the L.A. Metro commuter railway, as well as major bus lines and freeway junctions leading in all directions. On their way home from work, people who don't have a car of their own wait for the bus or the train at Slauson and Crenshaw on their way to diverse destinations all over Los Angeles county.

The intersection became known for robberies,[22] especially on the first and the fifteenth of each month when people collected their paychecks and government assistance—high season for hustlers.

Slauson also serves as a line of demarcation between some of South L.A.'s most infamous gang territories. Driving eastbound from Slauson and Crenshaw, you pass through Rollin' 60s, followed in quick succession by Van Ness Gangster Brims, Harvard Park Brims, West Side Neighborhood Crips, and the Hoovers—and those are just a few of the West Side sets. After crossing under the bridge that supports the 110 freeway, Slauson continues through a crazy-quilt patchwork of East Side hoods.

As Nipsey pointed out in his music, making a wrong turn off Slauson can teach you a life lesson. Apart from Google Maps and graffiti, there are few visible clues to navigate by in the real world. Area residents must keep the matrix of borderlines fixed in their minds. When the people are gone, what remains are the stories—the heroic exploits and tragic losses, the loyalty and the betrayal, the incalculable human cost of half a century of gang conflict, passed down from generation to generation.

🏁🏁

Ermias learned at an early age that deserving respect and receiving it are two different things. He was fifteen when he stopped attending Hamilton High, but contrary to popular belief he didn't exactly drop out. "I got put out and went to boot camp for a little bit," he said in a 2010 *Complex* interview. "They tried to say that I was involved in a robbery at the school. There was a computer lab that was broken into, and all the computers got stolen."

Despite his well-documented interest in computers, Ermy proclaimed his innocence—"I didn't do it!" he told *Complex* with a laugh.[23] Taking him at his word—because honesty generally was his policy—Hussle's first brush with the law was getting blamed for somebody else's crime.

After an emotional hearing, Ermias had no choice but to take it on the chin and keep pushing. "My mom went to my court date and expressed her frustration," he recalled. "They were like, 'We got a place for him, don't trip.'" He went to a juvenile program run by the Lennox sheriff's station. "It wasn't no penitentiary," he said. "If you fuckin' up in school, you get put out."[24]

Never one to bow down to authority, Ermias was finished with traditional education, but his hunger for knowledge remained. "I didn't wanna be looked at as no idiot," he told *Complex*, "and I didn't wanna feel like I was uneducated, because I really stopped going to school at fifteen. I was never ignorant, as far as being experienced in classrooms and learning about different subjects and actually soaking it up."[25]

He enrolled himself in a West L.A. community college, signing up for classes in psychology, English, and philosophy. Although his attention was divided between hustling and music by this point, Ermias managed to earn A's and B's. Still, the educational system continued to underestimate him. "My English teacher got at me and was like, 'Are you plagiarizing this shit?'" he recalled. "'You're fifteen and quoting Plato in your essays. What's going on?' I was like, 'Nah, I'm just into it.'"[26]

By the time he turned fifteen, Nipsey was getting into more than Plato. Conflicts with his stepfather were coming to a head at home. In his song "It's Hard Out Here," released on the first *Bullets Ain't Got No Name* mixtape, Hussle spoke about those difficult days, saying that his mother kicked him out and changed the locks. But as he said in the song, he forgave her.

These days Ermias was staying at his granny's house full-time. He was supporting himself on his own, with occasional help from Sam, whose street retail movement with Fatts was growing stronger than ever. "I kinda came into my manhood, or what I thought was my manhood, early," Hussle explained. "I had to make sure I had gas money, food money, rent money, clothes money—everything was on me, startin' at that age. So that's what led me to hustlin'."[27]

Ermias preferred surviving by his wits as opposed to anything that involved robbing or hurting others. "My mom taught me the difference between right and wrong off the top," he said, "but when I was in the street daily, full-time, twenty-four/seven, it's the standard that we follow, and I had to adopt that in order to hold my own."[28]

Still unaligned with a gang, Ermy ran the risk of being jumped. After one too many close calls, he started carrying a pearl-handled .38 for protection. "Growing up in L.A. you learn that you need guns early," Nipsey said. "Because people get shot. People that don't gangbang get shot. People that aren't a part of it, 'cause it's profile. You fit the profile. You a young Black person in L.A., you a young Mexican person in L.A., you get targeted."[29]

But Ermias had other concerns as well. Running around the streets in survival mode wasn't getting him any closer to achieving his dreams. "At that point, I kinda went through my struggle," he reflected later. "A lot of people get stuck in that zone right there and never transcend to the next stage, which was realizing who I am, what I wanted to do, where I wanted to go, and makin' decisions based on that instead of bein' like a leaf on a tree, gettin' blown whichever way."[30] The winds of change were blowing, but an unexpected opportunity would soon present itself.

In 1999, Dexter Browne and his wife, Lisa, moved to Hyde Park and purchased a Crip-blue house on Fifty-Eighth Place. Oddly enough, their real estate agent never mentioned a word about the Rollin' 60s to the young couple from out of town. Born in Trinidad, Dexter had a lot to learn about his new neighborhood, but he was a quick study.[31]

Dexter had attended Howard University on a swimming scholarship and graduated with a degree in civil engineering. He was working as a swimming coach at Howard while dating Lisa, a graphic designer he met in college. They eventually got married and moved to Houston, where Dexter oversaw a major construction project and she became an art director for Rap-A-Lot Records. Founded by the self-made music mogul J. Prince, Rap-A-Lot put Texas hip-hop on the map, launching stars like the Geto Boys, Scarface, and Devin the Dude. While living in Houston, Dexter bought a camera and fell in love with photography. He quickly mastered the technical side of the craft and soon realized that he'd been blessed with an "eye," that instinctive sense of composition and knowing when to squeeze the trigger so as to capture what Henri Cartier-Bresson called the "decisive moment." Lisa hooked him up with a gig shooting album covers for Rap-A-Lot, and a new vision began to take shape.

"We figured out a way to get transferred to Los Angeles," Dexter recalls. "Because of our past experiences, we decided that we wanted to live in a predominantly colored neighborhood. We were fortunate enough to get a house in Crenshaw, where I wanted to set up a studio and hopefully get to shoot some of the hip, rich, and famous in L.A."[32]

Excited to start a new life, Dexter and Lisa converted the guesthouse in their backyard into a studio and awaited the bookings that would surely roll in. But after sending his portfolio around town, Dexter began to grow disenchanted with the reception he was getting. Having prepared himself for a career in photography, he refused to miss out on the opportunities he sensed were all around him. Inspired by Gordon Parks and Che Guevara, Dexter saw himself as a "digital guerrilla." He wasted no time adapting to his surroundings, which a military strategist might describe as a "target-rich environment." There was a certain militancy to the rigor with which Dexter approached his work. His motto: *Don't wait to shoot; shoot and wait.*

"I decided to try a revolutionary effort to create a relentless continuum of undisturbed content," Dexter explains. Possessed by an independent spirit, he abhorred gatekeepers and middlemen. Before the advent of social media, he arrived at the idea that releasing raw and uncut culture would "serve to break the chains of digital slavery already upon us."[33]

In addition to his work as an engineer, Dexter launched a campaign that he dubbed ButterVision. His idea for a pre-YouTube video streaming platform to be called MyDBTV would fall by the wayside because coders were expensive to hire and investors couldn't see Dexter's vision. Still, he pursued plans to document a slice of L.A. life "from the hood to the hills" through video and photography. Working the grapevine, he started getting bookings with Black celebrities and aspiring models, juxtaposing their images with glimpses of Crenshaw street life. His larger agenda was to promote "democratization of media for underrepresented communities while inspiring others to do the same." A visual philosopher of sorts, Dexter was all about promoting unity in the community. He was fond of quoting the Swahili proverb *Vita vya panzi ni furaha ya kunguru*: "War among grasshoppers delights the crows."

As fate would have it, Cuzzy Capone's grandmother and aunt lived on the same block as Dexter and Lisa. Born and raised in the Crenshaw District, Cuzzy was a fixture in the neighborhood,

an extremely talented rapper who got down with the Rollin'
60s as a teenager, ignoring the advice of Baby Gooch, an older
homie—also down with the set—who'd looked out for him since
they were kids. "You know when you're young you don't listen,"
Gooch recalls. When Cuzzy got older and started to gravitate
toward the streets, Gooch tried to warn him. "Hey, this is not the
way," he said. "It's rough out there." But Cuzzy was hard of hearing. "We had many arguments and almost had fights," Gooch
recalls. "When you're young, you just wanna rebel. And I'm like,
You just don't get it!"[34]

Gooch had been around long enough to notice the hood
changing over time. "There was a lot of people in jail," he says.
"And this was before the riots." One by-product of the wide-
spread incarcerations was a loss of experience and knowledge
within gangs like the 60s. Gooch tried to impress upon Cuzzy
what went along with the lifestyle. It wasn't simply a matter
of claiming the hood or repping the hood, Gooch stressed. "If
you're around and something happens," he told Cuzzy, "you gotta
be ready to take part and . . . *do* something." But there was nothing he could really say to stop Cuzzy. He would make his own
choices, just as Gooch had done before him.

But Gooch and Cuzzy had something else in common—
hip-hop. Driven by sheer love of the art form, they would mess
around at various makeshift home studios when Cuzzy wasn't
locked up. Although Cuzzy had worked with Dr. Dre and
provided security for Irv Gotti and Murder Inc, he was so deep
in the streets he didn't consider hip-hop a viable career option.
"I had sat in the crack spot for sixteen months to get off parole,"
Cuzzy recalls. "Once that shit got raided and shut down, I ended
up comin' back to the block. I was forced back to Granny's house
because I didn't have nowhere else to go, and I was just coming
outside during the day. That's when I met Dex."[35]

His first impression of Dexter Browne was a spicy aroma. "Who is this nigga standing in the middle of the block, cooking curry and shit?" Cuzzy asked himself. He had to admit the Trini cuisine smelled pretty good, so he decided to step up. "Boy, gimme one of them plates!" Cuzzy said, and the two got to talking. Dexter explained that he was a photographer, new to the neighborhood.

"I've been shooting some celebs," Dexter told him, "but where can I get to photograph some Crips and Bloods? You know, some hard-core L.A.?"

"Well, Dex, isn't that your house right there?" Cuzzy asked between bites of curried chicken. The photographer nodded. "I hate to break it to you, but you're smack dab in the center of the 60s."

Dexter's heart began to race. "What you talkin' about, twenty, thirty guys?" he asked.

"No, Dex, try about three thousand deep."

"They say be careful what you wish for," Dexter says now, looking back on that moment. "Funny enough, I saw it as an opportunity. I understood that it was going to be very risky and I understood that there were no guarantees. But I had taken some risks previously in my life and I believed all the events leading up to that point had prepared me, particularly me, to try that crazy endeavor."[36]

Dexter invited Cuzzy to come in. They walked to the backyard where there was a guesthouse. Inside, Cuzzy was astonished to find brand-new professional recording equipment, untouched, still covered with protective plastic. "I couldn't believe it," Cuzzy says. "This nigga had a full-blown studio with real pieces and didn't know how to work that shit!"

It was as if the two were meant to find each other. Although Dexter had no musical aspirations himself, he knew that hip-hop was part of ButterVision's creative DNA. Cuzzy had the talent and the drive but lacked resources. A chance conversation led to a discovery that seemed like a dream come true. Before long, Cuzzy was spending his nights sleeping on Dexter's floor and his days recruiting people to join the musical movement.

"What Dexter did was help me create my own space and be able to work on some shit for real instead of just being young, running around," Cuzzy says. "I wasn't truly serious with music until Dexter's."

"ButterVision was a creative camp," Dexter says with evident pride. "We gave Cuzzy and others a unique opportunity to side-step the system." In doing so, Dexter also opened his family's home up to everything that was going on in the streets—just as his wife was pregnant with their first daughter.

"It was real Crips floatin' through that motherfucker," Cuzzy recalls. "There was fights in the backyard and the front, guns getting pulled. We went through it all at Dex's house because it turned into the hangout." Meanwhile, Dexter's photography business was picking up as word spread through Black Hollywood.

"He had five, six model bitches coming through every day," Cuzzy remembers. "Some of the women you see now, he was shooting their first head shots and shit. Or you might see Rick James and Katt Williams. I seen Scarface and J. Prince walk down the driveway—all types of shit."[37]

While Dexter's profile was rising, Cuzzy was busy building a musical team. His first call was to his friend Gooch, who wasn't so sure about the whole ButterVision thing at first. "I'm like, *You better bring your ass over here*," Cuzzy recalls. "He didn't want to, but I told him, this dude got all this equipment and we're at your house recording with the mic taped to the vacuum cleaner!"[38]

"I didn't know Dex," says Gooch, "and from what I understood about studios back in the day, when you create at somebody's place, they have part ownership or they want input. I didn't understand how he would be interested in hip-hop when he wasn't a rapper, didn't make beats. I was like, 'If we're over there at his place making music for free, he's not charging us, he's gonna want *something*.' "[39]

Dexter had reservations of his own. "His homie Gooch was looking a little rough," he recalled, "but Cuzzy said 'Don't worry DB, I got it.' Cuzzy never let me down. He was that guy who knew how to bridge different worlds. I always say he was a Crip with the charisma to go to Hollywood."

Once Gooch had the chance to chat with Dex, his issues were resolved. "I realized that he was just trying to have a creative outlet. We understood the gatekeepers of the industry, and we wanted to express ourselves freely. That's why we came together. Everybody had like minds. And Dexter was a guy who really understood. He read more than we did about photography and branding—a lot of different things. Dexter was like the manager that most artists wish they had. We had a kinship, friendship, and it became like a family thing."[40]

With the endorsement of Gooch and Cuzzy, Dexter became privy to a whole new world. "Many times the 60s would let me walk into any of the houses, anywhere," said Dexter. "Whether it was one of the homies cutting up crack or two guys in the alley fighting with teeth scattered on the ground. I could observe, and in many cases, document."[41]

As Dexter became more familiar with the neighborhood, he noticed this one slim kid who kept popping up at all hours of the day. Dexter might be shooting outside with people like Da Brat and Al B. Sure!, and somehow this kid and his friends would always be there, walking up and down the street. "I would see him passing by on weekdays," Dexter recalls. "So I gathered that he was a street kid who didn't go to school." The kid was Ermias Asghedom, accompanied by his trusty sidekicks Rimpau and Ralo Stylez.

"Dexter had models laid out in the middle of Fifty-Eighth in bikinis," Ralo recalls. "The homies would be down the street. That was like some movie shit."

After much observation, Ermias finally approached Dexter in front of his house and offered to sell him some computer software. "He came with his long jacket and *bam*! He opened it up and there was all these discs hanging inside," Dexter recalls. "He sold me a burned copy of Photoshop and Fruity Loops. I already had the programs, but I was so impressed with the presentation that I purchased two copies."

Dexter was intrigued by the fact that Ermias had studied him as a potential customer, sizing him up and bringing him things that would be useful to a photographer and music producer. "He was customizing his offerings digitally," Dexter recalls. "I just thought that was cool."[42]

Around that same time Cuzzy ran into Ermias walking down Fifty-Eighth with Ralo and Rimpau. When he wasn't out hustling bootleg software, movies, music, or maybe a little weed, Ermy was at Ralo's mother's house working on beats. "I approached them niggas," Cuzzy remembers. "I knew they did music because Ralo had an MPC under his arm. I didn't know how to work it, but I had been around that shit enough, so I knew what the fuck he was holding."

"We greeted each other, introduced ourselves, and it went from there," Cuzzy says. "I'm like, 'What's up with y'all? What y'all doing?'" He didn't have to ask twice.[43]

"I loved Cuzzy from off the jump," Ralo remembers. "Just like his character and his demeanor and shit. He was depressed. He wanted to do a song. And I'm like, 'Nigga, I do a song a night. Let's go!'" The three friends went back to Ralo's house, gathered up more equipment, and went straight to Dexter's.[44]

"I promise you we was making music that same night," Cuzzy recalls with a smile. "Ralo snatched the plastic off the equipment and we got a couple records done right away."[45] In between takes, Cuzzy regaled the young homies with stories of the hood and his adventures in the rap game. Ermias was soon calling him "big bro," and Rimpau felt the same way. "Of course niggas looked up to Cuzzy," said Ralo. "Cuzzy is the archetype, if you will . . . As far as givin' a nigga the confidence. I mean, we would spit and all that, but he's from the hood. So it's a conviction about the way he said shit."[46]

The appreciation was mutual. "Once I had them little niggas over there I was like, 'Damn—we got something here,'" Cuzzy said.[47]

"Our decision to bring Ermy and Ralo and them in was an organic decision that happened at street level," says Dexter, whose neighbors tried to talk him out of having anything to do with young Ermias.

"Absolutely not," he remembers them telling him. "Dex, that one there in particular is going to be problems. Don't bring him in!"[48]

The neighbors knew Cuzzy because he'd grown up on the block. Gooch was another local fixture to whom they'd grown accustomed. "But Ermy and them seemed like the young crowd coming up with their bandannas and everything," Dexter recalls with a laugh. "They just looked a little worrisome. It wasn't that they were afraid of Ermy, but they felt that as soon as he came in, the rest of the streets would follow." Which, to be fair, is exactly what happened.

Still, Dexter had a feeling there was something special about this quiet, skinny teenager. Intrigued by the creative connection among him and his friends, Dexter paid a visit to Rimpau's house, just a few blocks from his own, to see the young artists in their own element. "I went over to their place and got a really prolific piece of video where we all put up money to buy a pizza," Dexter remembers. He preferred capturing verité moments to more contrived footage, and what he was witnessing was very real indeed. Ermy's whole circle was in attendance that night— Rare S, Daddy O, B Side (now known as Kid Ink), Ed Wriott, and Steven Biz.[49]

"We had a gang of niggas from Watts in Rimpau's house on a school night," Ralo remembers. "His brother and sister in the living room trying to do homework. And we got five niggas from Grape Street in his room and we playin' beats loud. Dexter was like, 'Y'all are trippin'. I got a whole back house just for this.'"[50] Rimpau's mother was in the kitchen trying to cook. Ralo knew something had to give. "It just looked like the regular life was being heavily imposed on by music life," he said. "Once we went to go fuck with Dexter at his house, it just all blossomed—all the people that he brought to the table, people that we brought to the table. That meld of those two worlds was rich."[51]

"I was so impressed with what they were doing back there— all the music, the energy, the posters of Biggie and 2Pac on the wall—I made a crazy decision," Dexter recalls. "I said, 'Guys, I will take you all in.'"[52]

Dexter soon made a trip to Guitar Center on Sunset Boulevard to supplement the studio setup with keyboards and drum machines. At the time he was working both as a civil engineer and as a photographer, so he had some disposable income. "We outfitted the studio with a proper booth with some sponge on the walls and a microphone," Dexter recalls. "And within ButterVision we now had a new crew. We called them the BV Boys."[53]

Dexter will never forget the first time he heard Ermias rap. One day in early 2002 Ermy arrived at ButterVision headquarters with Ralo and Rimpau. "I walk up the stairs with them and they all have a seat," Dexter says. "I put on one of Gooch's beats and Ralo started freestyling, and then Eve D." Erm wouldn't say anything at first. "He just had to get warmed up," Dexter recalls. "But when he finally got around to saying something it was one of the most prolific set of words I've heard come out of a young man's mouth." Dexter's hunch had been right. There was something special about this boy.[54]

They soon fell into a routine of studio work every day. Ermy wasn't rapping much yet, but he had become quite skilled on the MPC after all those weekend classes at the Watts Towers. He and Ralo focused on making beats for Cuzzy's first project, which was to be called *Journey of 1000 Miles*. "Cuzzy was the headliner back then," Dexter recalls. "He was more prolific at that point musically. He would get X-ed out and freestyle for forty-five minutes with his eyes closed." Ermy's producer name at the time was Mav. "We did a bunch of work on Cuzzy's project and somehow we didn't put the project out," Ralo remembers. "At this time we didn't have any real information on how to distribute digitally. We were literally at the frontier, right at the cusp of everything."[55]

"It's funny, when we started off, them niggas used to look up to me," Cuzzy recalls of those early days with the BV Boys. "When they met me, I used to be in the room telling stories about the rap game and they eyes would be big as fuck. And eventually that shit turned all the way around to where I was lookin' at my little brother like that. You know what I'm sayin'? Shit is crazy."[56]

That transition began the day Cuzzy challenged him. "Ermy," he said, "are you ready to rap?" The young apprentice stepped up to the mic without hesitation. "Ermy had been writing for years," Dexter says. "He had all his little notebooks and all that." When he started spitting, the whole place went quiet. Everybody in the room realized they were in the presence of a rare talent. "I would never misrepresent that he first started making music at Butter-Vision," says Dexter. "I think he was a superstar from the time I met him."[57]

Fueled by years' worth of pent-up desire, Ermy never tired of putting in long hours at ButterVision. During his downtime he and Dexter started to talk more, getting to know each other. "He told me that his mom and dad did not live together," Dexter recalls. "He told me his father was a revolutionary from Eritrea. It seemed as though Ermias respected him, but I could tell at his age he needed some male guidance. By circumstance, I kind of found myself in that role." Ermias taught Dexter how to play basketball. Dexter taught him to play soccer. Ermy loved table tennis and chess. "He was always doing something," Dexter observed. "It was very rare that you would see him just sitting there."[58]

Although Ermias was supposed to be staying at his granny's house, the late-night sessions kept stretching out, day after day. While others slept on the floor around him, he'd stay hunched over the drum machine, finishing a beat.

By exposing Ermias to new situations, Dexter noticed two things straightaway: one, he soaked up the knowledge like a sponge, and two, everywhere he went people would notice him.

"We'd crack jokes and call him 'the Golden Boy,'" Gooch remembers. "We used to have photo shoots with people comin' up that was in the industry, or wantin' to go to the industry. Everyone was fascinated with him." Ermias wouldn't even have to talk. They'd just see him and ask, "Who's that?"

"Oh, that's my buddy Erm," Gooch would reply.

"He looks important," people would say. Or, "He looks like somebody I know." Or, "He looks like somebody that's on TV or something."

"There was something regal-esque about him" is how Gooch puts it.

Dexter was developing a strong respect for Ermias and felt a sense of responsibility for him and his talent. "I understood that he had to be facilitated carefully," Dexter said. "We used to joke around a lot in the studio just to make time fly," says Gooch. "But me and Dexter out of everybody, we knew what was actually transpiring. We had this feeling that we was onto something big."

The first musical breakthrough came when Ralo was working with a family friend named Zayd Malik, godson of Mtulu Shakur, Afeni Shakur's husband and Tupac's stepfather. "Afeni belonged to that same organization as my mom and Mtulu, and a bunch of other people I could name but I won't," says Ralo. "They're college professors, doctors, and lawyers who are all revolutionaries but they assimilated." Mtulu encouraged Malik's aspirations to become a rapper, and invited him to contribute a track to the Tupac tribute album *Dare 2 Struggle*. In 2001, Ralo produced the song, titled "Somethin' Ain't Right," and recorded a guest verse. He invited Ermias, aka Concept, to lay down a dazzling feature that juxtaposed police sirens, dark streets, and the philosophy of Marcus Garvey. "I blame the system for birthin' niggas like me," he rapped. "I'm the rebel, Concept forever the ghetto's poet / Black life treated like weed, light it, puff it, then blow it / But not me . . ."

Afeni was so impressed with the song that she invited Ermias, Ralo, and Rimpau to Georgia to perform with Zayd at the release party for the Tupac album *Better Dayz*. As Afeni drove with them from Atlanta to Stone Mountain, her phone rang. It was Mtulu Shakur, Tupac's stepfather, calling from a federal correctional facility. For no apparent reason, he asked to speak with Ermias, although they had never met before and there were three young visitors in the van. "Just the fact that that happened was supernatural," says Ralo, sounding shocked years after the fact. "These two people raised the most influential rapper of our generation who got gunned down and [Nipsey] took the fuckin' torch." That night Zayd, EQ, and Concept performed inside a tent and rocked a crowd of Tupac's family, friends, and fans—in the same city as Stone Mountain Park, the site of historic Klan rallies and the "Mount Rushmore of the Confederacy," the world's largest monument to White Supremacy.

Ermias began making regular trips to Atlanta after that, staying with Zayd and immersing himself in Southern rap— Gooch remembers him bringing an early T.I. mixtape back to L.A.—and the teachings of the Black nationalist organization the Republic of New Afrika. "They had like minds and they used to talk about a lot of deep shit," Gooch recalls. "Like Malcolm X–type stuff, Geronimo Pratt, and COINTELPRO, the FBI." Nip started reading books like *The Spook Who Sat By The Door* and he set up a base in ATL, doing some hustling and getting his own apartment. On his song "Crenshaw & Slauson (True Story)," Hussle rapped about "Real estate in Atlanta but ain't nobody know."

"What I'm telling you is prior to everything," says Ralo. "Nobody in the music indusry who wants to lie about what they witnessed or what they may not have witnessed has any point of reference in regards to this story. He didn't even exist. We weren't on that radar yet."

Ermias needed a new a rap name. His Concept days were coming to an end. His first BV Boys demo disc didn't have any name on it at all. "We used to just call him 'Erm' or 'E' for short," Gooch recalls. He and Dexter would talk about it. They wanted a name that would stick, something that could become a brand. "We was up on brandin'," Gooch says. "We was tryin' to throw some ideas around and I was like, 'Don't worry about it, man. I'll put it in the universe. It's gonna come to me.'"

One night out of the blue, it did. The way Ermy tells the story, he walked into a ButterVision session and was christened with his new identity on the spot. They had all been grinding in the studio for a few days and everybody's funds were low. "None of us had no hustle," Ralo admits. "We'd wait for Gooch to make a swerve." If Gooch didn't bring back some Chinese food from Yee's, Dexter or Lisa might cook for them. It was hard to be inspired on an empty stomach. One day Nip got sick of sitting and waiting.

"I'd go hit the block until I got enough for some weed and some chicken," Hussle recalled. "And I'd go hit the studio right after that." In various retellings, the spoils of his hustle expanded to include a bottle of Hennessy. Whatever Ermy brought back to the lab that night, it was enough to spark Gooch's imagination. He looked up from his mixing board and said, "I got it—Nipsey Hussle!"

Too young to get the reference at first, Ermias thought Gooch was joking around. "He was like, *What?*" Gooch recalls. "And I told him the story about Nipsey Russell, and how he used to do the scattin' and everything." The name just sounded phonetically pleasing—and it stuck. "When I said it aloud I knew it was meant for him," Gooch says. They discussed alternate spellings over Louisiana Fried Chicken and blunts. "We weren't gonna spell it 'Hustle' because, you know, we wanna be Ebonically correct," Gooch says. "And when you're doin' something that's equated with money, you put the dollar signs in there." They finally decided to go with Nipsey Hu$$le. "After that point he ran with it and really embraced the Hussle ambition," Gooch says. "It was his identity."

"Nipsey always wanted a lot of money," says Gooch. "He was like the Jay-Z type of person. I'm more like a 2Pac. I love money, and I know money. I want to be successful. But Nipsey was a monetary person. Everything he seen and everything he did, he had to equate to money. It was crazy to see a young person like that who was conditioned. It had a lot to do with his brother, Blacc Sam. He's a nonstop hustler."[59]

Sam and Fatts were still setting up their table every day in the Louisiana Fried Chicken parking lot, selling socks, T-shirts, CDs, and DVDs. But they'd been having trouble with the cops. "Three days in a row police came, pulled up, took all our shit," Sam recalled in a *WorldStar TV* documentary. "We went back, re'd up. They pulled up again and took all our shit. Third time they put us in cuffs." Sam challenged the police officer, who was Black. "Man, what's goin' on?" he asked. "We tryin' to make some money, man! We all Black, man."

"Shut the fuck up!" the policeman said. If they wanted to sell, they would have to do it like everybody else. "Go open up a store and lease it and pay rent," he told them. Then he uncuffed them and confiscated all their merchandise.[60]

Sam and Fatts sat on the curb, dejected. Once again, everything was gone. They were tired of taking L's. "Right when we look up, across the street is a big-ass 'For Lease' sign," Sam said. "That was God tellin' us we need to be in that lot. We need to pay some rent, stop getting harassed by these police." And so their first store, Slauson Tees, was born. The simple shop did a brisk business right away and soon became a neighborhood hangout, especially when Ermias was hanging out. "Even since we had the first shop," Sam said at the memorial service, "we didn't want all the homies hangin' out in the front. Soon as Nip pull up, he's there for 10 seconds—I don't know, phone calls is bein' made, the whole hood is there. It's 100 niggas in the front, 20 guns, and uh . . . We just knew that about Nip, man. He attracted people."[61]

Over time the T-shirt money began to stack up in a major way. "That nigga Nipsey was a pirate," says Ralo. "Blacc Sam was a pirate. Rimpau is a pirate. We bootlegged software. We bootlegged music. We did it in high school. We did it after high school. Blacc Sam literally poked a hole in the movie industry. I sold dope for like two days and I just . . . My heart hurt too much. I was like, 'Damn, it's somebody mom.' Selling CDs was way more. . . . You gonna get way better rest."

Before Nip's music career took off, Sam surprised his mom with a black BMW. "It was all hard-earned street cash," says Dexter. "He was prolific that way. They were good, hardworking boys that really loved their mom. And those were the kind of things that endeared me to them. They were tough in the street, but they never forgot their family."

At the same time ButterVision was bubbling, there were numerous other independent rap crews popping up around Los Angeles, rebuilding the West Coast hip-hop scene after the fall of Death Row. Top Dawg Entertainment was starting a movement in Watts around Jay Rock. The Game and his brother Big Fase 100 were dropping Black Wall Street mixtapes in Compton. Aside from ButterVision, the Crenshaw District boasted at least two other local sound labs, Scatter Brain's Rich Rollin' Records and Claustrophobic Studios.

One day Nipsey and Cuzzy took a break from the action at ButterVision and ventured over to Claustrophobic. The two went back and forth over the Neptunes' beat from Jay-Z and

Memphis Bleek's "Excuse Me Miss" remix on a freestyle they called "La-La-La."

"That was what skyrocketed Nip and Cuzzy as far as bein' around the Claustrophobic scene," Hoodsta Rob remembers. "When we put that mixtape together, that song went crazy! Everybody was lovin' it."

"We smacked that record," Cuzzy said. "That shit is a classic." The song's buzz in the streets highlighted Cuzzy and Nip's creative chemistry.

A local producer named Robin Hood was impressed with what he saw that day, not only Hussle's skills on the mic but his whole demeanor. He would eventually become Nip's road manager. It was Robin Hood who connected him with Larrance Dopson, the young musician who went on to start a production team called 1500 or Nothin. The name was inspired by the price they demanded for their first-ever live showcase, backing the R&B singer Bobby Valentino in the early 2000s. Their price would go up in due course, but even as 1500 expanded their client roster, working with many of the biggest stars in the music industry, they maintained a close working relationship with Hussle throughout his career.

Back at ButterVision, production was ramping up. Cuzzy was finishing up his mixtape *Journey of 1000 Miles* while Nipsey was laying down tracks of his own for a BV Boys compilation with Ralo and Rimpau supplying most of the beats. "It was a little gangbang rap camp," says Cuzzy with a smile. Dexter didn't ask anyone to sign contracts. He saw himself as a mentor, not a manager. All he asked was that they sign releases to be filmed for his ongoing ButterVision documentary project, and contribute the occasional soundtrack cut for his self-produced DVDs like *Beats and Babes*.

Hussle's formative years as an artist coincided with an implosion of the record industry due to online digital piracy. "One of the main things that we [understood] at ButterVision was that music in itself was losing its value as an asset," Dexter says. The launch of Napster in June 1999 had ushered in the MP3 revolution, causing a rapid decline in CD sales. It would be three years before Apple launched iTunes, so the music industry was in a state of free fall. "Music was valuable to everyone," Dexter said, "but because it was so accessible and nobody was willing to pay for it, we had to find ways to leverage the music for different stuff. That was the cornerstone of our whole philosophy."[62] Hussle soaked up all the information around him, storing it for future use. He also made sure to stay up to date with all new technologies and media platforms. Hussle used to communicate with Gooch on Napster chat.

In early 2000 Gooch put out his own independent album *YG* through ButterVision. The project featured beats by his boy Floss P, a talented producer who went on to work with Dr. Dre. Floss was responsible for "Phone Tap" by the Firm among other bangers, and he brought heat to Gooch's album as well. Despite the quality of *YG*, the grassroots project stalled due to lack of distribution. "We didn't have the access," Gooch says. "It was the gatekeepers."[63]

Dexter was adamant that ButterVision remain a self-sustaining entity independent of Hollywood and the music industry. "I told Nipsey that under no circumstances would they sign any deal with anybody," he says. But Nipsey could still hear that clock ticking in his mind. Now that he could make his own music, his dreams of rap stardom seemed closer than ever. More than anything he just wanted his shot at the big time.

"Nipsey actually begged me to give him a chance just to prove that he could get a deal," Dexter recalls. "I told him no problem, let's go up to Interscope. I know some guys there." Dexter had done some photography for Kevin Black, who started as a roadie with Run-DMC before moving on to street marketing at Def Jam for the likes of LL Cool J and Public Enemy. Black went on to become a senior vice president at Interscope who worked with Dr. Dre and helped break Eminem and several other big-name acts.

Nipsey went with Dexter to the Interscope Records office in Santa Monica, demo in hand. Kevin Black's office was just like Nipsey pictured it—walls covered with gold and platinum plaques. They sat and played a few songs from Nipsey's demo. "Kevin told him he had a cool look, but the music was rough," Dexter recalls. "He said he needed to go to the gym, put on a little lean mass, and work with a choreographer for some dance moves."

Nipsey stood up in the office. "Yo, DB, let's go, man," he said, disgusted. "Let's go."[64]

The disappointment of that day fueled Hussle to go harder. "We went to Interscope, hollered at Kevin Black early on," Nipsey said later in a ButterVision interview. "He kinda like wanted to change what we was doin'. So it's like, we ain't mad at none of them niggas. We tryin' to change what *they* listenin' for instead of havin' them change what we doin'. 'Cause we standin' firm on ours."[65]

"I knew what was happening," says Dexter, who filmed the whole meeting. "I was trying to dismantle Hollywood. We were guerrillas. We were fighting for equality and more inclusion within a sphere that wasn't properly divided."[66]

Such experiences informed Hussle's very first self-produced project, which was recorded in the guesthouse at Dexter's and sold on the street hand-to-hand. "I'd like to welcome y'all to my new mixtape, *Fucc tha Middleman*," Hussle said over a funky interlude. "All you record execs, cock-blockin'-ass CEOs and shit, Fuck y'all! We don't need y'all."[67]

The concept behind the project was self-explanatory: "We gonna put out our stuff until they can't ignore us anymore," said Dexter, "or until we get a partnership deal that we deserve." Dexter says he coined the term "Fuck the Middleman" but couldn't trademark it because you couldn't trademark the word "fuck" at the time. (The Supreme Court reversed this policy of the U.S. Patent and Trademark Office in 2019, overturning a federal law against "scandalous" or "immoral" trademarks.)[68]

Fucc tha Middleman kicked off a particularly prolific period for Nipsey. He soon began working on a project called *Rapsploitation*, both of which were burned at ButterVision and distributed in the streets by hand.[69] He followed up these projects with *Slauson Boy Vol. 1*, which is generally considered his first "official" project, still available on DatPiff, iTunes, Spotify, Tidal, and other streaming platforms. The credits of this still widely slept-on project say that *Slauson Boy Vol. 1* was recorded in a little-known studio known as The Kitchen. "The Kitchen is my house," says Dexter. "For obvious reasons I didn't want my name on there. I'm a professional civil engineer—still am—and also a certified swim coach. So I'm truly a Renaissance person, but sometimes it's a problem. Some of the world don't understand other parts of the world."[70]

Dexter appears on the mixtape at the start of track 5, in the skit that opens the song "Wrap It Up." He's the guy with the Caribbean accent from whom Hussle cops his weed in bulk.[71] "I got some shit goin' down outta town," Hussle tells him. "I need some of that green." His godbrother Adam, now a partner in All Money In, plays the suspicious hustling partner who walks with Nip while he does the deal. "You know I got the fuckin' best dread," Dexter replies as the six-minute song begins.

And what a song it is. Hussle's tale of a small-time herb man's hustling mission—"Set up shop, shut 'em down"—segues into the poignant testimony of a young man caught up in the drug game as he tries to make it off the boulevard.

The standout track on *Slauson Boy Vol. 1* is "Cali," a profound portrayal of L.A. street life from a critical perspective that's streetwise and "woke" at the same time. "I live life between Slauson, a prison and coffin," Hussle raps. "Stuck on the block, I ask God for the option to profit." If his bars about hustling sacks, busting a MAC, and tucking packs in a pay phone sound vivid, that's because they're based on a true story. With dreams of a big record deal on hold, Hussle had to get his grind on for real.

But first he took a moment to celebrate the release of his mixtape. "We did the first performance on the outskirts of Culver City in a little hall next door to a bowling alley," Gooch recalls. "Everybody had the *Slauson Boy* CD and they was bumpin' it. So they were like 'Aw, if y'all do a performance . . .'" Everybody wanted to go. The crowd was mostly homies from the hood, some girls, and other people Nip went to school with. Gooch remembers how crazy it was seeing Nip perform, like, "Oh shit, he's actually onstage!"[72]

It was really Nip's show, but of course he invited all the BV Boys.

There was no DJ, just a sound guy playing the CD from a little switchboard in the corner. "They didn't have no dance area," says Gooch. "It was a place where you do karaoke. But Nip performed like he was performing at the Staples Center." Everybody knew everyone there. Everyone knew all the songs. Nipsey just wanted to say the words in front of people. Sometimes he ran out of breath, but if Cuzzy wasn't sayin' his words, everybody in the audience was. "Oh shit!" Nip said to himself. "They actually singin' it word for word."[73]

CUZ, BLOOD, AND WHO KNOWS WHAT
THEY ALL THROWIN' UP SOMETHIN' BUT WE READY TO BUST
—Nipsey Hussle, "Cali," *Slauson Boy Vol. 1* (2005)

"I met Nip when he was about fourteen years old on Crenshaw and Slauson," remembers Cobby Supreme, a young neighborhood celebrity who would eventually join Hussle's group the Slauson Boyz. Also known as G-Bob and Money Man, Cobby was a few years older than Ermy. He pulled into the ARCO station and noticed the tall skinny kid selling CDs. "I was familiar with the hustle, and I respected it," Cobby told *GQ*. "When he tried to hand me the CD, I was like, 'No, I don't want to buy no CD.' But I still gave him $5. Told him, 'Keep the CD, just make your money.' And he smiled."[74] Something about the young man intrigued Cobby, a certain charisma. He called Ermy back to the car window and asked if he was Rollin' 60s.

"He shook his head and told me no, but he kind of did it with a grin," Cobby recalled.

"I'm like, 'You sure?'"

"'Nah.'"

"'You going to be 60s?'"

"'Nah,' Ermy repeated, grinning again."[75]

The question was inevitable for any young man from the neighborhood. "It was all like family," Cobby explained of the ties that bind the set. "We weren't basing none of the things we were doing on following traditional gang life. It was like, if you was in this, like anything else—a basketball team or whatever— you're going to be loyal. That's basically what it is."

Cobby describes himself as "the first little nigga probably thirteen years old with a car." By the age of sixteen, he says, he was "driving in Benzes and BMWs and wearing jewelry like grown men." He figures that's why Hussle gravitated toward him. "You know," he said, "that's what kids like."

The next time Cobby spoke with Hussle he was just back from an extended trip out of town, driving down Slauson, when he saw a group of thirty young guys. "They was over there doin' what they do in the neighborhood," Cobby recalled. He summoned Nip over to the car. "I was like, 'You from the hood now?' And he did that same smirk and then shook his head, and was like, 'Yeah.' I was like, *I knew it*. And then I drove off again . . . That neighborhood is real influential."[76]

Described in a 2004 newspaper article as being "the size of an Army brigade," the Rollin' 60s are one of the oldest and largest Crip sets in Los Angeles. According to press reports they are heavily armed and associated with drug trafficking, robbery, carjacking, kidnapping, and homicide.[77] Such press clips reflect the dominant narrative about gangs, but of course there's more to the economic and social realities that gave rise to these community-based organizations. Active members often wear white T-shirts and specific baseball caps—typically the blue Seattle Mariners cap with a big *S* for "Sixties."[78] Something as simple as wearing the wrong cap in the wrong neighborhood could lead to serious repercussions. Gang culture is so much a part of life in the area that many people in the neighborhood, affiliated or not, would say they "grew up in the 60s."

Though he was born and raised in the community, Ermias had no family ties to the set. His dad was a first-generation immigrant, and his mother's side of the family was unaffiliated, giving him a bit more leeway to choose which path to follow. Not that it was an easy decision.

"The culture of my area is the gang culture," Nipsey explained. "So by being outside, being involved with hustling, being in the hood, doing things to try and get money, being young . . . We were just raised like, 'If you're with me, if something go down, I'm in it.' Whether I'm from this shit or not. So after a while it just be like, you're always in the middle of some shit. You might as well."[79]

"Most kids start banging at around like fourteen, fifteen," says Justin Lamarr, who attended View Park Preparatory, an accelerated charter high school on Crenshaw Boulevard, during the mid-2000s. "You're not an adult by then, but you should be able to determine right from wrong and what's gonna get you in trouble." When Justin joined the high school football team as a freshman, he estimates that half the team were Crips, and half Bloods. "I've had multiple teammates who got shot," he says. "It shouldn't be normal," he says, but repeated experience has a way of normalizing extreme situations. "Like, 'Aw well, he didn't die, so . . .'" Justin and his brother were among those in the neighborhood who opted out of the gang. Nevertheless, Lamarr says he and his classmates used to admire Nipsey when they saw him in the parking lot across from school selling CDs and T-shirts, especially knowing he and his family had their own shop there. That example inspired Lamarr to launch his own marketing agency in later years. He says Hussle "became a hero to people like me who didn't gangbang but were from the neighborhood."[80]

Contrary to LAPD assumptions and popular belief, many households in communities like Hyde Park and Crenshaw made a point of steering clear of gang involvement altogether. "No male on my mother's side of the family has died from gang violence or gunfire—period," Ralo says proudly, adding that his mom's family has lived in Los Angeles for over 100 years. "I gotta keep that energy. To be from where I'm from, that's a hell of a stat."[81]

Ralo's perspective on gang culture is informed by growing up in a family steeped in education, progressive politics, and community activism. Prominent former gang members like Sanyika Shakur fka Monster Kody of Eight Trey Gangster Crips and Cle Shaheed Sloan fka Bone of the Athens Park Bloods used to come over for Kwanzaa parties at his parents' home in the heart of Rollin' 60s territory. "I feel like where I come from has produced one of the most despicable group of African-Americans to ever exist," he says now.[82]

According to Dr. Melina Abdullah of Black Lives Matter, even young people who stay out of gangs can get caught up in the LAPD's anti-gang tactics, whether implemented by the CRASH unit or its successor, the Gang and Narcotics Division. "Starting in the 1980s, the police created gang databases and placed what they called 'gang injunctions' on certain neighborhoods," Dr. Abdullah explains. "Anybody who lived in a so-called 'gang neighborhood' became gang affiliated even if they weren't engaging in crimes. So if you live off Crenshaw in a Rollin' 60s neighborhood, you were automatically affiliated with Rollin' 60s. They had these books called gang books, and if they caught you on the streets, they would take a Polaroid picture and put it in the gang book." To this day, other U.S. cities continue to struggle with criminalization of communities by use of such gang books and databases.

The smallest infractions could be considered a violation of the gang injunction: riding a bike, wearing certain colors, having a pager or a cell phone, associating with other people in the gang book. All these became grounds for arrest and jail time. Over time the Polaroids were replaced with digital imagery and the gang books became computerized databases. Studying the LAPD's gang databases, Dr. Abdullah has found children as young as one year old. "People are being criminalized from birth for simply living in particular neighborhoods," she says. "There's dozens of them under one year old. It's not a mistake. This is what they're doing."[83]

🏁🏁

Ermias Asghedom was blessed with more abilities than opportunities in life. In many ways the odds were stacked against him, although he often said he had it "better than some and worse than others."[84] He chose what he considered the best option available to him: to follow his passion for music, committing himself to making his dream a reality by all means necessary. Somewhere along the way to that goal he made another choice, to get down with the Rollin' 60s. Both of these choices impacted his life in profound, interrelated ways.

"I wanted to be a rapper all of my life," Hussle said. "Since I was like eight or nine years old I wanted to do rap music. I didn't always have the means and the options and the resources to do it, so I fell by the wayside at a point in time. My outlook on life was hopeless. I ain't see no pot of gold at the end of the rainbow."[85]

He got into hustling as a way to provide for himself as a teenager. At first it was about "wantin' to get shoes when they came out and wantin' to be fresh," as he put it.[86] But there was something deeper driving the Hussle. By the time he reached his teens he'd come to some conclusions about the world and his place in it. "It was niggas that was havin' it and it was niggas that wasn't, and I didn't wanna be one of the niggas that wasn't," he said. "I seen a long time ago, if you ain't got no money, you really ain't got no position out here. You ain't got no place in this world. So you know, that was my thing—school and all that was cool. But I felt like I was to the point I need to start making my own moves and making money."[87]

Getting money wasn't just a question of flossing. It was about the ability to put his ideas into action at every level. From selling bootleg CDs and incense, he graduated to having his own weed spots. "Nigga done dabbled in a little bit of everything," he said, "but my main hustle was producin' music and sellin' my music. I did that for years on Slauson and Crenshaw . . . Police used to come bump us up and kick us out and take us to jail all the time and all that."[88]

"I had my concerns about his strong allegiance to the street life," said Dexter, who was aware Nip was hustling but didn't press him for details.[89] Gooch was one of the first to notice the signs that something was happening in the young man's life.

"I don't know if he got put on yet," says Gooch, "but I remember he started changing his attire. He started wearing the hood shit. Blue rags, shoelaces. He was doin' his hood politics. Hustling, connecting with people. And they respected him—because of his music, because of his introduction to the hood and the way that he handled it, and because of his energy. People just *knew* he was somethin'. He was a cool dude, but you knew he wasn't a punk."[90]

When asked about his decision to get down with the Rollin' 60s, Hussle sometimes explained his choice as being made "out of frustration from not having outlets and studio access."[91] But it wasn't as simple as that, as he had a number of underground studios at his disposal by that time.

Just as he'd done with Cuzzy years before, Gooch tried to caution Nip about what he was getting into, even as he understood the forces drawing him into the 60s. "It's problematic to grow up as a young Black male in America, let alone that you don't have the money," says Gooch. "So I tried to keep that instilled in anybody that was around me: That that's not the way to go. But if you're gonna do it, these are the things that you have to beware about."

It wasn't as if Nipsey had no other talents. "Quiet as kept, Nip could have did anything," Gooch says. "He didn't have to be a rapper. He could have been just as successful as a fricking doorbell salesman or an entrepreneur—which he was. So I just wanted to let him know that. 'Don't do it because you feel that there is no other way. Or this is your only way.' Or 'Don't do it out of gratification or an easy fix to something.'"[92]

Even though Gooch was down with the hood himself, he didn't want to see anybody he cared about start gangbanging. "When Nip was becoming more acquainted with the hood, I was like, 'Hey man, we're doing this music,'" he recalls. "I *understood* that it's hard, and it was gonna be a struggle. But I knew Nip would be able to make it—somehow, some way. Because of the effect that he had on everybody."

Looking back, Gooch could point to key turning points in Hussle's evolution toward the hood. One of the biggest was buying his first car, the one immortalized in his song "Summertime in That Cutlass." Driving around Crenshaw in a blue Cutlass Supreme was like walking around waving a gang rag. "You're automatically gonna get stopped by the police," Gooch says. "And he didn't have a license." If the cops didn't catch him, there were always rival gang members to worry about. "If enemies come into the neighborhood, and they see you in that car, they're not gonna ask any questions. They gonna shoot you up." Gooch was like, "Hey, man, you sure you want this car?" But Nipsey's mind was made up.[93]

"Anyway, Nipsey got the car," Gooch says. "He's growing his hair out, driving around the neighborhood with other dudes that didn't have a car. He got this sense of power. He didn't tell *me* if he was riding around with a gun and selling weed and hanging out with thugs. But I knew he was gonna be *on* one day."[94]

This was the early 2000s, around the same time period when Nipsey met his girlfriend Tanisha Foster.[95, 96] Fatts gave her the nickname Chyna Hussle. She had just gotten her own apartment, which gave Nip a place to stay and a sense of adulthood. "Things were working," Gooch recalls. "His ideas were coming to fruition." Tanisha had a son and a daughter, ages six and eight, who would come over to ButterVision. She and Hussle had their issues, like any couple, but he always got along with the kids. "He was playing daddy," says Gooch. "It was cool."[97]

Not long after that, Nipsey hit a run of bad luck. A close buddy of his was killed. A couple of the friends he was getting money with got caught up and jailed. Six months after that he was in a store, and the owners thought he was stealing something because of the way he was acting. He had a gun on him—it was small, but his pocket looked heavy. The store owners called the police. He got "gaffled up" and went to jail.[98]

Gooch and Nipsey used to have conversations about the choices Nip was making. Gooch made a point of never telling him not to get down with the gang. His approach was more pragmatic: "Hey, you can do what you want to do, but just know you can ruin this," he would say. "There's baggage that comes with this."[99]

Surely the rapper who spit bars about COINTELPRO changing the Black Panthers into Crips and Bloods on his song "Cali" understood that baggage from the outset. Dexter believes that Hussle's decision to join the gang was strategic. "Nipsey understood the power of being dead center," he says. By getting down with the set, Hussle was "centralizing himself in a way that says, 'I can go up to the hills, or I can go down in the hood.'" Although Dexter's was an outsider perspective, he spent years of his life immersed in Rollin' 60s culture.

"I think there was a bit of a sort of flirting with the forbidden, in a sense, with the gang culture," says Dexter. "He felt that would leave his persona without any . . . misunderstandings. He is who he said he is." Dexter vividly remembers when 50 Cent dropped the song "Wanksta" and proceeded to dismantle Ja Rule's credibility. "We all lived through that in the back studio," Dexter says. "Nipsey was determined to make sure that would never be a topic of discussion when it came to him."[100]

Ralo emphasizes that his friend was no make-believe gangster. "Nipsey was full-throttle with all of the bullshit—every piece of it," he says. "There was no ulterior motive in his thug. You feel me? Nipsey was no cut. He could go left fast. Like *fast*, bro. That nigga had a hairpin fuckin' temper. And there's not a lick of fear in the boy's heart as a kid. Let alone once he became a man. Everybody wants to believe Nip was flappin' around with wings and shit. But that nigga, he could have been completely the problem had he not had a paradigm shift at whatever point it happened. That's what made his impact more. So authentic. Not contrived. This was the real deal. Nipsey stopped a lot of shit from happenin' because he was official. He was able to impact our community 'cause he was official."[101]

"I believe he wanted to speak for the people," says Gooch. "I think Nip made that conscious decision. Like, 'You know what? What better way for me to speak for the people? If I'm going to be successful, to be successful as part of the hood.'"[102]

Before the rise of Nipsey Hussle, the motherland of West Coast "gangsta rap" was Compton, a city in Los Angeles County that lies ten miles from South Central Los Angeles. By representing Slauson and Crenshaw, Nip was doing something that had never been done before. To do that required a different level of commitment. "You stand up in the middle of your hood and you decide that you wanna voice your opinion," Ralo said. "And you want the respect of your peers. That's not something that you can do from a studio. Not from where we come from. You can't go to the studio and create a relationship with a disenfranchised group of people. You have to actually be out there with them. And the only way you're gonna be able to lead them, or even have any modicum of influence in people's lives, is if you *become* them."[103]

"My opinion personally, ain't nothin' wrong with a gang," Hussle said back in 2008 during one of his first interviews in New York after signing his deal with Epic Records. "Everybody's a gang. Epic is a gang. Democrats and Republicans is a gang. You feel me? What your objective is—and what you represent and what you doing. All right, now that's where the problem come in. If all you doing is bringing violence to your neighborhood and terrorizing your folks, that's where the problem exists at. So the problem ain't the gang; it's the motivation and objective." Hussle went on to explain the vision behind the Slauson Boyz, tying the group's name to a larger movement and legacy. "I got a group that I'm also a part of called Slauson Boyz. That's our block, that's where we all started at, on Slauson. And that's like some throwback L.A. shit too—that one of the first gangs in L.A. after the Black Panthers. The Businessmen, Slauson Boys, and a couple other gangs. So us growin' up on Slauson, and bein' from that, naturally we gravitate toward the name."[104]

Cuzzy came to see a larger motive behind Hussle's choices. "He changed what it meant to be around these motherfuckers," he says of Hussle's impact on the 60s. "He brought the specialness back. We was missing that shit for years. Then Nip come and turn into this golden child—*Slauson Boy nigga!* The world is like, 'What the fuck just happened?'"[105]

In interview after interview, Hussle spoke about nothing less than a redemption of gang culture. "No matter how hood you is," Hussle said in 2010, "how much of a killer you is, how much dope you done sold, how much shit you done robbed, how much you do it from your shoulders—a motherfucker don't want a negative lifestyle. A nigga sometimes wants better for himself . . . We did that outta lack of choices . . . If a situation present itself to give you another lane, why wouldn't you grow?"[106] Four years later, he told DJ Vlad, "Our generation was kinda responsible for, like, putting it on the map in terms of hustling and business. Making moves outside of the streets, and taking it to a corporate level."[107]

Still, there was no getting around the harsh realities of getting jumped in to the 60s. "You gotta fight," Hussle said. "It's different for everybody. It's basically whoever like orchestrating your put-on. Sometimes it be young niggas putting you on and you just get in a ring and fight till niggas feel like you done fighting. Sometimes it's somebody that got a little bit more love for young dudes and a little bit of compassion, and you might have a different experience. Some niggas just get they ass beat because it was young niggas putting 'em on and didn't give a fuck about 'em."[108]

Hussle's put-on was orchestrated by Herman "Cowboy" Douglas, whose hood name was Thundercat. Cowboy was an aspiring rapper who linked up with Nipsey when he came home from the penitentiary in 2003. "I met cuz in the hood," Hussle recalled in an early Kev Mac video. "He came to the studio, seen the music we was doing and all that . . . I laced cuz to the recording get-down, and the recording process—as far as how to do Pro Tools shit, how to do song structures and all that. Feel me?"[109] Armed with the knowledge he acquired at ButterVision, Cowboy started his own independent production called Hood

Unit.[110] Sometimes Nip would go over to his place to write and record. Hussle even got HOOD UNIT tattooed on his hand.[111]

"People used to think [Cowboy] was Nip's big brother," Gooch remembers. "They look alike, kinda skinny, they both rap, and girls liked them. Plus they could both fight." The 60s used to have meetings which would include friendly squabbles. They called them Thunderdome after the movie *Mad Max Beyond Thunderdome*. Two members of the 60s might say, "Let's thunder," and then go at it.[112]

Cowboy was Thundercat, so Nipsey became his little homie, Lil Thundercat.

"I named Nip, then I tell him how the hood go," Cowboy said in a Kev Mac interview. "Tell him all the foul shit. I taught him about a lot of shit before I could lace him on the hood. I talked to him for a couple days—laced him on how the hood go. Gave him the rules, the regulations. Cuz went down and got put on, squabbled up."[113]

Behind the buildings was where the put-on took place—younger cats would thunder for respect while big homies observed. More than a physical contest, it was a test of heart. "Niggas went, squabbled, got they respect on their own," said Cuzzy. "Every day—behind this building, behind that building. I couldn't find niggas for a minute. Niggas emerged back up, scraped up, bruised up, with Seattle Mariner hats on and blue rags."[114]

"I have on tape where he confronts the gang to be Thundercat," Dexter recalls. "Nipsey taking off his sweater to fight some seasoned prisoners. He had balls like nobody you ever knew, that boy. And he was willing to live his convictions. I will definitely say that about young Ermias." Dexter recalls the transition vividly, and not without some misgivings. "The 'Six-Owe' started coming out of his mouth. When they greet each other they threw up the two-finger sign. You can't use that sign until you're on."[115]

Some thirty years after the Crips were first established, the risks of membership were realer than ever. But Hussle didn't get into the set alone. His homie Rimpau jumped off the porch with him. And despite his misgivings, Ralo went in back of the buildings too. "I know lookin' in from the outside it sounds ridiculous, but it's just about being loyal to the soil," he explains. "That level of camaraderie—even if it is a dead-end route." Ralo is a big guy—6'3", 300 pounds—but things did not go as planned when he squabbled up. The older dudes told him, "Hey, that's not you. That's not who you are. You're not a dirtheart." Ralo thought about it afterwards. "While I was in my parents' care, never was our electricity ever off," he says. "There was never not food. If there was, my mom wouldn't let me know. We weren't a part of the narrative of lack. There's something about gangbanging that bothers my spirit, but it never settled correctly with me that I never got put on the hood."[116]

"When you chose the street life I used to always be worried about you," Rimpau wrote in an Instagram post to Nipsey a few days after his friend's murder. "I always felt like you was too comfortable with this bullshit. But like a brother I followed right behind you. I know you was just as worried about me as I was for you."[117] Rimpau wasn't the only one concerned about Hussle's safety. "I know Blacc Sam was always worried about niggas," Rimpau said in an interview. "He was even worried about me, and that's not even my blood. He used to always tell me be safe and move a certain way."[118]

"I tried to do as much as I can," Nipsey's big brother said at the memorial service. "To keep him out of the front line and keep him out of the streets and out of the gangbanging as much as I could. But there really was nothing I could do."[119]

Chapter 4

ЄＰＩＴＰЄＡ

THINK IT'S TIME WE MAKE ARRANGEMENTS
FINALLY WIGGLE OUT THEY MAZES
FIND ME OUT IN DIFFERENT PLACES

—Nipsey Hussle, "Blue Laces 2," *Victory Lap* (2018)

When Dawit Asghedom was finished speaking at his son's memorial service at the Staples Center, he raised his fist and uttered the words *"Awet n' hafash."*[1] It's a safe bet that few people in the arena, or even watching at home, were able to understand what he was saying. In the Eritrean language of Tigrinya, this phrase means "Victory to the people."[2]

During the thirty-year guerilla war Eritrea fought for independence from Ethiopia, the phrase could be seen printed on posters everywhere. For many Eritrean soldiers who lost their lives in the war, these would have been the last words they ever spoke. Between 1961 and 1991, more than 150,000 Eritreans died during the conflict with Ethiopia's army and air force, not counting those who perished due to forced relocation and deliberately man-made famines that killed more than half a million.[3]

Dawit Asghedom was one of many who fled the conflict to save his life. He came to the U.S. at age nineteen seeking asylum and started a new life in Los Angeles.[4]

By the time Ermias was roughly the same age, his father was concerned that he was heading down the wrong path in life. "My mom is American," Nipsey explained in 2010, "so I was raised in her household in my formative years. But as I got older, my pops tried to keep me involved with the culture by telling me the stories of the conflict between Ethiopia and Eritrea, how he came to America, and about our family back home, because all that side of my family, my aunties, grandparents, is in Africa."[5] Seeking to help his sons connect with their heritage, Dawit Asghedom decided to take Samiel and Ermias on a trip back home to Eritrea for three months during the summer of 2003.

"As his dad, I wanted to make sure he saw the place that raised me," his father would later recall in an interview with *GQ* magazine. "It's good to know your origins. I always wanted to get them back there. I wanted them to know the family—their cousins, grandmother, uncles, and relatives they only knew by telephone. And I wanted them to see it was different in Africa."[6]

Sam and Adam were also concerned about the lifestyle Ermias was living. "I was very worried about my brother," said Sam. "Adam would have conversations with my brother like, 'Do something positive, because we're not gonna last out here. Nobody lasts out here like that.'"[7]

And then one day Hussle told Dexter, "Me and my brother is going to be taking a trip to go back to Eritrea with Dad." He packed his bag and set off to celebrate his nineteenth birthday in Africa. Until that time the farthest he'd ever traveled was to Atlanta.[8]

"It was life-changing when I went to Eritrea," Nipsey told me. For one thing, seeing a country run by Black people fundamentally changed his perspective on life in the U.S. He noticed that there was "no racial class" in his father's homeland and that "everybody feels a part of it."[9] The trip changed him in other ways too: by stepping outside of his daily reality, Ermias gained new perspective on himself. "If you don't know your full-throttle history, the whole story of how you came to where you are, it's kind of hard to put things together," he said. "That filled in a blank spot for me, as far as understanding myself."[10]

At first, Hussle didn't really want to be out of town for long. "I didn't even know I was goin'," Nipsey recalled during a *Victory Lap* promo stop at New York's Hot 97. "Out of the blue my brother just was like, 'Bro, we're about to go back home.' And I had a spot at the time. I was hustlin'. I had a studio. I was, like, knee-deep in some young nigga shit." But his paternal grandmother was sick, and she'd never met her grandsons. Ermias and Sam had no choice but to make the trip. "I was like, three months is a long time!" Hussle recalled.[11] But the experience would prove so transformative that he planned to make a movie about his first journey to the Continent.

"I was sick the first two weeks," he said. "I was like, cultureshocked, depressed. I ain't understand. I ain't really know what to do out there. In L.A. I was smokin' weed every day, ridin' around the hood in a car with rims. I just had a different comfort zone. And once I got out of that, after the first two weeks I embraced what was goin' on. And I just had to let go of what made me comfortable." He missed his cell phone, the internet. "That shit we rely on day-to-day out here—email and your females," Nipsey recalled with a laugh. "It's all cut off once you get out there. It's more about interaction with the people."[12]

"I love my culture. It was just a lot to adjust to," he told me.[13] But spending time with the African side of his family changed his perspective on life in many ways. "More than anything, my respect for women," he told Charlamagne Tha God on *The Break-fast Club* radio show. "I came in the house and they had food ready for me. And they wouldn't let me lift my hand to do no work . . . Literally when I came in to eat, they washed my hands for me. So I felt obligated to do my part as a man. Like, can't nobody disrespect my cousins. They don't gotta do no hard labor that men supposed to do."[14] Coming from a broken home, he gained a new appreciation for the dynamic of a family relationship.

"I had seen a place—and I'm just being honest—where the family structure wasn't devastated," he said. "Out here it's just a different dynamic between our families, and even the dynamic between men and women. I was raised in South Central L.A., so my perspective of women was a little fucked up, to be honest. I didn't *think* it was, but when I went out there and I seen how different the dynamic was. After being out there a month, I was ready to kill behind my female homegirls. You better not play with my cousins. I'll do something to you behind these women. Just the confidence they had in supporting me, and taking care of me. It was just like a mutual respect that made the relationship much different."[15]

He was also inspired by learning about his father's homeland and its history firsthand. "Eritrea is a small country, and it was formerly a part of Ethiopia," he told me. "Civil war happened thirty-four years ago, and Eritrea got its independence. They've got a very independent spirit. Fought for a lot of years for its independence. The United States backed Ethiopia. So Eritrea was against world superpowers and somehow came out on top, so there's a real sense of pride."[16] Another source of pride was the fact that Ethiopia and Eritrea are widely respected for being African nations that resisted colonization. "Even Jamaicans and Rastafarians identify with the culture," Hussle noted.[17]

Although he was a long way from L.A.—8,735 miles, to be exact—Hussle felt surprisingly at home once he got over the culture shock. "Asmara is a beautiful city for real," Nipsey added. "It reminded me a lot of L.A. It's like seventy degrees almost year-round. When you go down, it's like a road that goes down thousands of meters and then you end up inland—and that gets really hot. But in the actual capital city it's beautiful year-round. I was really informed by goin' outside. Like, *Dang, it's crackin' out here.*"[18]

Home videos show Ermias and Samiel in their baggy jeans and oversize T-shirts organizing smaller kids in games of stickball, using a tire for home base—or sitting with their cousin sipping soft drinks and admiring the panoramic view from an old city with modern architecture perched on a lofty plateau amidst volcanic mountains.[19]

Spending time in the Eritrean capital gave Hussle a new perspective on gang conflict in L.A. "You had your fake little pop-up gangs," he recalled, "but that wasn't the culture of that place. It was an actual conflict over land, over the border. A generational, decades-old conflict. That was more or less the culture of the young people. It was like, 'I'ma go to war, fight, and go to the front lines for my country.'"[20]

Ermias, Samiel, and their father visited Massawa, a port city on the Red Sea coast with Italian, Egyptian, and Ottoman architecture. They saw the imperial palace on Taulud Island and the monument to those who died in the civil war. They went to Sawa, where Eritrea's young people receive military training to prepare them for national service, during the festival for the National Union of Eritrean Youth and Students.[21]

Overall he considered his trip to Eritrea a mind-expanding experience. "I swam in the Red Sea," he said. "The shit that Moses parted in Exodus, I swam in that real quick, homie."[22]

More than that, it gave him a sense of belonging that he never experienced in Los Angeles. "It was really eye-opening, and I came back a different person. A lot of what you would call 'third-world countries' will be poor in resources but rich in ethics. Don't accept the propaganda. Go see for yourself. Inform yourself. The media does have an agenda."[23]

Contrary to images of famine and desperation in Western media, Nipsey found that life in East Africa could be very comfortable. "When you think of America, they don't market Skid Row," he told me. "They market Hollywood. They market Wall Street. I could take you to a place in New York that look a lot like the poverty of Eritrea. It's a little bit more extreme in terms of no plumbing. But in terms of the type of person that that makes, you may not be as critically affected because the wealth gap is not so vast. You might see a homeless man outside a bank on Wall Street. Skid Row is right down the street from Hollywood in L.A. But in Africa they market the famine or the poverty a little more for whatever reasons. I can't speculate on the agenda. But when I went, I was like, 'Man, they got plumbing and stoves and hot showers, and king-size beds, and cable and DirecTV, and Mercedes Benzes.'"[24]

When Hussle went to what would be considered "the hood," he found it to be a little bit more concentrated and a little bit more intense. "But the level of violence is not near what you'll encounter in the hoods of New York or L.A.," Hussle said. "There's not a culture of gangbanging and killing and extreme violence. So how is the poverty affecting them, is the question? And why is it affecting them different back home than here? Maybe because you don't see nobody worth $500 million individually, when you know that you can't even buy food. I'm not an expert on this, but my experience informed me a little bit. And man, it ain't no robberies like that. And if you hungry you can probably get you some food. You can probably say, 'I'm hungry, bro' and get you a plate. It's communal eatin'. We eat off one plate. So if we was all at lunch together, we go wash our hands. If it's your house, your wife will wash our hands as we walk in. And then they'll put the food on one plate, and we eat off one plate together. It's just different."[25]

Just as he would in L.A., Hussle made sure to bring his music with him. "He took *Fucc tha Middleman* and a lot of the songs he was doing," Dexter recalls, "and he told us 'the people in the streets was loving it.'"[26] Seeing the impact of his music in Africa expanded Hussle's sense of possibility. "That really opened my eyes to how global and worldwide hip-hop has become," he said in a 2006 conversation with Davey D. "People gotta express their struggle. When you ain't got no other means of liberatin' yourself, it's through spoken word and expression. You feel me? So it's relative out there as well. They relate to our struggle."[27]

Hussle's time in Eritrea was not entirely stress-free. Dexter remembers Hussle coming back from Africa with a broken arm. "He told us he got into an altercation when he was over there with some dudes and it got hectic," he recalls. "Nipsey was very charismatic with girls, so there were sometimes situations where girls were drawn to him who thought he was cute . . . That could be the grounds for some kind of conflict."[28]

Nevertheless his experience in Eritrea left him thinking of Africa as a second home. "We look at America like we got it right out here and the other countries don't," Hussle reflected years later. "But it's not no schools getting shot up back home. You know what I'm saying? So it just gave me a different perspective and something to think about. Man, these traditions been going on for thousands of years. And over time you work out the kinks. So for these customs and traditions to be thousands of years old and they're still in practice, that must mean they working to a degree."[29]

More than any one tradition or cultural experience, what resonated most was his overall connection to Eritrea. "It's devastating if you can't connect to a country," he reflected. "'Cause we know we're not from America for real. I was raised under my mom's understanding—being a Black American whose mom came from New Orleans, Louisiana, and a couple generations back they was exposed to slavery. So to have an understanding that there's a whole thousands-year-old tradition that we connect to. I'm fortunate 'cause my dad was born over there. So I connect to it in one generation. So I met my grandmother and I seen her way of livin'. It's my dad's mom. This is my immediate family, so I connected to it easier maybe than somebody who does their ancestry and figures out where they're from and then goes to visit—but don't got nobody that really love 'em."[30]

His experiences in his father's homeland stuck with Ermias over time, shaping the way he thought about life back home. "I think family is way higher on the list of things that are important in terms of Eritrea compared to America," he said later. "Out there family is the equivalent of how we feel about material things out here. That's what drives our culture. That's what drives our whole philosophy is material gain. And I feel like out there what drives their whole culture is family—family well-being and family togetherness. That's really the main difference, just the value system, what's important. And you would think that the country that has less would feel that getting things is more important."[31] In fact it was the exact opposite.

When Nipsey returned home from Eritrea, his friends noticed something was different. "When he came back from Eritrea, he was a totally different individual," remembers Killa Twan, who had known Ermias since middle school. "You could say he went as a young street thug and came back as a grown man. I really don't know what happened out there. I guess just seeing his people and opening up that third eye. All that stuff about the Marathon, I can say that's when he figured that out. It made him wiser and stronger."[32]

Nipsey felt it was time to make some hard choices about his life. "I think it brought me into being—I don't wanna say 'positive,' but more conscious of my decisions. I couldn't embrace the narrative of 'This how shit go' and 'That's how it is.' That wasn't really it to me no more."[33]

Nipsey's father couldn't have been more pleased. "Here it is very money-oriented and about material objects," he said. "I wanted them to see the richness of those differences. When we came back, Ermias said, 'What do I want to do with my life? Do I want to continue doing this, or do I want to go to a different direction?'"[34]

Years later Hussle posted an Instagram video of himself, Sam, and his father sitting by a fountain in Asmara. "My favorite part of *The Godfather* movie is when Michael Corleone had to go back home to Sicily, Italy and lay low because of some dirt he did in America," he wrote. Hussle wasn't exactly laying low, but he did take the opportunity to regroup and adjust his priorities. When he searched his heart, he realized that his true calling was music. "There was only one record store in town and I use to go there every day and tell the owner I'm a rapper and I'ma blow up in America when I go back," Hussle wrote on the Gram. "I spent 90 days out there and will never forget that summer."[35]

There are moments in life when you know you've reached a turning point. Nipsey's return home from Eritrea was one of those moments. But change does not come without sacrifice. "I realized I had to take two steps back," he said, "to take ten steps forward."[36]

Chapter 5

HUSSLE IN THE HOUSE

SPOKE SOME THINGS INTO THE UNIVERSE AND THEY APPEARED

I SAY IT'S WORTH IT, I WON'T SAY IT'S FAIR

FIND YOUR PURPOSE OR YOU'RE WASTIN' AIR

—Nipsey Hussle, "Victory Lap," *Victory Lap* (2018)

After celebrating his nineteenth birthday in Eritrea, Hussle touched down at LAX airport with renewed focus. Before the trip, he'd been full-time hustling and part-time rapping. Lacking an outlet to get his music heard, he was content to pop the trunk and sell CDs hand to hand. He knew how to get money, and he got a lot of it, but his actions were not aligned with a larger purpose. "I wasn't making a million dollars in the streets," he said. "I ain't gonna tell that lie." Over the years he had amassed well upward of six figures. If he wasn't on Crenshaw and Slauson he was on Brynhurst or Tenth Avenue. He knew what it was to go out of town, get money, do shows. He and Ralo and Rimpau and Fatts had plenty of stories about their missions to Atlanta or Las Vegas, but he had to make a decision. There came a time when he truly had the game on smash, moving up the supply chain to the point where his daily routine

131

was driving around the hood in his white Lincoln, picking up bags—$500 here, $1,000 there. It wasn't a bad life. But even at nineteen, Hussle had seen too many of his friends sent away to do football numbers behind bars. He knew he had to fall back for his own good.[1]

After going hard for the past few years, Hussle had moved enough packs and stacked plenty of paper. He felt he could afford to focus on the music again—and go full throttle with it this time. No matter how much he tried to avoid the issue, it was obvious by now that hip-hop was his true calling. It had him stuck like Don Corleone in *The Godfather Part III*—just when he thought he was out, rap pulled him back in. He prided himself on never lying in his raps, but getting into shootouts between studio sessions was a little *too* real. It was time to put his balling on pause and lock into a creative zone.

"It was hard for my ego," he admitted. "I was used to being that young fly nigga, taking my pick of whatever female I want. At all the parties, all the clubs, all the spotlight was on me." No more smoking Kush all day and balling at night. Success wasn't going to come without sacrifice.[2]

Hussle was known all over the city for his white Lincoln with Alpina rims—the kind with the lock and key. "Them was like name-brand rims," he explained with a smile on the *Rap Radar* podcast. "You couldn't even get to the lugs without unlocking 'em. That was some teenage baller shit." That Lincoln was so famous that girls wanted to ride in it and his business associates wanted to buy it. "I ain't sellin' this car," he told himself. "I'm winnin' in this car."[3]

That was when he experienced what Jay-Z would call a "Moment of Clarity." It happened, as so many things did, right in the parking lot at Crenshaw and Slauson. Leaning on his Lincoln, he pondered what he would come to recognize as "my little adolescent dream." He felt like a star. He had thousands in his pocket, and the confidence that came with it. But he wanted something more. He thought about that record shop back in Eritrea, how he'd told the staff he was going to blow up in the rap game. He thought about the grandmother, aunts, and cousins he'd just met, and how they would feel to hear he got locked up, or worse.

"I'm at that level where I was trying to get at as a teenager," he reflected. "I could either go to my next level with this . . . or I could fuck with what I been having a *itch* to do, which was the music."[4]

Before his trip to Eritrea, Hussle had completed his *Slauson Boy Vol. 1* mixtape at ButterVision, a musical milestone. But while he was away the studio was burglarized. "They broke in, they stole a keyboard I had all my beats on," said Ralo. "A very expensive keyboard that Dexter purchased. It was a multi Yamaha 88."[5] Dexter says he never really pressed or investigated. "We almost had to pretend like it didn't happen," he says. "I knew where I was."[6]

The violation of the studio put a damper on the creative magic that had been going on at ButterVision. Dexter started shooting downtown at another location. "My wife was doing graphics there and administration and I was the lead photographer," he says. "We would take Nipsey in our Land Rover."[7]

Hussle knew it was time to set up shop for himself. Standing there in that parking lot, he decided he needed his own studio. He made one phone call to his man D-Mac—who had been trying to buy the Lincoln—and asked if he was still interested. D-Mac didn't give him a chance to change his mind, and soon pulled up in his lowrider with a bag full of money. "He gave me the cash," Nipsey recalled. "I gave him the key." Nip sold most of his jewelry too—those Cuban links were just like stocks and bonds, but Hussle needed liquid assets right now. He was done flossing for the time being. He was about to tap into his higher purpose and get back on the Marathon.[8]

The next call was to his brother. He told Sam he was going to Sam Ash to buy some equipment. "How much you got?" Blacc Sam asked, then offered to match him buck for buck. "I'ma meet you up there."[9]

Between the two of them they had just enough to set up a studio. Nipsey couldn't afford to pay a studio engineer, so he taught himself how to use Pro Tools. "I had no training on it. I just was like, *I need to record*." The skills Hussle picked up back at the Watts Towers and sharpened at ButterVision were coming in handy. He knew how to connect equipment, how to chop samples and build drum loops. The next step was to master basic recording techniques in Pro Tools. "If my engineer was bullshitting with me or acting like he was doing something that was rocket science, I'd just tell him, 'Watch out, my nigga. I'll handle it.'"[10]

For this next leg of the Marathon he needed to keep the energy pure. Hussle thought about who was serious about music like he was. He hit up J Stone, a young MC who'd been making mixtapes in elementary school on a karaoke machine. Hussle met him on some street shit, but when they took time and chopped it up he could tell Stone was not playing.

Stone told Hussle how his older brother got killed when he was thirteen. Stone made a tape in his honor called *The Streets Ain't Safe* and passed them out at Crenshaw High. "That's when my music changed," said Stone. "It started coming from the heart. That's where the pain in my music came from."[11]

They talked about their goals for the future. "Man, this is what I'm on," Hussle said. "I'm trying to have my own label. I wanna name it Slauson Boy Records." J Stone's vision was similar.

"Yo that's tight. I wanna start my own shit too," he said. "I wanna start Low Down Records. I wanna have artists too."[12]

When he wasn't making music, Hussle was out doing promo. "I remember years ago when Nipsey was posting his own flyers on the poles around the neighborhood," recalls Choc Nitty, an MC/producer/entrepreneur from Watts. "I used to be like, 'Damn, I see you everywhere, bro!' And he'd be like, 'Gotta hustle, gotta hustle.'"[13]

By this time Nipsey was working with a team, anchored by Fatts and Adam. "Adam didn't rap," Gooch recalls. "He didn't gangbang. He just wanted to know what he could do to help." Adam might take Nip to go get posters printed, or drive the people who put the posters up all over the hood. "He also had a business mind, so he started taking phone calls and handling business as an A&R," says Gooch. "He could talk that vernacular, and you don't let people talk to the artist."[14]

Along with Sam they would eventually become the foundation of All Money In. "He printed business cards that said 'Slauson Boy Records,'" Sam remembers. "We paid money out of our pockets to get radio advertisements."[15] Hussle's team was magnetic, attracting people who were willing to do whatever they could just to be associated with the movement. "The people rallied around him," says Sam. "It motivated him."[16] This was before the T-shirts and the merch took off. Nipsey was always reaching out to people from the hood and giving them jobs or helpful life advice. "Instead of doin' this, you should do that," he would say. That sort of direction helped to change the lives of people like Slauson Bruce, a familiar face in the community who used to walk around the neighborhood recycling cans. "Man, come clean up the parking lot," Nipsey used to tell Bruce.[17] He wanted his win to be a victory for the whole hood.

FIRST GET YO' GRIND ON, THEN GET YO' SHINE ON
WE COME THROUGH DAYTIME WITH THE LIGHTS ON

—Nipsey Hussle, "Hussle in the House," *Bullets Ain't Got No Name Vol. 2* (2008)

Despite the disappearance of the keyboard, Dexter was still going hard with his photography and video production. One day an unexpected visitor knocked at his door. He opened the door to find a towering man with a bald head and powerful eyes. Dexter looked up at him and said, "You must be Big U."

"I am," he said. "I heard that you're doing a movie."

Soon after Big U got out of jail, he headed over to Dexter's house. "I guess he heard that somebody was making a film about the 60s," Dexter recalls, "which wasn't true."[18]

"No," Dexter replied, "I'm facilitating the progress of the kids in a way that would allow them to be who they want to be. When you look at the albums we recorded at the Kitchen, the guys' names are all listed as the executive producers—not mine. But it was done at my house at my cost."[19]

Big U had been incarcerated since 1991 for the attempted robbery of an undercover sheriff's deputy posing as a drug dealer.[20] He returned home fourteen years later determined to turn his life around. During his time away he'd written the proposal for the program that became Developing Options. "Almost everything to a T that I'm doing to this day, I wrote it out—helping the kids, doing the music, the movies."[21] Having previously managed Kurupt, he saw music as one of the main options that he wanted to develop.

Big U took an immediate liking to Dexter, who shared his expertise and knowledge as generously with him as he did with Cuzzy, Gooch, and Nipsey. Dexter shot portraits of Big U and his family at the house, and taught Big U and his team how to use video editing software like iMovie and Final Cut.

Dexter explained how he saw things. "I told Big U and his friends they needed to start making use of the things that were right in front of them," he says. "'Crip' is just as famous a word in China as 'Coca-Cola,' so why are you not leveraging on it?"[22]

By this time, Dexter and his wife were raising three young daughters, all of whom had been born in the neighborhood. It wasn't always convenient for a young family to have Big U and his friends, including former Death Row CEO Suge Knight, hanging around the home. "My wife was terrified," Dexter admits. "They would come and pick me up sometimes. Big U was like, 'I just want you with me, DB. I like your creative spirit.'" Sometimes Nipsey would come along on these outings. During one meeting at the Beverly Center, Suge pounded the table with his fist and everybody's food and drinks flew up in the air. "Who at this table made two hundred million dollars?" Suge wanted to know.[23] The company he'd built, one of the most successful labels in rap history, was in steep decline by that time—and Knight's legal issues didn't help matters. In 2006 Death Row would file for bankruptcy.[24]

Like many entertainment executives from the 1990s, Suge did not fully grasp how to navigate the internet environment. "He knew hit records," Dexter said, "but not what the digital democracy was coming with." That was what he had prepared Nipsey for—the change that was coming. Dexter taught him why it was important to retain ownership, and why he should hold out when the offers started to come.[25]

The first person to mention Nipsey Hussle to Big U may have been his nephew, Tiny Drawz, who met Nip at Claustrophobic Studios in late 2003. "Bear Claw had put out a big compilation for the homies to show their talent," Drawz said in a Kev Mac video interview. "I just happened to be one of the young homies that was lucky enough to get on there along with Nip." Drawz was already familiar with Hussle thanks to his pop-the-trunk distribution methods. "He had a hustle plus he had a flow."[26]

When he came back from prison, Big U—who was also known in the hood as Big Draws—asked Tiny Drawz a simple question: "Who home?" There was a lot of meaning packed into those two little words. Asking "Who home?" reflects the reality of high incarceration rates, the knowledge that at any given moment a considerable portion of one's community will be stuck behind bars. Having recently returned home himself, Big U wanted to know who was the hottest talent that was not currently incarcerated and ready to make moves.

Tiny Drawz let him know. "You need to mess with Nip," he said. "Nip might be the next one for real—the flow, the hustle, the image, everything." Big U said he would check him out and Tiny Drawz kept reminding him until he did. "Music-wise," he says, "that changed the hood a lot."[27]

Soon after Big U came home, he called a meeting with G Bob—known to Nipsey Hussle fans as Cobby Supreme. The purpose of the meeting was to identify potential musical talent to work with Big U's company Uneek Music. "Unc was like, 'If I'm trying to get a deal, I can't go up in the building saying I'm representing this and I got this and I got that,'" Hoodsta Rob recalls. Instead he suggested consolidating all the best talent under one name. Various suggestions were thrown out and shot down before someone pointed out that Nip already had the ball rolling with Slauson Boyz. Suddenly the idea seemed so obvious. "Why don't we just do Slauson Boyz?"[28]

Cuzzy says he was the one who first came up with the concept of a rap crew named Slauson Boyz, in honor of the iconic L.A. street organization.[29] "The Slauson Boyz is basically for the day-one people that was there from the beginning," says Hoodsta Rob. "It's a little seniority with us." The key players, he says, were picked based on work ethic. Nipsey was the main guy. J Stone and Cuzzy were core members too, and Tiny Drawz became one as well. Hoodsta had the studio, where he was constantly working and recording everyone. "It was a big thing, bro," says Hoodsta. "It was fun!"[30]

After returning from Eritrea, Hussle went to a local tattoo shop and had SLAUSON BOY inked in huge letters across his back. Dexter was taken by surprise when Nipsey removed his shirt to show off his new tattoo. "I was speechless, 'cause I knew what it meant," he recalls. "Hold on," he said after a moment. "Let me just go get my camera." There was no avoiding the issue now. Nipsey had quite literally put the hood on his back. Years after the fact, Dexter cannot conceal his misgivings. "It was something he wanted," Dexter says. "My perspective was 'It's a reality around you and you could leverage it, but I don't feel you should go so deep into it.' Nipsey had his own thoughts about that. He was very focused about how he wanted to shape his persona. Nobody told him to go put Slauson Boy on his back. He did that. It was part of him taking ownership of this brand that he was prepared to live and die by. I wasn't overly thrilled with it. I felt it was kind of maybe starting down that path a bit too much, and maybe should have stayed along more musical lines. But I suppose there will always be different perspectives on that."[31]

According to Tiny Drawz, the Slauson Boyz ended up signing with Big U as a group. "I'm not sure if they got another deal," he says, "or if [Nip] was going through a situation—then everything branched off and separated." Big U would later work with both Tiny Drawz and Nipsey Hussle as solo acts. "But in the beginning," he says, "Slauson Boyz were under Big U."[32]

Hussle had never met Big U before his return from prison, but was aware of Big U by reputation. He'd heard the stories like everybody else. Big U was a legendary figure in the streets. "Based on Draws's prior experience in the industry and also him being a figure in the hood," Hussle said, "when he got home he was like, 'Yeah, let's sit down and chop it.'"[33]

After spending three months with his sons in Eritrea, Dawit Asghedom wanted to keep in closer contact with them. He could tell the boys were going through a tricky phase in their development. Slauson Tees had been raided by police and shut down.[34] But as always, Sam found a way to rebuild, catering to a brisk market for DVDs. Meanwhile Nipsey was changing up the program by following his musical ambitions, but still navigating the perils of street life. After selling his white Lincoln, he bought an old Cadillac just to get around in. One day shots were fired and a bullet passed clean through the car without touching him.[35]

"That was a major turning point," says Gooch. "He was goin' the wrong way in the hood. It's hard not to get sucked in. It's like a black hole! The power, the energy is just—one little decision, another decision, one more decision, and before you know it, you're like, 'Oh shit! I done created a little windstorm.'"[36]

Being down with the 60s wasn't all about hustling for your own benefit. Everybody was expected to play their position and put in work for the set. Some people were hustlers. Some might have history in the hood but they straightened up, got good jobs, and made connections. Some people were just young and wanted to be known. Some people fought. Some people didn't know how to fight. Some were shooters. It was understood.

At one time the hood used to have regular meetings, but with so many arrests and the threat of gang injunctions, the leadership structure was breaking down. Knowledge wasn't being passed on as it once had been. The Crips were well into their fifth generation at this point. Gooch called it the "Tiny Loc Era." They were like the millennials of gangbanging—young, confident, self-motivated, making moves to the best of their ability based on their own judgment and intuition. "They don't have their parents tellin' them to go to school and do this or that," Gooch said. "It's like they're free thinkers. [Nip] was a free thinker that took advantage of it. And that's not easy to do that and be that way. *Shit*, that's difficult!"[37] That was Nipsey Hussle to a T. Still, there were times when you were called on to put in work for the set. Some of the things Hussle was asked to do bothered him, but he couldn't let it show.

"Deep inside my mind is buried crimes you can't imagine," he would later rap on the final track of *The Marathon*. "That I wrestle with at night, demons that I fight, I can't get past it."

At any given moment one car could drive up the block and turn an ordinary night into a nightmare. When the shots start to fly, nobody knows who the slugs will catch. It was a hell of a way to live, but at least Hussle could release the stress through his music. He recorded a song at ButterVision about some of his experiences in the field called "Bullets Ain't Got No Names." The play-by-play was like a flashback from a war movie, except this wasn't Vietnam or Afghanistan, it was daily life in a major American city:

> SIX MINUTES LATER, THEY GOT RIGHT BACK AT US
> TEN MINUTES LATER WE WAS RIGHT BACK AT THEM
> MY BURNER'S SO HOT, I PUT A HOLE IN MY MATTRESS

Sam decided it would be a good idea to put some space between Nipsey and the hood. The brothers purchased a house to live with their father over on Western Avenue. The house was four or five miles from the neighborhood, right on the border with the Eight Trey Gangsters, one of the 60s' most hated enemies. But that was kind of the point, to go where nobody expected them to be. It was time to change up the energy. And Hussle finally had a chance to set up his studio equipment.[38]

Ever since he was a kid, Ermias Asghedom had wanted to create his own studio. At the house with Sam and his father, he had free rein for the first time. "I'm OCD a little bit," Hussle said. "I gotta be able to create my space." Once he had everything set up, Nipsey called J Stone to come over and make some magic happen. "He ain't even have a bed up in there," Stone remembers. "It was just a table, computer and some speakers, and a microphone—that's it." Hussle slept on the studio floor.[39]

"We was kinda doing it ourselves," Stone says. "He didn't really know how to work Pro Tools like that. I didn't really know how to work Pro Tools like that. We started learning and just taught each other with no one else in the studio—just me and that nigga." On Mondays Hussle would rap and Stone would engineer, then on Tuesdays they'd switch places.[40]

Since they were recording in the Eight Treys they had to keep the music turned low. "It was people living across the street that we didn't get along with," Stone stresses. "We didn't want them to hear us."[41]

By this time Stone and Hussle had fallen all the way back from hustling so they could focus on music. "We knew we could hit the block and get dough," said Nip, "but we was tryin' to avoid breakin' the concentration. We was in a vibe. We had like a momentum goin', musically." Money got so tight they would chop up bits of candle wax to sell as crack so they could afford to buy themselves a little bit of weed for inspiration in the studio. "That's against the code, to sell a smoker some fake drugs," Hussle admitted.[42]

"We had some smokers pull up on Blacc Sam," J Stone recalls. "'Hey, man! Your brother in there? He got us for some money, man!'" Stone laughs at the memory. "We did it for the music, bro. All for the love of the music."[43]

Hoodsta Rob also came through to visit the house on Western. "This is how I know he was serious," Rob recalls. "Bro used to have vision boards to visualize what he was going to do in the future. He listed his daily things and certain words—the whole vision. Now that's a person who's serious about something. People don't have vision boards inside the studio. You usually see more weed than anything around studios. He had a vision board at the house on Western. I was like, 'Look at bro—bro *on it!*' Man, everything was falling into place too good for it to be bad."[44]

Nipsey drove his bullet-ventilated Cadillac to pick Cuzzy up and bring him to the house in ETG territory. "He wasn't on fire all the way," Cuzzy said. "He was just starting a little street buzz, but the city knew him." Hussle was supposed to keep a low profile, but he didn't seem to care.

Walking up the driveway Cuzzy could smell Dawit Asghedom's food in the kitchen. "Pops in there cookin' the Ethiopian shit with the *injera*," he said. "Pops like his shit *spicy*." He would greet his son's guests with a plate of food as soon as they came through the door. "That nigga was badder than us," Cuzzy said with a laugh. "It was always love and respect. Pops'll never trip."[45]

Between the music and the home cooking, the neighbors were starting to take notice. "Niggas started rollin' by," Robin Hood said in a Kev Mac interview. "Niggas was stopping. There was a couple niggas that stayed catty-corner to him that was coming on the porch." But Sam and Nip understood the risks and they were prepared to defend themselves with security cameras outside and firearms inside.[46]

Nip invited Dexter to the house to document him and Sam in their element. "I photographed them with guns in their hands, money counters," he recalls. "I'm the only guy they ever let do that. That was the depth of the relationship." In one of the shots, Hussle stands by the window, peering outside like the iconic image of Malcolm X, but he wasn't posing. "It almost seems like fiction," said Dexter. "The photos of Biggie and Tupac and Jay-Z and all of them were on the wall. That young boy that I photographed of looking out the window like Malcolm became what he dreamed about becoming."[47]

I CAN FEEL THE EXCITEMENT LIKE I CAN SENSE AN INDICTMENT
SWEAR I HOPE THAT I'M WRONG BUT JUST IN CASE I'M ON MY TIP
—Nipsey Hussle, "Outro," *The Marathon Continues* (2011)

The Asghedom brothers felt good about the new life they were building with their father. But between the disgruntled smokers and the Eight Trey Gangsters across the street, Sam and Nipsey knew things could go left at any time. Growing up in South Central Los Angeles, they were used to living with an element of risk, but at least Hussle was able to focus on his true purpose. "I was committed," Hussle said. "I was sincere. I was an artist *every day*. Even my commitment was influencing my homies to where they was coming to the studio and just takin' it serious. And bein' like, 'Fuck that, I'm about to just sit here every day with you. We goin' broke, but fuck it. We gonna make music!'"[48]

Part of what kept them going was the peace of mind that what they were doing was legal. "You ain't hear helicopters at night and think they was about to kick your door in," Hussle said. "You ain't have to have that paranoia that go with every other hustle that we was involved in."[49] Still, the raid did not come as a total surprise. It wasn't a drug raid, though. The cops were looking for DVDs.

Like the music industry, Hollywood had been struggling to keep up with what studios saw as digital piracy. Advances in technology made change inevitable, and a debate was raging in the film industry about how to respond. Some argued that bootlegging had a certain promotional value, building new audiences online and in the streets, but the Motion Picture Association of America didn't see it that way. Under pressure to crack down on DVD bootleggers, the LAPD set up a special antipiracy unit. They even arrested their own. Captain Julie Nelson, a twenty-eight-year LAPD veteran, was caught selling bootleg DVDs to an undercover agent in 2003. A search of her home recovered over 250 pirated discs. Possession and sale was a felony.[50]

Sam had a feeling he was being watched. Hussle asked Dexter to stash Sam's DVD burners and blank discs at the house. He'd come by every so often to pick up what they needed.[51] Although Sam had been trying to keep a low profile, the police raid on November 17, 2006 came as a devastating blow.[52] It wasn't his first run-in with police and they hit him hard. The brothers ended up losing their house and everything in it. "The police really boxed up all my music equipment," Hussle said. His Apple laptop with Pro Tools—gone. His hard drives full of music and videos— gone. "They took cars, jewelry, everything," he said. "You can get back cars, money, jewelry. But you can't get back a song. Or a visual. Niggas is dead. People that passed away and you got 'em on camera—a classic moment."[53] The police seized everything of value: the security cameras around the house, Sam's bullet-proof BMW 745, money stacked in safes, gold chains. The police also found a shotgun registered in Sam's name. "By me being on probation and havin' prior gun cases, they threw the gun on me," Hussle said. "So that was a major setback."[54]

It didn't seem fair. Not after all the work they had put in over all those years. Not after Nipsey had stepped away from hustling to focus on music. "I was really just in the house working," he said. "Nobody knows how pure you are but you. But I was really pure at that time. I wasn't doing nothing but music . . . I was confused. Where does the good karma pay off at?"[55] To lose it all and now to face criminal charges seemed too much to bear. Hussle's faith was shaken, but he didn't have time to mourn the loss. His brother had a case to fight. They needed money for a lawyer. He had no choice but to hit the block again.

🏁🏁

BEFORE I SELL MY SOUL, I GIVE MY LIFE
IT'S BEEN A MINUTE BUT WE GON' GET RIGHT, WATCH

—Nipsey Hussle "Love?" *The Marathon* (2010)

Hussle knew the drill. It never changed. Fifty homies outside on the same strip serving the smokers. Before he stepped away from the game, Hussle had elevated himself somewhat, but now he was hustling hand-to-hand—a harder job that paid less.

On his first day back, Nip's homie Tiny Bodee said what everybody else was thinking: *"Maaaaan,* your shit flop, bro!" His words had the sting of truth. "My shit *did* flop!" Hussle told himself. "I'm back out here swallowing dope when the police hop out."[56] It was enough to make him question everything.

Sam was convicted and sent to the penitentiary. Hussle moved into the guesthouse behind Dexter's place. Chyna Hussle was no longer in her apartment, so she and her two kids moved in with him. Gooch went half with him on an iron security gate. "That was the first time he ever paid rent and had a key," Gooch recalls. But it didn't seem like a moment to celebrate.[57]

"I was just confused," Hussle said. "I remember questioning everything. Like, 'Damn, I don't have no part of the game that braced me for that.' I don't have no mantras that I remember hearin'. I ain't got no answer for that one."[58] All he knew for sure was that taking losses was part of the game. He had to accept defeat and keep pushing. Most of all he had to find a reason to believe that all of his hard work and sacrifice would not be in vain.

Before Sam went to the pen, he gave Hussle his gold chain with a diamond-encrusted Malcolm X pendant, one prized possession that wasn't lost in the raid. Sam had designed the piece himself and had it custom-made by a local jeweler.

"Malcolm X is somebody we got a lot of respect for, a lot of admiration for," Hussle said. "I respect what he represented. I respect the 'by any means necessary' philosophy. I respect his transition from bein' a street dude to bein' somebody that had discipline and stood up for a cause that was real, and is still real."[59]

"You can have that," Sam told Nip. To him it was more than a piece of jewelry.

"Just a little something," Hussle said. "Five hundred grams, fourteen-karat gold, half a kilo. It's all material, my nigga. That ain't what it is. It ain't on me. It's in me."[60]

Veteran artist manager Steve Lobel grew up in Queens, getting his start in the rap game with Run-DMC. "I was carrying bags, driving vans, whatever I had to do," says the man who lives by the motto "We Working."[61] He worked his way up in the industry, specializing in classic New York boom-bap—the Beatnuts, Frankie Cutlass. He introduced Fat Joe to his future wife and helped multiplatinum producer Scott Storch get his life and career back on track after battling cocaine addiction. At the indie label Relativity he worked with stars signed to Eazy-E's Ruthless Records: Bone Thugs-N-Harmony, Three 6 Mafia, and Tupac's group the Outlawz. "I've had a thirty-year career, known a lot of artists," says Lobel. "I can say with confidence that Nipsey was the smartest artist I ever worked with. He was a learning machine. He read books and he sought knowledge where a lot of people don't."[62]

Back in 2004 Lobel was hanging out at Summer Jam, the annual concert thrown by L.A. radio station Power 106. "I was in the back leaning on the wall," he says, "and this big guy comes to me—white T-shirt, glasses. He's like, 'Hey, you Steve Lobel?'"

"It all depends on who wants to know," Lobel replied. He often says that he fears no one but God, but you can never be too careful.

"I'm Big U," the man said, and mentioned a familiar name. "At that time I was dating his wife's cousin's niece," Lobel explains. "The whole time he was locked up on a fourteen-year bid, they were telling him about this white guy who's engaged to such-and-such living in L.A."

Once he said that name, Lobel said, "Oh, you're family."[63]

Big U explained that he'd just come home and was looking for artists. "Yo, come see me in my hood tomorrow," he said. As promised, Lobel drove his Range Rover Sport from the Valley to South Central, where Big U gave him a bunch of CDs to listen to. Nothing caught his ear at first, but he kept coming back. "Then one day he gave me a CD that said 'Slauson Boyz' in Magic Marker," Lobel remembers. He popped the disc in while sitting in traffic. "I was stuck on the 405 with my man Mexican Sean, and we're listening to this CD," Lobel says. "This song comes on called 'Bullets Ain't Got No Names' and I'm like, 'Wait a second, man—this is the West Coast 50 Cent! He's spittin' street shit but he's singing hooks.'" Once they heard another song called "I Don't Give a Fucc" Steve picked up his phone to call Big U. "Bro, I think we found something!"[64]

Steve doubled back to the hood to find out more about these Slauson Boyz. He was asking around until he found Cowboy, who walked them to a liquor store. Using a wire coat hanger, he reached behind the bulletproof glass to pull the last Slauson Boyz DVD out of the display case. Watching their no-frills music video, Lobel loved what he saw. "Yo, this guy looks like Snoop Dogg," he said.

"Yeah, that's Nipsey Hussle," Cowboy told him.

"What? I love that name," Lobel said. "Like Nipsey Russell, the comedian. I gotta meet this guy." Cowboy called his little homie.

"He pulled up about an hour later in a Caddy," Lobel recalls. "He had that Cuban link chain, long white tee, Dickies shorts, and high socks."

"See, that's what I loved about Nip," says Lobel at the memory of that first meeting. "He never changed nothing but the size of his clothes. As he grew, he wore tighter shirts, but he never changed who he was. Everywhere he went he banged the hood. Everything about him was the truth, from gangbanging and business and rapping to his hustle, his work ethic."

"Oh shit," Hussle said as he hopped out the Caddy with the bullet holes. "Steve Lobel!" An astute student of the game and avid reader of rap magazines, Hussle was well aware of Lobel's work.

"Yo bro, I think you're a superstar," Lobel told him, and they started rocking from there. The industry veteran wasted no time leveraging his relationships to hook Hussle up with his first paying gig—in Japan. "They paid me to rap for the first time," said Hussle, who collected a check for $10,000 plus another 20,000 yen to perform on a Japanese TV show. "I ain't have no hell of a name," he said. "I don't even know if they knew the song I was performing." All he knew was he got a check to go to Japan.

Hussle wasn't sure he really wanted a record deal. Based on his own research he knew that Harlem rapper Juelz Santana—who made his name off mixtapes before signing a short-lived deal through Roc-A-Fella Records—was earning $15,000 per show, which didn't sound bad at all. He had a map on his wall to help him track his plan to sell a thousand units of his next independent release in every state. Between that and show money, he figured he could achieve his initial goal of making half a million dollars no problem.

"My whole movement was independent," he said. "My big homie came home from the pen and was like, 'Let's go get this deal.' And I was so stubborn, like, 'Nah. We finna be independent.' We had the same concept, we just had two different ideas of how to do it."

Lobel set up meetings with all the major labels on behalf of Big U to land a deal for Hussle. "I brought Steve in to be our front man," Big U said. "You know how hard it was to be Big U, my reputation precedes me. I had to put a white face in front of a Black situation."

Everybody passed. "I ain't going to say names because I'm not a snitch," said Lobel. "But everybody passed. As soon as I left the meeting, they'd call my phone.

"'You're by yourself?' they'd ask.

"I'm like, 'Yeah.'

"'Steve, are you out of your mind? This guy's a Rollin' 60s Crip! They're the most notorious gang in L.A.'

"I'm like, 'So? I fear no one but God.' I believed in this when nobody believed in it."

Hussle listed the labels that turned them down in his song "Keys 2 the City." By 2006 all the meetings were done, and

Hussle was planning to get back on his Slauson Boy Records mixtape grind. J. Stone's full-length project *Tears of a Hustler* was scheduled to hit the streets on May 21, 2016, to be followed by Nipsey's *Slauson Boy 2* dropping on the Rollin' 60s' Hood Day, June 10 (6 x 10). Then one day Hussle was out on Brynhurst Avenue with a bunch of his homies when his phone rang with an unfamiliar number.

"Who is this?" Hussle said.

"What's up, man?" said the voice on the line. "This is Angelo Sanders. I'm A&R at Aftermath Records. I've heard you got some dope music. Could you pull up on me?"

"Hell yeah I'll pull up!" Hussle said. "Where you at? I'm comin'!" It was the moment he'd been waiting for.

Hussle headed straight to the meeting and played a lot of the music that would end up on his first mixtape, *Bullets Ain't Got No Name Vol. 1*. "I feel what you doin'," Angelo said. "I'm gonna bring this to Dre." When he got back from the meeting, Hussle couldn't contain his excitement. "We about to be signed to Dre!" he told the homies. "It's crackin'!"

🏁🏁

THIS LIFE IS SHORT, LET'S MAKE IT WORTH IT, NIGGA

WE ALL SO FAR FROM PERFECT, NIGGA

THEM CAMERAS ROLLIN', NO REHEARSALS, NIGGA

—Nipsey Hussle "Count Up That Loot," *Mailbox Money* (2014)

Life on the streets of Crenshaw wasn't waiting for a record deal. On June 10, 2007, one of Hussle's little homies from the neighborhood, Boss Hoss aka BH, got shot in the back of the head. "I was sixteen years old," BH recalls. "I went code blue. I bounced back. Man, I was fucked up!"

BH promised God if He would give him another chance to live, BH would change his life totally. Sure enough, he started bouncing back. "I learned how to walk again," he says. "Once Nipsey found out I was back okay, he pulled up to my house. He was just so in shock, like, 'Bro, what the *fuck*? We got a call you were *dead*.'"

"I was," BH said.

"You only sixteen, nigga!" he said. "You almost lost your life! It's time for you to change, bro. You gotta come to this studio. You gotta do *this* shit."

From that day on, Nip took BH under his wing. "I had already told myself I'm not fucking with these lowlife stupid motherfuckers no more," he said. "I almost lost my life dealing with everybody still doin' dumb shit. It ain't even worth it." They set up a makeshift studio inside his mother's house on Sixtieth Street. "I made my first song in this room right here," BH says. "Me and Nip used to sleep in here on the floor, bro." They covered the bedroom walls with motivational phrases. Some were slogans like *All Money In, Stay Focused, Quitting is not an Option!!, Don't Talk About It—Be About It*, and *How Hard Are You Really Going?* Others came from the pages of books, complete with citations. "So much depends on reputation. Guard it with your life!!" from Robert Greene's *The 48 Laws of Power*; "Don't wait! The time will never be just right" by Napoleon Hill. There was even a paraphrased passage from *Walden* by Henry David Thoreau: "Go in the direction of your dreams! Live the life you've imagined." Hussle described the quotations as "different things that you wake up to when you on this Marathon."

A month after their meeting, Angelo called Nipsey back. "Dre's gonna fall back," he said. "He's not gonna make a move on that." Hussle told him it was all love. "I just didn't know if it was the music, if it was his history with my neighborhood," he said after the call. After all, Dre had been through a lot of drama between Suge and Death Row. "I ain't know what the reason was, but I respected Angelo for being a bridge, for getting him to listen."

Dre wasn't the only one listening. Jonny Shipes, the founder of Cinematic Music Group, had recently landed himself a situation at Epic Records. Shipes had discovered Sean Kingston, a Jamaican teenager living in Miami whose song "Beautiful Girls" blew up to become a massive pop smash. But what Shipes really wanted to put out was some dope rap music. Though it was just getting started at the time, Cinematic would eventually become one of New York's premier independent hip-hop labels.

"Charlie Walk at Epic had given me a label deal and he was like, 'Go find some stuff,'" Shipes recalls. "At the time West Coast hip-hop was not cracking. I called DJ Felli Fel in L.A. and I was like, 'Bro, what the fuck is going on? Where is the hot shit?'"

"Felli was like, 'Well, there's this kid Nipsey Hussle, but he's deep in the streets. I don't know that you're going to want to fuck with that. He's a real one.'"

Shipes googled Nipsey Hussle and a Myspace page popped up. "There was one or two songs on there," he recalls. "'Bullets Ain't Got No Names,' and maybe he had 'I Don't Give a Fucc' too."

Shipes listened and he got chills. "I felt like I was on Sixtieth and Crenshaw with him," he says. He fell in love with the rawness of the tracks, the hard deliveries and singsong hooks. Hussle was painting pictures with every word he spoke. "It was the rawest shit I had heard in years." He hit Felli back, and twenty-four hours later he and his partner Harlem MC Smoke DZA were on a plane to L.A. to meet with Hussle and his team.

"He had a very clear vision from the beginning, which was very similar to me," Shipes recalls. "For all intents and purposes, me and Nip kind of started together. Nip was like, 'All right, this random kid from New York is going to take a chance on me.' And Nipsey took a chance on me too, because back then I wasn't where I'm at today." At the time West Coast rap was not popping like it is now—The Game had blown up as part of G-Unit and then fallen out with 50 Cent. TDE and Kendrick Lamar had yet to emerge as a major force. "It's crazy that no one would put Nipsey on in his own state," Shipes says. "It took a white kid from 3,000 miles away that had nothing to do with Cali culture. And then from there everybody jumped on the bandwagon. People thought I was crazy. I would get calls from executives like, 'Are you fucking nuts fuckin' with them?' And I was just so young and coming out of the streets myself, it didn't even faze me."

Shipes remembers the first time he told Epic president Charlie Walk about his new discovery. "Charlie," he said, "I got this artist named Nipsey Hussle."

"Wait, like Nipsey Russell?" Charlie replied.

Shipes said, "Yeah."

"I love it," Charlie said. "I don't even need to hear the music, just sign him."

Before the Epic deal was finalized, Hussle and his management decided to put together a mixtape. They called it *Bullets Ain't Got No Name Vol. 1*. Steve Lobel had a good relationship with DJ Felli Fel at Power 106, who was also a producer and recording artist. He agreed to host the tape. "Nipsey had a certain it factor," said Felli. "He had a ton of music, but a lot of it wasn't radio material, to be honest with you. For me it was just seeing that there was something special about Nip. I just gravitated towards his stuff."

Hussle still wasn't 100 percent sold on the Epic deal. He kept pushing his management to negotiate better terms because his goal was always to stay indie. But then a situation came up that forced his hand. He and some homies got caught in another police raid, and this one was messy. They'd been caught on a surveillance camera with guns while partying with a girl in a thong who turned out to be underage. "They charged a nigga with some bogus charges, homie," Hussle explained in an early Kev Mac video. "A nigga never did nothin' with the girl!"[65] he said.

One of Hussle's friends was arrested, and he figured he would be picked up soon. He spoke to Big U, who helped him hide out. They decided to take Epic's latest offer and just get the bag. Years later, on an internet loosie called "Respect Ya Passion," Hussle would rap, "My first record deal probably saved my life, so shout-out to my nigga Draws and Jonny Shipes."

"When I did my Epic deal, you know, I was on the run," Hussle said later. "I had a case pending. My crimie was in jail. I thought I was about to go do a lot of time." Just to secure the deal, he sat in the house for three months waiting for the paperwork to be finalized. "I figured if I went to jail and it was a real case, that's gonna be the end of my opportunity." In January 2008, when Shipes told them the paperwork was ready, Hussle and Robin Hood flew to New York to sign the contract.

After the deal was done, they caught a flight to Jamaica. Sean Kingston was shooting a special there for MTV's *My Super Sweet 16* and it seemed like the perfect place to celebrate—especially since Hussle might be facing jail time when he returned to L.A.

Jamaica was nice—the ganja, the jet skis—but as soon as Nipsey came home, cops heard he was back in town. They were waiting at Slauson and Crenshaw the next day to take him to jail. One of the world's largest correctional facilities, The Men's Central Jail ranks among America's worst prisons, with a long history of documented abuses. Hussle had money to bail out because he'd just signed a major label deal, but he couldn't access it because he was on probation and the authorities had put a hold on his funds. To make matters worse, when he reported to jail a fight broke out in the holding tank. The situation got serious and Hussle found himself outnumbered by a bunch of Bloods. "You already know the county jail," he said later. "Six-Owe ain't got no homies in there. My mentality was I was expecting that anyway. We had a couple little melees, but I ain't get packed out, I ain't get blasted, so I did all right."[66] Hussle lived to tell the tale thanks to a Blood from Inglewood who showed compassion for the young Crip.

After processing, Hussle was sent to the secure housing unit (SHU), also known as solitary confinement. The psychological pressure of being locked up with no human contact is usually reserved as punishment for inmates who violate the rules. In Hussle's case, he was sent to the SHU for a medical reason. A spider had bitten him in Jamaica and the bite grew into an abscess on his leg. County jail inmates with any medical issues are put on twenty-three-hour lockdown. Hussle had to eat in his cell, shower in his cell, and only come out for one hour a day. "That was a little struggle for me," he said.[67]

Sitting in that solitary cubicle, Hussle had time to reflect on some of the choices he'd made. "I was feeling like I fucked off everything I had worked all my life to obtain," he said. "I was sitting in my one-man cell punchin' bricks, just out of frustration."[68]

One day during his two months behind bars, Hussle received a visit from the gang investigation unit. He imagined they would question him about incidents in the hood, trying to implicate him or pressure him to give up information about his homies. When he was escorted into the gang unit's office, he was surprised to see his Myspace page pulled up on the jail computer. "They had my YouTube playin'," he recalled with a smile. "They was singin' the songs too—by heart." You know you're hot in the streets when the gang unit loves your music. Hussle didn't know whether to laugh in their faces or sign autographs.[69]

During his time on the run, he had received word that Tanisha was pregnant with a baby girl. He chose a name while he was behind bars, deciding to call her Emani Dior. "Her name means 'beautiful faith' in Swahili," he explained. "I chose Emani for a few reasons." He had just signed a record deal. He was in jail and didn't know when he was going to get out. He had a child on the way and was not on the best of terms with the baby's mother at the time. "It was a lot on my mind," he said. "And I think that faith represented where I was at. And it was beautiful 'cause I ended up gettin' out of that situation and movin' forward. Other than that I just liked how it sounds. My name start with an *E* also."[70]

I. Mark Bledstein, the lawyer Big U connected him with, beat Hussle's charges on the second court date. (Nipsey would stick with Bledstein for the rest of his career, and featured him in the opening scene of his 2018 music video for "Hussle & Motivate.")[71] "That feeling that I had for them days is something I never wanna go through," Hussle said after the fact. "I would hate for anyone else to experience that ever in life. The feeling of regret, the feeling of frustration and the consequences of your decisions. And sometimes, homie, you ain't gonna get out. You ain't always gonna *get* away when you do your dirt. You might have got away in the past, but it only takes one time until they will book you down and hold you, my nigga. And then it'll be a wrap."[72]

The realization that he was about to become a father was both exciting and worrying. "My life did a complete perspective change because now . . . you are accountable," he said. "You are accountable for the well-being of something outside of yourself. This is a person. Things can happen that you cannot fix. That you can't take back. You have to seriously protect your kid from certain things. So my whole priorities, perspective, agenda flip-flopped a little bit. I won't say that my who I am and what I do took a 180-degree turn, but my priorities and my perspective definitely did. The decisions that I make, the process now, there's another element, there's another factor in my decision-making process. And that's my daughter's well-being. So it was definitely a paradigm shift in the way I think."[73]

Fresh out of the county jail, Hussle heard his voice on the radio for the first time. "I had a team around me that had a good relationship with Felli Fel at Power 106," he recalled. "He played 'Bullets Ain't Got No Names' probably about two weeks after I got out of jail. You sound different on the radio, and you know that a million people plus are hearin' it. I was just like, *man* . . ."[74]

Hussle flew back to New York for label meetings and to work on new music. Shipes booked him into a recording studio at the Manhattan Film Center, located at Sixty-Third Street and Park Avenue on Manhattan's upscale Upper East Side. Working in the next room over was Harlem rapper Shiest Bubz from Purple City Productions, who kept Hussle laced with good smoke when he was in town. Hussle was having a hard time concentrating because every time the studio door opened he could hear the beat Bubz was working on out the side of his ear. It was a supercharged flip of one of Hussle's childhood favorites, "Jump" by Kris Kross. "This shit crazy! I hope this nigga don't finish this song," Hussle thought. "I hope he sleep on this beat." He waited around two or three hours until Bubz was ready to go home, then approached him. "Bro, what you doin' with that beat?" he asked.[75]

"I ain't doin' shit with that," said Bubz. "This sound like some L.A. shit. I was gonna rock to it, but this sound like it's up your alley."[76]

Nipsey did his best to play it cool, but inside he was celebrating. The beat was coproduced by Don Cannon and a Detroit-born producer who went by Detroit Red, adapting Malcolm X's old street hustler name. "We slid that beat to 50," Don Cannon told Hussle later. "He picked another one." Hussle smiled and said, "50 slept, man! Nah, that was dope, man. Thank you."[77]

"Hussle in the House" dropped in 2008 as the lead single to Hussle's hardest mixtape yet, *Bullets Ain't Got No Name Vol. 2*. His first breakout street record flipped Kris Kross's lighthearted pop hit into a gangbanger anthem. Radio was loving it until stations started getting phone calls complaining about the song promoting Hussle's affiliation.[78] It was one thing for N.W.A to release a record saying "Crazy motherfucker named Ice Cube, from the gang called Niggaz Wit Attitude," as they did on their 1988 classic "Straight Outta Compton." As much as the city respected Cube as an artist, the streets knew he wasn't really a gang member. At the end of the day N.W.A was really just a rap group, despite Eazy-E's bonafide credentials. It was a whole different matter for Nipsey Hussle to come out in 2008 rapping "Crazy motherfucker named Nipsey / I'm turned up 'cause I grew up in the 60s."

"That was never done before," says Ralo. "An active gang member from the city of Los Angeles on the main stage of hip hop? No. That never happened."[79]

Although he rapped with a gruffness reminiscent of The Game, Nipsey was more often compared to Snoop Dogg. They shared a striking physical similarity and cool demeanor, and eventually became good friends. They also shared a Crip affiliation, but Snoop reps Long Beach whereas Game reps Compton. While rap legends Ice-T and WC do claim strong ties to South Central Los Angeles, both were born out of state and neither declared their gang allegiance as boldly as Hussle.

"Nobody said no hoods before Nipsey," Big U stated in a Kev Mac interview. "That was the problem they was givin' me in the industry with Nipsey . . . he's saying 'The 60s.' He's not sayin' a city. He's sayin' a gang. And get this—if Nip wouldn't have been signed to me, he wouldn't been able to say Six-Owe this, Six-Owe that."[80]

Hussle had a friend at KDAY, one of L.A.'s biggest radio stations, who tipped him off about calls the station was receiving from mothers. "Do you know what this record is saying?" they would ask. "He's from the 60s. Playing this record is promoting the stuff going on in L.A."[81]

"In my eyes, it's like, 'Nah, I'm not promoting it. I'm just speaking on it,'" Hussle said. "The radio people had to heed to that pressure and cut it off a little bit."[82] Hate it or love it, "Hussle in the House" was as unapologetic as Hussle himself. He wasn't trying to hide a damn thing. As its chorus clearly stated, the song was "Just a small introduction to this Nipsey Hussle music."

Chapter 6

ALL MONEY IN

**BLUE RAG, S-HAT, GOLD ON MY NECK FAT
GUNS CASE, CATCH THAT, THIS NEIGHBORHOOD, I REP THAT**
—Nipsey Hussle, "Hussle in the House," *Bullets Ain't Got No Name Vol. 2* (2008)

O ut by the Shell station on Crenshaw and Slauson, Nipsey Hussle sipped a Red Bull and puffed on a blunt as festive red and yellow plastic streamers fluttered overhead. He was pondering a question posed by a correspondent from *Wink$* DVD magazine, aka "the hottest shit in the streets." At that moment, in November 2008, Hussle's mixtape, *Bullets Ain't Got No Name Vol. 2*, actually *was* the hottest shit in the streets of his city. He could have been doing anything he wanted right then, and what he chose to do was to answer the question "What attracted you to the game?"[1]

The answer seemed so obvious that another artist might dismiss it, or respond with some half-hearted cliché. But not Hussle. He clearly put a high priority on interviews, considering how many of them he crammed into his schedule.

"*Shit*," he began. "I mean, the same thing that attracted every other nigga to it. First and foremost I love the music, though.

161

I been doin' music before I planned on gettin' rich from it. But other than that, obviously the financial benefits and the monetary gain. You feel me? And bein' able to, like, really, really ball and shine like I wanna shine—without havin' to worry about the Feds kickin' a nigga door in, motherfucker waitin' in the bushes to knock your head off."

"He always said that he was gonna have a *lot* of money," Gooch recalls. "Like, you know, millions. Like, 'Man, I'ma go to Saks Fifth. I'ma be shoppin' there all the time. I'ma have Bentleys—all of that.' I'm like, 'Damn, this nigga right here!' He said it like he knew it. Not like wishful thinkin'. Not like, 'I'ma *take* it. I'ma do it by any means.' No. He was like, 'I *know* I can get it.'"[2]

It was clear to anyone paying attention that Hussle's affiliation with the Crenshaw District was 100 percent authentic. And by 2008 that neighborhood was changing rapidly. Plans had just been announced for a high-speed light rail running from LAX to Crenshaw, bringing an influx of new visitors and new money into one of L.A.'s oldest Black communities. Gentrification was on the way. Could a skinny 60s Crip be the champion Crenshaw was longing for?[3]

Controversial or not, *Bullets Ain't Got No Name Vol. 2* was swiftly solidified as a hood classic. "When that mixtape came out I was still living in Leimert in South Central," recalled L.A. rapper and entrepreneur Dom Kennedy, who was then building his own independent movement. "It was Christmastime and that's all cars played. Every morning I was by the window and people was driving by playing it. That one had the love of the streets."[4]

There is much more to Nipsey Hussle's artistry on the *Bullets Ain't Got No Name* mixtapes than recycling "gangsta rap" clichés. A close listen to tracks like "Payback" and "Questions Freestyle" reveals his political awareness and capacity for critical thought. Still, there's no point trying to sugarcoat the nihilism of the title track that opens *Vol. 1.* And the song's video, full of guns and body bags, is hard to watch now.

As Nipsey's profile in the rap game elevated, he began to be acknowledged by his peers. Snoop was impressed by Hussle's confident demeanor before he even heard his music.

At the Staples Center memorial, he reminisced over their first encounter. "Most rappers when they push up on Snoop Dogg with a tape, this is their line: 'Hey Dogg, listen to my music, I can make you a million dollars.' Nipsey's line was: 'Hey homie, listen to my music. Just give it a listen.'"

"That's it?" Snoop queried. "No record deal? You don't wanna get put on?" By skipping the sales pitch, Hussle declared that he wasn't looking for a handout but simply confirmation that his music was dope. Right from the start he distinguished himself as a man of respect.

"Just listen to it homie."

When Snoop finally listened, he said, "Cuz *hard.*"[5]

Nip's introduction to The Game took place in the realest way possible. Game was driving his white Range Rover along Crenshaw with a Glock in his lap. Nipsey was out on the block with his homies when they spotted him. "That's Game over there!" he said.

After Dre, Snoop, and Pac, Game was the next big name out of L.A. "Everybody looked to Game—'Hey, listen to my tape, woo woo woo,'" Hussle said. So naturally he decided to approach the car.[6]

"I would drive through L.A. purposely not getting on the freeway 'cause I wanted as many views," Game later told Big Boy. "This was before Instagram. I was getting likes in the street."[7] He was on the way to get his Range washed at the same spot where he used to sell his CDs. Along the way he was hoping to impress some ladies on the Shaw.

One thing that Game, a Blood from Compton, was *not* trying to do was get approached by a bunch of Crips at a red light on Crenshaw. So he was less than overjoyed to see Hussle and friends walking toward his vehicle. "It was him and a few of Nip's homies, who I now know to be J Stone, Rimpau," Game recalled. "It was like ten of 'em and they all walkin' up."[8]

Game cursed his luck. "Nah man, come on, man," he said to himself. "I'm just tryin' to rap, live my life." As Hussle got close to the car he reached to pull out a CD.

"What's up, Game?" he said. "I'm Nip! We the Slauson Boyz."[9]

Everything was chill after that. Game asked if his demo had a phone number on it. Hussle said it did. Game called Snoop Dogg to check Hussle's credentials and Snoop gave him the big cosign. Before long Hussle and Game were in the studio laying down tracks together. "Game was always open arms," said Hussle. He respected Game's musical accomplishments, and also the fact that he rolled through the hood solo with no security, burner on his lap. "He saw I had a Glock," Game said years later. "I could see in his eyes that he said to himself, 'Game a real nigga. He out here.'"[10]

That was how Hussle preferred to move—by making real, spontaneous connections. He had no patience for that fake "my people will call your people" Hollywood nonsense. Although he'd seen a lot of setbacks in his life, moments like these gave him hope that doing things his way, the Hussle way, might just work out.

On the day of the "Hussle in the House" video shoot, photographer Jorge Peniche was hoping his plans to photograph Nipsey would work out. A tech-savvy sneaker head with an eye for design and a hustler's spirit, Peniche established a niche for himself doing creative work without ever taking a full-time job. Hustling was a necessity because Jorge's parents had brought him to America at a young age without official documentation.[11] Having bought his first camera to photograph the sneakers he sold on eBay, Peniche broke in as a photographer working with multimedia entrepreneur DJ Skee, and went on to shoot with major artists like The Game. While mastering the craft, Peniche stayed on the lookout for new opportunities.[12] A friend of his, the Mexican American rap artist Mr. Don't Know, introduced him to Hussle's mixtapes and he was "completely blown away" by what he heard. "He's got all the intangibles," Peniche reasoned. "He's got a crazy perspective. Super articulate. Super intelligent. Authentic. Comes from a place that people are interested in."

Peniche contacted Hussle via Myspace in January 2009 and received a quick response. "Let's definitely connect," Hussle wrote—perhaps impressed by Peniche's eighty thousand Myspace followers—and invited him to the shoot for his new music video.[13]

"Absolutely, consider it done," Peniche replied. Unfortunately he had a college midterm that same day, and the professor was not willing to reschedule. After racing through the exam, Peniche and a friend headed down to Crenshaw and Slauson. "It was quite the sight to see," he recalled. "Every car driving by was playing Nipsey full blast—*Vol. 2* or *Vol. 1*. The whole city was out there to champion him. The guy was an undeniable star, a legend. The great things that we've heard of Nipsey, he possessed those qualities before people might have acknowledged them."[14]

The first time Peniche saw him, Hussle hopped out of a white Bentley wearing Monarchy jeans, Prada shoes, a navy-blue All Money In Brink's truck T-shirt, long braids, and his signature Malcolm X chain. Peniche introduced himself and found Hussle just as affable amid all the excitement of the video set as he had been on Myspace. "He's been respectful since the day I met him till the last time I saw him," Peniche recalled. "Always super humble for the giant that he was. Just really an overall good guy.

The things you're hearing from people now is not out of sympathy or a by-product of tragedy. It's genuine love."[15]

Shooting on location—with available light, in between takes—presented a challenge, but Peniche was determined to make it work. "We took different photos at Master Burger," he recalled, "at Slauson Donuts, on Sixty-Third and Brynhurst, and literally in the middle of Crenshaw and Slauson as he was filming the video." The pictures were beautiful, especially the portraits of Hussle and his crew rocking the royal-blue crewnecks that were made specially for the shoot with *Crenshaw* written in gold cursive, like the Coca-Cola logo. Having gotten their grind on, it was time to get their shine on. The All Money In team was definitely shining that day.

BULLETS HAVE THE DOGS HOWLIN' AT THE MOON AT NIGHT
MAMA, IT'S COLD OUTSIDE, AIN'T NO HOPE OUTSIDE

—Nipsey Hussle, "I Don't Give A Fucc," *The Marathon* (2010)

Hope is a hell of a thing. As Barack Obama said in a speech back in 2004, remaining hopeful was nothing if not audacious. "Hope in the face of difficulty," the Illinois state senator said in front of the Democratic National Convention. "Hope in the face of uncertainty. The audacity of hope!" Ermias Asghedom could relate when Obama spoke about "The hope of a skinny kid with a funny name who believes that America has a place for him, too." And when a man with a father born in Kenya ran for president of the United States, Hussle mustered just enough hope to register and vote for the first time in his life.

"I never thought I'd see that day," Hussle said after Obama was sworn in as America's forty-fourth president. He thought about his granny, and what it must mean for her to see a Black man elected leader of the free world. "I couldn't even trick myself into thinkin' it was gonna fly," Hussle said. "Even after he was gettin' close to winnin' and I seen all the publicity around the campaign." But now that it was real, this thing called hope might start to spread.[16]

Hussle was filled with another kind of hope in February 2009 when Vlad TV asked him to name the "Top 5 Chicks You Want to Smash and Why." Encouraged by the reporter to "speak it into existence," he rattled off a fairly predictable list of names— Beyoncé, Halle Berry, Ashanti, Kim Kardashian. There was only one woman he spoke about at any length—Lauren London— in fact, he went on and on about her. "Little Lauren got it!" he said, apparently unconcerned by the fact that she was in a relationship with Lil Wayne at the time. Hussle seemed particularly impressed with her performance as New New in the movie *ATL*. "She was lookin' kinda fly in that little pool scene," Hussle said. "Lip gloss poppin' and all that." Despite declaring "I'm not into chasin' no female," he wrapped up the segment by saying, "Lauren London, come holla at me!"[17]

At that point in his career trajectory, Hussle didn't have much time for romance. Snoop had publicly cosigned the young rapper and offered him a feature spot on one of his albums. The Game called Nipsey "the next biggest thing in L.A., I swear before God." And then the Compton rapper backed up his statement by inviting Nipsey to become an opening act on his nationwide *LAX* tour.

"We did fifty-two cities in like fifty-five days and we all was opening for free," Hussle recalled years later. He took Cobby and J Stone with him on the cross-country adventure. Along the way they got to know the Top Dawg Entertainment family, including Jay Rock, TDE's lead artist at the time, and Kendrick Lamar— then known as K.Dot—who was his hype man. "We all was in it to get to this level and continue to grow in the game," Hussle said. "But obviously to see what K.Dot doin' [now], to see what Jay Rock doin', what we doin', we all paid a lot of dues and put in blood, sweat, and tears."[18]

Steve Lobel rode along with Nipsey and his Rollin' 60s homies from coast to coast in a camper van. "He gave me the name 'Maniac' because of the Game tour," Lobel recalls. "After forty dates, Nip was like, 'Man, I'm done!' I'm like, 'Nah, nah, nah, nah. We going to continue this whole tour.' He's like, 'You're a maniac!'"[19]

"It was eighteen of us to start—all of my homies," Hussle recalled. "We had more people than we needed. We had one bed in the back. I had a bed every night. The homies were figuring it out." When they went through Minnesota the heater broke in the RV. "They was sleepin' on the floor and it was freezing," Hussle said. "It was so cold the windows were sweatin'."[20]

During the Rhode Island tour stop, Nipsey and Cobby spoke with a local video program about their experiences on the road and what the tour meant to them. "Shout out to Game, all of Black Wall Street," Nipsey said. "They Damu, we Crips, we fuck with the whole Black Wall Street gang."[21]

Game had taken a lot of pressure on his shoulders bringing Nipsey along on tour. "A lot of people don't know I fought my own homies," he said years after the tour wrapped up. "I damn near died taking Nipsey and the whole 60s on tour. And when the 60s came on tour, sixty 60s came on tour! Niggas had they own bus, they own shit, put up they own money."[22]

At the time, it was rare to see members of rival gangs moving across the country in unison. Game, both of whose parents were Crips, was used to crossing color lines. He had toured with Snoop and opened his 2004 song "Westside Story," a collab with 50 Cent, with the words "Crip niggas, Blood niggas, éses, Asians." Counteracting the forces of division, Game strategically calibrated his music to appeal to listeners from every hood. The *LAX* tour took that intention to another level.

Hussle and Cobby were very much on the same page. "New World West coming right now," Cobby declared during the Rhode Island video interview. "Every nigga from the West Side—Crips, Bloods, wherever you from, niggas is getting together. We from the 60s, and if niggas fuck with us, shit, we all might as well be together. It's one big movement—Slauson Boyz. Holla at us!"

"Cobby said it all," Hussle affirmed. "One West *Movement*, my nigga—we united, my nigga. Niggas is doin' some shit that the feds, the state police, the local police, and everybody else couldn't do. And we doin' it on our own. We uniting our Black folk from L.A. We been divided from the 60s, homie. Rap music was what it took for niggas to come together and put their petty difference to the side . . . One West is taking over!"

"We don't need police," Cobby said. "We police ourselves. Real niggas do real things. It's all one love, my nigga. They wanna keep the beef crackin', we're trying to stop it. And it's the music that's doing it."[23]

By rising above long-standing neighborhood conflicts, Hussle and Game were doing more than making music together; they were empowering each other as well as their respective communities. Besides hitting the road together, Hussle and Jay Rock collaborated on a few tracks and did some memorable radio freestyle sessions along with Kendrick Lamar, who would later appear on Nipsey's debut album, *Victory Lap*. Listening back to their sessions with DJ Kay Slay and DJ Green Lantern, it's thrilling to hear three future giants in action together.

While Hussle was on the road with The Game, the video for "Hussle in the House" premiered on BET's daily video showcase *106 & Park*. Cohosts Rocsi & Terrence J. rolled the clip out with all the bells and whistles, encouraging the show's young viewers to vote if they loved it. It was just the sort of video that got BET in hot water with critics for promoting the "gangsta" lifestyle to school kids, but the Epic Records marketing department was thrilled to launch the artist on such a major platform.[24]

Watching from the state penitentiary, Blacc Sam was proud to see his younger brother on national television. In the video, Nipsey maneuvered around his section in a Mercedes S-Class, the Malcolm X chain Sam gave him hanging down to his belt as two long braids swung behind his ears. But what made the biggest impression were the Crenshaw crewnecks.

"That shit hit me strong," Sam said. "I looked at the video and was like, 'Oh, this is serious.'" Sam wasn't the only one struck by the Crenshaw shirts; so were his fellow inmates. "Everybody in there also, all races—everybody was like, 'That's huge,'" he remembers. "That *was* huge. That was one of the defining moments I could say in Nip's career."[25]

The iconic blue-and-gold colorway was inspired by an old Crenshaw High School uniform worn by Darryl Strawberry. "All the homies—Nip included—had the crewneck on in the video and it just hit," said Sam. "It was authentic. The video was a strong representation of what's going on. And everybody right there was just attracted to that. They wanted that Crenshaw sweater." Once Sam made it home and got back on his feet, he never forgot the impact that design had on him in prison. It was Sam who led the charge to develop that Crenshaw shirt into a powerful design, which would become a cornerstone of The Marathon Clothing business.

"A lot of people were attracted to that Crenshaw," he said. "It became kinda like to me our Brooklyn shirt, or our New York shirt. Everybody wanted a Crenshaw shirt."[26]

Back in Los Angeles in the summer of '09, Hussle hit the ground running. His movement was building momentum, generating a magnetic energy that attracted new supporters every day. "L.A. was turning back over," says Dom Kennedy, who would frequently collaborate with Hussle. "It was a pivotal time and he was one of the first people to really kick it off."

As the LAX tour was wrapping up, Nipsey got a Twitter shout-out from Drake, who was fresh off the success of *So Far Gone*, one of the biggest mixtapes in rap history. "Nipsey Hu$$le is the hardest out!" tweeted Drizzy, and the two were soon making plans to collab. Their song "Killer" was recorded for Drake's debut album, *Thank Me Later*, but instead they opted to let it leak online during the height of the blog rap era. The song got play on L.A. radio, and when Drake's tour came to town he invited Hussle out to perform "Killer" at the Nokia Theater. Hussle prowled the stage in red Crenshaw gear with his iced-out Malcolm X chain swinging, while Drake told the crowd, "Tell your favorite rapper . . . my nigga Nipsey is a killer!"

YOU GANGBANGIN' EVEN THOUGH IT GOT YOUR FAMILY SICK
NOW WHAT YOUR LIFE ABOUT? DOES MONEY MOTIVATE YOUR ACTIONS?
—Nipsey Hussle, "Questions Freestyle," *Bullets Ain't Got No Name Vol. 1* (2008)

Dressed in a black Alife cap and matching sweatshirt, Nipsey Hussle rolled up a Swisher Sweet as he watched the KCAL channel 9 evening news on TV. The hosts were talking about a show at which he was supposed to perform the night before. "L.A. police crashed a huge party for one of the city's most notorious gangs this morning," said the blond anchorwoman. "KCAL's Mark Coogan is in South L.A., home turf for the gang. Mark?"[27]

The news cut away to a middle-aged white reporter standing on the street with a microphone. "Everyone celebrates birthdays, but when street gangs celebrate theirs—and they do— oftentimes the LAPD is not far behind," said Coogan. "That's what happened early this morning when one big South Los Angeles street gang tried to dodge the cops by moving its party way uptown." The news showed Nipsey's name—misspelled "Hustle"—on the marquee of Platinum Live nightclub in Studio City, "a long way from the hood," as the reporter noted. "Rollin' 60s turf is over the hills and ten miles south of Studio City, in the Hyde Park area of South Los Angeles," Coogan said. "For the last several years, L.A. police have tracked and raided so-called 'hood parties,' making numerous arrests and confiscating guns. That crackdown prompted the Rollin' 60s to move their party out of the hood."[28]

Before Hussle arrived at the event celebrating the Rollin' 60s' unofficial birthday on June 10 (6 x 10), gang officers from the LAPD's Seventy-Seventh Division raided the Ventura Boulevard venue, arresting seventeen people, with more arrests pending for probation violations. "Police say that hood parties—gang birthday parties—often end in drunken violence," the reporter stated, parroting the LAPD's talking points. "They say many of the attendees are under parole or probation restrictions not to associate with each other, and that makes them subject to arrest."[29]

Sparking the blunt, Hussle exhaled as he processed what he'd just seen. "God willing I wasn't there," he said. He was still on probation himself, and had Hussle been in the house as planned, he could've been on his way to jail right now. "At the end of the day it was a paid gathering," Nip pointed out. "So if they gonna say every one of the shows I'm supposed to perform at is a 'hood function,' that's gonna hurt not only my career but the fans."

The larger implication for Hussle's future was that the police war on gangs was becoming a war on him too. "I don't wanna make it seem like I'm just some super-active nigga out here in the streets," he said. "I do music full-time. But at the end of the day, police got where I come from on they list, and under their target. So it is what it is."[30]

As Hussle noted, the news described the event as a gang gathering—"like there was some big to-do or some type of violence goin' on"—but no weapons were seized and everyone Hussle had spoken to said the event was peaceful until a small army of cops showed up. "Granted, people was probably smokin' weed," he said. "But you don't need helicopters and SWAT teams for that. To my knowledge, they didn't make arrests for no guns, no dope, no major violence or none of that. So a lot of the city's resources was devoted to somebody's personal agenda."[31]

Judging by the LAPD's actions, that agenda was simple: to lock gang members behind bars. While Hussle understood the need to prevent bloodshed, he felt the "lock them all up" approach was a bit extreme. "I think they should be a little more precise on they judgment of how they go about fightin' that problem," he said. Based on personal experience, Hussle knew that many gang members were born into a way of life that they didn't create. "I'm a full-time artist," he said. "I do music. But at a point in time I knew that lifestyle. I was around that. So I wouldn't condone it and I wouldn't perpetuate it or promote that, 'cause at the end of the day that's wrong." All the same, there was no getting around the fact that gang culture was a reality in Los Angeles, one that had existed for many decades. "The young kids that's gangbangin' is a product—not the source or the cause," he said. "They're the effect of what was goin' on for years."[32]

Given the chance, Hussle wanted to jump-start a transition out of self-destructive conflicts and into a spirit of cooperation among rival hoods. "I tell my homies we on that same page. We ain't gonna be no aggressors. We ain't gonna be the ones to start a problem." This mindset trickled down to the streets through artists' crews and fans. "Young dudes that's lookin' up to they homeboy that doin' music see that," he said. "We might get some money together. We might can just have a mutual respect for each other from a distance."[33] Respect, even grudging respect, was a lot better than revenge, but improving the situation in the streets wouldn't be possible without securing his own situation first.

There are times in life when the energy is just right and the universe seems to bring good fortune to you. Some call it dumb luck, but Hussle knew that luck is when opportunity meets preparation.

Case in point: When Ving Rhames, the famous actor from Hollywood blockbusters like *Pulp Fiction* and *Mission: Impossible*, grabbed an iPod loaded with his stepdaughter's music on his way to the airport. All he wanted was something to listen to during a long flight to South Africa. He had no idea what music was on there. He'd never heard Nipsey Hussle before. While flying to the continent he ended up listening to *Bullets Ain't Got No Name Vol. 1* and *Vol. 2*. The music spoke to him, sparking his imagination.[34] "It was nothin' but God," Hussle says. "And I don't call myself a particular religious sect or none of that. I just believe in God."

"I was connecting to your story," Ving told him.

"I ain't had no Top Ten singles on my mixtape," said Hussle. "My shit was for niggas like us, just talkin' about the shit we go through as street niggas—Blood, Crip, neighborhood, gangsta. Whatever you is, my nigga—we go through the same shit where we come from."[35]

Ving Rhames grew up in Harlem. His knowledge of L.A. street gangs came through popular culture. Inspired by Hussle's rhymes, Rhames wrote a script. He reached out to Big U and Steve Lobel and asked Hussle to costar with him in the film. Although Hussle had no previous acting experience, he accepted the challenge. He would be playing a character very similar to himself.

They shot for ten days in July 2009 and the film—originally titled *Wrath of Cain* and later renamed *Caged Animal*—came out the following year. Ving played an OG locked up in a penitentiary whose two sons—played by Hussle and Gillie Da Kid—are rival gang members who don't know they are brothers.[36]

"Aside from the movie, I connected with Ving 'cause he's a sincere, A-one nigga," said Hussle. "The whole concept of the movie is just based on what he heard on my project." The experience of acting in a film opened Hussle up to new possibilities. The story of the film itself highlighted some hard truths about the generational cycles of gang violence. With all these ideas bouncing around his brain, Hussle got to talking with Gillie one day during a break in shooting. A video blogger from the website Rap Status happened to catch the convo, and as usual Hussle was dropping jewels.[37]

"If you a young nigga comin' up and this what you plan on doin' full-time, just go turn yourself in," Hussle said. "Save yourself the headaches and heartache, my nigga." Hussle then proceeded to break down the reasons why the realities of gang life were a losing proposition in the era of cell phones, surveillance technology, and L.A.'s strict new anti-gang laws. Distracted by the subtle nuances and intricacies of gang life—Crips always wore their rags on the left side, they celebrated C-Days not B-Days, and never spelled words using the letters "CK" which stood for "Crip Killer"—it was easy to overlook the big picture. Something as simple as gang tattoos, for example, could effectively lead to a life sentence.

"Everybody's so quick to go get their hood blasted on 'em,'" Hussle said. "But niggas gotta understand, like I tell my young niggas, you gon' get more time for your tattoos than you gon' get for your crime." A friend of Hussle's had just been sentenced to 117 years for a fight. "He didn't kill anybody," he said. "They alleged that he had a fight with a nigga, and caused what they called 'great bodily harm'—which can be a bruise, a broken jaw, a busted lip." Because he was a confirmed gang member, so-called "gang enhancements" allowed gang members to be prosecuted as domestic terrorists. "They got new laws, especially in Los Angeles for the gang problem, that make it impossible, homie." Hussle's own transition was already underway. Now he wanted to show others the way out.[38]

Hussle would soon drop the third installment of the *Bullets Ain't Got No Name* trilogy, setting the stage for the release of his planned debut album *South Central State of Mind*. Featuring collabs with Lloyd, Snoop, and The Game as well as production by the Runners, Scott Storch, and J. R. Rotem, the album was slated to drop by the end of 2009. Hussle had been speaking about the project for more than a year, building anticipation in countless promotional interviews.

But after an executive shakeup at Epic Records, the team responsible for bringing Hussle into the building was on their way out. Charlie Walk was replaced by career songwriter Amanda Ghost, who would end up getting fired after just twenty months on the job. "The new CEO was like, 'Oh, let's put Nipsey in with this big EDM producer,'" Shipes recalls. "And we were like, 'What the fuck is going on? This kid's got the biggest buzz in the streets. Just put the fucking album out! Let's go!' They didn't understand."[39]

Hussle had started his professional rap career at a time when the entire music industry was in a tailspin, struggling to adjust to the digital revolution. "I feel like we had to fix the engine while the plane was in the air," he said. "The game changed right when we got in, so our whole strategy was null and void. It wasn't about droppin' a big single and puttin' an album out no more."[40] During this time of uncertainty Hussle bumped into Big Bob Francis, an old friend of Dexter's, who gave him a simple piece of advice. "Don't think of yourself as a rapper," Big Bob said. "Think of yourself as a brand."[41]

His logic was simple: There were no rules to being a rapper. But branding was a science that had been perfected by giants like Nike and Apple. He recommended Hussle read a book called *The 22 Immutable Laws of Branding*, which broke it all down. The second page of the book changed his way of thinking about business: "Selling, as a profession and as a function, is slowly sinking like the *Titanic*," wrote the coauthors, a father-and-daughter team named Al and Laura Ries. "Today most products and services are bought, not sold." In that respect it wasn't so different from moving crack rocks: you had to make the customer want to come to you. "Branding 'presells' the product or service to the user."[42]

Hussle grasped the concepts in the book straightaway, and as with all his personal breakthroughs, he shared what he'd learned freely with anybody who would listen. "That's what America's about—brands," he started saying in interviews. "That's why you charge a hundred and fifty dollars for some Nikes, and the shoes at Payless cost two dollars and it's made from the same material. 'Cause of the brand value. Once I got laced to that, I'm like, 'Lemme start developing the brand.'"[43]

The key was to focus on unique core strengths, and to amplify the qualities that distinguish your brand from the competition. Always a voracious reader, Hussle soaked up the knowledge and set about distinguishing his brand, All Money In, No Money Out.

"That All Money In shit was really his life," says Cinematic Music rapper Smoke DZA, who met Nip in the Slauson Tees era, prior to the establishment of The Marathon Clothing. "Before he incorporated the LLC, he was saying 'All Money In, No Money Out.' We're not spending no money. We just in the shit to make money. We gonna run it up. He always had the vision too. Since I known him, he was the first nigga I knew that had a kilo on his neck. The vision was always ownership for him."[44]

Even while he was still signed to a major label, Hussle never lost his indie mindset. Dexter's "fuck the middleman" ethos was deeply ingrained. "I've been writing raps and going to the studio to record them since I was like twelve," he explained as the relationship with the label began to fray. "I signed in 2008 and before that, I was local with it in the hood—on Crenshaw and Slauson out my trunk. Then I made sure everybody in L.A. know. I was staplin' posters myself, me and my homeboys. Me and my daughter mama was hoppin' out the car, staplin' posters and all that. Me and my brother was spending our fives and tens, bringing our little brown paper bags of money and doin' what we do with it. But once we signed with Epic, they started spendin' so I can focus solely on being creative."[45]

The old record-biz model was on its way out, replaced by a new set of rules: build a buzz, drop a mixtape, go on tour, establish brands outside of your music. As the business was changing, more than ever it seemed that the middleman was getting squeezed out—although not everybody was on board with the new rules of the game.

"The younger generation tried to be like Nipsey," said Steve Lobel, "and there is nobody like him, but they were trying to follow the blueprint of independence, do-it-yourself, fuck the middleman, get it done. I didn't respect the fuck-the-middle-man thing, because we all have middle men. Even if you're a drug dealer you got to get a middle man. Someone's got to give it to you off the boat. But at the end of the day he empowered everybody, which was great."[46]

Tick-tick-tick.

As much progress as Hussle had made toward his goals, he still heard the sound of that ticking clock in the back of his head. His most precious resource was time and it was passing him by. He had to get busy updating his blueprint.

🏁

"Don't shave years off your life with them blunts!" Curren$y implored Nipsey Hussle inside a cloudy Manhattan recording studio. Wiz Khalifa and Jonny Shipes were in there too, somewhere behind the ganja haze. "Papers—I'm tellin' you, dog," said Curren$y. "We'll smoke like an ounce in two days, me and him. Like a zip—don't even feel that shit. Blunts make your back hurt and everything. We smoke Kush, sour diesel. We don't burn no trash, never."[47]

It was January 2010 and Nip was in town for the *XXL* Freshman Class cover shoot the next day. Tonight he was locked in the lab to "Spit that pistol-grip poetry" on "I Don't Fucks with Em," which would become a standout track on Curren$y's crucial *Smokee Robinson* mixtape. The New Orleans rapper also known to his fans as Spitta Andretti had been signed to Master P's No Limit label and made records with Lil Wayne and Cash Money before opting to go solo. Like Nipsey, he used dollar signs to spell his name, and was all about developing his own brand, Jet Life. The two got along right away, even before Nip laid down his verse.

Though he surely caught a contact, Hussle was the only one in the studio not smoking that night. On probation since 2003, he hadn't smoked for seven years lest he fail a drug test and extend his obligation to the Los Angeles County criminal justice system. "Probation, man," Hussle said, exasperated. "It's like you got a tail on you and they can snatch your tail any time they want to. You don't even have to break a law to violate probation. That's some bullshit."[48]

If everything went as expected, Hussle would soon be completing his seven-year stretch. He was planning to celebrate by getting FREE AT LAST tattooed on his thumb and lighting up a Crip stick—two blunts rolled end-to-end.[49]

The next day Hussle was right on time for his first big magazine shoot, the *XXL* Freshmen issue. He was sharing the cover with Wiz, J. Cole, Big Sean, Freddie Gibbs, and Jay Rock. It was a huge milestone in Hussle's career, marking the moment when Neighborhood Nip was officially anointed as the next big thing out of the west.

"Nipsey was the star of the day," recalls Vanessa Satten, *XXL*'s longtime editor in chief. "He got the most prominent placement. It was all coming off his relationship with Snoop and bringing the West Coast back to relevancy. Him, Cole, and Wiz were the biggest priorities that day. Even if you look at the way Nipsey was styled, he stood out from everyone else." Everyone else on the cover was asked to wear black. "Nip clearly said, 'Fuck the system, I'm going to wear my blue flannel,'" Satten recalled with a laugh.[50]

"The first thing I got from Nipsey Hussle was how intelligent he was," said Wiz after hanging with him the night before. He was impressed to see Hussle step in to help the engineer during the session. "This is a straight hood nigga from Crenshaw—a real Crip—but he knows technology!" Wiz marveled.[51]

J. Cole missed a flight and was almost eight hours late for the shoot, but everybody remained chill throughout the day. Then in its third year, *XXL*'s Freshmen issue had never been a bigger deal, now solidified as the premier showcase for rising stars in hip-hop. "They were all happy to be a part of it," says Satten. "I remember Nipsey being easygoing that day and everybody getting along well." Kendrick Lamar rolled to the shoot along with his TDE comrade Jay Rock, and offered to take Cole's place when the North Carolina lyricist was late. Satten assumed he was joking, but he probably wasn't. She made it clear they were going to wait for Cole. Kendrick told her, "I'm going to be on this next year."[52]

"Okay, that's good," Vanessa replied. "Thank you for telling me that."

And sure enough, in 2011, Kendrick did make the cover. For the first time since the heyday of Death Row, L.A. was on the rise once again. "As New Yorkers we're always excited about the west coming back," says Satten. When that issue dropped, *XXL* readers could feel it happening, with Nip Hussle leading the way.[53]

Playing on the high school theme, each of the artists on the cover was given a superlative, the same way some seniors are in their yearbooks. Hussle was nominated "Most Determined" that year, which felt appropriate. There was no shortage of determination in the room at that cover shoot, but Hussle had been blessed with more than most. Determination would be a big part of what shone through during his journey forward, considering all that he was able to accomplish as an independent artist without a major label release. Speaking of which—*South Central State of Mind* never came out.

After countless promises and pushbacks, including a mention in the *XXL* cover story, Hussle's highly anticipated project fell victim to restructuring after the Epic Records regime change. Shipes would help Hussle negotiate for a release from his contract. Hussle was even able to retain control of all his master recordings, including the *Bullets Ain't Got No Name* sessions that the label had quietly funded. Shipes and Hussle parted ways amicably and all parties kept it moving. A new leg of the Marathon was about to begin.

Chapter 7

MARATHON MODE

ALL MY NIGGAS IS GONE, BUT I STILL EXIST
SO I GOT ON MY KNEES AND I TOLD HIM THIS—"I REPENT"
—Nipsey Hussle, "A Million," *The Marathon* (2010)

ipsey Hussle felt like crap when he got a call from Steve Lobel one February morning in 2010. "Nip, pull up!" said his manager, who would sometimes invite him on unexpected adventures like going BMX riding at the Fantasy Factory, a funhouse run by professional skateboarder Rob Dyrdek.

"I'm sick, man," Hussle replied. "I'm in bed."

"Nah," said Maniac Lobel. "Get up right now. Pull up!"

"Must be serious," Hussle said to himself, and made his way to the address Lobel provided. "It was all bigwigs there," he recalled later. "I seen Babyface and motherfuckin' Celine Dion. Man, *everybody* was there. If they ever bombed that it was over."[1]

Just when he was thinking, *What the fuck am I doin' here?* he saw a familiar face: Snoop.

"Cuz!" Hussle said, heading over to the big homie, whose handlers immediately said, "Nip ain't supposed to be here."

"Well shit," Snoop replied. "Me neither!" When they insisted that Snoop was indeed supposed to be there, he said, "Well fuck it—we both supposed to be here!"

Just then Hussle saw his friend QDIII, the producer of a track for what would be Nipsey's next independent project. QDIII introduced him to his father, the legendary Quincy Jones. The man who produced "We Are the World" to benefit Africa back in 1985 was now doing another one for Haiti twenty-five years later. And for some reason he wanted Hussle on the record—and in the video.

"Go get in it!" Q told Hussle, pointing toward the studio.

"I'm cool," Hussle said. "I'm just coming to show respect."

Q insisted. "Nah, go 'head!"[2]

Hussle kept resisting, saying he didn't know the words to the song, but Quincy can be very persuasive. Before Hussle knew it, he found himself surrounded by hip-hop icons, laying down vocals with the likes of LL Cool J, Busta Rhymes, Kanye West, and Snoop. Despite his best efforts to fade into the background, Hussle stood tall above the crowd, unmistakable in his gray hoodie and iced-out Malcolm X chain. He even got caught in the moment and threw up the 60s hand sign. When *Saturday Night Live* spoofed the song that weekend, they poked fun at "half-famous randos like Bizzy Bone and Nipsey Hussle."[3]

Hussle wasn't even mad when *SNL* cracked their joke. Since leaving Epic, he'd spent considerable time thinking about his brand, and he was clear that it didn't depend on being as famous as possible. "Nipsey Hussle can't be Nipsey Hussle if he doesn't celebrate his successes but also his strategy," said Jorge Peniche. "I think that's what people gravitate to. Nipsey is just by nature a motivator."[4]

Even when he was still signed to Epic, Hussle would grind like an independent artist. "I'm in overdrive, my nigga," he said. "A lot of artists get the deal and get comfortable. You feel like that's what they came for. I didn't come for the deal, homie. I came to connect to the people."[5] As he entered a new phase of his career, everything from his music to his interviews spoke of empowerment and redemption, sharing his journey as a young independent artist who was determined to make it, no matter how long it took.

"Really I just wanna say what I got to say and talk to my people. And give 'em some game and entertain 'em and tell 'em my story. I got a lot off my chest. I been through a lot. It's a lot of my homeboys who ain't got no voice. This story got to be told."[6]

That story is the Marathon.

🏁

SEIZE THE OPPORTUNITY, BELIEVE AND TAKE CONTROL OF IT
THEN GET ON YOUR MARATHON AND GRIND IT TILL IT'S OVER WITH.

—Nipsey Hussle, "7 Days a Week," *The Marathon* (2010)

Locked into his Twitter feed as usual, Hussle was aware of the critics and disappointed fans, complaining that they were not going to get *South Central State of Mind*. But truthfully, it was probably for the best. Hussle's departure from Epic realigned his brand with core values of independence and entrepreneurship. "Just like any business, some things work really well, and other things don't," said Peniche. "It's up to you to understand when to pull out of a situation before you cause damage to your brand." Hussle was an artist who actually stood for something beyond fame. "It was bigger than celebrity. Bigger than monetary gain."[7]

That summer Hussle and Fatts hit the road for a mini-tour through Europe and the UK. August 2010 found them in London for Notting Hill Carnival, Europe's largest street festival, performing at an event for Eritrean youth. As usual he had video cameras following his every move.

"Sup with it y'all?" he said as he made his way through the streets of Ladbroke Grove. "It's your boy Neighborhood Nip. We out here in London, gettin' it in carnival weekend. Fresh off the train from Germany, just killed the shit last night. On a Marathon. Shit don't stop!"[8]

The road was taking its toll on Fatts. "Long-ass fuckin' journey," he moaned. "This is bullshit. It's cold out. We on a Marathon, though. Tryin' to get it, man. Neighborhood."

After rocking the show, Hussle stopped by somebody's flat for a candid video interview, sharing his thoughts on the return to indie life. "We got the hard part over with, my nigga," he said. "Climbin' out the grave and gettin' into this game is the hard part." The trick, as always, was to reach the next level, and the next, and the next after that. "You don't have to know exactly how you gonna play it," he said. "You just have to know where you wanna be." One thing Hussle knew for sure was that "the shit get way bigger." Later that night, inspiration struck and Hussle set up a laptop recording session in his hotel room. He always carried a high-quality studio mic with him for moments like this.[9]

Upon his return to the States, Hussle kept going hard, using every spare moment to record new music and set up his business. He didn't mind working hard on something he loved so much. "Success to me is just being able to do what you love to do and support yourself off it," Hussle said. "Live your dream and do what you love to do every day. So I'm successful in my eyes. I don't sell dope. I don't go to work. I do music and I love to do it and that's all I have to do to maintain." The secret to his success was "an aggressive, full-throttle approach" Hussle called The Marathon. "Every day I run a lap and it don't stop."[10]

"The Marathon was this energy that Nip brought to the table when he'd come to the studio," said J Stone. "When he toured overseas off the mixtape that's when he knew. He was like, 'Damn they love us.' He'd tell us it's a marathon, we can't stop. We kept recording and recorded damn near every day. He'd release and keep going, saying it's a marathon. So he named his tape *The Marathon*."[11]

Hussle made sure his inner circle was part of the Marathon sessions. Along with J Stone he reached out to Cobby, Cuzzy, Twan, and BH. There was another homie in the neighborhood who made an impression on him, a heavyset kid who went by the name of Pacman. He and BH were neighbors who went to Crenshaw High together. Every day he'd be out there on Eighth Avenue in the same spot with a pistol hidden in a Doritos bag. He bought a 1960 hoodie from Hussle's shop. "I was just trying to be creative," he said. "Just some gang shit."[12]

One day Pacman was out there grindin' and Hussle pulled up. He was shooting a video for "The Hussle Way," a song off *Bullets Ain't Got No Name Vol. 3*. "I was on the block doin' what I do and he asked me to do a scene for the video," Pacman recalls. They shot it then and there, a quick street transaction. The video never came out, but Hussle and Pacman exchanged numbers and kept in touch. "He always used to call me 'The Truth,'" Pacman recalls. "No flaws on my resume as far as street shit. That's something they admire about me—I'm a solid nigga. Held my own." It was BH who first invited him to the studio, and even though he was skeptical at first he loved hearing the sound of his voice over a beat. Soon he was buying his own equipment and setting up his own home studio, applying the discipline of the block to a new hustle.[13]

Since Hussle and BH helped Pacman turn his life around, Pacman has done his best to block out any haters and pay the blessings forward. "If you want help I'll help you," he says. "I ain't gonna conceal the game from you. If you wanna grow, you wanna do better, come on. I'll bring you to the studio before I give you a gun now."[14]

When Hussle wasn't locked in the studio with his partners in rhyme, he was huddled up with Peniche perfecting the aesthetics of the All Money In brand. "With him going independent it was such a big deal," Peniche said. "I was super excited to be part of that because it's like we had free rein to do as we pleased and innovate as we pleased and take our time to really roll out these elaborate or very comprehensive ideas that some people might not necessarily understand."[15]

A fan of the photojournalism that used to appear in print publications like the original *Life* magazine, Peniche suggested taking a page from the classic weekly as a way to distinguish the brand. "Maybe that's kind of the push that we take," Peniche said. "How 'bout we take it to something that looks a little bit more classic?" He shot black-and-white portraits of Hussle on 35mm film with a Canon AE-1. "It was fly-on-the-wall photojournalism at its finest."[16]

Peniche knew Hussle was a devoted dad and wondered if he would feel comfortable being photographed with Emani. "I asked what him and his daughter loved to do. He said she loved to be with him, and especially loved sitting on his lap, pretending to steer the wheel of his car." Peniche's gritty black-and-white photographs of the father and daughter riding through South Central were later exhibited as part of the hip-hop photography exhibit *Contact High*. Emani wore heart-shaped sunglasses and a huge smile as she gripped the wheel. "The image to me was a homecoming of sorts, and an homage to success and fatherhood."[17]

Peniche maintained the classic aesthetic through the design and typography as well. "The Marathon logo was inspired by *Life* magazine's colorway and font," said Peniche. Instead of physical

CD liner notes, Hussle asked Peniche to design a digital book-let that fans could download with the free mixtape—after enter-ing their contact information so Hussle could keep building a relationship with his fans. He had some things he wanted to explain.[18]

L.A. hip-hop underwent a complete transformation after the Death Row era. Apart from Game, who benefited from the Dr. Dre stamp via 50 Cent, "gangsta rap" was not popping. "The clubs didn't support anything that was goin' on," recalled Chuck Dizzle of *Home Grown Radio*. "They wouldn't let these dudes do shows 'cause of the post–Death Row shit. West Coast hip-hop specifically, it had a negative connotation from the gangbangin' shit. These dudes couldn't do shows, they didn't get radio play. So it just dried up. And it was a circle of people like, 'What the fuck are we gonna do?'"[19]

Heading into 2010, L.A. rap was caught up with the jerk movement, with dance-driven acts like Cali Swag District and the New Boyz coming to the forefront. "This new generation starts to come out with the dancing and the skinny jeans," Dizzle said. "It opened up the doors for people to spend money and say, 'Okay, this is fun. I can invest in this' . . . Versus the stigma of gangsta rap that they were trying to get away from."[20] Street-oriented artists like Jay Rock, Glasses Malone, and Nipsey Hussle faced resistance from the industry and law enforcement alike.

In late 2010 Cinematic put together a Smoker's Club West tour, running from Vancouver down to Arizona featuring Hussle, Curren$y, Dom Kennedy, and Smoke DZA. Everything went pretty smoothly until the December 8 show at the El Rey Theatre in Los Angeles. The LAPD began pressuring the promoter about Nipsey Hussle's appearance.

"I didn't know about how the gang injunction shit worked,"

Curren$y recalls, "but when we got to L.A., we couldn't have Nip at our show. Nip was the one who let me know, like, 'Yeah, if I come, they're gonna shut it down unless you have the LAPD come do whatever.' I guess they hit him and the promoters and was like, 'Y'all can't do nothin'.'"[21]

Curren$y wasn't going for it. "Fuck all that," he told Hussle. "I need you to come rap 'Diamonds On My Neck,' bruh." Spitta loved the *Bullets Vol. 3* track with the Biggie Smalls sample in the hook. "It was the shit he was saying," Spitta recalls. "The beat hard, plus I had just gotten a big-ass chain." Inspired by Hussle, Curren$y copped his own chunky Cuban link. "There's a feeling you get when you know your jewelry is real," he explains. "I didn't have a chain until I could get a real chain. Motherfuckers fuck around and get bullshit. So when you get that motherfucker and you *know* for sure . . . It's bigger than just the chain, you know what you had to do to get it. You know you put in real work, you know how much that cost. It sound like some dumb hood shit, but it's way bigger than that."[22]

When the show went down, Hussle didn't perform his own set, but Curren$y brought him out to do that one song. "This is your town, bruh," he said. "You *got* to come out." Due to relentless police harassment, Nipsey Hussle concerts had become a rare treat in L.A. So when he came out of nowhere rhyming "Break the beat up, wake the street up with my potent flow," the crowd was—in Spitta's words—"excited as fuck."

"That's why I knew it had to happen," Curren$y says, looking back on a perfect moment. So perfect he was willing to chance getting his own set shut down, and Hussle was willing to risk getting arrested. "But he was like, 'Fuck it, dog,'" Spitta recalls with a smile. "He came and did that shit."[23]

Two weeks later, on Tuesday, December 21, 2010, the first fully independent release from All Money In, No Money Out was made available for download via iHussle.com. According to the mixtape's cover art, the official title was *The Marathon (Music)*, but most people referred to it simply as *The Marathon*. To access the content, new users had to register with Hussle's website, entering their contact information and receiving a welcome email that explained the mindset behind the project: "The Marathon is all about the work before the celebration, the test of endurance that separates the winners from the rest."

The actual mixtape came as a zip file containing eighteen MP3s and a digital booklet in PDF format with photographs by Peniche along with track list and credits, and a note from Hussle. Blacc Sam, Fatts, Adam, and Nipsey Hussle were listed as co-executive producers. Ralo Stylez was credited as executive music producer.[24]

"He gave me that title because the level of contribution I was making was not just engineering and not just producing," Ralo says. "I'm recording songs, I'm mixing songs, I'm also bringing some of these compositions to the table. We created a sound on *The Marathon*. It was a minimalistic approach where each sound would debut at certain parts of the loop, and it would create this, like, narcotic effect. We were onto something."[25]

"Yes, it's rap and its hip hop," said Peniche, "but if you were to put it into its own genre, it's Marathon Music. From 2010 forward, that was kind of the philosophy or the mindset that we had, like, 'We're gonna create Marathon Music' . . . music that not only inspires but educates."[26] The beat selection on *The Marathon* included Wiz Khalifa and Curren$y ("7 Days a Week") and Kanye West ("Mac 11 on the Dresser"). "Call from the Bank" was built around a sample from MGMT, the indie rock band known for collaborating with Kid Cudi and being sampled by the likes of Mac Miller and Frank Ocean. Hussle took the extra step of crediting MGMT as a featured artist in the track listing, emphasizing the fact that he was stepping out of the "gangsta rap" box.

"The beat might be different from what they normally hear me on," said Hussle. "I always felt like if anything it'll make you curious. Like, 'What he about to say on this?'" When Hussle listened through his catalog he was proud of songs like these, what he called "the *musical* flexes." More than anything he wanted to be fearless enough to try anything. He never wanted to be accused of playing it safe, or as he put it, "exercisin' a sellable cliché."[27]

The *Marathon* digital booklet contained Hussle's essay explaining why he decided to go independent. "As is the case with most people in this game," he wrote, "I am driven by both financial and creative motives. The decision I had to make recently is to which motive I would give priority in my career." Despite naming his company All Money In, Hussle chose to prioritize creative integrity over chasing commercial hits. He said you could always tell when artists are reaching for radio records and club bangers. Kanye West produced a song called "Encore" from *The Black Album* where Jay-Z says "When you first start to come in the game they try to play you. Then you make a couple of hits, look how they wave to you!"

"Nipsey would always quote that," says Ralo. "Cause it's never enough. You make a hit record, then you gotta make another hit record. Then you make another one, now you need a whole album full of them. And your visual support better be impeccable too."[28] Pretty soon you were stuck in a box.

"My biggest disappointment with the label," Hussle wrote, "was the separation of the processes it takes to develop and release something special: the music, the pictures, the videos. It was all being created and released from separate points of reference, therefore confusing the consumers about the identity and integrity of my brand."

The next line of Hussle's essay was so important that he asked Peniche to set it in red capital letters: "I WILL NEVER SAY SOMETHING I DON'T AGREE WITH OR BELIEVE IN . . . even if the reward is massive!" He went on to underscore the principles behind his decision, which was not made without sacrifice: "I always told myself that if I make it here I would keep it true to my heart and soul," he wrote. "I will not break my word for anyone."[29]

The video for "Keys 2 the City" showed Hussle taking off in a helicopter and stunting atop a skyscraper looking down at the L.A. skyline and the Staples Center. The message of the first official single off *The Marathon* was clear: Neighborhood Nip was on a higher level now. The song's lyrics detailed all the labels that had fronted on him in the past, singling out Dr. Dre by name.

On "Mr. Untouchable," the first track to leak before *The Marathon* was released, Hussle rapped "High till I die so it's motherfuck a *Detox*," a reference to Dre's much-hyped "final album," which was first announced in 2002, eight years earlier. Hussle even got Kokane, an L.A. funk vocalist who'd put in work with Dre, Snoop, and N.W.A, to sing the hook.

"It ain't a shot, cause it doesn't say 'fuck Dre,'" Hussle explained on the day *The Marathon* dropped. "It ain't nothin' personal to Dre, it ain't nothin' personal against *Detox*, it's just I'm on this All Money In shit . . . Niggas take it how they take it. I'm out here in these streets . . . It was just me speaking my mind at that moment. Basically I'm on some 'If I can't get money wit'chu, it's fuck you.' It ain't nothin' personal."[30]

Having built his own movement and stepped away from his major label deal, Hussle embarked upon *The Marathon*, declaring his independence as he laid out a long-term vision for success. In setting up All Money In, he'd studied the blueprints of pioneers like James Prince, E-40, Master P, Jay-Z, Biggs, and Dame Dash as he drew up his own master plan. "Not one person can make or break what I'm doing, except me or God," Hussle stated proudly. "Not the label, not Dr. Dre, not Snoop, Game—and much respect to all them niggas, but as a man that's not how I was raised."[31]

Soon after *The Marathon* hit the streets, Blacc Sam came home from the pen and got right back on his grind. Hussle's big brother had taken some hits, but he was a survivor. "The house got fore-closed on," Hussle recalled. "That shop that he had originally, he lost it." Although Sam "had money put up," some of the plans he'd put in place were shaken. "He thought he had a situation to get back on his feet," Hussle said. "All his credit lines went dry. He had a foreclosure on his credit because of, you know, the situation with the law."[32]

In the *Victory Lap* song "Young Niggas," Hussle speaks about Sam burying a quarter million dollars in cash in their mother's backyard. "It was in an airtight safe, wrapped in plastic, fireproof safe," Hussle told me. "When he dug it up, you know, unlocked the safe, a good portion—a little bit less than half of it—was molded. Just imagine like a book, a molded book, that you can't even turn the pages in the book. It was devastating."

Hussle and his sister and mother plugged in blow dryers and helped Sam try to salvage as much of the cash as possible. "It was wet and mushy and soggy," he recalls. "I didn't even wanna say nothing, 'cause it was real hard to come across that kind of money back in the day. It was a painful moment." The smell of molded cash lingered in the house. Some of the money had to be thrown out, while some of it was borderline usable. Hussle took some of it to the Slauson Swap Meet, making the best of a bad situation.[33]

Following his release, Sam hit the ground running, getting Crenshaw shirts printed up as seen in the "Hussle in the House" video. He set up a table at the bus stop on Crenshaw and Slauson, selling socks, T-shirts, and those Crenshaw shirts, in small batches at first—as many as he could afford. "We didn't make that a business at all," Hussle recalled. That part of the vision was all Sam, and as usual his instincts were right on the money.[34]

The Crenshaw shirt became a hot item in the streets, selling out quickly each time Sam printed more. "His first $2,000 he made, Sam got the shop back," said Hussle. It was a different space this time, but in the same shopping plaza with the same landlord. "The landlord knew he'd pay the rent on time," said Nip. "He was a good businessman. He got the shop, and moved the table inside the shop. He didn't buy no furniture, just moved it inside the shop and opened the door." Sam's hustling ability— a rare blend of work ethic, business acumen, and personal style— was nothing short of miraculous. Dollar by dollar, he reinvested back into his business. By sheer force of will, he and his brother set about building The Marathon Clothing from the curb up.[35]

Starting a business in South Los Angeles was not easy, but that was only half the battle. Once you built it you had to defend it from every angle. Hussle had this in mind when he described his hometown as "a city where you either gonna stand up to it or kneel down to it."[36]

"Before I met Nipsey I didn't know how to secure the bag," said Ralo. "One thing about L.A. is this: You acquiring a bag is gonna be met with violent opposition. Period. Every time. All the time. You gotta be ready for it or it's not yours. And if you're not sober and into it about that fact, you're gonna be putting everybody in harm's way. Cause you're the weakest link, putting everybody in harm's way."[37]

DOUBLE UP, THREE OR FOUR TIMES I AIN'T TELLIN' NO LIES
I JUST RUN IT UP, NEVER LET A HARD TIME HUMBLE US

—Nipsey Hussle, "Double Up," *Victory Lap* (2018)

On the afternoon of March 18, 2011, officers from the LAPD's Seventy-Seventh Division responded to reports of a disturbance at 3420 W. Slauson Avenue. According to the official police report, a "gang fight" had broken out in the alley that separates the Shell station and the shopping plaza.[38] "When the officers arrived, they saw about 10 gang members fighting and heard gunfire," the report states. "They also noticed one of the fighters, 29-year-old Samiel Asghedom, was in possession of a gun." Among the people fighting were Nipsey Hussle and Big U, who had worked closely together for many years. As tough and experienced a fighter as Hussle was, his skinny frame was no match for Big U, a powerfully built martial arts expert. According to sources in the neighborhood, Blacc Sam fired a shot in the air in an attempt to end the conflict. Officer Salvatore De Bella opened fire in Sam's direction. "Emptied a full clip," Hussle recalled. "Police is trained shooters, police don't miss . . . and he didn't hit my brother at all."[39]

After the gunsmoke cleared, five people were arrested and held at the Seventy-Seventh Street station, including Big U, Hussle, and his brother. On the evening after the incident, Hussle took to Twitter to dispel any rumors that might be going around: "I ain't dead . . . I ain't in jail . . . and I ain't on tha run. TMC."[40]

"We been through so many different tumultuous situations in the parking lot," Hussle said later. "It was a higher purpose, I believe, for what we doin' over here. It wasn't to get in trouble with the police. It wasn't to be a menace to the area. It wasn't to continue a tradition of self-destruction. It was to build."[41]

Exactly what caused the issue between former business partners remains unclear. In one interview Big U described the incident as "a family dispute," emphasizing how much he cared for Hussle. "That's my little brother," he said. "I love him to death . . . But it's like any- and everybody else. Sometimes you have a dispute and you gotta get an understanding." Big U pointed out that all families have their differences, and that he and Hussle came from a place where things like that happen. "If he got a problem, I got a problem," Big U said. "And if I got a problem, he definitely gonna have a problem."[42]

Having differences is one thing and having problems is another. While taking part in a panel discussion after the incident took place, Hussle was asked if he found it difficult to keep up relationships in his local community as he became more successful. "Your best friends can turn on you and get jealous," a member of the audience stated. "And it turns into a group of people tryin' to hold you back and keep you at the level you are."[43]

"That's another of the big struggles you gonna deal with as an artist," Hussle replied. "Especially if you come from L.A. or especially if you come from the streets in general. You got a lot of people that feel entitled to your success—on *they* timeframe."

Diagnosing the problem was one thing; dealing with it was something else. "It's a process," Hussle added. "Hopefully you don't go to jail reacting emotionally," he said. "Or get—God forbid . . ." He stopped himself from speaking the worst-case scenario out loud, finding another way to finish his thought. "We all know what can happen, the downfalls out here," he said. "But it's an art in surviving that transition."[44]

Without mentioning any names, Hussle described an incident that sounded similar to he and his brother's run-in with Big U. "Recently we had an altercation with this dude we used to do business with," he said. "It was all over the internet and all that. But the bottom line with that was it became a situation that couldn't be avoided. It had to be addressed."[45]

The falling-out between the partners took place three months after the release of *The Marathon*, while the dissolution of the Epic deal was still being finalized, as well as the end of Hussle's working relationship with Big U and Steve Lobel. The fact that Hussle and YG had recently been in the hood shooting a video may not have helped matters. "It was a situation where parties involved wanted to take advantage," says one member of the set, who spoke about the situation on condition of anonymity. "The way that shit was set up, you would look like a bully just outta nowhere. So you had to find a reason. And this was one of those things. 'Oh, you got a Blood in the hood shootin' a video?'" The bottom line, as this Rollin' 60s member saw it, was that Hussle and Sam and their father were determined to stick together and stand up for their rights no matter what.[46]

"We were aware of the altercation between Big U and Nipsey when it occurred," said Dexter Browne, who moved back to Trinidad with his family in 2007 when he and his wife were no longer comfortable raising their daughters in the neighborhood. "Certain persons called me to tell me what happened. I just felt good to know that they were able to get to a point where they were amicable. When I was able to talk to Nipsey, he told me that they had gotten to a place where they could disagree but not be so disagreeable—and so I felt very good about that. I felt that meant he would be able to balance both of those worlds, which is a very hard balancing act—that nobody has been able to pull off so far."[47]

SEE, IT'S A COUPLE NIGGAS EVERY GENERATION
THAT WASN'T SUPPOSED TO MAKE IT OUT, BUT DECODE THE MATRIX

—Nipsey Hussle, "Loaded Bases," *Victory Lap* (2018)

LeBron James was in the zone. Standing in the home team locker room at Miami's AmericanAirlines Arena on June 12, 2011, he nodded his head to the song pumping through his black head-phones, tuning out the pressure, ignoring the cluster of cameras and members of the media watching his every move as he went through his pregame preparations. Tonight was a must-win for the Miami Heat: game 6 of the 2011 NBA Finals. After a three-game series on the road against the underdog Dallas Mavericks, the "Super Team" featuring three franchise all-stars—James, Dwyane Wade, and Chris Bosh—had returned home trailing 3 games to 2. They had to win tonight in order to force a deciding seventh game and claim the NBA championship they believed was rightfully theirs. The pressure to win was nothing new for James. He was accustomed to that. But this season had been difficult for other reasons.[48]

Ever since his stunning 2010 announcement that the two-time league MVP would be leaving his hometown Cleveland Cavaliers to "take his talents to South Beach" and join the Miami Heat, LeBron James was suddenly unpopular. Jilted Cavaliers owner Dan Gilbert called him a coward, a traitor, and a narcissist, but the "bad guy" role didn't suit James at all. "During my first seven years in the NBA I was always the liked one," he said. "To be on the other side, they call it the dark side, or the villain, whatever they call it . . . It was definitely challenging for myself. It was a situation I had never been in before. I took a long time to adjust to it. It didn't feel good." He felt as if he were turning into somebody else. "I started to buy into it," he said. "I started to play the game of basketball at a level or in a mind state that I had never played at before. I mean angry."[49]

Sure, the Heat had made the finals his first season, but there was no satisfaction in advancing this far. During an over-the-top welcome party for the "Three Kings" (James, Wade, and Bosh) LeBron was asked if he'd come to Miami to win championships—plural. Thousands of Heat fans cheered as he responded, "Not two, not three, not four, not five, not six, not seven." Anything less would be an embarrassment. And now the Heat was one game away from the unthinkable.[50]

Before slipping into his jersey, LeBron took off his headphones and hung them on the handle above his polished hardwood locker. Nipsey Hussle's voice filled the Miami Heat locker room. "Look, I'm from Westside California, they run up on ya / Ask you where you from and check yo' tats under yo' clothin'." Facing unbearable pressure, James was preparing for the biggest game of his life by listening to *The Marathon*.[51]

At the time, Hussle and James did not know each other, but Nipsey definitely saw the clip when it made the rounds on the internet. "He ain't talkin' to reporters or nothin'," Hussle said proudly. "He's just locked in."[52] It was the kind of endorsement money couldn't buy, one of the most famous professional athletes in the world cosigning an independent mixtape rapper. And while game 6 didn't work out the way James hoped—Dirk Nowitzki and the Dallas Mavericks won 105–95, sealing the Mavs' first-ever

NBA championship and humiliating the Heat—LeBron's cosign couldn't have come at a better moment for Hussle.

"'Bron a hip-hop head, truthfully," Hussle reflected later. "And 'Bron from the hood. He come from the struggle. So I think anybody that is a hip-hop head *and* you come from the struggle, Nip Hussle is gon' be one of your favorite narratives, and one of your favorite approaches to hip-hop. So I think that he fit who I'm speaking to . . . he's been on a marathon and he raised his own personal standards and clearly challenged himself to be better than his environment expected him to be. So I think he relate on them levels. And that's my perspective on it. I ain't never asked him, but that's what I think."[53]

Given the meaning behind *The Marathon*, it was no surprise that athletes resonated with the message. "They go through the same struggle," Hussle said. "They just attackin' it through they gifts on the field, and we doin' it through the art and through the music. So I think whether it's the message of motivation— if they apply it to sports or if they apply it to just the pursuit of becomin' better, and bossin' up and bein' successful, maximizin' your potential and challengin' yourself—I think those things is in the music and in the message of *The Marathon*."[54]

July 2011 found Hussle posted up at the luxurious Palms Casino Resort in Las Vegas courtesy of resident DJ Clinton Sparks. Around 5 a.m. Hussle took a break from shooting hoops to talk about the new music he'd been cooking up in the studio. "My last project was called *The Marathon*," he said. "I'm workin' on a group of records right now. I ain't titled it yet, but I might call it *The Marathon Continues*. But it's gonna be a free release. It's comin' out in the next two months at the latest—it might come out sooner dependin' how we work it . . . I'm in the studio every day. Not too many features on this new one. Everything kinda like in-house."[55]

Hussle also had a show in late July at the Las Vegas club Déjà Vu Showgirls, for an event billed as the Strip Hop Topless Party. 50 Cent and Floyd Mayweather Jr. were in attendance when Hussle hit the stage. Between the rap stars, boxing champs, expensive bottles, and topless showgirls, everything seemed to be going well—until Cobby Supreme noticed some people in the crowd acting shady.[56]

"We did our song and shit," Cobby recalled. "While we was onstage doing it I noticed that it was a pack of guys in the crowd that wasn't dancing. They was just lookin' kinda mean and shit while everybody else in the party was goin' crazy to the song." Cobby gave Nip a heads-up, like, *Watch these guys right here.* Once their set was finished, Hussle went to take photos with fans while Cobby let their boys know there might be some trouble. "The pack of like ten or thirteen guys— whatever it was—they approached him," Cobby recalled. "And while they approached him you can see the girls that Nip was taking a picture with run from up under his arms. At that time I proceeded towards where the pack of guys was. And I could see Nip's face being seriously bothered, like the guys said something bad at Nip, and he was gettin' ready—like he was gonna have to take a blow or he was finna give one."[57] Hussle said he was in the VIP section letting his chain hang when a dude standing near him asked where he was from—always a loaded question in gang culture. "I'm from L.A., bro," Hussle replied, but his facial expression didn't sit well with Cobby, who launched a preemptive strike.

"Niggas tried to rob us," Hussle said in summary, adding that one of his homies ended up "reversing the charges."

"I kinda caught it before it happened," said Cobby with under-stated pride. "We fought our way out that club successfully."[58]

"Somehow a melee broke out," said Hussle, "and it ain't go in they favor, the niggas that started it."[59] A massive brawl ensued. Dozens of Las Vegas police officers responded to Déjà Vu Show-girls. The first officer on the scene was met by a club employee yelling, "Officer, help! My security is getting beat up by a bunch of guys inside the place!"[60] One man was knocked unconscious either before or after being thrown through a glass table.

Hussle recounted the incident in a verse from "Grinding All My Life" on *Victory Lap*:

LAS VEGAS, STRIP HOP, YEAH YOU CREAMED THEM PUNKS
AFTER ALL THAT LOOKIN' TOUGH ALL HE SEEN WAS STUMPS
50 CENT AND MAYWEATHER FLEED THE SCENE WITH US—TRUE STORY!

🏁

Life kept moving so fast, there was no shortage of lyrical inspira-tion. But somehow there were never enough hours in the day to lay down all the rhymes that came to mind, no matter how much time Hussle spent inside All Money Business recording studio in downtown L.A.[61] There came a time when he had to stop recording and choose a release date for *The Marathon Continues*. Hussle and his team agreed on November 1, 2011—the numeri-cal symbolism of 11/1/11 was too powerful to pass up.

Hussle hadn't dropped any new music since *The Marathon* in late December, creating a deliberate dry spell. "The new music has a different sound," Hussle explained. "I kinda wanted to shock people with it as opposed to drop leaks and warm 'em up to it."[62] Response to *The Marathon* suggested that he was developing a passionate, highly engaged fan base. "Now kids tell me I'm the reason that they finished school," he rapped on "Road to Riches," a new song for *TMC*. "And if it wasn't for *The Marathon* they wouldn't have made it through it." Hussle felt a sense of responsibility to maintain that standard, no matter how long it took.

Just days before the November 1 release date, he was still compulsively recording new material for *TMC*. "We almost done," he said. "We gettin' there. We basically got what we need. But I'm just the type of artist I like recordin' to the last minute . . . my team might be a little upset, 'cause we got hard deadlines and stuff. But it seem like in crunch time you get some of your best material."[63]

TMC's bold new sound was evident on the mixtape's second track, "Who Detached Us?," which was built around a sample of "Rocketship" by Guster, an alternative rock band from Boston. Hussle's lyrics posed big questions about how his generation had lost its way, in terms broad enough that anyone could relate, whether they grew up bangin' in the hood or chillin' in Hollywood. "We used to be connected, who detached us," Hussle asked. "We used to be respected, now they laughin'." Hussle said "if it was up to me I'd rap like that on every song,"[64] suggesting that he had been suppressing this side of his intellect to conform to the expectations of his audience. He wasn't going to do that anymore.

Although Steve Jobs was credited as a featured artist on *TMC* just like YG, Rimpau, Cobby, and Dom Kennedy, the Apple founder didn't actually spit a verse on "Who Detached Us?" Instead, his voice appears via a sample of his 2005 commencement speech at Stanford University. A college dropout himself, Jobs used the speech as an opportunity to reflect on some of the choices he'd made in his life. "Death is the destination we all share," Jobs stated, his ice-cold candor resonating with Hussle. "No one has ever escaped it. And that is as it should be, because

Death is very likely the single best invention of Life." The sentiment hit different for a technologically gifted kid who grew up in
the 60s. Jobs's ultimate advice to the graduating class of the elite
university was to be brave enough to think freely and trust your
instincts. Hussle wanted that same freedom for himself, and he
was willing to risk everything to have it. The song closed with a
line borrowed from the final edition of the 1970s counterculture
journal *The Whole Earth Catalog*: "Stay hungry, stay foolish."[65]

Tick-tick-tick.

On November 4, a few days after *TMC*'s release, Hussle
celebrated with a live gig at the House of Blues on Sunset
Boulevard, backed by the band 1500 or Nothin'.[66] Hussle
had known Larrance Dopson of 1500 since Robin Hood first
introduced them, and the production collective made a profound
impact on the sound of *TMC*.

"We been knowin' Nip for a while," said Rance, a drummer
turned keyboardist who was raised "in church in the hood" and
segued into production when he learned that it paid more. "That's
our brother," he says. "We grew up together. You know, we've
always been doing music, but it was a time where Nip was makin'
his own beats. And we always had a mutual respect for each
other. And we all took the stairs, so we was just climbin' all at one
time."[67] By that point 1500 or Nothin' was a bit further along in
their climb than Hussle, who described the band as "legends in
the makin'." They were highly sought-after, working with artists
like Will Smith, Jay-Z, Kanye West, even Dr. Dre's mythical
Detox project. "They damn near worked with everybody that's
anybody in the hip-hop world," Hussle said. "Their whole squad
is over-talented. And they're young and they're hungry. So I'm
fortunate that I come from the same area as them. I don't have to
pay them 30, 40 thousand for the beats! We in-house."[68]

Chapter 8

PROUD 2 PAY

THEY TELLIN' ME THEY BELIEVE AND I GOT STYLE FOR DAYS
AND WHEN I DO DROP AN ALBUM THEY'LL BE PROUD TO PAY

—Nipsey Hussle, "Outro," *The Marathon Continues* (2011)

Bouncing on the balls of his feet like a center just before tip-off, Nipsey Hussle swayed to the woozy beat of "All Get Right," track 5 off his *Crenshaw* mixtape. With a cordless mic in hand, he parted the plush drapes from backstage just enough to peek out at the crowd of loyal fans assembled in the Hollywood nightclub Bardot for an intimate invitation-only event on May 26, 2014. The tattoo on his left thumb read FREE AT LAST, a permanent celebration of the moment in 2010 when he finished seven years of probation at age twenty-five. As DJ V.I.P. spun the record on his laptop, flooding the opulent space with sound, Nip could hear his own voice coming through the in-ear monitors. "I know y'all been waiting," it said. "My foundation's solid. Let's take flight."[1]

Tonight was the fulfillment of a promise, a secret show to reward the superfans who "kept it one hundred" and supported Hussle's game-changing Proud2Pay initiative, purchasing physical copies of *Crenshaw* for $100 each—and turning conventional wisdom about the state of the music business upside down. "Nipsey changed the game," declared veteran rap DJ and host Sway Calloway, who proudly paid Hussle $100 cash live on the air. "'I know y'all give it away for free—not me! I don't want $11.99! I don't want $15.99! I want $100 for my work!'"[2]

The idea came to him, like so many others, while reading a book. *Contagious: Why Things Catch On* by Jonah Berger was recommended to him by Big Bob Francis. In Chapter 2 Hussle read about Barclay Prime, a Philadelphia restaurant that made waves by charging $100 for a cheese steak sandwich. Philly cheese steaks were street food, but this was no ordinary sandwich. "It came with truffles and it came with a glass of champagne," Hussle explained. "It was a real elegant presentation, but they got all type of backlash because they charged $100 for a product that cost 3 or 4 dollars in Philly. But after a while it became like a status symbol. When you want to take a girl on a nice date, you take her to Barclay Prime and get a $100 cheese steak. Oprah came through and got one. Jay Leno got one. And it became a really big marketing tool for their restaurant, and a magnet to bring people in. So I just thought about hip hop, and I'm just like, our price point was come up by—*somebody*. We never came up with the business model."[3]

Dressed in black Crenshaw logo gear from head to toe, Hussle burst into the Bardot ballroom with a big smile on his face as the crowd broke into cheers, raising their smartphones to capture the moment. "Look!" he said, like he does to start most every song, by way of commanding attention—but this audience was fully locked in already.[4]

Although Hussle's long-awaited debut album, *Victory Lap*, would not come out for another four years, this night was a victory in and of itself. "My Cuban link, that's 14K," Hussle rapped, skipping words now and then to let his fans' voices be heard. "My presidential, I wear it every day / It symbolizes how I'm enterprisin' / I came from lint in Dickies pockets so I emphasize it." Hussle had picked up a few extra Cuban links since completing the *Crenshaw* tour, hosting pop-up events in major cities across the U.S. where crowds lined up to support his movement.

That night, there was no velvet rope, no stage; Hussle was standing on his fans' level. "Everybody in this motherfucker," Nip told the ecstatic crowd, many of whom were close enough to touch him. "I know you got that *Crenshaw* tape, so y'all gotta help me rap all these lyrics." As Nip's day-one homie Rimpau popped a bottle of Veuve Clicquot Rosé and sprayed down the crowd, Nip spoke from his heart. "Y'all helped us make history. We promised y'all we was gonna come through. We just celebratin' tonight."[5] After grindin' all his life, Hussle had earned the right to stunt. Everything seemed to be going his way, but less than a year before, the picture hadn't been so rosy.

"It's so many underlying events that took place back then," Hussle told me the week *Victory Lap* finally dropped. "Real-life things. Street shit that never really got written about 'cause it doesn't belong on the front page. You know—my brother going to the penitentiary. Me going to jail. Us getting raided. Us having real war in the streets. But I never went on camera or went on record and said, 'This is why it's taking so long' or 'This is what I'm going through.' *Nah.* I just dealt with what was going on 'cause it sounded like excuses . . . I was just trying to work through it, survive it."[6]

Whenever they were working on music Ralo and Hussle's connection was effortless. The two knew each other so well they barely had to speak in the studio. But life was more complicated than just making music. "I was starting to challenge him a lot and he would really be annoyed by me," Ralo says. "Nobody wants to feel like they've chosen the wrong path to live their life. And Nipsey was adamant about never being afraid of our people, and adamant about never turning his back on who we are and where we came from. I cannot say that I have that same level of commitment to any of those things. In retrospect that's not something that you can decide for anyone. The fact that I'm not into gangs, that shit is like a demerit on my manhood almost. Even though you're supposed to be a man first, and then make those type of choices. But it never settled correctly with me that I never got put on the hood."[7]

One day they were working on *Crenshaw*, and something happened at Tanisha's place. "We in there, we workin', smokin' weed and shit," Ralo remembers, then the next minute Nip received some news that broke his concentration. "Something in regards to where his kids were at, his stepchildren and his daughter," Ralo remembers. "Nip and Fatts were out of there."

Ralo couldn't stop them, but he hated to lose the creative vibe. "It was hard enough to get him to even work," Ralo remembers of those days. "'Cause he's a general and a leader who's called in so many directions on any given day. Getting him to focus on a rap would be supernatural in itself."

"Niggas left, when they came back they had blood all over they chest," Ralo remembers. "They both had chest wounds. And Nipsey wasn't in the same vibe that he was when he left." Ralo didn't agree with the decision, and he said something to Hussle. "That nigga got offended," Ralo says. "And I dig it now . . . I wasn't lookin' at things for what they really were. If you're not dead or in jail, then you gotta figure out how to let that decision of bein' in the gang not put you in those two places. And it's damn near impossible. The commitment that is required—to the graveyard or the penitentiary. And that's a motherfuckin' hell of a commitment, bro."[8]

"I'm single," Lauren London said with a smile. On March 28, 2013, she stopped by Hot 97 in New York wearing a Compton cap to chat with Angie Martinez and promote her new role on the BET series *The Game*, on which she premiered in March 2013. Somehow the conversation shifted to her love life.[9]

Despite describing herself as a "private person," the L.A. native had been in some high-profile relationships. She and Lil Wayne were engaged in 2007, and while they didn't get married, they maintained a strong friendship as she raised their son Kameron. During a recent interview with Trey Songz, the R&B star had told Martinez about a past relationship with London.

"I want a good guy for you," Martinez told London, who confirmed she was not in a relationship with anyone.

"Me too," Lauren agreed. "So we're gonna wait for that. The good guy with a little bit of flavor, though. 'Cause I might run all over the extra-ultra-nice one. Some strength in there."

Although she didn't mention any names that day, London may have had Hussle on her mind. While she was preparing for the first season of *The Game*, Lauren had been hanging out with Jackie Long, an actor she'd known since they both appeared in the 2006 film *ATL*. "The first time I ever even heard about Nipsey was from Lauren London," Long said in an interview. "I will never forget I went to her hotel to go over some lines, and she was like playing some music."[10]

"You know Nipsey Hussle?" London asked.

"Who is that?" Long replied.

"He from L.A.," she told him. "He a rapper . . . Ooh, I want him so bad."

"Let me see the nigga!" Long said. "So she showed me Nipsey in his tank top, all skinny and shit. I said, 'Okay! Why don't you go get him, then?'" Long was happy to hear that London had taken his advice. "I said, 'Sis got what she wanted,'" he recalled. "She said she was gonna get it, and honestly it was the most coolest thing."[11]

Long ended up meeting Hussle through another mutual friend, NFL star DeSean Jackson, who also grew up in the Crenshaw District. "Nipsey was a real cool dude," Long said. "He was always an intellectual dude. And he was always just telling you some knowledge when you seen him. It was never no bullshit . . . What I loved about him a lot, how he always carried himself. Whether in his gang attire or his business attire. He had his own moves, his own team, and everybody was just doing good."[12]

Lauren first approached Nipsey near the end of 2013 to purchase copies of *Crenshaw* as a gift for her costars on *The Game*. "She had reached out to support," Hussle recalled. "She's just like, 'I'm on set' at one of her TV shows. 'We're doin' a wrap party, and I wanna buy everybody Crenshaw stuff.'" Hussle almost gave them to her free—after all, Lauren London was a big star who'd caught his fancy the first time he saw her on-screen—but then he thought again. "Nah," he said to himself. "I'ma keep it business. Niggas probably always givin' her free shit. I'ma make sure I charge her."[13]

They laughed about it afterward. Hussle noticed that she'd started following him on Instagram and wasted no time shooting her a DM. "I was kinda aggressive after we locked in, though," he once told DJ Clue. "I wasn't tryin' to be on no friendly shit."

"Cuffin' right away?" Clue responded with a laugh.

"Yeah off the top," Nip replied.

"I ain't even mad at that."[14]

"Because we're both from L.A., we had a lot of friends in common," Lauren told *GQ*. "I had a couple of homegirls that had hung out with him and would come back to me like, 'Oh, my God! You would really like Nip! He seems like your type!'"

She picked up the box of CDs and Crenshaw merch in person. "I pulled up to his shop on Crenshaw and Slauson, and he was like, 'You want to hang out?'"[15]

On their first date she found out Hussle knew her aunt, and had arranged for them all to meet. They ended up eating at her house, then driving down the Pacific Coast Highway, listening to music and chatting. "Just kicked it on some regular low-key in the car, not havin' to be around anyone," she recalled. Sometimes they'd go to eat Ethiopian food at Merkato or London would make them tacos. "It was just . . . easy," she said. "It felt so natural for us to be in each other's lives."[16] It was that early exciting stage in a relationship when they were still getting to know each other. Lauren appreciated that he was polite, but no pushover. She noticed certain phrases kept coming up. "I'm like, 'How many times do you say "on hood"?'"[17]

Hussle appreciated her easy candor. She was an actor who moved through the world without pretense. "I like raw people," he said. "I like people that's one hundred. That's probably what I admire the most."[18]

In the wake of *Crenshaw*'s success, Hussle and his All Money In team finally had a little bit of money to work with. Labels were calling, and he took a few meetings but always made it clear that his terms were nonnegotiable. He understood how the game was played and he was only interested in a partnership based on mutual respect. Meanwhile he focused on perfecting *Victory Lap*.

With his profile rising, Hussle was starting to be respected for his opinions as well as his music. In June 2014, talk show host Larry King invited him on the air to debate the use of the N-word in hip-hop following a controversy sparked by video footage of Justin Bieber telling a racist joke. Hussle defended his own use of the word on both cultural and linguistic grounds.[19]

"Jews don't call each other 'kike,'" King pointed out. "Italian people don't call each other 'dagos.'"

"Right," Hussle replied. "And Black people don't call each other 'nigger.' They say 'nigga.'" Stating that he'd never been criticized for using the word in his lyrics, Hussle emphasized that the nature of segregation and racism had changed since his grandparents' time. "I think more than anything it's institutional now," he said. "It's not really overt. You learn about it when you go to jail or you go into a courtroom. Or when you make it to the county jail and you see the amount of Blacks and the amount of Hispanics as opposed to whites."[20]

He got a reminder of how the system worked around 11:30 p.m. on Friday, August 29, 2014. Hussle was looking forward to traveling out of town that weekend to perform at Jay-Z's Made in America Festival for the first time when police raided the family business on West Slauson. "Even though we pay taxes, everybody's on payroll, it's a completely legitimate store," Hussle said. "They still come in there and act like it's a dope spot. And come with fifteen police and kick the door down, search under T-shirts, don't find nothin'." After going through this sort of treatment over and over, Hussle lost his temper. "I was a little upset, so I just gave 'em a bar of how I felt," Hussle said, "and they booked me for some frivolous bullshit."[21]

That night a group of police from the LAPD's Seventy-Seventh Division showed up at the shopping plaza to check whether anyone in Hussle's crew was in violation of their probation. "Soon the entire party had been cuffed and detained by enough officers to field a football team," wrote *Streetsblog L.A.* "Hussle's clothing store was then searched for the next few hours." Nipsey showed no emotion whatsoever as he was escorted into a squad car, hands cuffed behind his back.[22]

Neighborhood residents saw what was going on and offered words of encouragement.

"That's bullshit!"

"Fuck 'em anyway, Nipsey!"

"Keep your head up, homeboy."

"That's okay, baby. You'll be out in a few hours."[23]

Released early on Saturday morning after posting $13,000 bail for charges of obstructing an officer, Hussle issued a defiant statement via Twitter.[24]

"I will be at my show in Reno today and also #MadeIn-AmericaFestival on Sunday #themarathoncontinues." Years later, a month or so before the release of *Victory Lap*, Hussle posted a photo of himself being arrested that night on his Instagram. "They gave it all they got and in the end they learned the devil will NEVER STOP GOD," he wrote in the caption. "We lost everything but our Honor out here . . . The Paybac deeper than Rap tho on my soul."[25]

A few weeks later Hussle flew to Atlanta one day after the BET Hip Hop Awards and stopped by DJ Drama's radio program at Means Street Studios, rocking an abundance of gold chains. Despite the success of *Crenshaw*, Hussle had not been nominated in any category and opted to skip the awards. L.A. was well represented, with DJ Mustard and Kendrick Lamar winning three and two awards respectively. And Dr. Dre was named Hustler of the Year. Best Mixtape honors went to Wiz Khalifa.[26]

Drama addressed the BET snub straight off the bat. "I gotta say this: we got robbed at the Hip Hop Awards, for *Crenshaw* not being nominated," said Drama, who hosted the tape.

"I felt that too," said Hussle, playing it cool. "I was gonna be quiet! I felt the same way."

"How does *Crenshaw* not get nominated for mixtape of the year?" Drama reiterated.

"Man, you know," Hussle replied. "It is what it is. It's opinion-based, so you know, everybody got their opinion. But I felt as far as impact, I don't think no mixtape impacted to the degree as what we did with that *Crenshaw*."[27]

Turning his attention to *Victory Lap*, Hussle downplayed any talk of pressure surrounding his debut album.

"Do you feel like you have a lot to live up to?" Drama asked. "A lot of eyes are on you."

"Majority of songs that I put on *Crenshaw* was records that I didn't feel was good enough for *Victory Lap*," Hussle said, adding that he had most of the album done before releasing the mixtape. "So nah, it's no pressure. I don't think anybody could put more pressure on me than myself and the vision I have for where I wanna be. And I say this all the time, where we started to where we at is a much further distance than where we at and where we tryin' to get."

"You're still independent?" Drama asked.

"Yup," Nip replied.

"And you get phone calls every day from all these labels," Drama said with a smile. He himself was an A&R at Atlantic. His cohost on the show, Don Cannon, held an A&R position at Def Jam.

"Yeah, man," Nip replied, poker-faced.

"I mean, what's goin' on? What you wanna do?"

"I like doin' my job first," Hussle said. "So they try to give you the check—"

"'Cause where I'm at they got a check ready for you. Where Cannon's at they got a check ready for you."

"Yeah, yeah, yeah," Nip said with a grin.

"It's a lot of checks ready for you," Drama said.

"I wanna do my job," Hussle repeated. "My job is to make the album."[28]

As soon as Drama went to the phone lines, callers from across the country dialed in for a chance to talk with Hussle. The second caller was legendary Houston rapper Scarface.

"Face, what's up?" said Drama.

"It's all good," Scarface replied, explaining that he was driving back from playing in a celebrity golf tournament. "I said let me call my nigga."

Hussle let Face know he was feeling A-1 and that he had something for him on his new album. "Y'all play my jam," Face said. "For the people that ain't really familiar with Nipsey, this little nigga go hard than a *motherfucker!*"

"Tell them niggas, man," Hussle said with a big smile, forgetting all about award show snubs.

"That's like one of the young ones that I really respect in the game, man, cause he *killin'* that shit," Scarface added, requesting a fairly obscure single called "Respect Ya Passion" produced by Bink! "Play that motherfucker right quick."

While Cannon scoured his laptop for the track, Hussle expressed his appreciation to the artist who brought new levels of psychological depth to "gangsta rap" on Geto Boys classics like "Mind Playin' Tricks on Me" as well as his solo masterpiece *The Diary*.

"We talked on the phone for some hours," Hussle said after Face hung up. "He's like, 'I wanted to call you and tell just on some rap shit, on some street shit, I salute and I respect.'"

"I feel like you get a lot of those phone calls from a lot of people," Drama said.

"I feel like we gotta carry on a tradition," Hussle replied modestly. "Just the real niggas that was entrepreneurs and lived by a code and represent good music. So that's kinda my DNA and what I'm tryin' to do."[29]

Being recognized by pioneers who inspired you early on is a special kind of soul vitamin that energizes all aspects of your life. "Comin' off *Crenshaw* I was just real confident," Hussle recalled. "It felt like I could say what I want to say. I ain't really have too much pressure on the next one."[30] While taking his time to perfect *Victory Lap*, he kept thinking about the implications of what he'd accomplished with the Proud2Pay model. As successful as it had been the first time, he wanted to try it again with even higher stakes. Instead of charging $100, Hussle decided to sell his next project for $1,000.

Even though the concept had been proven once before, Hussle's aggressive price point provoked cries of outrage. Not all of them came from the industry; some came from within the 60s. "We was having a lot of problems in our neighborhood and shit," Hussle's little homie BH said. "People was just hatin' on us. They was just trying to stop our shine because we wasn't dealing with people no more."[31] Hussle made the decision to tune everything out as much as possible. "I don't feed into doubt and negativity," he said. "The industry is changing, and it's not gonna make sense to do it any other way," he said. "This is the gold rush of our generation. This technology has empowered everybody. Giants crumble. Big companies have crumbled before."[32]

What Hussle understood before most musicians or executives was that selling albums was a thing of the past, like eight-tracks and gramophones. "Digital music is abundant," he said. "It's going against the laws of nature to charge for something that is ubiquitous. It would be like charging for air."[33]

Hussle felt another body of work taking shape, something distinct from *Victory Lap*. It was an unplanned release that took shape quickly. He decided to call it *Mailbox Money*, a term for passive income generated by an asset like real estate. "If you own publishing, you write your own records, and you ain't sold your publishing, that's mailbox money," he explained.[34] The Proud-2Pay model was a new way to access the value of that asset.

This time around, Hussle was more interested in building relationships with his core fans than he was in destroying the old ways of doing business. "The internet empowered the creators," he explained. "It hurt the monopoly, and I think that's good. I'm not saying that in a destructive way. I think it's a good thing that the people that make the art that the people love have the opportunity to distribute it to a global audience on the internet. We have access to owning what we make. That's why my project is called *Mailbox Money*. At the highest level of business, their model is equity, mailbox money."[35]

"I look at Proud2Pay like another retail outlet," Hussle explained. "You go to iTunes to buy music, traditional retail like Best Buy and Target; you go to Spotify to listen to music. If you want to release something on Google Play or at Walmart, those outlets all have price points and business models. I choose to release mine on my Proud2Pay outlet. It's just another retail platform to release it. It's about engagement. It's about people that are into collector's items. Like when someone buys a signed Michael Jordan jersey."[36]

The singer-songwriter, producer, and self-taught coder Ryan Leslie had developed an app called Disruptive Multimedia that allowed Hussle to keep in touch with every customer who spent $1,000 on his project from the moment it went on sale December 31, 2014. "Just your fans that really fuck with you and really believe in you," Hussle said. "You give them priority. They your base. These Proud2Pay, these are my real ones. This who I do it for."[37] With the help of Leslie's app, he was strengthening those relationships, and the database of diehard Nipsey Hussle fans was growing every day.

On February 23, 2015—not quite two months after *Mailbox Money* went on sale—Hussle and Cobby walked out of LAX rolling suitcases with a large cardboard box perched on top. A TMZ cameraman named Joe approached them on the sidewalk and Hussle slipped off his Beats By Dre headphones to speak with him. "You're selling physical copies of the new album for a thousand dollars apiece," said Joe the TMZ guy.[38]

"Yeah," Hussle replied.

"You only made a hundred copies," Joe TMZ continued.

"Yeah," said Hussle.

"Are people buying it?" Joe asked, "I mean, a thousand dollars is a lot!"

"Yeah," Hussle replied. "We sold like a little bit more than sixty of 'em so far.

"Wow!" Joe said. "So you got forty left? Are you gonna keep some for yourself like a collector's item?"

"Nah," Hussle said. Then he reconsidered. "I mean, I might keep one."

Joe could feel him warming up. "With art like this," he said, "you've created a piece of art that's going to exist forever."

"Right," Hussle said.

"They tend to go up in price," said Joe. "Do you think like a hundred years from now, they're going to potentially be valued like a Picasso?"

"All right, look," Hussle said. "You gotta look at shit like this. This how you determine value—scarcity, abundance." Gesturing with his left and right hands, Hussle illustrated the economic principles of supply and demand. "The less of something it is, the more it's worth. The more of something it is, the less it's worth. That's why diamonds cost money."

"I think it's genius marketing," said Joe.

"Thank you," Nipsey replied.

"I want one," said Joe, "but I can't afford it on TMZ budget. I'm ballin' on a budget."

Nipsey cracked a smile, raised his index finger, and stepped away saying, "Hold up." Walking over to Cobby, he picked up the cardboard box perched on top of his luggage and cracked open the packing tape. Inside the unassuming box was $100,000 worth of CDs.

Hussle pulled one jewel case out of the box and brought it back to the TMZ guy.

"You're kidding me!" Joe said. "You're giving me a thousand dollars!"

"I ain't given nobody *none*! It's the first one goin' out. That's for you!"

"Are you serious?"

"Fa sho'," said Hussle. "Get outta here."

The TMZ guy began giving an acceptance speech like he'd just received an award. "I'd like to thank my mom for raising a good kid."

Suddenly Hussle grabbed the camera from him and turned it around. "Neighborhood!" he yelled.

"This is a really good album," Joe said as Hussle zoomed in on the CD. "And I'd like to thank Mr. Hussle. Thank you, sir. I really appreciate that."

"Neighborhood!" Nip yelled, triumphant. "We out here!"[39]

Chapter 9

FDT

THIS REAL, THIS AIN'T RAP,

WHERE EVERYBODY WANNA ACT PRO-BLACK

THE LAST LIE YOU HEARD, THIS AIN'T THAT

—Nipsey Hussle ft. YG, "Last Time That I Checc'd," *Victory Lap* (2018)

During the early morning hours of Friday, June 12, 2015, YG was in Studio City wrapping up a recording session on his sophomore album, *Still Brazy*, when "a little incident" took place. His account of what happened can be heard on the second verse of "Twist My Fingaz," a song he recorded soon afterward.

"Got two motherfuckers wanna fight me outside," he chants (in the cadence of Malcolm McLaren's 1982 classic "Buffalo Gals") over a Mustard track so funky you might forget how serious the subject matter is. "Do your dance, YG, do your dance," the hook repeats over and over, then he gets down to the play-by-play. "I tried to pop first," he spits, "got popped back, got hit in the hip couldn't pop back."

Less than two weeks later he told a writer from *Billboard* that he was "hard to kill," explaining that the bullet that hit him "went in, went out, and went back in again," leaving three wounds. "I can't die," he told his team, who rushed him to a hospital, crashing their car on the way. After changing vehicles, they finally made it to the ER.[1] Fortunately, the slug missed his femoral artery and doctors wasted no time patching him up. After a quick interview with police—who described him as "very uncooperative"[2] —YG was able to check out of the hospital that same night.[3] (He wasn't any more forthcoming when recounting the shooting to *Billboard*: "It was not gang-related at all," he stated. "It just happened out of the blue. We don't know who did it, we don't know why. We don't know nothing.") The very next day he was right back at the studio on crutches, and Nip stopped by to make sure his homie was good. "I got shit to do," YG told *Billboard*. "This shit don't stop for nobody."[4]

As Brazy as that situation was, something altogether more bonkers was about to take place three thousand miles to the east at 721 Fifth Avenue in Manhattan, an event that would have a far greater impact on the entire world. Four days after YG's shooting, Donald J. Trump glided down the golden escalator of his fifty-eight-story skyscraper (whose height he exaggerates to appear ten floors taller)[5] to announce his candidacy for president of the United States.

"The Music of the Night," a creepy song from the Broadway musical *Phantom of the Opera*, played over and over in Trump Tower before the candidate's arrival. "Close your eyes, for your eyes will only tell the truth," the Phantom sang. "And the truth isn't what you want to see."[6] When Donald and Melania appeared at the golden escalator, the raucous sounds of Neil Young's "Rockin' in the Free World" rang in a different mood.[7] The Canadian singer-songwriter spoke out against Trump using his music, but his complaints were ignored until 2020 when Neil Young sued Trump in federal court for copyright infringement.[8]

Greeted onstage by his daughter Ivanka, Trump stood before a gaggle of media, curious bystanders, and actors who'd answered a casting call, earning fifty dollars cash to wear MAKE AMERICA GREAT AGAIN T-shirts and hold up signs of support. Then he uttered the first lie of his campaign. "Wow! Whoa! That is some group of people—*thousands*!"⁹

According to reporters who covered the event, there were maybe one hundred people in attendance to witness the billionaire trust fund heir and star of the NBC reality show *The Apprentice* kick off his run to become the forty-fifth president of the United States. From the start Donald Trump built his campaign on a bedrock of racist rhetoric. "When Mexico sends its people, they're not sending their best," he said that day, straying from the official talking points distributed by his staff, and presumably speaking from the heart. "They're bringing drugs, they're bringing crime, they're rapists. And some, I assume, are good people."¹⁰

The candidate's ignorant, divisive remarks were picked up all over the media, leading the Univision network to scrap a $13.5 million agreement to broadcast the Spanish-language version of Trump's Miss USA and Miss Universe pageants in protest.¹¹ His derogatory views should have come as no surprise. Trump had a well-documented record of racism dating back more than half a century.

In 1973 the U.S. Department of Justice sued Trump Management Inc. for refusing to rent apartments to Black tenants.¹² In 1989 Trump bought newspaper ads calling for the death penalty for the Central Park Five, teenagers of color who were falsely accused of rape and spent years in prison before being exonerated by DNA evidence. Even after their names were cleared Trump refused to apologize for stirring up what amounted to a media lynch mob.¹³ In 1991 one of Trump's top employees wrote a book quoting him as saying that "laziness is a trait in Blacks." During President Barack Obama's first term, Trump pushed the "birther" theory that America's first Black president was actually born in Kenya, making him ineligible for the office. When Obama finally released his birth certificate to refute the rumormongers, he referred to Trump as a "carnival barker."[14] The real estate developer and reality show star was now seeking to replace Obama as leader of the free world.

Although he was never before taken seriously, Trump had indulged his political ambitions as far back as 1988, seeking the nomination of the Reform Party in 1999.[15] After two terms of President Obama, perhaps he believed there were enough outraged white Americans out there that the country was ready for President Trump.

The mood on the streets of America was tense. During the summer of 2014 police officers asphyxiated Eric Garner on a sidewalk in Staten Island. Not even a month later the fatal shooting of Michael Brown in Ferguson, Missouri, led to two weeks of clashes between community activists and paramilitary police. That summer saw the rise of a nationwide Black Lives Matter movement, born in the aftermath of Trayvon Martin's killing by George Zimmerman. Black Lives Matter went on to rally support for residents of Staten Island, Ferguson, and anywhere state-sponsored violence threatened the safety of African Americans.[16]

Two months before Trump threw his hat into the ring, Freddie Gray died in the custody of the Baltimore Police Department, touching off several days of protests. Maryland governor Larry Hogan declared a state of emergency and deployed the National Guard. None of the officers charged for Gray's death were convicted.[17]

One day after Trump announced his bid for president, twenty-one-year-old unemployed ninth-grade dropout and avowed white supremacist Dylann Roof entered the Emanuel African Methodist Episcopal Church in Charleston, South Carolina—also known as Mother Emanuel—during evening Bible study and murdered nine Black parishioners with a handgun. He was apprehended peacefully the following day and confessed to the mass murder, revealing that the people in the church were so nice to him that he'd almost spared their lives. Prior to the bloody rampage, Roof had complained to a friend about the Freddie Gray protests and said that "Blacks were taking over the world." He is currently awaiting execution in a penitentiary in Terre Haute, Indiana. In January 2020, attorneys appealing his death sentence stated that Roof "believed his prison sentence was irrelevant because he would be freed after a coming race war."[18]

A couple of weeks after Trump started to take America on a long escalator ride down, Kendrick Lamar performed "Alright" live at the BET Awards. "Alls my life I has ta *fight*, nigga," the mighty MC roared, spitting truth from atop a graffiti-tagged prop police car, surrounded by explosions and flames, as a giant American flag waved behind him. Even after all the hard times, the bad trips, and the generally fucked-up state of affairs, Kendrick's song still found reason for hope. "If God got us," he declared, "then we gon' be alright."[19]

With lyrics like "And we hate po-po / Wanna kill us dead in the street fo' sho'," the song would soon be adopted as the unofficial Black Lives Matter theme song. Lamar's nationally televised performance of "Alright" struck a chord with his fans while striking a nerve with conservative culture warriors. Fox News commentator Geraldo Rivera blew a gasket the next day, declaring that "hip-hop has done more damage to young African Americans than racism in recent years."[20]

Expressing disbelief that Rivera and Fox could "take a song that's about hope and turn it into hatred," Lamar pointed out that the real problem wasn't him standing on a police car. That was a potent image, to be sure, one that was echoed in the song's music video. But the real problem wasn't defiance of police authority; it was "the senseless acts of killing these young boys out here." As a hip-hop artist, Kendrick felt a responsibility to speak on such outrages. "Yeah, we're angry about what's going on," he said. "But you can't take away our hope that things will be okay at the end of the day."[21]

Like every other rapper in Los Angeles, Nipsey Hussle was paying close attention to Kendrick at that moment. "You know we all conscious of each other's movements on the west," he told me a few years later. "What was dope about Kendrick to me is that he became such a commercial success but never really made commercial product, in intention. [His music] became consumable on the highest level, but I always respect when people find that balance."[22]

Although he initially signed a deal with Young Jeezy, YG had a self-made mindset similar to Nipsey's." "I'm the only one who made it out the west without Dre," he declared on "Twist My Fingaz." He went on to build his own 4Hunnid brand, and negotiated his own label deal for the release of *Still Brazy*. "Nip, we talked about a lot of family stuff, business stuff, life goals, brand goals," YG said.[23] Hussle shared insights gained from his reading, giving him a copy of *The 22 Immutable Laws of Branding*. Having survived such a close call, YG understood the value of building something that would live on after him. "You ain't gonna be here forever," he said. "So while you're here you wanna create something outside of your music that's gonna be able to take care of your family." YG considered Hussle more than a friend. "He ended up bein' like a big brother to me."[24]

The feeling was mutual. "YG represent a lot of things I represent," Hussle said. "He important not only to the city but to hip-hop. I got a certain respect and understanding with anybody that come from L.A. and the street culture of L.A. I feel like I understand you a little better."[25]

After dropping a number of successful records together, it was only natural for Hussle and YG to embark upon a collaborative project. They decided to call it *2 of Amerikkkaz Most Wanted*, inspired by the classic Snoop and 2Pac collab from *All Eyez on Me*. The hook on that song said, "Ain't nothin' but a gangsta party." But once these two locked in, their thing turned into a whole different kind of party.[26]

🏁🏁

WE THE YOUTH

WE THE PEOPLE OF THIS COUNTRY

WE GOT A VOICE TOO

—YG ft. Nipsey Hussle, "FDT," *Still Brazy* (2016)

On the last day of Black History Month, February 29, 2016, Donald Trump threw a campaign rally at Valdosta State University, located deep in southern Georgia, close to the Florida state line. Although the student body is now more than 34 percent Black, the school's website explains that "prior to 1963, the African American presence at Valdosta State was limited to staff in cleaning, cooking, and maintenance positions."[27]

A group of thirty Black Valdosta State students decided to attend the Trump rally that day, all of them dressed in black as a form of "silent protest." Earlier that week Trump had been endorsed by former KKK grand wizard David Duke,[28] and the students were understandably curious to hear what Trump would be saying on their campus. But they didn't get the chance. Before Trump began speaking, security guards asked them to leave the auditorium.[29]

"We didn't plan to do anything," said Tahjila Davis, then a nineteen-year-old Valdosta State student majoring in mass media. "They said, 'This is Trump's property, it's a private event.' But I paid my tuition to be here." Brooke Gladney, another Black student who was asked to leave, said, "The only reason we were given was that Mr. Trump did not want us there."[30]

Cell phone footage of the distraught Black students being escorted out of the Trump rally circulated on social media, along with reports that another group of Black students had been ejected from an earlier Trump rally in Virginia that same day.[31] Campaign mouthpiece Hope Hicks denied allegations of racial bias. "There is no truth to this whatsoever," she claimed. "The campaign had no knowledge of this incident."[32] Her statement was contradicted by Valdosta police chief Brian Childress, who checked with the campaign staff and confirmed that they requested the students to be removed from the event. "I'm not campaigning for anyone," the police chief said. "That's not what I do. But in this case I support [the Trump campaign]." Chief Childress also issued an official statement on the students' ejection: "To suggest that this incident was racially motivated is unfair and simply not factual."[33]

Tahjila Davis saw things very differently. "I think we got kicked out because we're a group of Black people," she said in a televised interview, wiping tears from her eyes. "I guess they're afraid we're gonna say something and do something, but we just really wanted to watch the rally. And to get kicked out because we're a group of Black people is really crazy. It shows you how racist our own school is."[34]

How could a candidate endorsed by the KKK get away with calling himself "the least racist person there is anywhere in the world"?[35] Part of the explanation was that the media did not take Trump seriously until it was too late, playing his presidential run for entertainment value and big ratings. By 2016, many young people were getting their news from comedy programs like Jon Stewart's *The Daily Show*. From Stewart's perspective, the Trump campaign was a gift from heaven—the jokes just wrote themselves. "I'm just really happy right now," Stewart said on the day of Trump's golden escalator ride. "A billionaire vanity candidate taking the escalator to the White House? Hey, only losers walk!"[36]

Another explanation for Trump's ability to fly under the radar for so long despite his racist track record was that hip-hop moguls were infatuated with the billionaire playboy whose name had been branded as a signifier of success. For many years Trump used to hang out with Puff Daddy and Russell Simmons at opulent rap functions.[37] Back in 2005 he stopped by 50 Cent's *G-Unit Radio* show to chat with DJ Whoo Kid and Tony Yayo. Donald said Ivanka was a big 50 Cent fan and Curtis Jackson himself soon called in to chat. "Let's do a song," Trump told 50. "Write up some good lyrics." Yayo and Whoo Kid laughingly suggested they could call the track "You're Fired." Trump was proud of his hip-hop clout. Mac Miller, Jeezy, Smif-N-Wessun, and Rae Sremmurd all released songs name-checking Trump in the title. "I'm in more of these rap songs," he bragged. "My daughter calls me up, she said, 'Dad, you're in another one!' "[38]

To Mac's credit, he was also one of the first hip-hop artists to denounce Trump's political career. In December 2015 he sensed that the joke had gone too far and tweeted, "Just please don't elect this motherfucker man." The late MC also appeared on Comedy Central's *Nightly Show* in March 2016 to emphasize his point. "I fuckin' hate you, Donald Trump," Miller said. "You say you wanna make America great again? We all know what that really means—ban Muslims, Mexicans are rapists, Black lives don't matter. Make American great again? I think you want to make America *white* again."[39]

Russell Simmons soon withdrew support for his "old friend," publicly backing Hillary Clinton before the election, as did Pusha T.[40, 41] Meanwhile, Killer Mike aligned himself with Bernie Sanders[42] as Kanye West began flirting with Donald Trump while struggling with mental health issues[43]—he would eventually rock the red MAGA cap on TV and on stage.[44] Azealia Banks also threw her support behind the Donald. "I think Trump is the only one who truly has the balls to bust up big business," Banks wrote on Twitter. "Donald Trump is evil like America is evil," she added. "I only trust this country to be what it is: full of shit. Takes shit to know shit so we may as well put a piece of shit in the White House."[45]

When Obama was running for president in 2008, the unified power of hip-hop helped lift him to victory. Endorsements by rappers from Jay-Z and Jeezy to Common and Will.I.Am—not to mention two cover stories in *Vibe* magazine—helped to mobilize record turnout among a coalition of young voters from various cultures, ethnic groups, and economic backgrounds.[46] Eight years later, America was faced with the most openly racist candidate in modern history, but the popular resistance was in disarray. Somebody needed to step up, harness the awesome power of hip-hop, and speak with a clear voice, calling Trump out on his bullshit.

YG and Hussle were locking in to start work on their collaborative album as outrage against Trump was reaching a fever pitch. "Everywhere I went, everybody's findin' out all the real shit about him," YG recalled. He and Nip were always talking about using their platform to make a bold statement about real issues. As YG put it, they aspired to do "stuff other motherfuckers are not doing. So we finally hit the studio and really did it."[47]

"Over the last couple of years Trump's been foreshadowing that he's going to run," Nipsey said. "I thought it was a joke. I knew he was a big celebrity, but I didn't know it was possible for him to become president." Hussle noticed that the power of the Trump brand was working in his favor. "When you think about the 2016 election, all you really hear is Trump," he observed. "You know Hillary, you know Bernie, but it seems like Trump's name and voice is louder than the rest of them. So it was like, *Are we actually taking this serious?*" For Hussle, Trump was "just a privileged rich dude that got an out-of-touch view of the world. That made me like, dude is definitely out of his mind and our country sounded crazy for even taking him as a legitimate candidate."[48] "We weren't feeling him," YG said. "The world wasn't feeling him."

Having grown up in L.A., both YG and Hussle found Trump's attacks on Mexican Americans particularly offensive. "I went to Paramount High School," YG recalled. "It was probably like 95.9 percent Latino . . . All my homies grew up with Latino next-door neighbors, tryin' to talk to they sisters and shit."[49]

Hussle had always discouraged Black-on-brown (as well as Black-on-Black) conflict. "That's divide and conquer, that's Willie Lynch," he told Davey D back in 2006. "I feel like we got a common enemy, so I don't feel we got time to be beefin'."[50]

In the decade since then, Hussle had put those views into practice, bringing different hoods and cultures together within his team, including his Mexican-born business partner and road manager Jorge Peniche. "The way Trump was campaigning was really affecting my guy," said Hussle, who gained a new appreciation for the impact of Trump's rhetoric. "His situation was really in jeopardy. And watchin' on TV, we like, 'That's not right.' This dude went to college. This dude is a good person. I saw it up close and personal."[51] Fortunately, Peniche was able to work out his situation, but as the son of an immigrant himself, Hussle knew that many others were still in jeopardy.

Moreover, Hussle had a sizable Mexican fan base turning out for his concerts and supporting his movement. "I felt like they needed somebody to ride for 'em," Nip said. "Because we relate in the struggle, and poverty, and not havin' shit, and bein' incarcerated—we relate. So that message ain't something we feel neither."[52]

By the time Black people started getting thrown out of Trump rallies, YG felt they had no choice but to act. Trump was taking it too far. One day he put it to Nip: "Look, bro, if we doin' a project called *Two of AmeriKKKaz Most Wanted*, we *gotta* have a song called 'Fuck Donald Trump.'"[53]

Nip thought the idea was "tight," like a 2016 version of N.W.A's "Fuck tha Police." His exact words, as YG remembered them, were: "Cuz, on Six-Owe, I feel you! Let's do it!"

Everything unfolded quickly from that point. YG knew exactly which beat he wanted to use. When he explained the concept to DJ Swish, the producer thought it was something YG was doing for fun. "I never thought this would be popular," Swish said, "but it fits well with the times."[54]

DJ Mustard and Young Thug happened to be in the studio when the vocals were laid down. "We heard it back through the speakers and we already knew this was powerful," Hussle recalls. YG thought Nip should be the one to rap the verses. "You always talk about real shit," he said. "I be on some turnt-up burnt-out shit." But Nip challenged YG to set it off.[55]

"Nah, you rap it!" Hussle said, and YG didn't hesitate. As soon as he laid down his first verse—evoking the Rodney King riots and saying "I'm 'bout to turn Black Panther / Don't let Donald Trump win, that nigga cancer!"—everybody started looking around like, *We should lock the door and finish this.*[56]

"Me as an artist, Nip as an artist, we very straight up and down," YG said later. "It is what it is. It ain't no hidden messages when we rapping. You gon' know what the fuck we talkin' 'bout." By the final verse, YG and Nip were going back and forth, making plans to form a coalition that would disrupt Trump's campaign by uniting the same people Trump sought to divide.[57]

"Hold up, Nip, tell the world how you fuck with Mexicans," YG said, after mentioning his Mexican plug and the Mexican mechanic who fixes the hydraulics on his lowrider. "It wouldn't be the USA without Mexicans," Nip replied—a statement that cut to the heart of Trump's xenophobic attacks, and one that rang especially true in border states like California, Arizona, New Mexico, and Texas. While calling for Black love and brown pride, YG and Hussle were also demonstrating the possibility of reconciliation between red and blue.

With inspiration flowing, the record was done in less than an hour. In case anybody missed the significance of what was going on, YG closed out the song with a promise to pay Trump a visit. "When your L.A. rally? We gon' crash your shit!" As soon as they knocked out the vocals, YG turned to Nip. "I'm like, 'Ay, bro . . . you ready?'"

"What you talkin' 'bout?" Nip replied.

"You ready for what might come with this?" he said, on a serious note. "Like, niggas gonna get banned from shows. All the police, all them people, gonna be on us."[58]

"We already get backlash. We already can't do this and this and this," Nip replied. "Fuck it. Let's make it worth something."[59]

I DON'T STRESS OUT NIGGA, POKE MY CHEST OUT NIGGA

—Nipsey Hussle, "I Don't Stress," *Slauson Boy 2* (2016)

They called the song "FDT" and dropped it on March 30, 2016. Hip-hop's powerful rebuke of the presumptive Republican candidate set the internet ablaze. The final version of the track included a sound bite of Trump talking about building his "great wall" on the Mexican border (and getting Mexico to pay for it!) as well as a clip of Tahjila Davis speaking about getting thrown out of the Trump rally. "We tryna touch the people," YG told *Billboard* after the song was released. "We tryna motivate all the young people to vote. Really take your time 'cause it's important, you feel me? If not, it could be all bad for us."[60]

"FDT" represented much more than just two rappers dissing a controversial politician. A Blood and a Crip had come together to make a song repping for Mexicans—whose L.A. street culture dates back even farther than the Slausons and the Businessmen. As hard as Nip and YG went in their verses, they still made space for open-minded white folks to join the movement. If historian Mike Davis was right when he said, "I don't think there's anything the police fear more than an end to gang warfare,"[61] then "FDT" had to be their worst nightmare.

Always using his music to motivate, Hussle invested every song with a sense of purpose. With "FDT" the stakes could not have been higher. It was one thing for Snoop to clown Trump after the election, but YG and Nipsey hit the candidate with a lyrical blast when it really mattered, rallying their fans to get involved in the election. "This was when he was still campaigning," Hussle said. "So we was just really trying to make sure he didn't win."[62] All they needed now were the visuals.

On April 3, 2016, YG and Hussle met up with director Austin Simkins, aka Salty State, to plan the "FDT" video in the streets of L.A. YG and Hussle shot the first scenes together on Fairfax, then split up to do separate shoots in different locations. There was no need to organize extras. As soon as they started blasting the song a crowd formed. The helicopters and squad cars were provided courtesy of the LAPD at no additional cost.

Hussle shot his scenes a few blocks south of The Marathon Clothing store, near Crenshaw and Florence Avenue. Cars were cruising by slow to watch the action as a group of young people hollered, "Fuck Donald Trump!" Somebody called the cops, who turned up in force. Cobby Supreme sat on top of his white Impala, waving his hands in the air as his homies climbed on top of the vehicle with him, enjoying the moment. A police officer approached him, pointing a green plastic Taser gun at him. "This is my car," he told the cop, who held his fire. But the squad cars kept arriving—as did the news crews.[63]

"Fucc Donald Trump video shoot was lit!" local artist J23 posted on Instagram. "@nipseyhussle had the whole city behind him. I been fuccin wit nip for a long time so I'm glad I got to be a part of it." As things were winding down the police stepped up the pressure. "First they pulled out tasers, then pistols, then SHOTGUNS," an L.A. artist named Mosaicc posted on the Gram. "Not sure any of that was necessary, but my nigga @nipseyhussle executed like a professional." In his Instagram video, Hussle can be seen stepping in front of armed police with his hands in the air to protect extras taking part in the video. "We was all in a peaceful FUCK DONALD TRUMP mood," Mosaicc wrote. "No rioting, no fighting, we were together. I guess expressing political views with togetherness requires police to pull out shotguns."[64]

An LAPD spokesperson stated that there was no violence on the set and no arrests were made but that hundreds of people were ordered to disperse.[65] Meanwhile YG and his homies were shooting their part on the East Side, around Fifty-Sixth and Central. "Helicopters were coming at us, the SWAT team was on us." They shut down the shoot while the cameras rolled. "We like, 'What's goin' on?'" YG recalled. "It was crazy."[66]

The whole spectacle ended up on TMZ, calling further attention to the "FDT" wave. On April 13, Kobe Bryant played his final NBA game, scoring 60 points at the Staples Center as he wrapped up a twenty-year career with the Lakers. Five days later the "F.D.T." video was released on the Worldstar YouTube channel. The visuals opened with a statement from both artists, spelled out in white type on a black background, clarifying the intention behind their song.

"As young people with an interest in the future of America," Hussle and YG asserted, "we have to exercise our intelligence and CHOOSE who leads us into it wisely. 2016 will be a turning point in this country's history. . . . The question is. . . . in which direction will we go?" The statement closed by urging viewers of the video to "register ASAP and choose wisely." The gritty black-and-white video—with occasional touches of red and blue—soon began racking up millions of views. It wasn't long before the powers that be took notice.

"Secret Service hollered at the label," YG told a TMZ reporter while waiting for a security check at LAX airport. "They asked if they could see the lyrics on my album . . . 'Cause I'm talking about it on my album, they gon' try to take it off the shelf."[67] Back in 1989 N.W.A's label Ruthless Records received a letter from the FBI following the release of "Fuck tha Police." The letter did not mention any particular song by name, not did it threaten any music being censored. That FBI letter did point out that seventy-eight law enforcement officers were "feloniously slain in the line of duty during 1988 . . . and recordings such as the one from N.W.A are both discouraging and degrading to these brave, dedicated officers."[68] But YG and Hussle had attracted the notice of another branch of the federal government. The Secret Service is responsible for the president's security. And they didn't bother complaining to YG's label Def Jam; they escalated the conversation to its corporate parent, Universal Music Group.[69]

"They were basically saying we were sending death threats to a presidential candidate," YG recalled.[70] "It was freedom of speech," Hussle said. "You know, we didn't make no threats—I didn't *think* we made threats."[71]

"When I first heard about it," YG said, "I'm like, 'How they bannin' this record? You feel me? Freedom of speech—this is America!' Then I go and listen to the joint. I'm like 'Oh, okay. Nah, it's a couple lines up in there.'"[72]

After reviewing all the lyrics on *Still Brazy*, the Secret Service came back with a list of specific concerns, like the part where YG says, "I'm surprised El Chapo ain't snipe you." Then there was the verse where Hussle says, "And if your ass do win, you gon' prolly get smoked." The Secret Service demanded that these lines be removed or else they would pull the album.

"I was just like, *Damn*," said YG, who considered leaving "FDT" off *Still Brazy* altogether. "I'm a square," he joked. His A&R Steve "Steve-O" Carless, who's also one of Hussle's business partners, convinced him to keep the song on the album.

"Ever since John F. Kennedy was assassinated there's somewhere in the law that you're not allowed to cite any type of violence towards a sitting politician or an incumbent politician," Carless explained in an interview with Genius. "We had to blank the lines out because someone from one of those government agencies called to the top of Universal Music Group and was just telling us that we can't have any violent connotations toward a sitting politician or . . . candidate."[73] They agreed to blank out the lines in question to keep "FDT" on the album. "It's still explicit," said Carless, "but it's censored because they just started tripping."

The requested edits were not limited to "FDT." The Secret Service also demanded that a line from the album's thought-provoking final track, "Blacks & Browns," be edited out. During his guest verse, the Mexican American artist Sad Boy Loko's voice gets drowned out by static and the missing words are left up to the listener's imagination. In his original verse, Loko says, "We're trying to make America great / Fuck you *ése*, somebody bring him to the Treces," a reference to the multinational street gang MS13. The record picks up again with " . . . just for disrespecting."

"That was real," YG says, "Donald Trump definitely heard 'Fuck Donald Trump.'"[74]

Even in its edited form, *Rolling Stone* hailed "FDT" as the summer's "most jubilant protest anthem . . . a catchy middle-finger track."[75]

YG says he and Hussle took the Secret Service scrutiny in stride. "Ay, it is what it is," he said during a visit to *Big Boy's Neighborhood*. "This how we took it: 'Them people's on us. They havin' conversations with the label about this record—*job well done.*'"[76]

Agreeing to government censorship didn't make it any easier to get the song played on the air. "We can't get it cleared," YG told Big Boy. "Radio stations banned the joint. It's understandable, though. I know why. But it's just some real stuff behind this song."

"To keep it real with you," Big Boy told YG, "Like *nine thousand* real—we got hit." Big Boy said he wanted to give the song some spins on Real 92.3 FM, but was told not to play it.

"I'm already knowing," YG said. "But still to this day we on some 'Fuck Donald Trump'—don't get it twisted."

"That's how we all feel," Big Boy replied.[77]

Undaunted by the radio blackout, YG and Hussle doubled down by dropping a remix of "FDT" featuring G-Eazy and Macklemore, spreading the message to fans of the clean-cut white rappers. (The original version remained far more popular on YouTube.) While Hussle and Boog stayed close to home awaiting the birth of their son, YG hit the road in the summer of 2016 for a nationwide Fuck Donald Trump Tour, pledging to donate a dollar from each ticket to victims of police brutality. He didn't want to be accused of trying to milk "FDT" as some sort of marketing gimmick. "Nah," he said. "I'm really out here for the people."[78]

YG was used to dealing with pushback from concert promoters concerned about his gang ties, but after "FDT" the pressure increased. "There's things we've done a long time ago or stuff that happened around us, but we were still able to do shows," he said. "Now, I don't know what happened, but one day they just started trippin'. My shows started getting canceled and I didn't do anything wrong."[79] Still, he made sure every "FDT" tour stop was lots of fun, celebrating Mexican culture by inviting fans onstage to smash a Trump piñata.[80]

When one reporter asked YG if he was actively pro-Hillary, he replied, "I ain't pro-nobody. I'm just pro–'Fuck Trump.'"[81] Inspiring young voters to say "FDT" would prove easier than inspiring them to register, vote, and support his opponent.

In between the Chicago and Minneapolis gigs, with another month still to go on YG's "FDT" tour, Trump won the presidency—despite Hillary Clinton earning almost three million more votes. Like George W. Bush before him, Trump had lost the popular vote but still won thanks to the murky mathematics of the Electoral College.

Hussle was shocked when he heard the results. "I be so busy working that I catch it as it's unfolding," he recalled. "They're like, 'The polls lookin' like he's gonna win,' and I'm like, 'He ain't finna win.'"[82]

Hussle's business associate, the marketing maven Karen Civil, had been working with the Clinton campaign. "She had the celebration set up for Hillary," Nipsey said. Like many observers, Hussle assumed Hillary had it in the bag. "When they said Trump won, I was in shock," he said. "Almost how I felt when Obama won, but at the opposite end of the spectrum."[83]

YG took the loss even harder. "It's not our land," he said. "It's not made for us." After all he and Hussle had put on the line, it hurt to see Trump win. "It's America, that's how it was designed," YG added. "We came here as slaves. It wasn't designed for us to win." Still, he felt good for speaking his mind. "That's what rap is made for," he said. "Too many rappers keep saying shit with no substance."[84]

As the shock of Trump's victory wore off, YG focused on "knowing my rights, chasing my dreams, and taking care of people." The "FDT" experience had a profound effect on him. "I'm on that positive [stuff] now," he said. "We're playing for keeps, for survival. We've got to play chess, we can't be playing checkers. We have to motivate, but we've also got to make our own moves and fight out there to keep our heads above water. What else can we do?"[85]

If there was any silver lining to Trump's win, Hussle appreciated a certain "era of honesty" that came with his election. At least there was no pretense of fairness. "He's not even hiding it," Hussle said. "His shit is coming out and he's sayin' *Fuck it.*"[86] And by the same token, that blatant racism motivated YG to push for them to make the bold statement they made.

Even after wrapping up the Fuck Donald Trump Tour, YG was not finished repping for the cause. In March 2017—three months into the Trump administration and a full year after the release of "FDT"—he was booked to perform at San Diego State University for a $60,000 fee. The promoter requested that YG not perform the controversial song, which had become a fixture in his live concerts. He went ahead and did the song anyway. According to the school paper, he still got paid.

As the Trump administration settled in, lying about the size of the crowd at his inauguration, detaining children at the U.S.-Mexico border, instituting a travel ban against primarily Muslim countries, "FDT" gained new resonance. "When he won, the song became that much more meaningful," Hussle observed. Global outrage over Trump's policies spread, inspiring Hussle to tweet, "A wall won't erase hate, only increase it. And a ban won't protect us, only divide us. These protests are proof hate can never drown love."[87]

Although "FDT" wasn't getting much support from mainstream radio programmers, enterprising hackers found a way to get the record played by any means necessary. In January 2017, regularly scheduled programming on WFBS FM in Salem, South Carolina, was interrupted for fifteen minutes while "an anti-Donald Trump rap song that contained obscene language" played on a loop, according to the Associated Press.[88] Similar incidents were reported on radio stations in Seattle, Louisville, and San Angelo, Texas. The song's music video was hacked onto a cable broadcast in Mooresville, North Carolina. Hussle posted news accounts of the guerrilla support for "FDT" on his social media, noting that a regional Mexican channel in Nashville and a Catholic programming station in Illinois were also targeted. Hackers exploited a security weakness in low-power FM transmitters. According to reports, some stations opted to shut down rather than get in trouble for airing the anti-Trump song. The South Carolina station identified the IP address of the suspected hackers, who were reported to the Federal Communications Commission. Addressing the incident in a Facebook post, WFBS stated, "If [the hackers] do not like President Trump, then get a sign and stand on a street corner."[89]

In some ways, the trajectory of "FDT" mirrored Hussle's own, thriving on fervent grassroots fans rather than mainstream support. The song has become a protest anthem alongside N.W.A's "Fuck tha Police"—and remains so even in the George Floyd era. Hussle's friend O.T. Genasis used the song for an Instagram post of him Crip Walking in front of the White House.[90] But mainstream radio stubbornly refused to play it.

In September 2017 Jorge Peniche showed Hussle video footage of the song playing at a rally in the streets and Hussle's frustration boiled over. "All you muthafuckin' radio stations, all y'all niggas is hos," he stated in a video post, tagging New York's Hot 97, Power 106 in L.A., and Hot 107.9 in Atlanta. "Y'all scared to play 'Fuck Donald Trump.' Y'all niggas supposed to stand up . . . Play that record, make that muthafucka the anthem. We did our job as artists. Y'all ain't doing your job as DJs and radio stations . . . Wha's y'all stance? Y'all not supposed to rep on Twitter, USE YO PLATFORM."[91]

The following day Hussle called in to Power 106 and spoke to J Cruz, the host of *The Cruz Show*, on which he'd appeared as a guest many times. "We gotta be radical sometimes," Hussle said. "All of us." During the interview he pointed out that he'd never complained about lack of support for his own records, but that he considered "FDT" an issue bigger than his own career. "It's something we stood out on a limb for."[92] Two months later Hussle would announce his Atlantic partnership, paving the way for the rollout of his major label debut. But at this moment, music industry politics were the farthest thing from his mind.

Taking a stand against Trump was more aligned with Hussle's values and principles than with his personal interests. "Truthfully, if a rapper that's been successful didn't care about his people it would make sense to get Trump into office," he said. "Because for a person who makes legitimate income, it would probably mean paying less taxes if Trump was president. It would probably be financially better for people like YG and myself."

Other rappers made their own calculations. Eminem dissing Trump in a BET Hip Hop Awards "freestyle" generated a lot of buzz for his comeback album *Revival*, which dropped two months later.[93] But he was silent when it could have made a difference in the election. Slim Shady has "Stans" all over the country. Who knows how many may have sat the election out—or secretly voted to make America "great" again? Hillary Clinton lost Marshall Mathers's home state of Michigan by just 0.3 percent in 2016—the slimmest margin of any state in the 2016 election.[94] Clinton sure could have used those sixteen electoral votes.

Shortly after the election, Kanye West expressed support for Trump while onstage during his Saint Pablo Tour. "I told y'all I didn't vote, right?" Yeezy told a crowd in San Jose. "But if I would've voted, I would've voted for Trump." The crowd booed and threw stuff at Kanye's levitating stage as West encouraged his fans to "stop focusing on racism . . . This world is racist, okay?"[95]

Kanye's ongoing support for Trump—the photo ops, the rambling monologues, the MAGA hat—would continue to confound faithful hip-hop fans, including Hussle. "I really am a fan of Ye's music," he said during a chat with Nessa Diab, one of the most politically aware personalities at Hot 97. "I really do think Ye is important to hip-hop. I just don't agree with that part of his convo."[96]

"The comments on TMZ were very hurtful," Nessa replied, referring to West's suggestion that four hundred years of slavery "sounds like a choice." Hussle agreed that he too was disappointed.

"One thing I know about us as hip-hop, we defend our own," Nip replied. "We don't let you talk bad about our artists. Man, you be on trial for murder, we gon' ride with you . . . So when somebody that you probably defended in the past, and rode with, does some shit like that, you like, 'Damn . . . That one I can't ride with. I can't defend *that* one, bro.'"[97]

The sole redeeming aspect of Yeezy's bizarre bromance with President Trump *might* be that it enabled his wife to secure a presidential pardon for Alice Marie Johnson, a former FedEx employee who served twenty-one years of a life sentence for her part in a cocaine smuggling ring.[98] Even still, West's support of such a dangerous and divisive public figure remains pretty much indefensible—especially from an artist who once excoriated a U.S. president on live television, saying "George Bush doesn't care about Black people" in the wake of Hurricane Katrina.

"Honestly, this is the truth," Hussle told Nessa during their convo. "Ye trollin' with that hat. We know that. He trollin' for some type of reaction." Raised to cherish certain morals and principles, Hussle could not relate to such a reckless bid for recognition. "I ain't even part of that culture," he said. "I grew up more offa like, respect, than just doing things because people pay attention to you. But that's the era we're in now."[99]

Growing up with real loved ones in his circle, Hussle knew he could expect a reality check if he ever got out of pocket. "Me personally, I gotta go back to a real place," he said. "I be in Hollywood, I be in this funny-style-ass music industry . . . no matter how goofy and weird the shit get, I can't make no move that my ground zero is gonna not respect. 'Cause I'm liable to them, still."[100]

It's possible that Kanye West is no longer liable to the kind of day-one "loved ones" who will keep it real with him when he needs it most. His bewildering behavior—up to and including plans to run against Trump for president in 2020—would suggest as much. But if nobody else in hip-hop was willing to check him, at least he could count on Nipsey Hussle to keep it one hundred with him. If Ye insisted on trolling the world with the MAGA hat, then Nip was ready and willing to return the favor and "troll the guy that's trollin'."

On April 28, 2018, Hussle was booked at Broccoli Fest in Washington, DC, performing for a crowd 33,000 strong. While he was in the nation's capital, it seemed only right to close his set with "FDT." Even two years after its release, the song always got a good crowd response, "whether it was Black, white, Asian, or anything in between," said DJ V.I.P., Hussle's official tour DJ. "People of our generation haven't seen any benefits of that, as far as Trump goes. So everyone was turned up, having a good time wherever we performed it." Fifteen minutes before Hussle made his way to the stage, his team noticed a photo of Kanye with the red MAGA hat trending on social media. "We changed up our visuals for that performance on a whim," V.I.P. recalls. "It was something that we were all joking about . . . and we ended up throwing it up on the screen." The crowd at Broccoli Fest booed the picture loudly.[101]

"We let the people react to seeing the hip-hop icon that Ye is represent somebody who is completely opposite of what hip-hop stands for," Hussle explained. "I don't do the subliminal. I'm not finna halfway diss you. I just thought that the picture had a lot of conversation around it. The White House is around the corner. I was gonna perform 'Fuck Donald Trump.' I wanted to create a moment."[102] Hussle posted a shot of the stage to capture said moment on his Instagram with the caption "Performed #FDT in Washington D.C. Picture Speaking A Thousand Words."

Whether the subject was Kanye supporting Trump or radio stations failing to support "FDT," Hussle had higher aims than maximizing his industry clout. "I think all of us as hip-hop artists, we gotta be liable," he told Nessa, whose partner Colin Kaepernick knows all about sacrificing career goals on principle. "Even if you don't come from the hood, or you're not from no block, or you're not from no area where there was standards. You a part of hip-hop. Hip-hop got a standard. And you gotta hold yourself to that standard or else you gonna be ostracized. And if you don't check yourself you might be revoked."[103]

Chapter 10

VICTORY LAP

THIRTY-TWO EXTENDOS IN MY MAC, NIGGA

SPEND A THOUSAND ON SOME T-SHIRTS UP AT SAKS, NIGGA

—Nipsey Hussle, "Rap Niggas," *Victory Lap* (2018)

A fter the success of *Crenshaw*, Hussle's phone was ringing off the hook. One of the meetings he took around that time was with 300 Entertainment, a new record label founded by veteran music executives Lyor Cohen and Todd Moscowitz.

"What's wrong with the record industry is the good records," Cohen told him. "It's easy to tell a garbage record. It's easy to tell a great record. You know them right away. But the good records are confusing." The "good records" were the ones that clogged up the pipeline, getting in the way of greatness. Hussle applied that principle to his earliest rough draft of *Victory Lap*. "I had a twenty-two-song playlist at first," Hussle said. Listening with Cohen's advice in mind, he decided he had only nine truly *great* songs. So he slimmed the playlist down and kept recording with the aim of creating more great songs. "That's the next move," Hussle declared with absolute certainty during an appearance on the *Sway in the Morning* show back in 2013. "It's gonna be *Victory*

Lap. The first single is called 'Rap Niggas' and it's coming top of next year."[1]

Hussle was right about one thing—"Rap Niggas" would be the first single from *Victory Lap.* There was never any question in his mind about that. But it would not be coming top of next year—or the year after that. In fact, "Rap Niggas" didn't come out until December 1, 2017. What happened during those four years is a story of dedication, perseverance, tragedy, and the triumph of willpower and creativity against seemingly insurmountable odds. In other words, the story of Nipsey Hussle's life.

"Nip always wanted 'Rap Niggas' to be his first single," said Rance of 1500 or Nothin', who updated the track repeatedly over a four-year period. "This is how I'm about to disrupt the whole music business," Hussle would say. "And let everybody know what time it is. And then after that I'ma get their attention and I'ma reel 'em into the real knowledge that everybody needs to know."[2]

"It ain't even a traditional single," Hussle admitted. "It's not for radio, but it need to be said. It's in context. It's everything that's goin' on. It's everything I represent right now."[3] What Hussle needed—more than having a hit single on the radio, more than being famous—was simply to say this: "I ain't nothin' like you fuckin' rap niggas."

"Rap Niggas" gets to the heart of the "gangsta rap" dilemma. As Black Sheep once put it, the choice is yours: "You can get with this, or you can get with that." Are you a rapper or a gangster? Is it even possible to be both? And why do people who are one try so hard to be the other?

The term "gangsta rap" is a straw man created by the mass media as a way of ostracizing rap as an art form when that still seemed possible, before hip-hop became the world's dominant mode of pop culture. Mostly used by people who don't actually listen to hip-hop, "gangsta rap" is a useful crutch for reporters who specialize in oversimplifying complex stories and repeating police talking points verbatim. Critics of "gangsta rap"—whatever the term actually means—make sure to overlook all the nuances.

When Hussle said, "I ain't nothin' like you fuckin' rap niggas," he asserted that he was really "about that life" in a way most MCs could never be. "Did niggas laugh at you in the beginning?" Snoop once asked Hussle as they discussed the unique challenges faced by artists who grew up in gang culture. Informing your homies in the set that you're about to become a rapper can be a delicate business. "I didn't even tell people at first," Hussle said. "Until I had good music that I believed in, I wouldn't even tell people that I rap. I felt like being in the streets, rapping is like outcasting yourself. Calling yourself a rapper, that's damn near like you retire. Like you ain't with this no more."[4]

"Like you done with the hood," Snoop said with a knowing smile. "You've found other things that are a little bit more relaxing, like golfing and rapping."

"Exactly!" Hussle replied. "You know, so I had to turn it up extra sometime, just to show, like, I'm not on no rap shit."[5] Then again, as Tupac once asked, "Is Frank Sinatra a gangsta singer?" He certainly knew a lot of mobsters, but he didn't sing about Sam Giancana. By the same token hip-hop is filled with studio gangsters who "wouldn't bust a grape in a fruit fight," as Jay-Z so memorably put it in "99 Problems."

Even before Hussle's *Marathon* series, his earliest raps offered an informed critique of gangster life, talking about problems and solutions from a firsthand perspective to help fuel constructive debate. "I got a lot of concepts and titles that revolve around the state of this violent world we live in," Hussle said during the *Bullets Ain't Got No Name* era. "One second I have this standpoint, but then on the next record I might take a different standpoint and speak on this topic from the perspective of intelligence, of somebody that wants to change this problem, somebody that wants to resolve the conflict."[6]

Songs like "Hussle in the House" are written from the position of "somebody that's actively involved." A song like "Hussla Hoodsta" speaks for somebody who feels trapped. "Granny, they still shootin'," he rapped. "I can't get no sleep / And it's too late to change 'cause I'm in too deep."

Rather than stirring up controversy for its own sake or getting caught up in media debates about music and morality, Hussle tried to show a bigger picture to people caught up in the gang lifestyle, as well as those who would judge them wrongfully. "A lot of my homeboys, including myself, at a certain point felt like there was no options left," he said. "Like, it wasn't no other decisions to be made than the ones we made as far as gangbanging, as far as being in the streets, bringing violence to other niggas that got the same color skin as you, that come from similar struggles as you."[7]

As the name of Big U's gang-prevention organization suggested, the solution was developing options. "Give a nigga another option," Hussle said. "Like open up the studio and give niggas some access, or lower the prices on cameras and make 'em available to niggas like us. Ninety percent of the time they gonna fall back and do that."[8] When Hussle drew a line in the sand distinguishing himself from "Rap Niggas," he wasn't making a distinction based on being more "gangsta" than another artist. He was speaking about his intention.

Decades of sensational media coverage around "gangsta rap," including some straight-up propaganda, spread misinformation. "The number-one misconception is that everybody in a gang is a mindless killer," said Hussle, "just an ignorant, self-hating nigga with an Uzi running around killing motherfuckers all day. I'm not gonna sit here defending what's wrong. Killing and gangbanging, that's just wrong. But at the same time, so is the way that adolescent teenagers get done in these courtrooms, based on, 'Oh, he's a gang member,' so he gets a trial like a terrorist."[9]

Hussle's most urgent message was that the current generation of gang culture in L.A. is the effect, not the cause. "We didn't wake up and create our own mind state and our environment," Hussle said. "We adapted our survival instincts. We don't want our mamas dressed in black standing over our caskets. And having to be a burden on our folks, calling collect and getting mad 'cause motherfuckers ain't writing you or visiting you and all that. That's not the lifestyle anybody want for theyself, but that's the results of the lifestyle we live."[10] For Hussle redemption was the real mission.

Mention the title *Victory Lap* to most rap fans and a particular image comes to mind: Nipsey Hussle leaning way back in his Maybach with the ceiling missing and one finger in the air as if conducting a symphony from behind the wheel of his European whip. The iconic cover art has become so synonymous with the Grammy-nominated album that it came as a bit of a surprise when Jorge Peniche posted his original *Victory Lap* CD booklet concepts on Instagram. The designs, which feature Hussle's handwritten lyrics to a still-unreleased song, speak volumes. "You could," he wrote. "I could too. I Hussled till I got it. Nigga you should too."

The Marathon was never a spectator sport. As implied by the name of his website—iHussle—Nipsey saw all of his true fans as people who were running their own races. From its inception, *Victory Lap* was meant to be a shared victory—for Hussle and his audience.

The concept resonates with Dr. Melina Abdullah of Black Lives Matter, who knew Hussle and had a chance to speak with him about cooperative economics. She feels that some of that sense of shared fate has been overlooked in the time since his passing. "That's something that bothers me about the aftermath of his death," she says. "They're trying to lift him up as this super-capitalist, which is not at all in line with what I know his intent to have been." Not that there's anything wrong with having nice things—Rolexes, Cuban links, and luxury automobiles are great. But Hussle's vision went way beyond building wealth for himself and his family. As Dr. Abdullah points out, "It was about empowering an entire community."[11]

Hussle said he began talking about *Victory Lap* as early as 2012, so it's possible that the meaning behind the title evolved over time. "I just know I wanted my debut album, the one we went to retail with, to be called *Victory Lap*," Hussle explained to me days after the album's release.[12] The victory lap or "lap of honor" is a tradition in the world of motor sports where the winning driver takes one last circuit around the track, usually at a reduced speed, saluting the crowd while soaking in their love. It was designed to be a shared experience.

There were so many victories to celebrate, starting with just being alive, handling business, and building an independent success. "Comin' off the major label," Hussle said, "havin' to rebuild the brand on my own, takin' risks, spendin' my own money, doin' things unconventional—like you said earlier, the hundred-dollar album and just bein' somewhat of a radical and it workin' in my favor."[13]

Six years after Hussle came up with the name, *Victory Lap* still ticked all those boxes. "But a lot has changed since I originally started promoting it," he told me. "Being clear that Nipsey Hussle has a clear lane in the game—and built it, and took the stairs. Had opportunities to be assisted, but chose to do it on our own"[14]

At first, Hussle saw *Victory Lap* as the completion of the

Marathon mixtape series, which proved to be a motivational accelerant for much of his fan base. "I wanted the album release to close off the *Marathon* trilogy," he said, "and to represent the end of the completely independent, doing-it-on-our-own mode, and going to a new partnership." The All Money In label's victory would be "establishing a new partnership that was in our favor this time," Hussle said. "And more in a direction of what we came in trying to establish."[15]

Hussle took his first meeting with Craig Kallman, the chairman and CEO of Atlantic Records, around 2012, well before *Crenshaw* was released. He respected the fact that Kallman was a former DJ who built his own independent label, Big Beat Records, and allowed Biggie Smalls to become a label boss in his own right, putting out artists like Lil' Kim and Junior M.A.F.I.A. "We had been talking for a while once I got out of the Epic situation," Hussle said. "I started doing the Marathon mixtapes and touring. I had certain terms that I wanted to come into the building with . . . At the time they didn't feel like I could justify my terms, which was probably true. So I kept working."[16]

Hussle started promoting *Victory Lap* as a mixtape after negotiating with a few major labels. He felt he was getting close to a deal, which he planned to announce after releasing *Victory Lap* and then transition into album mode. But Hussle began to realize that record companies were unwilling to give him any type of control over his creative output. "They wanna give you a check," he said. "I told them keep the check, give me an asset and just market and distribute my shit." Instead of a big advance, he wanted to be involved as a partner. "Niggas couldn't do that," he said. "And it's not because the people at the label didn't want to help me. It's because the corporate structure of their companies would not allow ownership. And I'm offended by that."[17]

Hussle changed plans on the fly. "I called an audible," he said. "I believed in my heart that I would be less of a man to not stand up for what I believed in. I felt like it was racist. Like, *I don't deserve some shit I just built by myself? You want to give me some money? Oh, because you don't think I know what the asset is? You think I don't understand where the real value is?*" His goal changed, his very definition of what would constitute a victory. "I didn't do a press release or tell nobody about it," he said. "I just let my demonstration speak." He said that his Proud2Pay model with *Crenshaw* was only the beginning. "That's just a small piece of what my plan is."[18]

After the *Crenshaw* breakthrough, Hussle and Kallman revisited their earlier discussion about a partnership at Atlantic. "We sat back down at the table and we figured out what the deal structure would be," he said. "And I did a couple more mixtapes and then we actually inked the deal."

All Money In quietly signed with Atlantic back in 2015, keeping the agreement under wraps. "It wasn't the illusion of independence," Hussle explained to Charlamagne, years later, on The Breakfast Club. "I realized people don't care about the deal. That's a business thing. People care about music."[19]

Hussle chose to hold off on the announcement until there was new music to release. "Nobody knew that," said Ralo. "But of course when you're with a label, it's gonna be in your best interest—not only in your best interest, but it probably is required—that you work with the producers that are already in bed with the company."[20] As a result, Ralo found himself on the outside looking in as work began on Hussle's major label debut. "Me and Nip, we weren't talking," Ralo recalls. But when he saw the track credits for *Victory Lap* he had to reach out. "I texted him and I told him 'Thank you,'" Ralo says. "I got surprised and two songs that are on the project I co-produced."[21]

Although he was more than capable of making his own beats and engineering his own sessions, Hussle had assembled a musical squad, the core of which was 1500 or Nothin', the production/composing team anchored by Larrance Dopson. Better known to Nip as "Real Rance Fresh," Dopson was Hussle's "day-one A-one," who put together a band with some of his musician friends from church, talents like James Fauntleroy, Lamar "My Guy Mars" Edwards, Charles "Uncle Chucc" Hamilton, and Brody Brown. Working with 1500, Hussle knew that he could rock with live musicians and still sound like a rapper. "I been up there where you get a band and, you know, it turns into the Playboy Jazz Festival," he once said with a smile. "And nothing against that, it's just the songs sound different."[22]

It was 1500 who introduced Hussle to Mike & Keys, the production duo formerly known as the Futuristiks. They first began working with Hussle on *Crenshaw* tracks like "Checc Me Out" and "Blessings." Since then he considered Mike & Keys "the home team"; now all they needed was their own playground. Fresh off the *Crenshaw* tour, Hussle invested a substantial chunk of the proceeds into a new studio he called "the compound." It was not cheap setting up his own studio, but Hussle always put a high priority on ownership. "I believe in investing in yourself when you make money," he said. "You could easily go a lot of places, but I just feel like your foundation should be strong."[23]

They found a spot in Burbank and spent a year and a half on renovations. "It was like an open space," he said. "We built the walls out, built all the acoustic from scratch."[24] The renovations took considerable time and energy as well as a six-figure investment. The compound had four rooms—two for producers and two for artists and songwriters—as well as two office spaces. "I had the logos on the wall," Hussle said. "I was taking all my meetings there. I had a whole video editing room. I had a plan of how I was gonna get this album done." The compound had facilities to shoot content and do postproduction as All Money In expanded into digital video and film.[25]

For Hussle the studio was the fulfillment of a vision he'd been longing to fulfill for most of his life. He set up his bookshelves and filled his whiteboards with short-term and long-term goals. He couldn't wait to start work. "Nip used to pick me up at seven o'clock in the morning every single day," recalls Money Mike of Mike & Keys. "Everything he did, he was already like three or four steps ahead of niggas on what he was tryin' to do. Even us creatin'. He made sure that we was always together. Nobody ever talks about that, you know, us being Black men. It's hard to work together and be in the same place."[26]

"It's super important to really tap in," said Rance of 1500. "Any artist that we work with, we live in that artist. And it's really just a soundtrack to life."

In addition to Mike & Keys and the 1500 or Nothin' team, Hussle brought in acclaimed producers like Bink! and L.A. legend DJ Battlecat to enhance the creative chemistry around *Victory Lap*. New songs were being laid down, and previously recorded songs were reimagined, expanded, and given new life.

One of the first songs Hussle recorded for *Victory Lap* was "Real Big," or "Rescue Me," according to the original session file name. "We had done it at 1500 studio in Inglewood and then we brought it to my new studio in Burbank to just add layers to it," Hussle recalled. "That's one of my favorite records off *Victory Lap*."[27]

1500 and Bink! decided to call some people in to give the record more texture. "I stepped out for a minute," Hussle said. "When I came back Bink! was in there. Battlecat was in there. Marsha from Floetry was in there. It was just like a room full of greatness that I just walked into. And everybody was like on a keyboard, Marsha was in the booth singin', Bink! was on the console. Battlecat was playin' the Roger and Zapp machine. And it just was like the record was comin' alive. Just walkin' in and seein' everybody workin' on my record was dope. That was something that I was real inspired by."[28]

"That was probably the most special song I feel like we did with Nip," said Money Mike. "When Rance made Nip record this song, we never woulda thought Nipsey would record on a beat like that, first of all. It's not even no snare, no nothin'—just a kick and a high hat."

"That's literally a storytellin' song, bro," Rance said, referring to Hussle as "one of the best storytellers alive" a full year after his death. "That's one of my favorite songs, 'cause he was singin' the hook. That was my favorite part 'cause that nigga could sing!"[29]

All the musical excellence pushed Hussle's lyricism to new levels. "I'm not even gonna front," he said. "I did go crazy in the process of making *Victory Lap*. I did. I just was a artist. So I didn't restrain. I didn't hold back and keep my business program intact or my business bedtime or my business wakeup time or my business daily program. I just turned into a pure artist."

Hussle was convinced he was doing the best work of his life. "That's what I'm proudest of is the radical exercise that took place on this project," he said.[30] Finally he was able to dive all the way in and show what he was capable of. "You gotta mine for diamonds in the earth, and that's a dangerous job," he said. "People die." Hussle thought of the creative process in similar terms. "To mine for your art—you gotta dig for 'em. Music is like that, but it's dangerous to go mine yourself for your value."[31]

Hussle considered making music to be a spiritual process. "Anybody that fuck with music long enough—if you don't cloud yourself and miss it—you gonna realize it's spiritual," he said. "If you in tune and you're present enough, it's vibrations, it's the word. So the power of the word is intense. It's real."[32]

More than anything, *Victory Lap* was a collection of stories about Hussle's life. "You've put out so much music," Elliott Wilson asked Hussle on the *Rap Radar* podcast, "how is there still so much that hasn't been expressed?"

Hussle's answer may have seemed obvious, but it was profound in its simplicity. "Man, it's just a lot of things that happened," he said.[33]

"It was thousands of murders in L.A. every year. And so to do what we did in that environment too. We wasn't removed. I'm removed a little now 'cause I'm successful and I've got places to go. But I wasn't removed in between making projects and going to the studio. I was right here. So all of that took place. It's a lot of stories."[34]

Even as he revisited the trials and tribulations of the past, Hussle's intention was to inspire. He told Mike & Keys, "I want a soundtrack for my penthouse. I want a soundtrack for my Maybach. I want a soundtrack for my office space. I want the way I feel when I hop in my car and wake up in my spot and look out the window . . . Not a nigga from the streets comin' and bein' successful but a pursuit, a long-distance pursuit. And at the end of it, embracing your victory. That's how I want the music to sound."[35]

The short-attention-span internet music media cycle is quick to throw around words like "classic" and "timeless," words that take on meaning only with the passage of time. But Hussle paid close attention to great music of the past when working on his debut album in an effort to give it more staying power. Although he had no way of knowing that *Victory Lap* would be the only album he would see released during his lifetime, he certainly put everything he had into it.

"When you think about the production that's popular right now, and when you make a project that doesn't necessarily sound like right now, I think that lends toward the music being received as outside of time," he said. "I study music and I study artists and careers. And when you look at albums that sold ten million— even outside of hip-hop—like Tracy Chapman, or Adele, or even Nelly or Eminem's second album, the production, ninety percent of the time, is not trendy. It's rooted in music. It's rooted in chords and instruments and the traditional greatness of music."[36]

In early 2015, Hussle and his team flew out for a European tour.

"I felt at home," said Hussle after an energetic performance at the O2 Academy in Islington. "I felt like I was in L.A. . . . To me that's the best part of this. You can get acclaim in the media, and you can get money—obviously money is the motivating factor. But when you get the love back from the people, and it's genuine. Somebody screaming your lyrics, that's genuine. That's one of the best payoffs of your hard work. It's reinforcement. That's why we do it."[37]

On his way back to LAX, Hussle was looking forward to getting back to work in his studio. He couldn't wait to see how the *Victory Lap* sessions were coming along and wrap up all the finishing touches on the renovation. But he would soon get some bad news about the studio. Hussle had been paying rent to a man he thought was the owner of the building. In fact, he was subletting the space. The All Money In team was still finalizing the construction when they received an eviction notice giving them days to vacate the premises. "It was just some political paperwork shit that went bad," Hussle said.[38]

He tried talking to the owners, explained that he didn't realize the space was a sublet. He offered to pay a year's rent up front. "They were just like, 'Nah, we cool. We ain't really fuckin' with you,'"

Hussle recalls. "They ain't really give me no reason." He went to court with paperwork, receipts, bank statements. "I never missed the rent. Everything was always on time," Hussle explained. "The judge like, 'Brother, none of that don't mean shit.'"[39] On the third day, police came in and evicted them from the compound.

"That set me back," said Hussle. "We had to recalibrate the whole approach. We took a big financial loss. Also we had got comfortable in the space working. It just all crumbled in the middle of the process, so that one really hurt."

The way a person handles adversity reveals more about their character than how they celebrate victory does. Hussle was offered all sorts of suggestions of how to seek revenge. "I'ma burn the building down," they said. "Let me fuck this building up." Hussle and his team had put the walls up, laid the floors down. It would have been easy to lash out. "I just told everybody *chill*," Hussle recalled. "We ain't doin' nothin'. We just gonna take that one for the team."[40]

As much as it hurt to lose the studio where he'd planned to complete *Victory Lap*, Hussle found another victory in the way he dealt with the setback.

"They robbed me, in essence," Hussle said. "They took something from me. They ended up keepin' a lot of the walls and the structure up for their next tenant." It wouldn't have been hard for Hussle to retaliate. All he had to do was say yes. But instead he chose to let the universe balance it out. "It's cool," he said. "I ain't even take it as nothin' but a higher energy movin' me out of that space."[41]

The *Victory Lap* sessions shifted back to 1500 Sound Academy in Inglewood. Hussle also rented space at Paramount Recording Studios. He threw himself into the creative process once more.[42]

On August 14, 2015, the N.W.A movie *Straight Outta Compton* hit theaters nationwide and topped the box office for weeks. A major production with a $28 million budget, the film was directed by F. Gary Gray and included Dr. Dre and Ice Cube among its producers.[43] For his entire career people had been telling Hussle how much he resembled Snoop. He was the obvious choice to play Snoop on the big screen. "Snoop called me," Hussle said. "Before Snoop, Ted called me—one of his business partners. Before Ted, Dre people had reached out. Before that, F. Gary Gray, the director." Hussle told them all the same thing: "Them dudes is icons and legends. And them is the people I grew up listening to and lookin' up to. But I studied branding. And one of the laws is, you don't walk in no great man's shoes."[44]

Hussle discussed his decision with Snoop at length because he valued his friendship so much. "I just had to respectfully say, 'Nah, I can't do it,'" Hussle recalled. "I think I coulda pulled it off authentic, 'cause I grew up on Snoop and I know his lyrics by heart," he added. "But I just feel like it's people in America, in the world that might not have heard of Nipsey Hussle yet, that might not have been exposed to what I do yet. That might be the first time they get exposed to it as an actor portraying Snoop."[45]

One by-product of the conversations around *Straight Outta Compton* was that Hussle finally got into the studio with Dr. Dre—a goal of his for years, whether he liked to admit it or not. "I just heard the soundtrack," he told Big Boy. "It's gonna be epic. And I would love to have been involved, outside of the capacity I was involved. 'Cause I done music on the soundtrack with Dre." But when Dre released his third solo album, *Compton*, one week before the film, Hussle's music was not included.[46]

Hussle did take on another acting role that year, however, appearing as himself in the pilot episode of Rachel Bloom's critically acclaimed CW musical comedy series *Crazy Ex-Girlfriend*. Hussle's memorable cameo poked fun at rap-star machismo in a musical number called "The Sexy Getting Ready Song." While Rachel's character Rebecca Bunch prepares to go on a date, squeezing into a pair of Spanx and tweezing and waxing hair, Hussle pops up in her bathroom rapping, "Hop on my dick in that tight little dress . . ." He then stops suddenly as he notices all the stuff spread out on her bathroom sink. "God," he says in shock. "This is how you get ready?" Rebecca nods. "This is horrifying. Like a scary movie or something. Like some nasty-ass patriarchal bullshit." Hussle excuses himself. "You know what? I gotta go apologize to some bitches."[47]

"He was so sweet and so funny," recalled the show's cocreator Aline Brosh McKenna. "He was just game," Bloom remembers of working with Hussle. "He brought his girlfriend on set, and I remember her thinking the song was so funny."[48]

The writers loved his performance so much that they came up with a closing segment for the show in which he works through a list of "Bitches to Apologize To" and calls them up one by one. Hussle phoned in the lines like:

Hey, Denise? It's me, Nipsey Hussle. I had an eye-opening experience earlier today. I'm calling to apologize for the way I treated you when you danced in my recent music video. Denise, I'm sorry that I showered you with Cristal. I didn't even ask you if you like champagne. And it probably messed up your blowout.

Anyway, Denise, hit me up whenever you get this. I'd love to discuss *The Second Sex* by Simone de Beauvoir, which I just read. You are beautiful inside as well as out. You are my equal.[49]

A few months after that episode aired, Lauren found out she was pregnant with the couple's first child. It was joyous news but forced a difficult decision. She had been handpicked for a major role in John Singleton's TV drama *Snowfall*. "It was her dream role," said Hussle. "It was the toughest decision of my career by far," Lauren told *GQ*. She turned down the opportunity and chose motherhood while supporting Hussle as he continued to pursue his musical ambitions.[50]

After putting so many years into *Victory Lap*, Hussle wanted it to exceed all expectations. In the process he was becoming an obsessive perfectionist. "I listened to Quincy Jones interviews," Hussle recalled. "I was listening to how he mixed *Thriller*, and how they had ten songs 'bout to mix. He listened back and he said 'What's the weakest three?' And they got rid of 'em. And because they got rid of them three, they got 'P.Y.T.' and they got like two other monster records that you probably can't even believe wasn't on the first round of the album."[51]

Quincy wasn't available to consult on *Victory Lap*, but when Lauren brought Hussle along to celebrate her friend Cassie's birthday on August 26, he caught the ear of another superproducer. "I've been knowing Puff, but at Cassie's birthday party we had a good convo," Hussle recalled. "He was just like, 'I'm in L.A., man, come through. Let's hear the music.' And so I brought the album over there."[52]

Puff liked what he heard—a lot. At first Hussle was hoping to convince him to hop in the video for "Rap Niggas." He mentioned Puff's role in the Nas video "Hate Me Now" as a point of reference. "I want you to put the mink on, get in the video, we gonna make a movie," Hussle said. Puff told him the backstory on why that video was so lit. "Bro, I bust a forty-million-dollar check a week before I did that video," Puff told him. "I went and spent all this dough on a chain and got tigers 'cause I got the biggest check of my life. We probably ain't gonna be able to re-create that energy."[53] But as Puffy listened to "Rap Niggas," he had some ideas. Hussle was all ears.

"Yeah, that shit tight, bro," Puff said. "But it's missin' something." Hussle was disappointed at first because the record was already mixed and mastered. "I see what you tryin' to do with this," Puffy said, then pulled up a record by Ice Cube and Dr. Dre called "Natural Born Killaz." It was ten times louder than Hussle's lead single. "This is your standard," Puffy told him. "Till your shit knocking like *this* it's not serving its purpose."[54]

Hussle called Rance and Mars from 1500 back to the studio to make it bigger and better. "This a West Coast anthem," Hussle said, and then played them "Natural Born Killaz" for reference. "They took the record to the next level," Hussle said, with obvious pride. "We thought we was done with it."[55]

By some improbable twist of fate, one of the most important West Coast rap albums of the last decade was shaped by a Harlem hitmaker—now living in L.A.—who was once at the epicenter of rap's bicoastal rivalry.

Puff advised Hussle to cut certain tracks from *Victory Lap*. "Nip, you got a classic album," Hussle recalled him saying. "A lot of legends don't got classic albums, bro. I don't just be throwin' that word around." Puffy told him, "I been ridin' to it in the Maybach. I been listenin' to it bar for bar. Take a couple of these songs off and it's gonna stand up." Hussle took his advice. Puff also called in Scott Storch and Mario Winans to play on certain records, and sat in to supervise a second round of mixing.[56]

Puffy's most memorable contribution was his vocal performance on "Young Niggas," a track built around a sample from
"West District" by PartyNextDoor. "This the one, bro!" Puff
exclaimed when he heard the song. "I'm hoppin' on this one."
Hussle made sure the energy in the studio stayed lit during Puff's
vocal takes.[57]

In summer of 2017 Hussle paid respect to Lauren with an
Instagram post: "My muse for the last 4 years . . . a lot of her
energy went in this new album . . . I prolly owe her some pub. I
gave her a baby tho so we even 🙏" Lady Hussle's contributions to
Victory Lap were not limited to serving as a muse. Her voice can
be heard saying the words "victory lap" between tracks. Hussle's
soulmate also lent her acting talents to several music videos.
"Man, she been makin' my shit go viral," Nip said. London also
made sure to express her opinions about the music. "Sometimes
she'll be in the studio and she won't say nothin' if she don't like
it," Hussle recalled. "If she feel it she'll say somethin'."[58] Among
the songs that got her seal of approval were "Rap Niggas" and
"Young Niggas." Listening to the album top to bottom in his
car, Lauren had to admit she was impressed. "This shit is a clear
elevation from what you've been doin'," she told him. "Not to say
that your shit wasn't tight, but you gon' wake a lot of people up."[59]

To create such a powerful body of work over a period of years
required Hussle to endure the loss of family time—time and
again. "How much did you have to sacrifice to get to this point?"
on-air personality Hardbody Kiotti asked Hussle when the
Victory Lap promo run stopped by 97.9 FM The Box in Houston.

"Man," Hussle replied, pausing to think for a moment.
"Everything."

As an artist, an entrepreneur running several businesses, and
a father, there were never enough hours in the day. "Everything

get tested," Hussle said in a matter-of-fact tone. "Your relationships get tested. All of that. The kids, it's hard to explain to."

Hussle said he used to keep Emani away from the studio. "It was a lot of men in the studio," he explained. "And it just was a certain energy I ain't want to necessarily overexpose my daughter to." But given how much time he was spending working on *Victory Lap*, he rethought his policy. "This my life," he said. "So I can't separate my kids. That can't be the reason we can't spend time." He thought about how many Bob Marley interviews he had seen where children were hanging around in the background. "It's gonna be weed lit," he said. "It's gonna be everything that you try to keep your kids away from. But the kids gonna be right there on deck."[60]

Hussle set up a special room for Emani to hang out in while visiting the studio, and he instituted some basic codes of conduct. "We ain't gonna talk like that with my daughter in here," he explained. Hussle arranged for someone to watch over Emani while he was working to keep her supplied with cartoons and snacks. "She can kinda peep what I'm doing and get a better understanding," he said. "'He ain't just avoiding me. He really in here working.'"

A former musician and rapper who transitioned into radio, Kiotti said one of his favorite songs on *Victory Lap* was "Dedication," for reasons that were obvious and not-so-obvious. "You gotta love this shit," he said. "It's a lot come with this."

Hussle agreed wholeheartedly. "One hundred percent," he said. "If you don't love it you gonna quit. You gon' hang the towel up, fa sho'. And if you ain't willin' to die and lose everything, you're not gonna make it. And you probably not gonna die. You know what I'm sayin'?"

"You gonna pass out before you die," Kiotti said with a laugh.

"But you gon' have to be comfortable with dyin' for this shit," Hussle said, not joking at all. "It's like gangbangin'. You can't be a real banger unless you're willing to die and do life. You're not gonna be able to function under this situation. Not to say that that's what you want, but you gon' have to accept that's a part of this life."[61]

One of the most powerful tracks on *Victory Lap*, "Dedication" was one of the earliest songs recorded for the project. Getting it finished was very much a Marathon in itself—and a team effort. Ralo Stylez made the original beat around 2012. Two weeks after *Crenshaw* came out, Hussle laid down a hook that felt important right away. "I knew that this message that I'm expressing or this group of words belongs on an album called *Victory Lap*," Hussle said. "I ain't even write the verses yet." Within a year or so he laid down a couple verses, but something about the song felt unfinished. "I know what it is," Hussle said, as if he sensed its potential. "I'm just not there right now to write it."

Hussle's music team would always ask about "Dedication" as mixtape after mixtape rolled out—*Mailbox Money* in 2014, *Slauson Boy 2* in 2016, *No Pressure* in 2017. "You sleepin' on that record, bro," they would say. "I'm not sleepin' on it," Hussle would say. "I'm just waitin' till I'm in the right energy to write the rest of the song."[62]

"We went through maybe at least like six different versions of that song," said Rance.

"This is one of them songs where he had one verse for like six years," added Money Mike. "And I remember we was sayin', 'We gotta get Nip to rap on it, bro. Let's just go in and press him right now.'"[63]

On June 14, 2017, Hussle attended the red-carpet premiere of the Tupac Shakur biopic *All Eyez on Me* accompanied by Lauren, his mother, and his grandmother. "Mom was always a big Pac fan," he said. "She told me she bought tickets to see the movie at the Magic Johnson Theatre. I said 'Cool, do that, but we gonna go to the premiere too.'"[64]

Walking through the parking lot, Hussle happened to see Kendrick Lamar, who had an even more intense connection to Tupac than most California MCs. As a boy, Lamar saw Shakur shooting a music video in his neighborhood. Since then, Pac had appeared to him in a vision, and his most recent album at the time, *To Pimp a Butterfly*, included an extended conversation with Tupac's ghost.

The two wordsmiths greeted each other.

"What's up, bro?" Hussle said.

"That verse comin' back, nigga," Lamar replied. "That shit fire!"

"Oh all right, bet! The 'Keyz 2 the City' record?" Hussle asked.

"Nah," Lamar said. "'Dedication.'"

Hussle was confused. *Damn, I ain't even send that*, he thought. But this wasn't the time or the place to ask questions.[65]

"All right," he said. "If that's the one you fucked with and you wrote a verse to it, dope."[66]

The premiere was packed with West Coast rap royalty. The movie, however, was just okay. As much as the lead actor resembled Shakur physically, no actor alive could replicate his magnetic charisma. During the course of the evening, Hussle had a deep conversation with Snoop, Lamar, and his label boss, Top Dawg of TDE.

"Top a Blood," Hussle explained. "He from Bounty Hunters. He from the Nickerson Gardens projects. Snoop from Long Beach, he from Rollin' 20 Crip. Kendrick from Compton. He grew up in a Piru neighborhood. I'm from the Rollin' 60s. So

Top and Snoop, in they era, the politics was so intense that no matter how powerful they were, it was things that was just taboo. You couldn't really get into them type of things. But now me and Kendrick, we from a different era." Hussle and Lamar listened to Snoop and Top while they discussed Death Row–era street politics, as portrayed in the film they'd just watched, which culminates with Shakur's murder at the hands of Southside Crips. "We saw what happened with Death Row," Hussle recalled. "We saw what happened when gangbangin' spills into music and when street politics make they way into power positions. You get the perfect storm for destruction."[67]

After a while Kendrick and Hussle spoke up, adding their voices to the conversation.

"Our generation, you see me and YG, how we politic," Hussle said. "You see how all of us represent our tribes, but we can coexist in the music space."[68]

TDE was another prime example. Bringing together Jay Rock from Bounty Hunters, Kendrick—a "good kid" from a Piru area—and ScHoolboy Q from Hoovers, their HiiiPower movement was all about unification for a higher purpose.[69]

It was a new era. And if unity was possible through music, maybe it could go further. "The time might be right," Hussle suggested, "for us to try to use our influence to evolve how we exist."[70]

The conversation made a deep impression on Hussle, and apparently on Lamar too. He sent back his guest verse on "Dedication" soon after the premiere, closing it out with an image of Tupac's spirit overseeing the group's conversation at his premiere. When Hussle heard it he was blown away.

He couldn't ask for more inspiration or motivation to finish the song. "I went back in and did my third verse," said Hussle. "Even in his verse it's like a conversation to me, like if an artist was talkin' to the artist he's featured on the song with. So I reacted a little bit to what was said. So it's just a dope record. It was a reason I couldn't write it for three years."[71]

Nipsey wasn't even mad they snuck "Dedication" to Kendrick behind his back. "That wasn't my strategy or nothin'," Hussle said. "It was just a combination of people makin' that record meet its destiny."[72]

By all accounts, the final "Dedication" session was an unforgettable experience. "It was probably one of the craziest nights ever," Money Mike recalled. "The energy in the room that night was so crazy, I think everybody had to walk outside and get some air."

"I remember Nip told us to take a picture that day, 'cause everybody was there," said My Guy Mars. "I came back, and that nigga was singin'! I was like, 'Wait—that's you singin', nigga? Let's go!' And I thought niggas were gonna change it. 'Cause you know how niggas be changin' shit. But for him to keep that and really show his musicianship—which a lot of people don't know he was a real musician. That nigga knew music, that's why he kept musical niggas around. So that song was definitely special."[73]

Hussle could have gone with the three verses he'd written years before, but it wouldn't have been this song. "I thrive offa that type of rap that's based on life," he said after the record was completed. "No disrespect to no one, but it's not just phonetics and aesthetics. It's real words behind an experience."[74]

THIRD GENERATION SOUTH CENTRAL GANGBANGERS
THAT LIVED LONG ENOUGH TO SEE IT CHANGING

—Nipsey Hussle, "Blue Laces 2," *Victory Lap* (2018)

Tick-tick-tick.

After all the years of planning and preparation that went into *Victory Lap*, looking for the perfect beat, the optimal mix, the ultimate moment of inspiration, there came a moment—as happens in every creative endeavor—when the sound of the ticking clock drowned out everything else.

Rance remembers the final *Victory Lap* sessions as a blur. "It was crunch time at the end of the album and we all went in and went crazy that last week," he said. By his estimation, as many as six songs were not going to make the cut, including some that became album highlights. "We had a bunch of radio songs on there," he recalls. "And we tapped into the culture and things came out how they came out—for real for real."[75]

"I had big records," Hussle said. "I had a record with Cardi B, I had a record with Future." Songs with such bankable stars were pretty much guaranteed to get heavy rotation on radio and splash on the pop charts, but Hussle was more concerned with the integrity of his vision for *Victory Lap*. "I wanted it to be just a person telling their life story over the course of an album,"[76] he said. That's why he always stressed that he was signed to his own label, All Money In, and partnered with a major label to make use of their resources, contacts, and expertise. Nobody was going to pressure him to change his artistic vision in a desperate reach for a club banger.

One of the last *Victory Lap* songs to be completed was "Last Time That I Checc'd," Hussle's collab with YG. "I wanted to create something for the West Coast that they felt like was specifically for them," Hussle said of the song, calling it "an anthem for the streets and my generation."[77]

But according to Hussle's production team, that anthem almost didn't get done. "I can honestly say, that was a song that never woulda happened if Rance never woulda pressed," said Money Mike. For nearly two years the track remained unfinished, just a funky 808 beat with a hook that referenced a line from Young Jeezy's ATL street anthem "Trap or Die."

"That was one of them songs that I believed in," said Rance. "It's just about timing. Sometimes it's just God's timing. And if you don't rush it, it comes to you. Power versus force," he said, referencing one of Hussle's favorite books.[78]

"Nip needed that extra inspiration," said Mars. "If we gave him the monstrah shit then he would come with an idea." At the last minute Rance put his foot down, like "Fuck that! This song gotta be on the album. I'm pressin'. Let's go!" Mike & Keys touched up the track to spark Hussle, who connected with YG in the nick of time to create a classic, bringing a strong message of unification to *Victory Lap*.[79]

"I understand art reflecting life, but we grew up on art *instructing* life," Hussle said of the song. Where some of YG and Hussle's records in the past had been on the ratchet side, "Last Time That I Checc'd" was written with the explicit intention to school a younger generation, showing them how two young Black men survived the L.A. streets and found a way to turn things around and live a more constructive life. "After a while," Hussle said, "I felt like it was almost a responsibility for me to give the game up."[80]

Having that track in place helped to fulfill a larger goal for *Victory Lap*, giving the project a sense of completeness. But there was still something missing. In order to tell his story properly, Hussle wanted to touch on certain key musical moments, milestones in the Marathon. He recorded sequels to two landmark tracks, "Keys 2 the City" and "Blue Laces," a Crip confessional that Hussle once planned to turn into a film.

He called Mr. Lee, the legendary Houston producer who made the original "Blue Laces." They had spent two weeks together in a condo in New York courtesy of Jonny Shipes when they made the first record, and had maintained a strong friendship over the years.

Mr. Lee was happy when Hussle rang him up in February 2017 and said, "Bro, make me a 'Blue Laces 2.'" Two days later Mr. Lee sent the beat back.[81] He returned to the same sample used on the original, "Hospital Prelude of Love Theme" from the *Foxy Brown* movie soundtrack.[82] This time around, Mr. Lee let more of Willie Hutch's vocal rock, speeding up the snippet where he says "Aw baby it's been so long . . ." until it sounded otherworldly, like angels speaking in tongues. As poignant as a bittersweet memory, the spellbinding instrumental evoked a tense atmosphere that got Hussle's juices flowing.

Big Reese, a member of Mike & Keys's production team, was in the lab that night. Hussle described him as an OG from San Diego who "turned into a real positive dude that came up out the struggle." They had become close and Reese had the kind of rapport where he could push Hussle creatively. "That's tight, Hussle," Reese said after the first verse was laid down. "Where you goin'?" Nip told him he was leaving and would return tomorrow.[83]

"Don't leave," Reese said. "Do the second verse right now."

Hussle got back in the booth and dug deeper, unleashing another stream-of-consciousness flow that spoke on Dr. Sebi, the herbalist and healer who died in a Honduran prison in August 2016. Lauren had introduced Nip to Dr. Sebi's dietary recommendations and he found they made him feel much better.[84] Upon researching him further, Hussle found his story intriguing, especially when he read about a court case where Dr. Sebi faced trial for practicing medicine without a license and allegedly proved that he could cure patients of AIDS using herbs and a nutritional regimen. Finding it odd that the story had not been more widely publicized, Hussle was planning to produce a documentary on Dr. Sebi's life, and had joked in interviews about threats to his own life because the pharmaceutical industry didn't want Sebi's herbal remedies to be publicized. "You know how they play," Hussle said in one radio interview. "Niggas is tweetin' me, 'Hussle, be careful! Your plane gonna go down.' I'm like, 'Y'all niggas better ride for me.'"[85]

"Blue Laces 2" was the first and only time he would speak about Sebi on record, stating that the herbalist's death in jail was some sort of punishment for "teaching health." (The doctor's family says he died of starvation due to poor prison conditions while incarcerated in Honduras.)[86] The rest of the verse touched on Hussle's admiration for Rick Ross, Hussle's business accomplishments, and his work with the Los Angeles City Council.

Big Reese was feeling a certain vibe in the air. "Blue Laces 2" was turning into a powerful testimony right before his eyes. "Damn, that's tight, bro," he told Hussle. "The second one is harder than the first verse . . . Finish the song right now, Nip. You've got a certain spirit right now. Don't leave."[87]

And then Hussle stepped back into the booth and delivered a verse unlike the two that preceded it. Rather than a series of vivid impressions, it was a flashback to a traumatic real-life episode, rendered in heartbreaking detail. "Sometimes you'll be in a luxury car or a penthouse or a first-class flight or a bomb-ass hotel somewhere and just remember the complete opposite," Hussle reflected later. "Bein' on the run from the police or driving your homie to the hospital bleedin'. Just thinkin' 'bout the struggle, really, and what we went through in the process of tryin' to get here."[88] The final verse of "Blue Laces 2" describes a gun battle on a beach and its tragic aftermath, trying to get his homie to the emergency room before he bleeds out while calming his hysterical girlfriend and evading police.

"It was hard for me to get it out," Hussle said. "I was overwhelmed because of how truthful it was and how real it was to him. I was in the booth having a moment." When he was finished recording the song, he thanked Reese for pushing him. "Damn, bro," he said. "You was utilized by some higher power today."[89]

As soon as that record was finished, Hussle felt that his work was done. "I knew that at the point I was at in my career, I wasn't gonna do nothin' else till I felt that I had an album with fourteen or sixteen great songs," he said. "My whole process was when it blow me away, I'ma be ready to move. When I listen to it top to bottom and I'm like, I get the chills from it and I hear a person in this music, then I'ma be ready to go. So when I heard it I'm like, 'Yeah, it's outta here.'"[90]

Wrapping up work on the album gave Hussle more time to focus on his expanding family. Kross "The Boss" arrived August 31, 2016—a Leo like his father, with a birthday two weeks after. Hussle always loved being a father, although it terrified him at first. "Nobody ain't ready for that," he said. "Hell no. You don't know what to do. But y'all gonna learn together. The mother number one got the instinct, so that's gonna kick in. And what's crazy about the kid is that the kid ain't really trippin'. A diaper, a bottle, the love—we cool."[91]

The hardest part was the choices. "The fatherhood part easy," he said. What was tough was being committed to the grind. "Dang, I gotta make hard decisions," he said. Birthdays and Christmas were nonnegotiable. "We'll miss the bag for that," he said. "But I'm sure I missed a cheerleadin' practice or a tournament, a parent-teacher conference—that's part of the game." He would explain to Emani when he had to be away during a special family moment in pursuit of an opportunity. He spoke to her like an adult, and even when she was disappointed he felt she could understand.[92]

Having two children of his own made him even more selective. "I'm a sniper," he said. "I got two babies now—I got a daughter and a son. If it ain't about no business or work, I can give that time to my kids." And he never questioned the sacrifices he made for family.[93]

Having Kross was a brand-new kind of thrill. "He was a little sumo wrestler," Hussle joked about his son. "He stretched out, though. I think he gonna be tall." Hussle himself stood six foot three after a late-teens growth spurt.[94] Seeing a little man around the house got his mind moving in new directions, including his views on life in the hood.

When people asked Hussle for advice, he took the responsibility seriously. "What I tell my young people in the area I grew up in . . . I talk to 'em like they was my son. I wouldn't tell my son to go be a reputable gang member because it's glorious. I would tell my son advice like I want him to win. You cannot even repeat the existing rhetoric. You can't. You gotta create your own understanding of the time." He would never advise anyone to get put on the hood anymore. Even though he had made that choice himself, he couldn't imagine Kross going in back of the buildings to fight and wear a blue rag.[95]

The same advice he'd give his own son was worth sharing with the world. "It's about money, it's economic," he said. "Without money your opinions aren't empowered. So my thing for my young people, is like—start." Get involved in music. Pick up a camera and make a video. Even if your father wasn't a rap star, creative fields were still entry-level meritocracies. "You can buy your laptop for a thousand dollars and attack it and start something," he said. "I feel like just empowering the ideas economically is the quickest."[96]

In April of 2018, Hussle, Sam, and their father made a second journey to Eritrea. This time around his experience was very different from the first trip home fourteen years earlier. "They had a minivan waitin' for me and I drove into the country," Hussle recalled. His passport and paperwork were handled VIP-style and his family stayed in a hotel. "It was dope just breathin' the air," said Hussle. Instead of three months, they spent just over a week, mostly in the capital city of Asmara. Hussle was pressed for time. As soon as he got home he would start preparing for the Victory Lap tour. He found time to meet with Eritrean president Isaias Afwerki, and of course he got to see his grandmother and his cousins, sharing some delicious meals with them. He stood on the cliffs of Asmara and looked down over his father's home village Adi Kefelet as he reflected on all the evolution he'd seen.

"Seeing the way the city and everything else has changed is gratifying," Hussle said in an interview with the national news agency *TesfaNews*. "I love to be here. The people, the food, the culture, and the lifestyle are extremely good."

As he'd predicted when visiting the local record shop during his first trip home, Hussle had made it big as a rapper in the U.S. His success had won him many admirers in Eritrea. Billion Temesghen, the *TesfaNews* reporter, had many questions about hip-hop and gangs in Los Angeles, and Hussle explained every-thing in great detail.

"What would hip-hop be in your own words?" Billion Temes-ghen asked.

The answer seemed so obvious that another artist might dismiss it or respond with some half-hearted cliché. But not Hussle. "It is a vocabulary, it is an art, and it is a culture that originally was only of young people in America but now has gone global," he said. "The neighborhoods from where hip-hop came out had unique environments and situations that made people search for a real and efficient form of expression. From police brutality to gang cultures, the riots, racial discrimination, and more unique events that urged the growth of hip-hop in terms of music and hip-hop in terms of culture and identity. The hip-hop community in every part of America spoke about events that took place all over the country. In New York, for example, there was a graffiti movement and break dance movement. So hip-hop was like CNN for what was going on in the streets. Each region had a specific approach but deep down it was all about the struggle for equality and respect for African-Americans."

Comparing hip-hop to jazz, Hussle pointed out that music in America was an expression of our struggles, being black in America. Even as an Eritrean-American, he felt connected to this aspect of African-American history.

"My father is from Eritrea and we have always been in touch with our Eritrean ancestry and culture thanks to him," Hussle said. "However, we still grew up in South Central LA all of our lives. So our exposure was to the culture of Los Angeles, which was gang culture. I was born in 1985 and grew up in the '90s. The LA riots took place in 1993. Rodney King, the brutality of LAPD, and all the social issues that took place back then happened in our backyard."

"Are gangs scary?" Temesghen asked. "Terrorizing?"

"If you come from areas in which gang activities are common then that becomes part of who you are," Hussle replied. "I guess the equivalent metaphor would be coming from a place of war. If you do you are conscious about war even as a child and later without even realizing it, you become part of it. Afterward, these people of war areas become involved in different ways. Some of them become fighters, some become writers, some sing about it, and some become politicians. Everyone, one way or another, creates a subliminal link to what he or she was growing up. And the gang culture is similar. It might have all started as self-defense but then everyone became part of it as it was the dominant culture

of South Central L.A . . . The word 'scary' or 'terrorizing' is for
people who are not familiar with it. But for those who grow in it,
it is just a serious matter. It has been there for generations. It is
dangerous. Black people were being targeted by white gangs. It
formed as a form of protection for your own Black people."

Since the reference to Nipsey Russell did not resonate in
East Africa circa 2018, Hussle's Eritrean fans took the liberty of
coming up with their own name for him: "Nebsi." In Tigrinya,
the word translates to "self," also slang for "homeboy" or "homie."
Temesghen explained that his Eritrean name was roughly equivalent to "self-hustle" or "the hustle of a homie." She asked if he
would like to correct anything for Eritrea's national newspaper.

"Absolutely not," Hussle said. "I was educated about the
Tigrinya link to my name recently and I am just so glad it makes
sense in Tigrinya. There is no need at all to correct it. Let it be
the way it is. That is how I want to keep it with my Eritrean
friends and fans."

"Ermias," Temesghen asked, "is there anything you want to
add before we finish our interview?"

"There is, actually. I want to say how gratifying it is for us to
be able to come home and be able to have a country that we can
call our own, where the leaders, the police, politicians, business
owners, and entrepreneurs look like us and are in charge of their
own destiny, and each has a say in the overall power structure. It
is just so impressive. We are not used to that in America. There is
a taboo that we are inferior."

"It is so sad that they make sure young African-Americans
grow up with that ideology," Temesghen said.

"Yes, sadly that is the reality," Hussle replied. "But here
in Eritrea, it is different. Had it been so in America too there
would have been less violence, less insanity, no drug addicts, and
no violent families. You might have the material advantage in

America but life is not all about that. The sense of family, peace, and respect is alive out here in Eritrea. You might think money is important but it's the togetherness of families being tight that makes life better. All we think of in America is a concrete reality in Eritrea. As for me to be part of it is a pride I carry profoundly."

Now that *Victory Lap* was finally complete, Hussle began thinking about people who had helped empower him along the way. One of the people he reached out to was Jonny Shipes. "From 2013 to 2016, we didn't really speak," Shipes recalls. "No bad blood, we just went our separate ways. He'd comment on my Instagram, I'd comment on his. But we just weren't the way we were before. For those five or six years, we were inseparable, talking daily, sleeping at each other's cribs, doing whatever we had to do to get by."[97]

Then in 2016, Hussle randomly hit him one day. "Yo man, you did everything you said you were going to do," he told Shipes. "It's so impressive to watch what you've done, and I never got to say this to you, but I just wanted to thank you." Shipes had worked with many people in the music industry and didn't expect spontaneous expressions of gratitude. It felt good. They caught up and made plans to connect. "Yo, next time you're in Cali, hit me," Hussle said. "I'll come out, scoop you." A few months later, Hussle met Shipes at LAX, picked him up in the Maybach, and took him to the studio to listen to *Victory Lap*. "I got to make sure I don't get choked up right here," Shipes says as the memories return. "The last two years was the same as the first five. Just totally normal, "Yo, come by the crib, come by the studio . . . It's Lauren's birthday, come by. We're going to have mad fun. I guess that was just his way of making sure me and him were good."[98]

Deal or no deal, Hussle was good. By the end of 2016, he was earning just under $1 million per quarter from streaming and downloads because he owned the rights to all his mixtapes. Before *Victory Lap* even dropped, he posted his Tunecore royalty statement on Instagram in the amount of $908,312. "No flex," read the caption. "For motivational purposes only. The money's in controlling ya catalog."[99]

After years of making enlightened moves behind the scenes and pioneering innovative approaches to the entertainment industry, Nipsey Hussle decided to formalize this aspect of his work, announcing the launch of the Marathon Agency in October 2016. The core of the team included Hussle's godbrother Adam Andebrhan and longtime Marathon partner Jorge Peniche, along with two familiar faces from Hussle's inner circle—marketing and branding savant Karen Civil and rap industry A&R Steve Carless, who worked closely with Hussle putting together *Victory Lap*. Civil and Carless had known each other for a long time, attending the same high school in Elizabeth, New Jersey, and working together on campaigns for YG and Jeezy. In a social media post, Hussle described the Marathon Agency as "the new home for the RADICALS . . . The REVOLUTIONARIES & THE GAME-CHANGERS that believe that they can do it their way."[100]

Before the agency was established, Peniche remembered being somewhat "protective and territorial" when Steve Carless first began working with team Hussle. "We gotta make sure that no one comes in and poisons the ecosystem," he remembers thinking at the time. "We created it, it's clean. And we know how to work in this ecosystem. So I was just wary at first, like, 'Aw man, Steve is comin' in. This guy has a label background.'" Despite his initial reservations, Peniche came to respect Carless. "I love the guy to death," he said. "And we operate at the same frequency, Steve-O and I—which is kinda crazy. We get along really well." Carless helped Peniche build on his photography and design expertise to become a full-fledged tour manager.[101]

"We collectively were a group that helped push Nipsey to the next heights," Civil told me. "With the Marathon Agency we were able to market and promote and help bring awareness for other artists. We worked with Nicki Minaj, YG, Dave East, and Teyana Taylor as well—different people who understood Nipsey's business model, and we helped them with certain projects." The Marathon Agency also consulted with Pusha T during the time when he was working in support of Hillary Clinton's presidential campaign.[102]

"Nipsey pushed you to want more, to become more," Civil says. "When I started working on the Hillary campaign I talked about it with Nipsey first. You always wanted to get your blessing from him—and not in the sense of just wanting to ask him. You always wanted his thoughts on it. Is this a good idea? A bad idea? When you second-guessed yourself, he was that voice of reasoning and understanding. He was our hope."[103]

There were other signs of hope in Los Angeles that fall. The same week that the Marathon Agency announced its launch, the American Civil Liberties Union filed a federal lawsuit against the LAPD, charging that the department's gang injunctions were violating thousands of city residents' right to due process. At the time of the suit, forty-six different injunctions were in force, affecting some ten thousand people within a seventy-five-square-mile area. People under injunctions can be arrested for wearing certain clothing or even socializing in public, and the process for challenging the injunctions is long and complicated. Violating gang injunctions can lead to charges of contempt, punishable by up to six months in jail. Residents of neighborhoods affected by gang injunctions were "basically subject to parole-like restrictions without any hearing on whether or not they are actually a gang member," said Peter Bibring of the ACLU. "That violates any notion of due process."[104]

Around this same time, just as *Victory Lap* was wrapping up, Hussle spoke with Vanessa Satten, the *XXL* editor who'd put him on the Freshmen cover. She had noticed the way he was connecting with YG and artists from other rival sets, and wanted to know whether that reflected larger changes happening within L.A. street politics. "We've always had situations where people from different sides of the tracks would be able to find some mutual ground," Hussle said. "You had Snoop and Suge Knight partnering up and building Death Row Records. Even my big homie Draws would be with Suge."[105]

"Was it different then?" Satten asked. "Is it easier now?"

"This gets tricky," Hussle told her, his relaxed demeanor switching up perceptibly. "Let me tell you a thing about gang-banging. Gangbanging is like a volcano. Don't ever get comfortable in a volcano. You know what I'm sayin'? It might could go. It could blow. So it's never like it calmed down. It's just placid. It's chill right now. It's gonna go up again, though. Not to just be grim, but that's kinda the reality of that. So it could seem like it calmed down and then it'll be a sick-ass summer like this summer. This past 2016 was a deadly summer in L.A. Niggas died. Gangbangin' was *crackin'*. It's just like, sometimes it flare up and other time it's chill."[106]

Part of the message of *Victory Lap* was that it was possible to make it out of the volcano alive. If Hussle could survive and thrive as a youth who grew up in the Rollin' 60s, maybe other people could do it too. "You can check the L.A. history," Hussle said. "My section especially is cannibalistic. You know what I mean? Feed on they own. We don't got nobody that really made it out from over here. That was born and raised over here. That walked to the liquor stores. Went swimming in the summer at the parks. Rode they bikes through these back streets. Fought in the back of these buildings. So the learning curve for the community, the learning curve for myself, was very, very intense."[107]

The 60s were not unique in this respect. Gang politics controlled much of Los Angeles. Asked to explain the city's identity, Chuck Dizzle of *Home Grown Radio* took a moment and then said, "We're survivors—in every sense of the word."[108] From the Watts Rebellion to the Rodney King Uprising, from police brutality to gangbanging, L.A.'s communities of color exist under constant threat. "There's families that actually feud because one's from one hood, one's from the other hood," Dizzle said. "The way L.A. is set up, this is one hood, this is another hood. You have to peacefully coexist. You have to figure the shit out. There's kids that literally go to school together—one side of the tracks is from here and one is from there . . . They go to elementary school together and when they hop off the porch—meaning they join a gang—they're forced to pick a side. We were homies. Now it's like—*Aaaah, well, those days are over.* And imagine if my relative gets killed and I know it was people from your hood."[109]

"That's how the streets is ran in L.A.," Hussle said. "Gangbangin'. Not hustlin'. You can be a successful hustler and have no say-so. You can have the bag and all that. It don't matter, bro. Niggas gonna take that from you. For real. Because that's not the structure in L.A. The structure in L.A. is bangin'. So it's like every community is controlled by a gang, and got a history. And got a narrative of what happened. And who did what and who stood down and who stood up and who did what they was supposed to. And as much as you be an individual, it's a way of life that—your granny knew about it. Your aunties and them knew about it. Everybody. The mailman know the difference between the neighborhoods he deliver the mail in."[110]

Understanding the pervasive nature of gang culture affords new perspectives on the best way to reach young people growing up within that environment. Influences like "gangsta rap" are not a cause but an effect. "It ain't like you wake up and decide, 'Aw that documentary inspired me. I wanna go bang,'" Hussle said. "Or 'I heard this album . . .' Or 'I seen the video, that's what I wanna do.' Not to say that's how other areas got it. 'Cause it's a lot of different reasons everybody do what they do. But just as far as L.A., the schoolteachers. It's the way of the streets, period. It ain't no alternative thing goin' on in the streets."[111]

Creating alternatives to illegal hustling was a matter of survival, so when California voters approved Proposition 64 in the November 2016 elections, legalizing the recreational use of marijuana,[112] Hussle and his team wasted no time getting involved in the green rush. Legitimizing the weed business had pluses and minuses. The people who had risked their freedom providing cannabis to the public when it was illegal had a hard time getting into the legal side of it. Hussle had a certain advantage due to his celebrity. "I've got a built-in marketing mechanism by me being an artist with fans and with a platform," he told me. "So I didn't have the same challenges that somebody that's just a hustler and was moving they packs would have. It's like a liquor license almost. There's a limited amount of licenses that they gave out, and if you don't have a partner with one, and you can't get one yourself, you're boxed out of selling liquor. Same with the weed. If you don't have a partner that there's a reason he'll partner with you, he'll just do it on his own."[113]

After sealing up a partnership with the California-based cannabis professionals at the Cure Company, Hussle and his team curated the cultivation of a special strain called the Marathon OG. He soon began opening dispensaries to distribute the product. Leveraging his star power to broker the legal cannabis deal, Hussle left the day-to-day operations to his team, including his childhood friend Stephen Donelson, affectionately known as Bolt da Fatts. Known for his loyalty, his winning smile, and his can-do attitude, Fatts had grown up riding bikes around the neighborhood with Nip and Sam. When Fatts and Nip got down with the hood, they had an understanding that they would never fight each other. They had been through so much, from missions out of town with a burner stashed in the air conditioner to helping Sam sell merch on the street before they opened Slauson Tees.[114]

"Fatts is a nigga who did a 180 in life," says Ralo. "He would be like Paul of the New Testament in the sense that he was on the road to Damascus to kill Christians. And then he ended up being blinded by the light and then he turned around and became a disciple. You dig?"[115] In short, Fatts was family. Hussle hoped the new dispensaries would provide a steady revenue stream while the All Money In team waited for the record deal to be announced.

"Cannabis is a billion-dollar racket, though," Hussle said, "so ya gotta understand it's really aggressive and it's really competitive. The goal is who gon' be Newport? Who's gonna create the brand that becomes the Newport or the Marlboro of weed?"[116]

Hussle's knowledge of branding and corporate strategy was on point as usual. But there were other types of aggressive competition in the cannabis industry. And the neighborhood had seen other types of arms races for quite some time. Fatts became the owner of Top Flight Collective, a cannabis dispensary with multiple locations, including one on West Boulevard at West Fifty-Ninth Place,[117] a few minutes away from the shopping plaza at Slauson and Crenshaw.

According to sources within the 60s, there was an attempted burglary at that location during the fall of 2017. "Whoever it is, whatever it is, if you've got somebody doing something that

you want to do, you might be envious of it," says one member
of the set. When Fatts and his team investigated the attempted
burglary, they wanted to know if the perpetrator had been acting
alone or if the attempt had been orchestrated. "They handled it
like motherfuckers that was tutoring us would handle it," says
one 60s member. "They went out and did what they was supposed
to do and that's what got 'em in the situation that brought all the
attention to all of it."[118]

On the evening of September 29, 2017, Fatts was standing
out front of Top Flight Collective. Around 10:45 p.m. he was
struck by gunshots fired from a passing vehicle or vehicles. Fatts
ran inside the dispensary, collapsed, and was pronounced dead
around 11:10 p.m.[119] "They aired my nigga out," says a knowl-
edgable source in the neighborhood who asked not to be identified. "They shot him over 30 times. It was horrific. I don't know
if I'm at liberty to speak on the way that it transpired. It was
betrayal and violence. How the characters in the parade play out
and everything, I don't know nothing."[120] There were two other
dispensary shootings around that same time along Crenshaw, but
no clear indication that they are related.[121]

A makeshift memorial of blue candles soon sprang up on the
sidewalk along the 5900 block of West Boulevard, along with blue
and yellow flowers and Mylar balloons fluttering in the breeze.
Services for Stephen J. Donelson were held at Calvary Baptist
Church on Fairfax Avenue just below Slauson.[122] The thirty-
year-old father was a cofounder and part owner of All Money
In Records, The Marathon Clothing, and other businesses in the
shopping plaza like Wireless Connection and Baba Leo's Fish
Shack, as well as Elite Human Hair, Fourth Ave Collective, and
The Marathon OG, an exclusive strain developed by Hussle in
collaboration with The Care Company. "You own 1/4 of every-
thing I'm a part of," Husssle wrote on Instagram along with a

photo of blue and yellow candles arranged to spell out FATTS. "Ima make that worth 100 mill before we meet again. 🏁[123]

"Me and your son missing you dearly Stephen," wrote Leneice Patton on his *Los Angeles Times* homicide report—which incorrectly identified him as a hired security guard rather than the owner of the dispensary. "Rest In Paradise my King . . . love you always, Sush."[124]

Hussle and his inner circle were devastated by the loss. "Fatts, you know that's one of my best friends," he said. "We just had a genuine friendship. And also one of the people that really believed that we could do something else besides gangbang." To lose a member of his day-one team just as their lifelong plans were coming to fruition cut him to the core. "I feel terrible that I'm the one who just gets to feel it," Hussle said. "Fatts don't get to feel it."[125]

His emotions were still raw a few months later. Hussle got choked up near the end of his *Rap Radar* podcast interview when Elliott Wilson asked about Fatts. "Man, that caught me off guard completely," Hussle said. "I didn't expect that at all. And the timing was crazy. We been sittin' on *everything*. We been just holdin' our punches just to do it all at once. We been all anticipatin' the moment that we get to enjoy. And it's a little fucked up—it's *really* fucked up that my partner and my homeboy ain't on this side of the dimension to experience it with us, and benefit from it. And, you know, from like . . ." He cleared his throat and paused, wiping a tear from his eye. "I don't wanna get too deep into it. I get emotional."

"I feel you," Wilson replied. "Respect. Respect."

"But his kids, his kids would be proud of him."[126]

On the credits to *Victory Lap*, Fatts is listed as one of the executive producers, and rightfully so. His contributions were invaluable to the ultimate fulfillment of the All Money In mission. Still, his death cast a pall over a major victory for the team, making the announcement of the Atlantic Records partnership in November 2017 somewhat bittersweet.

"The best day with Nip was when we got the Atlantic deal," said Hussle's bodyguard J Roc. "Nip did it the boss way and got what he wanted. And I was so happy."

"He said he couldn't fully be excited, because Fatts wasn't here," said his Atlantic Records PR representative Brittany Bell. "He felt bad celebrating such a moment, because the person who had been there from the beginning wasn't here."[127]

"I got regrets," Hussle said during one of his first interviews after the deal was announced. "I do. I lost one of my homeboys. And I feel like I might have stayed in the field too long. I mighta taken too long to just make this transition. But at the same time I can't think like that, but I do. Like, damn. About just how long it took for us to be comfortable to go ahead and partner up and make that next move." Ever the hustler, he did his best to use the tragedy as motivation. "We gonna have to keep raisin' the value of what he's involved in, which is the music and the label."[128]

Hussle and his team finally announced their multimillion-dollar joint venture deal with Atlantic Records in late November of 2017. He had done his research and put his faith in the executive team, consisting of Craig Kallman, as well as former Def Jam execs Julie Greenwald, Mike Kyser, and Kevin Liles, all of whom had impressive track records setting up joint ventures like Jay-Z's Roc-A-Fella Records and T.I.'s Grand Hustle. Atlantic stood by T.I. when he was imprisoned on federal weapons charges, and rocked with him as he rebuilt his career afterward. "That's honorable," Hussle said. "You don't see that." It didn't hurt that Hussle had known Dallas Martin, Atlantic's senior VP of A&R, since 2011, when he was working with Rick Ross at Warner Music.[129]

Despite living by the mantra "Fucc Tha Middleman" for years, Hussle did enjoy the idea of partnering with the iconic label that was once home to Aretha Franklin and Ray Charles.[130] Apparently the feeling was mutual. "He's really looked up to," said Kallman. "I think he's a true icon, and so culturally significant to the entire West Coast. I'm super, super excited about *Victory Lap*. I think you've made an incredible album and I can't wait to get it out there."[131]

"As youngsters, looking up at Snoop, Jay, Puff, and Master P doing things with the music and enterprising, we always wished and hoped to be in that position," Blacc Sam said. "And everything we had always admired other people doing, my brother was doing. From the store opening up to getting written about in *Forbes* and *GQ*."[132]

"We're finally getting the light shined back on us," said Adam. "'Cause you know, we all been listening to the Atlanta people. Even here in L.A. we're so soaked up with the south culture. It's like the light's been back on us now, and it's been awhile since it's been on us."[133]

Once Hussle locked in with Atlantic, everything started moving forward—fast forward. His team could feel the change right away. "He was just breaking down that wall of going to the real mainstream," says DJ V.I.P. "Not mainstream sellout, but just mainstream awareness."[134] As official tour DJ, V.I.P. saw the crowds at Hussle's shows increase by a factor of five to ten. "Once that partnership evolved and started to grow, that's when we were doing bigger festivals," he said. Hussle would soon land bookings on MTV's *TRL* and the BET Awards, and headline Broccoli Fest. "We had been at some of these shows before, on smaller stages," he said. "But not the prime-time slots."[135]

Hussle did not dip his toe into the mainstream. He and the

All Money In team dove in headfirst. Now that they were ready, every door was open to them. They would soon ink partnerships with Puma and Jay-Z's management firm, Roc Nation, kicking everything into overdrive. "We had Jay right there," says V.I.P. "Jay hadn't been fully invested in a West Coast artist like that ever. He was all hands on deck. He made his team and their assets fully available to us, and we were getting ready to start utilizing that. That would have single-handedly put us into nothing but arenas. We would have only been doing big tours, whether it was coheadlining or headlining. They just have the resources to put you in those big venues and sell out those seats."[136]

On Christmas Day 2017, Hussle and Boog went to the Staples Center to watch the Lakers play the Minnesota Timberwolves. Hussle was wearing his Wilt Chamberlain throwback jersey and a pair of Puma suedes in Lakers purple with gold stripes.[137] Despite rookie Kyle Kuzma scoring 31 points, the Lakers lost 121–104, but Hussle won. Just to be chilling courtside with his queen was victory. They'd had a bit of a rough patch over the past month. In late November he posted a tweet about them deciding to separate and focus on raising their children, then deleted the tweet.[138] A couple of days later his ex Tanisha, who still went by Chyna Hussle on Twitter, tweeted something about how they never broke up.[139] Social media can really make life complicated sometimes, especially when it comes to affairs of the heart. Somewhere along the way, reality always make a comeback, though, and pretty soon Hussle and Boog were good again.

Their courtside flex at the Staples Center had the paparazzi going nuts, and Hussle's choice of footwear was another strategic chess move, teasing the Puma collaboration they would announce on January 16, 2018. Hussle helped design the gear, and on his six-foot-three frame the tracksuits looked like formal wear. Hussle wore the designs on stage and in interviews. Puma sponsored his events, and contributed thousands to refurbishing the basketball court at 59th Street Elementary across from his granny's house. Granny even got to sip champagne on the jet.[140]

NBA All-Star Weekend is more like a full week of over-the-top parties featuring some of the highest paid athletes in the world balling out of control—in every sense of the word. It was also the perfect backdrop for the *Victory Lap* rollout. All week long there was no doubt that Nipsey Hussle was the king of L.A.

The only other pretender to that throne was New York rapper Tekashi 6ix9ine, a rainbow-haired prankster who spent the entire All-Star week trolling social media by talking slick about L.A. gangs, bragging that he didn't have to "check in" with any hoods.[141] Meanwhile the wildly successful artist was being extorted by members of his management team, affiliates of the Nine Trey Gangsta Bloods—whom he would later testify against in a New York courtroom.[142] All of Tekashi's All-Star bookings were canceled due to fear of retaliation and he avoided setting foot in any hoods, but he gained a lot of social media attention while making a mockery of a culture that Hussle respected.

Hussle had his own way of dealing with people like Tekashi. He would put them on "goofy time," meaning he'd ignore them until they self-destructed.[143] Whenever an interviewer asked about Tekashi Hussle refused to speak about him, knowing that trolls thrived on publicity, and any mention made or attention paid would only give his career more oxygen. Hussle did reveal some of his thinking in a conversation with his old friend DJ Drama.

"Tekashi is making a lot of headlines basically playin' with the streets," Drama said. "What are your thoughts on that?"

"I wouldn't speak on nobody specifically," Hussle said. "But just what you said about playin' with the streets, I wouldn't suggest it. I wouldn't play with Atlanta. I wouldn't play with New York. I wouldn't play with *any*. 'Cause it's real individuals everywhere, and if you disrespect somebody's home, they gonna feel you forced their hand. *Anywhere.* Not just L.A."[144]

When rappers travel out of town, they often "check in" with a local gang for protection. Referring to the practice as "friendly extortion," Hussle said he preferred to simply move with respect. "When I come to Atlanta, I show respect and I tap in," he said. "I'm not in my hometown. I got my jewelry on. I might be a victim if I don't walk and tread the right type of way. Much as we secure, you're not bigger than the program."[145]

Nor did Hussle advise those visiting Los Angeles during the All-Star festivities to check in. "You can't pay me for no love," he said. "I sell music and clothes and all type of other shit. I don't sell like, friendship or protection." But when it came to his real friends, that was a different story. "You can take my car," he said. "You can come to my store. You wanna know where to go eat at? You can meet my homeboys. You can get niggas' numbers. If any problems or whatever, just call in. That ain't because you had to. That's because it's strength in numbers and we only from one place."[146]

On the evening of Tuesday, February 13—three days before the album dropped—the same Brink's truck featured in the "Hussle & Motivate" video pulled up in front of a Los Angeles strip club. The truck was now painted black and marked with All Money In logos. The back doors swung open and out jumped

Adam, Cowboy, J Roc, Cobby, and Nipsey Hussle—all dressed in AMI hats and black *Victory Lap* T-shirts—with heavy bags of cash in each hand. "Neighborhood!" they yelled.

"Congratulations on the new album!" yelled a TMZ reporter on the scene. "What's up with the armored vehicle?"

"All Money In! That's what's up!" Hussle shouted. "Bags, nigga. Control the bags."[147]

After making it rain at the strip club that night they returned to the hood and parked the All Money In Brink's truck at Crenshaw and Slauson. Soon Hussle started getting phone calls. The truck had been towed. "Why?" Hussle wondered out loud. "What's the threat of this truck being parked right here?" He came to find out that police claimed the truck's registration was expired and that it was parked in a handicapped spot. But it was hard not to feel as if the LAPD was out to get him. "We got a long storied history with the Seventy-Seventh police department," he said. "They feel like it's a failure for them if we succeed, to a degree . . . None of us on probation, none of us on parole no more. We pay a lot of taxes. We employ a lot of people in the area. We are responsible for, I'm sure, this corner bein' a lot less crime-ridden. We pay rent on four different units on Crenshaw and Slauson."[148]

Making the best of the situation, they started a contest to win a 14-karat gold All Money In pendant. "Tha police buster ass towed our All Money In Brinks Truc," Hussle wrote on Instagram, instructing fans to pull up to the tow yard where the truck had been impounded and post a photo with the hashtag #FREE THEBRINKSTRUCK. "We had a lot of people come down," said the receptionist at Pepe's Towing on Boyle Avenue.[149] "It was three hundred, four hundred niggas outside the gate takin' pictures," Hussle stated. "We didn't take it too serious, though. We laughed it off."[150]

Out on the town the following night in a black du-rag, white Puma *Victory Lap* tracksuit, and mad gold chains, Hussle and J Stone and BH celebrated in the streets of their city. Even amid the jubilation of *Victory Lap*'s release, Hussle took the opportunity to speak on the police. "One thing we don't respect is how the LAPD came through and took our Brink's truck," Hussle said. "We puttin' on for the city, we showin' love. We raisin' the expectations of young niggas that come out the hood. And we don't understand *why* the police wanna hate on that. But guess what? We gonna turn a negative into a positive. So the Brink's truck is back in L.A. It's back in our possession. All All-Star weekend we turnin' up. *Victory Lap* is officially out."[151]

The first time Ralo had a chance to listen to the album in full, he noticed something unusual about the guest features. "Everybody's verse on *Victory Lap* was paying homage to Nipsey," he said. Hip-hop is a competitive sport. There's usually a bit of low-key one-upmanship involved whenever one rapper is invited to rap on another rapper's record. (Kendrick Lamar's song-stealing guest verse on Big Sean's "Control" being one extreme example.) "It's an honor to see that type of shit," Ralo said. "To have a debut album come out, and the features are that big, and his peers are just givin' reverence to this man. That shit was almost bizarre. Like they knew he was gonna die."[152]

Amid the strip club parties and gold chain giveaways, Hussle carved out time to cut the ribbon on Vector90, the coworking space, business incubator, and STEM academy that he cofounded in the Crenshaw District.[153] His business partner David Gross was on hand for the launch event, along with L.A. City Councilmember Marqueece Harris-Dawson and Vector90 board member Don Peebles, a self-made Black businessman who manages $5 billion in real estate. "He's building the tallest skyscraper on the West Coast right now," Hussle said. "And he's a first-generation success story. His dad was a mechanic, and he accumulated that type of success in one generation."[154]

While *Victory Lap* cuts like "Grinding All My Life" and "Hussle & Motivate" played in the background, invited guests and media toured the sleek space, absorbing information from an art exhibition highlighting the dearth of Black talent at high-tech companies like Google and Facebook. Vector90 was designed to help bridge the gap between South Central and Silicon Valley.

"It's a big problem in Silicon Valley right now," said Hussle. "It's a lack of diversity. It's a lack of our people in powerful positions in these billion-dollar companies that are poppin' up. And when people address the companies, the companies got an excuse. They say it's no pipeline from the inner cities to Silicon Valley."[155] As a young man who grew up in this neighborhood and had an interest in technology, Hussle understood what a difference a resource like this could make.

"I was never just . . . a completely self-destructive young dude," he said. "I was always somebody that was fuckin' with computers or tryin' to learn how to make beats or rappin' early. And I just got so frustrated with not havin' no outlet that I damn near threw the towel in on tryin' to be creative or trying to go against the grain of the culture I was surrounded by. So I know the pressure of havin' good intentions and then seeing nowhere for them to connect and saying 'fuck it.' So I think that to have those places where people can connect early, you'll save a lot of people."

"I grew up around here and there is absolutely no space like this," said Desha Greene, one of the first entrepreneurs to use the space. The single mom of twins was developing her own dating app, but had to go to coffee shops to hold meetings. Now she had a space where she could work without interruptions and network with like-minded professionals. Greene was planning to enroll her daughters in the STEM academy as soon as it opened.[156]

Later that night Hussle was backstage at the Hollywood Palladium as Rance and the 1500 or Nothin' band warmed up the stage. The official *Victory Lap* release party was a star-studded event. Hussle brought out Marsha Ambrosius to perform the song "Real Big" with him. He brought out Puffy to perform "Young Niggas." He brought out Sacramento street legend Mozzy. He brought out his day-one homeboy J Stone. And then, as a giant screen flashed the word VICTORY against a backdrop that alternated red and blue, 1500 started playing the beat for "Last Time That I Checc'd" and Hussle brought out . . . his daughter, Emani.[157]

"That was my favorite guest of the night," Hussle said. "She finished the set with me."[158] Casually dressed in a T-shirt and jeans, Emani gripped the mic and rapped the chorus with impressive authority for a nine-year-old as her father's voice played in the background. Apparently all those nights in the studio had not been lost on her. Hussle put his arm around his daughter's shoulders as she finished her bars, then gently guided her to the side of the stage before YG came charging out, greeting his homeboy with a pound so powerful you could feel it all the way in the back of the venue. Their explosive performance closed out the show with a mighty demonstration of unity, creating an indelible moment that will go down in L.A. rap history.[159]

Hussle believed *Victory Lap* would be the beginning of a whole new phase of his career. "I've learned a lot just putting this out," he said after the *Victory Lap* rollout. "This my first major label release. It's the first time I actually mixed and mastered a project. It's the first time we really did a full campaign and marketed an album and did radio runs and all that. I feel like 'Cool, I got it. I figured it out. I know the whole process. I know everybody at Atlantic. We got a working history.' The next one gotta be bigger. It gotta continue to grow."[160]

As a hustler, Nip wanted a platinum album so he could charge platinum prices. But more than money he wanted his respect as an artist, and as a man. "People know the name Nipsey," he said. "They know, like, he from L.A. He has respect in his city. He's made a couple moves . . . But as far as musically I haven't really been able to flex like that. And this album was an example of me goin' in that direction. And I still got a little space to grow and space to really just demonstrate what I'm capable of."[161]

Chapter 11

EXIT STRATEGY

EVERY NOW AND THEN I THINK IF WE CAN GET BACK TO
THAT BLACK SHIT, INSTEAD OF KILLIN' FOR BANGIN'
AND CRACK SHIT

—Nipsey Hussle, "Payback," *Bullets Ain't Got No Name Vol. 3* (2009)

"I always had a political opinion," Hussle said during a January 2017 panel discussion about mass incarceration and the prison industrial complex. "I always had some type of understanding. But until I had a voice, until I had a reputation as a successful artist, nobody cares about your opinion. It means nothing. People look at the car you're pulling up in, or where you're living at, or your economic status, and judge your philosophy based on how far it's taken you."[1]

By that point in his three-decade journey on earth, Nip's personal philosophy had taken him far. Reviled for most of his life by polite society as a Rollin' 60s Crip and a "gangsta rapper," he'd now earned the right to exchange ideas in a public forum at the historic Nate Holden Performing Arts Center alongside a California State University professor, a member of the Los Angeles police commission, an attorney and CNN contributor, and the Oscar-nominated director Ava DuVernay. On the poster for the event, a screening of DuVernay's eye-opening documentary *13th*, Nipsey Hussle was identified, without exaggeration, as a "business mogul, philanthropist, and community activist."[2]

In keeping with his Marathon mindset, Nipsey would never deny the rocky road he'd traveled and the obstacles he'd overcome to get to this point. "If you're a young Black or Latino male, going to jail is just something you expect to happen in your life," Nipsey stated. "The film gave a vocabulary to something we as young people felt and understood viscerally. We ain't naturally had the factual breakdown of it, but we felt this gotta be set up. This can't just be all coincidence. This gotta be by somebody's design."[3]

By way of illustration, Nipsey went on to share a recent experience from his own life. "I got a few businesses on Crenshaw and Slauson, in the actual strip mall right there," he said, and the crowd burst into applause. "I wasn't bragging," he added. "I wanted to make a point."

Before he could continue, Hussle's easygoing relatability inspired a member of the audience to share his own testimony.

"*That's what we need!*" a voice in the room yelled out. "That's what we need! More businesses. More solid businesses that put Black people first."

"No question," Nipsey replied.

"'Cause all them people want is money!" the brother went on, his voice rising.

"Yeah," Nip said, letting him vent.

"Y'all got the bread. Put it together! Like you doing at Slauson and Crenshaw." The *y'all* he had in mind were not, presumably, people on this panel, but other members of the Black community. People who hadn't shown up for this community dialogue.

"Absolutely," Hussle affirmed.

"We need solid, physical results," said the voice in the crowd. "It's time for our protest to match the physical work. You can't just be marchin' and then goin' home, and nobody putting money together to buy nothin'."

"Right," Hussle said, ceding the floor out of respect to the urgency of the man's message.

"The population of Los Angeles: 4.7 million white, 4.2 million Latino, and 800,000 Black," the man stated down to the decimal, as if all too familiar with the math. "A Black man can't rent a room nowhere!"

"Right," said Hussle.

By this point the audience member's voice was raw with emotion. The audience, the moderator, the other panelists sat in silence, witnessing a moment of public catharsis.[4]

"I can't rent a room," the man said, in summary, "because none of my people don't own no fuckin' homes!" What could be realer than real estate? The search for place was difficult, even in one of L.A.'s oldest Black neighborhoods, ravaged as it was by disinvestment and the forces of gentrification.

"Real shit," Nipsey replied, acknowledging the authenticity of the pain being shared. "Real shit. That's a good point you make." The air seemed to flow back into the room as he resumed his own testimony.

"The reason I brought it up," Hussle said, "I was in that parkin' lot just passin' through, and one of my people called me like, 'Bro, police over here got somebody hemmed up. Chill out.' So I kicked it at the gas station for five minutes." Then he thought about it again. "I'm not on probation," he said. "I ain't do nothin'."[5]

Relating to the feeling, the audience let out a burst of tense laughter.

"So I drove in," Nipsey continued. "Soon as I drove in the parking lot, the police pulled me over." He'd been through the routine so many times before that he engaged the cops in casual banter.

"I let 'em do their procedure," he said. "And as they was gettin' ready to leave, they like, 'Yeah, bro, I just wanna give you a heads up. The city attorney has your store as one of the top ten gang targets in L.A.'"

The audience let out a collective groan.

"So I'm like, 'Why is that?' And we just started talking." As he spoke, Hussle was back in that moment, stating his case all over again, this time to a more receptive audience.

"Number one, it's very, very hard to start a business and be successful," he said. "Especially if you don't come from business owners that have been successful." The crowd applauded in agreement. "So we already dealt with that. And we dealt with that without no help from y'all.

"Number two, everybody that work for this store is from this area," he stated. "And if it wasn't for this store, might be a part of your problem." Louder applause this time.

"Number three, they're doing a big development on Crenshaw," Hussle stated, referring to a $3 billion light rail project from LAX. "They got all type of stuff gettin' built. Only time it's a problem is when *we* doin' it?" Now the crowd was wide open. "What happen when they build a Shell gas station or a Hungry Harold's or any one of these businesses?" Hussle asked. "*That's* not a gang hangout?"[6]

Experience had taught Hussle that in the eyes of the LAPD, any man, woman, or child from this neighborhood could potentially be classified as a gang member, gang affiliated, or "from a gang area," regardless of their actual character or intentions. Even as the ACLU's federal lawsuit made its way through the courts, gang injunctions—and the beliefs that gave rise to them—were still very much in force.

"Your interests are not opposite to ours," Hussle explained to the police officers, reminding them that their mission statement—as painted on the door of every police car—was "to protect and serve."

"We've got a similar interest as business owners," he added.

The police officer in the parking lot told him that if the city attorney could hear him speak, he was sure that their opinion would change.

"But we don't get to speak," Hussle lamented to the crowd. "We catch a case, and they come shut our shit down, and we deal with reality. We deal with bills gotta get paid, overhead still real, and we got our legitimate operation shut down."[7] The cycle had played itself out more than once. What was Hussle's exit strategy? Could he actually break the cycle and transition from surviving to thriving?

Even after all the setbacks, Hussle remained in Marathon mode, willing to rally back and give it another try. "I know our generation, we got tired of trying," he admitted. "Or even watching people try and it not working. Even culturally, it ain't no Black Panther groups. Black Lives Matter is the closest thing to it. That used to be like a young person's outlet for their frustration.

"And now?" he continued. "You got gangs. Niggas is gang-bangin' as a result of sayin' 'Fuck it.' When you get tired of just tryin' to do right and bein' weighed down and feelin' the gravity of an uphill battle just to do right."[8]

But maybe, just maybe, it was time to try again.

Efforts like this panel discussion were a step in the right direction. Bringing scholars, professionals, and families together to look at Black history in hopes of charting a way forward. Watching and discussing DuVernay's searing film 13th allowed the public to confront the ways public policy and corporate interests have conspired to keep the legacy of slavery in place, and encouraged viewers to identify ways of breaking those cycles.

"How long does a moment last until it becomes a movement?" asked DuVernay. She spoke about the galvanizing effect of the brutal murder of Emmett Till, the fourteen-year-old boy from Chicago who went to visit family in Mississippi in 1955.[9] While stopping by a grocery story, he allegedly offended a white woman named Carolyn Bryant, who would later admit that she lied about some details of her story. Emmett Till was abducted from his great-uncle's home by Bryant's husband and his half brother. They beat the boy, shot him, and tied barbed wire around his neck, attached him to a heavy metal fan, then sunk his body in the Tallahatchie River. Three days later his body was recovered and returned to Chicago, where his mother, Mamie, insisted on an open-casket funeral. Tens of thousands came to see Emmett Till's disfigured body, which was even photographed for *Jet* magazine with his mother looking on. A white jury acquitted Till's killers expeditiously. Outrage over the boy's lynching helped galvanize the Civil Rights movement. Later that same year the Montgomery Bus Boycott brought names like Rosa Parks and Martin Luther King Jr. to prominence.

"I think Trayvon [Martin] was our Emmett Till in terms of a real activation around outrage that instigated action," said DuVernay. "Unfortunately, we've had a steady diet of horror and terror and trauma that continued to push us to a place where it wasn't enough to rage against it. We've organized against it. And now we have a president who is I don't think doing anything really new. He's just being louder about it and talking about it on Twitter."[10]

"When we talk about the history of our Black liberation movement," said Dr. Melina Abdullah, "which began, as

Angela said, from the moment we were stolen from the shores of Africa, we resisted." The chair of Pan-African Studies at Cal State University, Los Angeles, and cofounder of the L.A. chapter of Black Lives Matter spoke about the importance of the Black Arts movement to the struggle. "W. E. B. DuBois said 'all art is propaganda,' and we need our artists to recognize their roles," mentioning poets Amiri Baraka and Sonia Sanchez.

"Be careful," the moderator of the panel said to Hussle. "You might have to rap that song that I like."[11]

"She talkin' about this record called 'Fuck Donald Trump,'" he said with a grin as the room filled with applause. Hussle said films like *13th* help people of his generation connect the dots of their own history. "You might have an understanding of one of the issues," he said, "which was the increase of incarceration over the decades." Learning more about the political mechanisms and corporate interests behind the prison industrial complex gave Hussle more confidence.[12]

With the launch of The Marathon Clothing smart store in the summer of 2017 paving the way for the rollout of *Victory Lap*, Hussle was accumulating the financial wherewithal to express his viewpoints and make sure that people were listening. He wasn't just making songs. He was opening businesses and providing jobs at a time when many Black-owned businesses were being priced out as investors prepared for the arrival of the light rail and the football stadium being built in Inglewood. He was working with the L.A. City Council on a public arts project called Destination Crenshaw to help stave off the process of cultural erasure that went along with gentrification. To really make a difference for people like the man who spoke up during the panel discussion, someone had to create affordable housing in the community. There was so much to do, and so little time.[13]

Tick–tick–tick.

On July 7, 2017, Sean Mack, the twenty-four-year-old brother of David Gross, was murdered in Inglewood. "My younger brother was born after I left L.A. and we developed our relationship from afar," said Gross. "When I moved back to L.A. we became very close. He worked for me and we spent a lot of time together." Sean Mack was an aspiring rapper and a member of a Blood set. "Just a really cool, dynamic, and charismatic kid," Gross said of his little brother.

"I wish I could go back and rewind time and show my older brother something different," Gross said. "He wouldn't be in a jail now. I wish I coulda grabbed my younger brother and showed him a different opportunity. He wouldn't be in a grave right now."[14]

Gross and Hussle sought to galvanize a movement starting in their hometown and spreading across America's Black metropolises—Oakland, Chicago, Detroit, Baltimore, Philly, Atlanta, Memphis. "The idea of buying back the block, I don't know where that started, but it's been ubiquitous in our culture," Gross said. "Black excellence and ownership are what Nipsey preached and rapped about for his entire career. We figured the quickest way to shift the mindset, and then shift the culture, was to have a lot of the people who helped move culture." What Nip is to South Central, T.I. is to Atlanta, Meek Mill is to Philly. Imagine if they were all working together toward a common goal.[15]

Except that his vision wasn't imaginary at all. It was already happening, and of course Hussle was a driving force behind it. Just as the NBA has a players' association, hip-hop had become big enough and powerful enough that it made sense for groups of artists to come together and make sure they were aligned for their best interests. Roc Nation was a prime example of what was possible, but there was much more work to be done.

"When somebody get in, we gotta leave the door open," Hussle told *Fader* in January 2017. "We gotta carry this shit the right way. That's why me and YG—we saw what happened with Death Row out here. The street politics wasn't all the way sustainable so it crumbled. So with YG being a Blood and me being on the Crip side, we had to make sure, as leaders, it was the right way to do it, from an L.A. perspective. And with hip-hop in general, I fuck with Meek Mill. We was just at the table yesterday. That's the type of conversations we having—Drake was at the table, Meek was at the table, T.I. was at the table, J Prince was at the table, Mustard was at the table. It's almost like some Corleone, Five Families shit if niggas really do it the right way. We can definitely come at it like a player's association and make sure that it's fair."[16]

Now that Hussle had decoded the matrix of the music industry, his restless creativity was toying with other types of ventures. The next logical step for the kid who built his own computer to make his own beats was to make a foray into technology.

"I wanna get into tech for real," he said. "I got ideas that I'm really passionate about. It remind me a lot how I used to look at hip hop . . . I know I could add value. So that's something that I wanna use my platform as an artist, and as someone that's got music attention, to set the meetings up and have them convos. And just do my due diligence and learn also." Although the mental divide was huge, Silicon Valley was just an hour away from L.A. by air. "We supposed to be involved," Hussle insisted. "We grew up in the generation of there was no computers at one time—and then there *was* computers. You feel me? And I seen how me buyin' a computer and gettin' Pro Tools changed my life. And me learning how to engineer my own recordings impacted my life, in a major way. So I wanna be involved in that."[17]

Hussle saw how much massive tech companies relied on hip-hop, which was now the number-one genre of music on streaming platforms. "Dr. Dre was one of the first ones in that space with the streaming service that turned into Apple Music, and the hardware too, the headphones," said Hussle. "Any one of these billion-dollar platforms, a lot of the value comes from the people of influence that use the platform. And those people are never involved in the business. But the attention that they garner is bein' leveraged."[18]

Hussle was always meeting interesting people at Lakers games. He had good seats at the Staples Center, so the people sitting next to him were usually worth talking to. At one game he sat next to Sean Rad, the founder of Tinder, who explained how an app is valued. "He told me an equation," said Hussle. "Basically, there's a certain dollar amount for every user on an app. If you want to go sell your app, the value of your company is based on users times this dollar amount." When you add up all the Twitter users who have 10 million followers, you can calculate the value of the company that way. "So when Twitter gets evaluated at so-and-so billion, the model is an eyeball monetization, an attention monetization model," Hussle explained. "And who's the reason that they are paying attention? The celebrity. The artist."[19]

Driven by a sense of responsibility, Hussle lived according to codes and principles that included giving back to the community. "You can't break the rules, the fundamental rules," he said. "Be a man of your word. Do what you say you gonna do. Respect people the way that you would like to be respected." He never forgot that it wasn't Jay-Z who put him on in the game. It was the people who paid five dollars for his mix CDs when he was standing in the plaza at Slauson and Crenshaw. "People supported me when they didn't have a reason to," he recalled, all these years later. "You know what?" they said. "You're a young person trying, and I support the ambition."[20]

As successful as they'd become, All Money In and the Marathon brand remained a family business. "My dad is part of The Marathon Clothing," said Hussle. "He work every day at the shop. My brother is my business partner. My sister work with us. Moms. Everybody." For Hussle, that feeling of family extended to the core team, and from the team to the community that supported the overall operation. The fact that the community was intertwined with an intricate gang hierarchy that had its own set of internal politics never seemed to deter him.

"It's all real businesses that have employees," said Hussle. "That takes administration and take everybody being committed. I definitely feel responsible, because everybody's committed to my dream."[21]

Beyond being a musician, entrepreneur, and activist, Nipsey Hussle was an innovator. Constantly seeking out knowledge, he found new ways to look at old problems, devising fresh solutions that he shared with the world. At Vector90 he was experimenting with ways to go beyond financial incentives and extract value from the community's knowledge base in other ways. Volunteering to share expertise at the STEM academy downstairs could earn people credit to use the coworking space upstairs. Cultural experience was what people wanted more than anything; that was the true source of inspiration. "If you focus and zero in, you can inspire a person to a degree that they work for the movement," he said. "You planted somethin' in 'em. They walk into a room, and if there's nine people that don't know about you, they feel like they got a dope opportunity to gain currency with nine people by puttin' 'em on somethin' dope." His quality-over-quantity approach was paying off in the long run.

The challenge, then, was to be the best version of Nipsey Hussle. To embody everything that meant to the world, and live up to it every single day. "I think we represent inspiration," he said. "I think we represent stayin' down. I think we represent pulling yourself from your bootstrap. I think we represent one of the main core principles of hip-hop." A key component of that was remaining loyal to the soil. "I started on Crenshaw and Slauson," he said. "I'm on Crenshaw & Slauson now. The Marathon continues."[22]

Hussle took a decade to deliver his debut. Now that he had his situation set up, and was putting the finishing touches on yet another recording studio—with the most state-of-the-art equipment in a secure location this time—he was not trying to waste any more time.

"Me and Nip were texting once or twice a week," says Ralo. "He was heavily pursuing me, sending me pictures of the new studio." He had recently signed a ten-year lease on an entire floor in the building where they completed *Crenshaw*. "He was having showers installed and there was an SSL board and at least five or six different studio rooms that had been built out with the bass traps, mixing consoles, vocal booths—everything's professional, the lighting was dope as fuck." Hussle wanted Ralo to come back and lock in on production for All Money In. "Look, we're gonna work until you need a break," Hussle told him. "We're not gonna burn ourselves out on each other. We're gonna get what we came for, then we're gonna go on about our business."[23]

The release of *Victory Lap* was just the beginning of Hussle's strategy. "The focus was to get the album out but we had an in-depth plan of what we wanted to do," he said, "and so part of that is gettin' the label really solid." He was planning an All Money In album featuring artists like Killa Twan, Pacman, J Stone, Cobby, and BH. "We gon' come with the original home team of my homies that grew up in the section with us and built the sound with us," Hussle said. It would be a return to making music collectively, just how they all began, but on a whole new level.[24]

"I'm gearin' up to start recording again for the next one," Hussle told DJ Drama. "I'm tryin' to come back ASAP. I took so long to make my official debut we gotta gas now. It's about music. I got a whole goal about how I wanna deliver the albums that's under this deal. I wanna do this in a concentrated window. I don't wanna get on no two-year hiatus and shit."[25]

"I got an album concept called *Exit Strategy*, that might be one of my last ones," Hussle said. "It's a term they use in business when you build companies. You create an exit strategy as you make a company. You don't wait till you're five years in it . . . So the exit strategy for a lot of companies is to go public, or to sell." The concept was rooted in the idea that any brand peaks during a specific time window. "As an artist, as a brand, as a rapper, as a musician, you got a window and a lot of people—even an athlete—they don't have no exit strategy. It's just living in the false reality that it's going to be like this forever. From their lifestyle, the way they spend money, everything. I don't feel comfortable moving like that, so I have an exit strategy."[26]

Knowing when to bow out was all-important—in music, in business, in the stock market. "It's not called quitting if you quit while you ahead," he said. "It's about being aware and being strategic enough to know that you got to get out the pool at some point. You got to put your clothes back on and dry off."

On *No Pressure*, a collaborative mixtape Hussle recorded with a young artist named Bino Rideaux and released on Novem-

ber 25, 2017, Hussle rapped about being "Stucc In The Grind."
On *Victory Lap*, of course, he would rap about "Grinding All
My Life." Hussle combined the two songs into one official music
video, emphasizing the relentlessness of his work ethic. He often
spoke about grinding extra hard while the spotlight of fame was
shining so that there would be enough to sustain his family when
that light began to fade.

At the time *Victory Lap* was released, Hussle estimated he
had another fifty songs in the stash. "I got the album *done*, like
mastered in my hand," he said. "All right, what we gonna do
now? We gotta shoot some videos, we gotta do the marketing
and figure out the release. I wanna stay in music mode. Yeah,
so . . . we got a ton of music." He had at least two other collaborative projects with Bino. He had the Future record, a record
with Hi-Tek on the beat, James Fauntleroy and Daz Dillinger
on vocals. He'd gotten in the studio with Meek Mill as well.
And then there was the Cardi B record. Despite a minor internet hubbub when Hussle questioned Cardi's decision to use
disrespectful gang slang on social media, Hussle and his daughter were both fans of her music. "Number one, she's a woman,"
Hussle said. "I'm not even into addressing women in any other
way but with love and respect—that's not what I do."[27]

More importantly, they had gotten into the studio and
collaborated on a record called "I Just Wanna Know" with a beat
by Mars from 1500 along with a producer named Lil' C. "It's a
banger," he said. "It's a fuck anthem." Hussle sent it to Mike Will
to touch up the production and give it a little extra bounce. "She
kilt the verse," Hussle said. "In her verse she say, 'Can a Crip
nigga fuck with a Blood bitch?'" The song took Hussle and YG's
message of unity to a whole different level. Hussle said he'd love
for it to come out. He'd also been recording with a new artist

from L.A. who Dallas Martin had discovered by the name of Roddy Ricch.[28]

Hussle wasn't sure which records were going on which project, but he knew how he wanted to close it all out. "I'ma name my last album *The Spook Who Sat by the Door* when I finish our situation with our partnership at Atlantic," he said. "Anybody who hasn't seen that movie or read the book, it's about a gang member from Chicago, who presented himself in a way. He never caught no cases. He had a clean-cut look. And he infiltrated the CIA. He became educated and basically he used their agenda, which was to have a token nigga in the CIA for political purposes—he used it against 'em."[29]

Whereas Dan Freeman, the antihero of *The Spook Who Sat by the Door*, blended into the background at the CIA, Hussle wasn't exactly clean-cut. "That's one of the reasons why I was so vocal about where I was comin' from and where I represented, because I knew who I wanted to mobilize," he said. Distinguishing between the culture of hip-hop and "the power structure of the music industry," Hussle played the part of the average "gangsta rapper," but with a whole different agenda. "They got prescribed personas they expect from us," Hussle said. "So I feel like the way he use their intention against 'em was one of my underlying strategies."

"You got to put the medicine in the candy," said Charlamagne Tha God of *The Breakfast Club*, who picked up on the Spook reference in "Blue Laces 2" because he'd read the book and seen the movie. "What's interesting about that book, all his people used to call him an Uncle Tom and a coon and a sellout. And he was there workin' for them the whole time."

"I don't wanna blow nothin' up like he did in the movie," Hussle replied. "But just in terms of bein' able to mobilize his homies to a higher cause, that's somethin' I feel like we all gotta do. Kendrick talk about it in 'Dedication.' Me and Kendrick and Top and Snoop, we had a convo at the Pac premiere. Just about a little bit of what we talkin' 'bout."[30]

Hussle's exit strategy was unfolding to perfection. He just needed a little more time. In one of his last interviews, Hussle stopped by the KRRL FM radio station where Big Boy asked him how much of his iceberg was above the water. "For real, I would say just the tip of the iceberg," Hussle replied. "It's so crazy 'cause how long we been pushin' and how much ground we covered. I was playing with a handicap the whole time. I been telling people I been paid to practice for real. I ain't know how to do nothing. We learned on the job. And to be where I'm standing now? With the information I have and the resources and the relationships. If we could do what we did standing way back there. And here what can we do?"[31]

On the afternoon of September 14, 2018, Blacc Sam found himself dealing with a life-or-death situation on Slauson and Crenshaw. Gunshots rang out in the shopping plaza parking lot. A member of the Rollin' 60s had shown up at the Marathon Clothing store, looking for trouble and a fight broke out.

Police responded to find blood on the ground. All witnesses on the scene were uncooperative at best. Police interviewed a man who had been stabbed and beaten so badly that he needed nine staples in his head. He claimed that he had been assaulted by Blacc Sam, and struck with a metal pipe, but would not answer questions about how the conflict started. He denied that any gun had been involved or that there was even a shooting, although multiple witnesses heard gunshots. Video footage showed the "victim" arriving in a red vehicle and taking something out of the glove compartment before walking toward the store. A few minutes later he can be seen returning to the car, bleeding, and pursued by a group of people whose faces are not visible.[32]

Despite the contradictory evidence, Blacc Sam was arrested for assault and locked up for a month. "Honestly, bro, that situation was just a case of the police just bein' devilish," said Hussle,[33] who was three thousand miles away at the time attending Rihanna's fourth annual Diamond Ball at Cipriani Wall Street. "They see what we doin'. They see what the energy is. They see what direction we goin' in. And just the history of where we come from, they still hate that. And so they take opportunities." The incident prompted E. Y. Song, who managed the shopping plaza for its owners, to file an eviction proceeding seeking to kick out all of the Asghedom brothers' businesses, including the Marathon Clothing smart store.[34]

A month after his arrest, Sam posted his own $1 million bail and went to court, where his charges were dismissed. "The victim's account is somewhat contradicted by other evidence and reports from anonymous witnesses," wrote Alice Kurs of the Los Angeles District Attorney's Office. "At this point it cannot be ruled out that the victims went to the location armed with a gun to confront the suspect and the group of men hit the victim in self-defense (or to wrestle the gun away from him)."[35] Hussle and his brother boarded the Puma private jet with their grandmother and flew to Las Vegas for a charity event, giving sneakers to high school students. "You know I gotta talk some shit," said Sam on his way to the jet. "A million-dollar bond. Nigga, what you talking about? We in Vegas already."[36]

BEEN TRYNA CHANGE MY LIFE BUT IT'S AGGRAVATIN'
MAKIN' THE SAME MISTAKES TWICE, I'M SHACKLED TO SATAN

—Nipsey Hussle, "Mac 11 on the Dresser," *The Marathon* (2010)

Driving through South L.A. in Hussle's Maybach, BH didn't have a care in the world. "Our hood went through some crazy shit in the last twenty or thirty years," said Nip's young apprentice. "It kinda was like a black cloud over our whole hood." After he got shot, he'd decided he was done with his old lifestyle. "It ain't even worth it," he says. "I almost died. And what did I almost die for? Nothing!"[37]

He and Nip would always talk about how to make things better for the kids coming after them. "It ain't about us no more," Hussle would say. "Let's motivate 'em, Hogg. Let's just keep going! We gotta motivate these kids to know where they can do this shit too. They ain't gotta go to the streets. They can look up to us and see, 'Damn, that nigga successful! But they come from nothin'! They from the block, but they havin' it their way.'"

That was the reason Hussle stayed grounded at Crenshaw and Slauson. "He was trying to make this shit better," says BH. "Nip had started opening all the businesses right there. But one thing I always used to always tell Nip, is like, 'Bro, now that we got these businesses and shit established, get the fuck from over here, bro! Like, don't even be over here like that. 'Cause we already done did what we did. They already know it's our shit.'"[38]

BH will never forget his last conversation with Hussle. "He came to get me, and we just ridin' and talkin'."

"BH, you done made it hard on yourself," Hussle told him.

"What you mean?" BH replied.

"Bro, all you do is drive Lambos, Rolls-Royces," he said. "You can't go back now—*Boooy*, you gotta keep going! But I know you can do it, nigga. Just keep going, bro! You can't turn back now."

They started laughing as they cruised through the streets of South Central. The lights of downtown were twinkling in the distance.

"One more thing," Hussle told him. "What you gotta understand too, bro, the hood look at you like a mirror—and look at me like a mirror."

"What you mean by that, bro?" BH asked him.

"The reason we get so much hate in the neighborhood is not because they hate us," he said. "The people that's over here, everybody has the same dreams, but everybody didn't accomplish their dreams. They didn't accomplish their goals. So now that we drive down Slauson and we in the Maybach or a Rolls or whatever the hell it is, now they mad at us because they look at us like a mirror. Because they didn't accomplish the shit that they wanted to, and we did."

"Up till this day," BH told me, "I feel what he was saying."[39]

Chapter 12

TOO BIG TO FAIL

HOW MANY TIMES HAVE YOU GONE TO GOD IN PRAYER WITH A NEED IN YOUR LIFE JUST TOO HARD FOR YOU TO BEAR?

—Myrna Summers and the Voices of Bountiful Blessings Temple of Deliverance Choir, "Oh Give Thanks," *Come to Jesus Now* (1980)

IF YOU GO TO CHURCH TODAY, PRAY FOR US.

—Pacman Da Gunman, Twitter post (March 31, 2019, 3:10 a.m.)

"Don't cheat!" Lauren London scolded her man, seated across from "the amazing Nipsey Hussle the Great" on the set of *GQ*'s *Couples Quiz*. "I was just looking down at my jewelry," Hussle replied with a grin, leaning forward in his director's chair against a backdrop of soft pastel colors. "I wasn't looking at the questions."[1]

In her hands London held thirty index cards, each inscribed with a query designed to test how well her beloved truly knew her. Unfazed by the pressure of undergoing such an intimate interrogation by his significant other—on camera, no less—Hussle stepped up to the challenge with a spirit of playful competition. "See, he *stays* ready," Lauren said with an adorably affectionate inflection, "so he doesn't have to *get* ready."

"You got the script down!" Hussle replied, impressed. It should have come as no surprise. That's what happens when you fall in love with an actress.[2]

"This was a man who was proud to be with his woman," says Vanessa Satten, the *XXL* editor who put Hussle on the cover in 2010. "You see a lot of rappers proud to have many women. Nipsey and Lauren's relationship looked like genuine love for each other, and the timing of that beautiful fashion shoot of them together was so poignant."[3]

Posted on March 28, 2019—a month after Hussle and Boog's epic *GQ* spread first appeared—the charming eight-minute clip was viewed some 15 million times in the space of a year. It soon became one of those moments that seems destined to endure forever, or as long as YouTube shall live. There's an irresistible joy in watching two people so perfectly in sync bantering with each other, even when you know the greatest love stories seldom have a happy end.

Where did we first meet? "On Crenshaw and Slauson at my store."

What did I think of you? "She was head-over-heels sprung."

Correction: "I thought he was very tall."[4]

"Career-wise, Nipsey Hussle and Lauren London occupy the same branch on the pop-culture tree," Mark Anthony Green wrote in his *GQ* profile of the couple. "I call this branch: *The Branch White America Hasn't Exploited Yet.* It has its pros and cons."[5]

The pros—autonomy, authenticity, awesomeness—are self-evident. Dealing with the cons can be easier once you manage to decode the matrix (the *whole* matrix, all the way from the Spook Hunters to the Proud Boys—not to mention the prison industrial complex and the music industrial complex) and devise a strategy to short-circuit the machinery of exploitation.

Accomplishing that improbable feat made Hussle more apt to punk CEOs than to diss fellow rappers. "I'm integrated vertically, y'all niggas blew it," he boasted on the title track to *Victory Lap*, secure in the knowledge that he owned not *only* the rights to all his raps but *also* the delivery mechanism—The Marathon Clothing smart store.

When Hussle and David Gross named the STEM center at Vector90 "Too Big to Fail," they were borrowing a phrase popularized during the financial crisis of the late 2000s to justify government bailouts of failing Wall Street firms using taxpayer money. In the words of Federal Reserve Chair Ben Bernanke, "a too-big-to-fail firm is one whose size, complexity, interconnectedness, and critical functions are such that, should the firm go unexpectedly into liquidation, the rest of the financial system and the economy would face severe adverse consequences."[6] By reclaiming that term and applying it to residents of South Los Angeles, Hussle and Gross were saying that people can be as important as financial institutions. They had the audacity to suggest that the people of this neighborhood in particualr were too important, too interconnected, to let them fail.

On Saturday, March 30, Hussle made a quick run to Puerto Nuevo Coffee on West Slauson to pick up some green juice. Always eager to maximize family time, he brought Emani along for the ride. "Do you know how kids spell love?" he often said. "T-I-M-E." Between studio sessions, video shoots, promo, and his various businesses, finding personal time was a constant challenge. "That shit ain't easy," he said. "But it's worth it 'cause what you're actually doing is extending your presence here. You extending your legacy. It ain't gonna be one-sided. You get a reward offa that."[7]

Unless he was out of town, Hussle would drive Emani to school every day, and he tried to make the most of every minute they spent together. "We have a little convo before she get out of the car," Hussle once said while comparing notes on fatherhood with NBA star and devoted dad Stephen Curry. "She get sick of me runnin' the script," Hussle said with a smile, "but I pound it in her head."[8]

"What is integrity?"

Integrity is doing the right thing when nobody's looking.

"All right, are you a leader or a follower?"

I'm a leader.

"What's the difference?"

Think for myself.

"All right, do you have confidence?"

Yes.

"What's confidence?"

Believe in myself.

"That's our script every morning," he said. "And it seem basic, but I want her to get older and look back on the things that I thought was important. That my dad always put into me: integrity, confidence, and bein' a leader. Regardless if she can't really embrace those ideas right now, when she get older and do an evaluation of what the message that I wanted her to receive direct, she not gonna forget that. That was what my dad thought was really important was the integrity and leadership and confidence."[9]

While Hussle and Emani were at the counter of Puerto Nuevo waiting for his freshly squeezed juice, someone tapped him on the shoulder, trying to walk past in the little coffee shop.

"What up, Nip?"

He turned around to find a face he hadn't seen in many years.

"Your name Firebugg, huh?" Nip said.

"Yeah," the man replied. He was a similar age and height as Nip, a bit more musclebound, short hair, neatly trimmed beard. The tats on his skin spoke to his affiliations. The expression on his face spoke of humility and strength.

Nip smiled. "You from Centinela Park?"

"Yeah."[10]

The Centinela Park Family is a Blood set from east Inglewood whose territory borders the Rollin' 60s'. The rival sets have been mortal enemies for decades. Nipsey's song "Bullets Ain't Got No Names" recounts an episode from the days when he was in the field and his set went back-to-back-to-back against Centinela in one hellish night. "My hood is warring, so ain't no warnings," he rapped in a verse that was, like most of his music, based on a true story.[11]

On March 30, 2019, the energy in Puerto Nuevo was completely different. By chance or by destiny, Nip and Firebugg had bumped into each other in a neutral setting—Nip with his daughter, Firebugg with his girlfriend. The stage was set for a powerful convergence, a spontaneous meeting of the minds.[12]

Just as Hussle's worldview had evolved profoundly since his days of "putting in work" for the set, Firebugg had undergone a transformation of his own. "Twelve years in prison instilled something in me," he said. "Brought me up and awakened me as a grown man to see the bigger picture. So when I look back in hindsight I know that meeting was kind of like a blessing." He thought he was just stopping off to get breakfast, but when he walked in the restaurant, he recognized Hussle right away. Under the old way of thinking, he'd caught Hussle "slippin'" by walking up on him from behind. But Firebugg wasn't on that vibe anymore.

"Any type of destructive, any type of violence, anything like that was never on my mind," he said. Firebugg had watched Nip's success from behind bars, feeling a sense of pride that someone who survived a similar lifestyle could better himself, build businesses, and give back to the community. "Off top, I'm lookin' at a man that came from the same blocks that I came from," he said. "Different color, different side, but transgressed to a level in the game that—I'm not even talkin' about the millionaire status. I'm talkin' about the humanitarian on the blocks where we from. So when I walked up on him from behind it was like, *Wow, it's Nip*."

Hussle was similarly impressed. "I be seein' you on IG," he told Firebugg with a smile. "Real nigga shit . . . You know my niggas be payin' attention. We don't be pressin' the like button. You know what it is." They decided to sit down and chop it up.

As Hussle joined him in the coffee shop booth, he shook Firebugg's hand and noticed a tattoo on his arm. "Is that Malcolm?" he asked. "Bro, I've been waiting on you." He held on to Firebugg's hand with a firm grip.[13]

"Bro, I got a vision and I been needing a nigga who hold a voice and solid mind state," Hussle explained, reminding him of the last time they met. The year was 2007; the place, Los Angeles Men's Central Jail. Hussle had been on the run when he signed his recording contract, celebrated for a week in Jamaica, then returned to L.A. to turn himself in. The first *Bullets Ain't Got No Name* mixtape was yet to be released. His girlfriend Tanisha Foster was pregnant with Emani. He had so much to live for, but on that day everything was hanging in the balance.

"When I first fell I was in the holding tank," Hussle said, maintaining his grip on Firebugg's hand. The Centinela Park Blood remembered him vaguely. He'd seen a million people inside, gone through so much himself. "Nah," Hussle insisted. "You was in the holding tank. One of my homies had packed out one of your homies . . . Your homie jumped my homie so he jumped him back." Although prisoners in county jail are generally separated according to gang affiliation, when they first come in for processing they're all grouped together in the "holding tank," a place where anything can happen. Fights are not uncommon. Sometimes those fights can be fatal, leading to an inmate's body being "packed out." Firebugg was starting to remember. The young Crips were outnumbered. They wouldn't stand a chance. What was the point? In that moment he had the authority to stop the attack, and he used that authority.[14]

"We came in and you told your homies, 'Nah, we ain't about to jump them,'" Hussle told him. "I never forgot that, bro."

"He never let my hand go," Firebugg recalled. "And he just took me on a whole journey." They spoke about the drive-bys that inspired the song "Bullets Ain't Got No Names." Hussle told him he remembered being on the block with the homies saying, "Watch that corner." Enough time had passed that they could laugh about the memory now.[15]

Always a man who preferred demonstration over conversation, Hussle was making his moves more strategic than ever these days. There was so much he wanted to do, and so little time. "I'm with everything," he said, "but I don't have the energy for nothin'." His words resonated with Firebugg. The dumb shit. The fake shit. The buster shit. Snitchin'. They had neither time nor energy for any of that.

They never spoke of a "peace treaty," because that had been done before. Gang treaties never seemed to last. Whether police broke the truce or somebody else did something to someone, somehow the pressure always kicked in and the drama kicked off all over again. The solution wasn't another treaty but ownership, economic empowerment. Buying back the block, as Rick Ross put it in a song, with Hussle on the "Refinance Version" remix. "Operation buy back the 60s," Nip spit, before outside forces could "gentrify the whole inner city, genocide the whole inner city."

Hussle felt good walking up Slauson and seeing businesses that he and his brother had opened, knowing that they'd created jobs for people from the neighborhood. Now he was sketching out a vision for developing South L.A. that was bigger than Hyde Park. "I'm tryin' to do that all the way to the beach," he told Firebugg. "But between me and the beach is Inglewood . . . I've been waitin' on somebody to tell it on your side. Who else gonna tell the story better than you?"

The busy coffee shop was quiet now. It felt like the whole place was leaning toward their booth to catch the convo. "We both acknowledged the fact we was sworn enemies by gang rights but we said we was born brothers by essence," Firebugg wrote on a photo he posted on Instagram of the two of them together. "Let's get this flick and fuck the streets up," Hussle told him, then he and Emani made their way back outside. "I felt like I just witnessed two kings at a sit-down," Firebugg's girlfriend said afterward.

"When you cross paths with another real individual," Firebugg reflected after their meeting, "the word 'peace treaty' will never have to come up. Because we already know the level that we on in the game. And when you go deeper than that, a prophet knows when he sees another prophet. When he seen Malcolm on my arm, he's got a chain of Malcolm. I only think about that in hindsight. It didn't hit me till later on."

Hussle told Killa Twan about his meeting with Firebugg soon after it happened. Hussle's childhood friend grew up in a Blood neighborhood, so he and Nip had been crossing gang borders for years. Twan understood the significance of what had taken place. "These two done fought each other before," Twan said. "They done shot at each other before . . . If it was another weak individual, that would be a bad situation. But by him being another strong man how he is, they was able to sit and talk and eat and converse as men, instead of as an Inglewood Blood and a Crenshaw Crip."[16]

SITTIN' ON THE STEPS FEELIN' NO FEELINGS
LAST NIGHT IT WAS A COLD KILLIN'

—Nipsey Hussle, "Victory Lap," *Victory Lap* (2018)

Angelique Smith couldn't get a good night's sleep. After tossing and turning until the early morning, Ermias Asghedom's mother finally dozed off just before sunrise on Sunday, March 31, around 6 a.m. A highly spiritual person who regularly attended the KRST Unity Center of AfRaKan Spiritual Science, she lived her life according to the principle that "everything is in the divine perfect order of our creator." Angelique always had an extremely strong connection to her son Ermias, who was conceived on her birthday. For the past two weeks she had felt an unshakable sense that something wasn't quite right.[17]

Hussle wasn't supposed to be at The Marathon Clothing store on the afternoon of Sunday, March 31. He had no set schedule, but his usual routine was to stop by most weekday mornings after dropping Emani at school. Unless there was a public event planned, his bodyguard, J Roc, rarely came with him—especially on a Sunday.

"Always by hisself," said Cowboy, also known as Big Thundercat, the man who made music with Hussle and sponsored Lil Thundercat's put-on with the hood during the mid-2000s. He now worked full-time at the shopping plaza. "Only time he ever really had security is when he was on the road or on tour," said Cowboy. "As far as being in the inner city or coming to the job, he never had security ever."[18]

"Nobody's ever at the shop on Sunday like that," says DJ V.I.P. "Sundays were usually deemed for our families and for personal stuff. We try to make sure that we always had those days, because a lot of people had a girl, kids, things like that, so that was important to him. Nipsey made sure that not only he had time for that, but we all did."[19]

This particular Sunday was special for a few reasons. Hussle had been out late the night before, celebrating his godbrother Adam's "C-day" at the stroke of midnight. Their business partner Jorge Peniche credits "Dammy Dam" Andebrhan as "one of the guys that helped shape a lot of the sonics of the Nipsey Hussle brand and music."[20] Hussle posted a photo on Instagram showing him and Adam dressed in white with gold chains on, looking strong and prosperous. In the caption Hussle saluted him as "Day 1 wit this all $ In Shit! 🏁 "[21] Like Hussle, Adam had grown up with Fatts, and they had both made sure to take care of his family ever since his death a year and a half before.

Before Adam's C-day festivities, Nip had driven out to Anaheim on Saturday evening to watch the Texas Tech Red Raiders beat the Gonzaga Bulldogs and advance to the Final Four in the NCAA Men's Basketball Tournament. It was a long drive through rush hour traffic, but Hussle couldn't miss this game. He'd been invited by his old friend and mentor Big Bob Francis, the man who gave him the book *Contagious*, inspiring Hussle's Proud2Pay play, as well as *The 22 Immutable Laws of Branding*, which encouraged him to think of himself as a brand rather than just an artist. Big Bob's son Brandone Francis, a second-string forward for Texas Tech, had bragged to his friends that his favorite rapper would be in the building, and Hussle arrived just in time to see him come off the bench to drill a three-pointer. Brandone finished the game with six points, which was his team's exact margin of victory. Hussle cheered as loudly as anyone in the Honda Center. "He's forever gonna be my big brother," Brandone said. "I'm excited that he was part of the historic moment that we had as a team."[22]

Hussle's chance meeting with Firebugg the day before had Nip's mind racing with ideas. The two had been texting each other ever since he left the coffee shop. Firebugg had lost one of his closest homies during Centinela's wars with the 60s. For him to put that pain aside and embrace the vision of unification was a major step forward.

On Monday, April 1, Hussle was scheduled to join a meeting set up by Roc Nation with Los Angeles Police Commissioner Steve Soboroff (also a billionaire real estate developer credited with building Staples Center) and LAPD chief Michel R. Moore. "Our goal is to work with the department," the Roc Nation letter read, "to help improve communication, relationships, and work towards changing the culture and dialog between LAPD and the inner city."[23] After so many years of harassment by police, Hussle was somewhat skeptical, but he did his best to remain open-minded. The police were going to be either part of the solution or part of the problem, but at least it was worth a try.

On his way down Slauson toward The Marathon Clothing flagship store that Sunday, he passed by the corner of Crenshaw, where construction crews were working on the new light rail line that would speed passengers from LAX to this storied neighborhood where Hussle had staked his claim. Nip had worked closely with Councilmember Marqueece Harris-Dawson to develop the concept they called Destination Crenshaw, conceived as both a celebration of culture and a bulwark against gentrification.[24] The multimillion-dollar project brings together local artists, curators, and Zena Howard, a Black architect at Perkins & Will, the firm responsible for designing the Smithsonian National Museum of African American History and Culture.[25] Hussle remained actively involved in planning for the 1.3-mile "unapologetically Black" open-air museum designed to chronicle the story of African Americans in Los Angeles. Thanks to the community art intitiative, passengers riding the Metro rail, whoever they are, and wherever they're going, would be immersed in the story of Black people in L.A. as they ride through the Crenshaw District.[26]

These and countless other thoughts crackled through Hussle's brain at 2:53 in the afternoon as he pulled up to the Marathon store in his black Maybach with All Money In logos embossed and embroidered throughout the interior.

While sitting in the parking lot, Hussle posted a cryptic tweet: "Having strong enemies is a blessing." He knew that most of his followers would miss the veiled reference to Firebugg, but as with so much of Hussle's life and work, those who knew would *know*. He could not have foreseen the events that would unfold over the next twenty-nine minutes. *Tick-tick-tick.*[27]

"Sam was with Granny at the crib," says V.I.P., who was in North Carolina at the time in a private session. "Nip was just stopping by the shop to help the homie get some clothes. He just pulled up to look out for somebody from the neighborhood who just got out—and shit happened."[28]

The homie in question was fifty-six-year-old Kerry Louis Lathan Sr., aka Cousin Kerry. Born in Houston, he had moved to Los Angeles as a child and joined the Rollin' 60s. After catching four previous felony drug charges, he'd gone to prison on a murder conviction in 1996. Though Hussle didn't know Kerry—being just eleven years old when he got locked up— shortly after he came home on parole, Nipsey sent him a care package of Marathon gear as a gesture of goodwill "on hood." Kerry was trying to get his life together, put his family back together, and adjust to a whole new world. That day he said he needed some clothes so he could console a friend who'd just lost their father. "My nephew was complaining that I'm not in prison anymore so I don't have to wear the same shirt," he said. " 'You're free.' "[29]

While waiting for Cousin Kerry to arrive, Hussle signed autographs and shot selfies with customers at The Marathon Clothing store, and chatted with Cowboy and Rimpau, his old classmate and longtime musical collaborator. "I was just telling him how proud I was of him," Cowboy recalled later. "It felt like the old times again, just talking and reminiscing."[30]

🏁🏁

NIGGAS KILL THEY PARTNERS AND BRING YAMS TO THE REPAST
BUT STILL TO THIS SHIT I PLEDGE ALLEGIANCE

—Nipsey Hussle, "One Take 3," *The Marathon* (2010)

Before Kerry arrived, a white Chevy Cruze pulled off Slauson at 3:05 p.m. and parked in front of the Master Burger. Hussle recognized the face in the passenger seat. "Is that Shitty?" he asked. "I don't think nobody had seen him in some years," Cowboy said later while testifying before a grand jury. "He's from the neighborhood, one of the homies from the hood."[31]

Born Eric Ronald Holder Jr., the man Hussle knew as Shitty Cuz was a member of the Rollin' 60s as well as a wannabe rapper who recorded under the name Fly Mac. Rumors that he was once signed to All Money In were denied by Hussle's estate, and few of Hussle's inner circle remember the guy at all.

"A couple people tell me I knew him and I seen him before," says Cuzzy Capone. "He might have been in my presence, but he wasn't somebody that I knew. He definitely wasn't a factor in my eyes and in my life. Just a complete nothing-ass nigga. I don't know this nigga from shit."[32]

"I never heard him rap," says Gooch. "But I know that there was some people on the block that he used to hang with in the neighborhood. It was like two or three dudes over there that was rappin'. If he was that good I would have known of him. People say he came over to the studio before. I can't remember him bein' over there, but it was so many times that people came to the studio, didn't know how to rap, we're writing music, we're trying to create. And they hear a beat, and just 'cause a beat playin' and ain't nobody sayin' nothin' y'all wanna rap. And it's like, while you're rappin' out loud, we're tryin' to write. It's fuckin' us up. So I used to be like the security, like, *Nigga, shut the fuck up.* And I even beat a few people up or just made a few people leave sometimes just because of that aspect."[33]

Judging by his SoundCloud page, Shitty Cuz wasn't particularly talented or focused, uploading just five lackluster tracks over a span of four years. Nevertheless Fly Mac added the slogan "plenty niggas hate cuz I'm da great" to his 2015 SoundCloud profile. Hussle had long referred to himself as "Tha Great" in real life and on his Twitter profile. But Hussle backed up his claims of greatness with compelling lyrics, a distinctive voice, a sense of flow and melody, charisma, integrity, and determination— qualities sorely lacking in the handful of Fly Mac tracks to be found online. Just four years younger than Nip, Holder failed to achieve even a fraction of the success Nipsey Hussle had attained in the rap game.[34]

Holder exited the vehicle and went into Master Burger to order some chili cheese fries, then he walked toward The Marathon Clothing store, where Hussle, Cowboy, and Rimpau were standing together. The weather was hot and sunny, and Holder was shirtless with a black bandanna tied around his neck, flaunting his gang tattoos—H6OD CRIP at the top of his chest and SIXTIES across his stomach.[35]

According to Cowboy's memory of the conversation, Hussle's demeanor remained cool as Holder approached. "Hey, man, what's up," he said. "Where you been, bro?"

"I've been out the way," Holder replied.

"Man, you know they got some paperwork on you," Nipsey told him. "I haven't read it, you know. Like, you my bro. Maybe you need to take care of that."[36]

In this context, "paperwork" is a term for court documents that would suggest someone in police custody had struck a deal to reduce their penalty. In other words, that paperwork would label him a "snitch." Within street culture, where loyalty is everything and snitching can be a matter of life or death, "paperwork" is taken very seriously. It gets downloaded, printed out, passed around, tampered with, and discussed in hushed tones. The repercussions for messy paperwork can be severe, often leading to a "DP," short for disciplinary punishment—a beating, or worse.

Neither Holder nor Hussle was heard to mention any specific names or cases as they spoke, but the implication was clear: these rumors of paperwork were a serious matter that needed to be addressed.[37]

"Oh yeah, motherfuckers be hatin' on me," Cowboy remembers Holder saying.

"So you know what I'm talking about?" Nip responded.

"No," Holder repeated. "People be hatin' on me."[38]

Around that time, the woman who had driven Holder to the shopping plaza got out of her Cruze and walked toward the group of men, intent on taking a selfie with Nip. The woman's name has not been released because she later became a snitch herself, making a deal with the Los Angeles County district attorney to testify against Holder. She's identified in court transcripts as "Witness #1."[39] Under the terms of her agreement with the DA, the driver received immunity from prosecution for anything she spoke about on the witness stand, as long as her testimony was 100 percent truthful. If she was caught lying about anything under oath she could still be prosecuted.

According to Witness #1's sworn testimony, as soon as she turned into the plaza from Slauson Ave she noticed Nip standing outside. "Ooh," she said. "There goes Nipsey Hussle. He look fine. I want to take a picture." She had seen him in a movie on BET and heard some of his music. "He's cute," she added. "He's handsome." Holder—whom she'd been dating for about a month—said nothing, giving no indication that he knew Hussle.[40]

As Witness #1 approached for her selfie she says she overheard some of Holder's conversation with Hussle. "He was asking Nipsey if Nipsey ever snitched," she claims. "He was like, 'Well somebody said . . .' but I didn't really hear the name. And Nipsey was like 'Chill.' Like 'No, no.'" Witness #1 testified that Holder asked him over and over, "Have you ever snitched? Have you ever snitched?"

"Nipsey wasn't really talking," stated Witness #1. "But his 'no' was just like, 'This dude needs to go' . . . That's how I kind of took it, like trying to brush him off. You know how somebody keep asking you something and you probably don't want to keep answering the same question? Nipsey was just kind of like that."[41]

That's when Nipsey turned to her and said he was ready to take a picture. "I felt honored," said Witness #1. "He didn't turn me away or nothing." Hussle leaned against a parked car and put his arm around her as she raised her phone to snap the selfie. Then she went back to her own car without speaking to Holder at all. As soon as she got back to the Chevy Cruze she posted the photo on Facebook to show her friends. "I thought it was gonna be a boring day," she said, "but it turned out cool. Everybody was having fun."[42]

Reading through the Grand Jury transcripts of Witness #1's testimony, at times she sounds like a starstruck groupie. At other times—such as the portion of her testimony where she deals with the fact that she appeared to tell investigating detectives that

Eric Holder said he wanted to do a drive-by, but then seemingly changed her story and insisted that he never expressly said that—some feel she sounds very much like an accomplice to a murder. "Why does she have immunity?" Ralo asked after discussing the transcripts. He wanted to know why the DA didn't press Witness #1 about a mysterious meeting by the side of the road with two men shortly before driving to the shopping plaza. "He had guns in her car," said Ralo. "The bitch even hopped out the car to take a picture with the nigga. Do you know how fuckin' heinous that is? If you know this nigga's about to get flipped and you hop out and take a picture with him? That bothers my spirit. And the fact that she has immunity speaks volumes for crime fighting in this city."[43]

Given her extensive contact with Eric Holder, the driver offered police a great deal of information, but Ralo is not the first to question her credibility. Meanwhile there were many other witnesses in the parking lot who have not testified. While Hussle, Holder, Cowboy, and Rimpau were talking in the parking lot, standing nearby was another fan, Joshua Baerga, an aspiring actor from New York who goes by the name Kid Flashy on Instagram. Speaking from behind bars via three-way phone call, Kid Flashy spoke to the YouTube vlogger L.A. Show.[44] (Although there is a lot of nonsense on the internet about the case, the L.A. Show stands out for doing original reporting.) Flashy said he had been in Los Angeles for an audition—G-Unit Films was casting for a new TV series about the notorious street gang BMF, or Black Mafia Family. Afterward, Flashy says he decided to stop by The Marathon Clothing with a friend. "It looked like a heated conversation," Flashy recalled. "'Cause when I walked up to try to get a picture at first, I heard Nipsey tell him, 'You can't even be here right now.' So I kinda backed up 'cause it wasn't really the time to ask for pictures."[45]

Cowboy described the temperature of their convo differently. "It was no hint of any animosity," he said. "Had they had any type of words I would have escorted him out. Had they had, you know, any type of argument . . . Nipsey was basically looking out for him, telling him, you know, 'I haven't read it, I don't know if it's true or not, but you need to address it.' That's what Nipsey was doing."[46]

According to time codes pieced together from various security cameras around the shopping plaza, Holder's conversation with Hussle lasted approximately four minutes and fifteen seconds. Near the end of their discussion, Cowboy says, Shitty brought up his music.

"He asked had we heard his rap," Cowboy recalled. "He said, 'Yeah, I've been in the studio. I did my new song.'

"He asked us had we heard it and we're like, 'Nah, we haven't heard your song' or whatever." Then Shitty walked away and headed back to Master Burger.

At 3:08, while Holder and Hussle's conversation was winding down, a black SUV pulled into the plaza parking lot carrying Cousin Kerry, driven by his "nephew" Shermi Villanueva. (Familial terms like cousin, uncle, and nephew are also used to describe relationships between members of the gang in ways that can be deliberately confusing.) When Holder walked away, Kerry approached Hussle with a warm greeting, then asked Cowboy about his lunch. "We was talking about a chicken fajita that they sell over at the— what is it? El Pollo Loco or something. It had chicken and avocados in it. I'd never seen one—I've been gone twenty-five years."[47]

Standing by parked cars in front of The Marathon Clothing entrance, the Grammy-nominated rapper continued chatting with starstruck fans and signing their merch. "He was taking photographs with a little baby," Kerry recalled in an interview.[48] "His mother asked for a selfie with her son. He was gonna turn three the next day."

Eric Holder came out of the Master Burger and told Witness #1 that he needed two dollars to pay for his food. She handed him a five and he completed the chili cheese fries transaction. Then he walked back toward where Hussle was standing.

"I want to call your attention now back to the top of the video at the Master Burger door," Deputy District Attorney John McKinney said to Herman "Cowboy" Douglas as he sat on the witness stand during grand jury proceedings on May 6, 2019. "It appears that Holder walks . . . back over to your group again. Do you see that? He looks like he shakes Rimpau's hand or daps him up, meaning kind of giving him a pound. And then he immediately leaves with something in his hands back toward the white car. Is that what the video shows?"[49]

"Yes," Cowboy replied.

"Do you recall that happening?"

"No."[50]

Once Holder returned to the car, he told Witness #1 he wanted to eat his food. "Not right here," she told him, according to her grand jury testimony. "Well, we could just drive around," she says he suggested. She pulled out of the parking lot and turned right on Slauson.

At 3:17, five minutes after Holder and Witness #1 drove off, Cowboy walked into The Marathon Clothing store to take a lunch break, leaving Hussle in the parking lot with Rimpau, Cousin Kerry, Shermi, and an assortment of fans. Kerry did not go inside with Cowboy to get the new shirt he said he needed to visit a grieving friend.

During Cowboy's grand jury testimony, McKinney, a young Black prosecutor from the Major Crimes Division of the L.A. County District Attorney's Office, asked whether there was anything about Holder that made Cowboy want to get Nipsey away from him. "I felt something in my gut," he said. "At that split second I asked myself, Why do I feel this way? . . . Just his presence made me just—I had an uneasy feeling about him, his demeanor and the stuff he was saying."[51]

On the witness stand and in various on-camera interviews, Cowboy consistently referred to Holder's attack as "a straight snake move," second-guessing his own decision to take a lunch break at the exact moment he chose. "I just replay it over and over," he told the TV show *Extra*. "And I wish I could have done something different. I wish I woulda never left his side. You know, it was never no drama, it was never no argument, never no dispute. It was nothing. It was an all-out sneaky snake move."[52]

Rimpau did not testify before the grand jury and has given no interviews about the events of that day. "I beat myself up about MARCH 31st everyday I wanna do something but ain't nothing I can do to bring you bacc," he posted on Instagram on April 26. "I wanna juss Shyne wit you one more time Brodee I worked so hard to get my shyt together bro and I'm glad you seen my progress I thank you for pushing me for the discipline you instilled in me." He ended his post with "LLKingNH," *Long live King Nipsey Hussle*.[53]

After pulling out of the parking lot, Witness #1 circled the block in her Cruze, turning right on Crenshaw and right again on Fifty-Eighth Place. They made another right into an unmarked alley between Crenshaw and West Boulevard that separates the shopping plaza from the Shell gas station on the corner. That's when Witness #1 says she first saw the gun, a black 9mm pistol.

"As we driving he's pulling out the gun," she testified, "I saw him loading the bullets into the magazine . . . kind of holding it towards the window but not, and I was just like, 'You're not gonna do a drive-by in my car.'"[54]

The DA asked where he got the gun from. "He pulled it out so fast I don't know where he got it from," she said. Nor had she noticed the semiautomatic weapon earlier that day when she picked him up shirtless in a nearby town to take a half-hour road trip to Los Angeles.

In earlier testimony the driver mentioned that she'd seen him carrying a similar gun over the past month, which he'd said he needed "for protection."

She said he usually kept it tucked in his waistband. She also claimed not to know he was a gang member, despite the unambiguous tattoos all over his upper body.

"Did he say anything to you about Nipsey Hussle?" DA McKinney asked. "Did he seem angry with anybody?"

"No," she replied. "It seemed like his normal self to me."

"Okay," the DA replied, pushing toward his point. "Why did you think at that moment that he was gonna use the gun to shoot somebody?"[55]

She said she'd never seen him load the gun before. "Every time he be with me he will just have it on him," she said. "I never actually seen him fixing stuff, putting it in there. I never seen him playing with it. Like he's about to get ready to use it."

After she let Holder know she would not tolerate any drive-by shooting in her car, Witness #1 says Holder put the gun away. The DA didn't press her further about why the idea of a drive-by would even cross her mind. In her initial interview with detectives from the Seventy-Seventh Division, she reportedly said Holder asked her to take him around the block so he could do a drive-by. She later claimed that she'd been confused by the detectives' questions during her five-hour interrogation.

As they circled the block a second time, Holder told her to stop the car on West Fifty-Eighth Place in the parking lot behind the Fatburger restaurant where all the employees' uniforms are cobranded with The Marathon Clothing's iconic Crenshaw logo. "Pull over in here," he said. "I want to eat." The front of her car faced the alley that led to the shopping plaza.

Chewing on some chili cheese fries, he slipped on a red T-shirt. Witness #1 said she asked if Holder was ready to go yet.[56]

Something about her testimony was not making sense. McKinney challenged Witness #1 again: "You didn't say to him, 'Why did you bring a gun in my car? I could get in trouble for this if we get stopped.' Anything like that?"

"No," she answered. "I just wasn't thinking about it . . . I was telling him is he ready to go and . . . started moving my car towards the alley. And then he was like, 'Wait. Don't go nowhere. I'll be back.'"

"All right," she says she told him. "Hurry up."

Many parts of Witness #1's testimony seemed to invite a suspension of disbelief. The prosecutor needed her to make the murder case stick, but some of her answers certainly appeared strained. "Didn't you wonder, 'What is he talking about?'" McKinney asked. "'Where is he going?'"[57]

Once again the driver dismissed what would appear to be obvious, commonsense responses. "No," she said. "I just thought maybe he probably was gonna go get something or whatever. Maybe he forgot something or wanted to buy something."

"What direction did he go in?"

She said he went down the alley, "towards Slauson way."

"Did you see him with the gun at any time?"

"No," she said. According to Witness #1, the only thing he was carrying was a takeout container of chili cheese fries. As he was walking through the alley toward Slauson he put the container on the hood of a white truck that was parked, she said. Then he turned the corner toward the Master Burger—back into the parking lot where he last saw Nipsey.[58]

Meanwhile, in front of the Marathon store, Hussle was still chatting with fans, and Cousin Kerry had made no progress toward getting the new shirt that was supposed to be the whole reason why Nipsey came out on a Sunday.

"Yo, Nipsey man," Kid Flashy said to him. "I'm out here for the BMF audition with 50 Cent. Mind if I take a picture with you and put it up?"

"Yeah, no problem," he said. "Come on."

They posed for one last picture, just outside the entrance to The Marathon Clothing store, which had a big #CALIFORNIA-LOVE hashtag on the plate glass windows in honor of Hussle and Boog's *GQ* spread. Nipsey grabbed Flashy's hand with a firm grip, standing tall in the blazing Los Angeles sunshine wearing an immaculate white T-shirt, white du-rag, and red shorts with a white drawstring. On his left wrist was the gold Rolex Presidential he wore every day.

Soon after Kid Flashy snapped his photos, he noticed someone approaching. "The kid came back around the corner," Flashy recalls. "I passed right by him, and I felt like something was goin' wrong. But I didn't really pinpoint it. Then I seen him pull out and start hittin' him."[59]

Cousin Kerry and Nipsey were standing face-to-face between two parked cars when all hell broke loose. "A guy just came around shooting," Kerry said. Just before the shots rang out, the gunman spoke to Hussle, Kerry told the grand jury. "I believe he said, 'You're through.'"

In the heat of the moment, Kerry didn't see the gunman's face. "The first thing I saw was gunfire," he said. "I looked up and saw him shoot and that was it . . . I saw the flash . . . When you see gunfire at one o'clock you too close to the gun. So I ran."[60]

Holder stepped toward Hussle, his arms fully extended. In his right hand was a silver revolver, in his left hand a black semiautomatic—both firing at close range. One of the first bullets struck Kerry in the back just below his belt, chipping a piece of bone off his pelvis. "When I turned to run, it knocked my legs from up under me," he said. "It was hot. Fire hot." He fell to the pavement facedown. "I was moving my feet to see if my legs still worked."

Hussle went down just after. Kerry could see part of his body lying on the ground past the car tire that obstructed his vision. He heard the gunman shooting. He heard women screaming.

DA McKinney asked if it was a continuous pattern of shots or more staccato.

"It was like one, two, three, then it stopped," Kerry recalled. "And then it came back—one, two, three more—then it stopped. Then it came back again. I was like, 'I'm sure this guy's gonna finish me off. 'Cause I can't move.' But he didn't." Holder fired no less than ten bullets in three bursts of gunfire.

Kerry heard Hussle say three words to Shitty Cuz: "You got me."[61]

Then Shitty ran up to Hussle and kicked him once in the head before running away.

Inside the Marathon store breakroom, Cowboy was eating his fajita bowl when the sound of shooting interrupted his meal. "I heard maybe a few gunshots," he said. "I started running out to the front. I heard some more gunshots." He burst through the front door just in time to see Holder running around the corner and Nipsey lying on the ground.[62]

Besides Hussle and Kerry, Shermi Villanueva was also struck by a bullet. Miraculously the slug hit his belt buckle, leaving him stunned but without serious injuries. "Who did this to you?" someone called out to Hussle. Kerry heard him say a name but he couldn't make it out.

Sitting in her car with the engine running, Witness #1 was checking social media on her phone when she heard the gunshots. She couldn't see the plaza from where she was parked, but she did see a man running from that direction. "I was just like, 'Oh my God,'" she remembered. "'What's going on? I hope you're okay. You need to hurry up!'"[63]

"Let me get out of here" was the first thought that crossed her mind. But she didn't. "I didn't know like if he got hurt or something happened," she testified. "So I waited on him."

District Attorney McKinney asked the obvious question. "Did it cross your mind that the gunshots you heard were fired by him?" Her answer, once again, was no.

Then she saw Holder running up the alley. "What's going on?" she asked as soon as he got in the car. "Drive," he said. "Drive before I slap you." He'd never spoken to her like that before. "What's going on?" she pressed. "You talk too much," was his reply.

"I just kept driving," Witness #1 testified. "I didn't want him to hit me or nothing like that."

Although security camera footage downloaded by LAPD investigators showed that Holder was carrying one gun in each hand, the driver says she saw nothing until after he got in the car. "He had the revolver like on this side of him," she said. "Like he didn't want me to see it." He stashed the semiautomatic in the bag that his chili cheese fries had come in.

"You knew something bad happened in that parking lot at that point, didn't you?" the DA asked. "What did you think happened in the plaza parking lot?"

"I just felt like I know there was shooting going on," she said. "I didn't know if he was the shooter. I didn't know if he was getting shot at. I just know something had happened."

Sam picked up when the phone rang at Granny's house. "He got the call and he ran out of here so fast," Margaret Boutte said. "He never does that." As soon as he left, she picked up the phone and called her daughter. "Angel, something must have happened," she said. "Samiel jumped up. He didn't take his shower. He got out of here so fast."[64] Sam punched the accelerator and flew down Slauson, running red lights all the way to Crenshaw.[65]

"I ran over to Nip and held him," Cowboy said. "He had a pulse, you know, in and out of consciousness. But he fought, he fought hard." There were red stains on his T-shirt. Cowboy applied pressure with his hands to slow the bleeding. "He was still breathing, biting his tongue a little bit," Cowboy recalls. "If his eyes started to roll back a little bit I said, 'Nip, wake up!' And he'd snap back out of it." There wasn't much more Cowboy could do but pray and wait for the paramedics.[66]

Blacc Sam got there first. He had worried about something like this happening to his little brother for years. "There's no reason for him to still be alive," he said to himself, noticing bullet wounds in Nipsey's leg, stomach, and under his left armpit. Sam tried to block out the chaos around him, listening carefully to the 911 operator and counting chest compressions.[67]

"Nip is sporadic," Sam would later tell the *Los Angeles Times*. "Nip gonna pull up and hop up out of the Jordan Downs projects, Nickerson Gardens, in any 'hood in L.A., Compton, Watts— solo with $150,000 of jewelry on his neck and $80,000 Rolex with no security. That's why the people loved him."

When the paramedics finally showed up, Sam let them take over. The EMS team administered an IV and breathing tube, trying to stabilize Hussle. They didn't notice the wound to his head until they lifted him onto a stretcher.[68]

Killa Twan remained calm when he first heard Nip got shot. He'd just gotten off the phone with Hussle an hour and a half ago. Twan had been at The Marathon Clothing store picking up shirts and socks and just missed him. "It's so much we done been through," he told himself. "He's all right."[69]

Then somebody showed him an Instagram Live post and told him, "Nah, bro, you need to go check." He raced all the way from Watts to Crenshaw, arriving just as his friend was about to be rushed to the hospital. Twan's cousin who lived in the neighborhood grabbed him, like, "Bro, you don't wanna see."

"Huh?" he replied in disbelief. "But he gonna be all right though, right?"

His cousin shook his head quietly. "Nah, bro gone."

"Are you sure?" Twan asked.

"Man, we know," his cousin said. "We seen that shit too many times. We have seen too many lifeless bodies. Fuck what they talkin' 'bout. He's gone already."

Twan caught a glimpse as the paramedics were carrying Nipsey away. "I remember the white turban he had on his head," he says. "As they was puttin' him in the ambulance I saw how red it was. I was like, '*Hell* nah.'"[70]

By the time Angelique Smith made it to the shopping plaza, her son had been taken away in an ambulance. "What happened?" she asked a police officer at the scene.

"Someone was shot," the cop replied.

"Who?" she asked.

"Nipsey Hussle."

"My spirit said 'Oh, oh. That's it. That's why'," she recalled during a memorial service at the BET Awards. "I was finished processing my son's assassination." Her choice of words—not *death* or *murder* but *assassination*—was notable.[71]

She soon ran into Rimpau, who had fled the scene when the

shots rang out and returned to the shopping plaza looking traumatized. She put her hands on his shoulders and tried to reach her son's friend. "Look into my eyes, Evan," she said. "You know that we are spiritual beings having a physical experience, right Evan? You understand that, right? So even though our bodies die—as they call it—on this side of eternity, our spirits live. We lift out of this vessel and we continue on." She felt a spirit of retribution and revenge surrounding him. "I don't even know what words I used because I was very frightened then," she recalled. But in the end she felt she had "chased those spirits away from him."[72]

YG was at DJ Mustard's house watching March Madness on TV. Michigan State and Duke were playing for the chance to face Texas Tech in the Final Four. YG had a bet on the game with Ty Dolla $ign. Jade, his "day-one homegirl" who worked at the Marathon store, called to say she heard something about Nipsey getting shot. As YG was telling Mustard the news, she called back again to confirm that he'd been shot four times. YG got in his truck and asked which hospital he was being sent to.

"And then she called back again and said somethin' else. I just got up and left. I went to get my truck. I hopped in the truck and I'm leavin'. I'm like, 'Where y'all goin'? Like, where bro goin'?' So then I passed by Mustard house and he had hopped in his car. He like, 'Shit, I thought you left already.' I'm like, 'Nah, hop in my shit.' So we all hopped in my truck. And they gave us the location where they was takin' bro. And we was on the way, and yeah, we was like fifteen, twenty minutes away. And they like, 'Homie ain't make it.'"[73]

Chapter 13

HIGHER AND HIGHER

I DON'T KNOW ABOUT HELL, I DON'T KNOW ABOUT HEAVEN

ALL I KNOW 'BOUT IS RIGHT NOW

AND THIS LIFESTYLE IS INTERESTIN'

—Nipsey Hussle, "Ocean Views," (2016)

Seattle-based hair stylist Tatum Herman was Hussle's favorite barber and braider. "She the truth," he used to say. He would take her on tour with him whenever she was available, although she didn't particularly enjoy life on the road.

When Herman was asked to braid Nipsey's hair for the wake, she was a little scared. "I brought his favorite tea," she recalled, "so that the whole room could smell aromatic. I brought a few crystals, some sage, palo santo. It was a ritual, because I knew I had to be in a certain space." She thought it would be harder that day, but she felt his presence in the room.

"Nip was very tender-headed," she said. "I mean, he would be moving around and he could not handle it. When I did the first braid, I swear to God I heard him say, 'T, this the first time it don't hurt.' His spirit was in there with me."[1]

Herman was not the only one who felt Hussle's presence

349

that day. Inside the Staples Center, Lauren's nine-year-old son, Kameron Carter, spoke to the capacity crowd. "On the night of April second I had a dream," he said. "I was in paradise and I was playing in the ocean water when Ermias popped up right behind me. He said, 'What up, Killa?' 'Cause that's my nickname to him. I turned around and I yelled his name and I gave him a hug. Shortly, he was gone but it was still cool I guess."[2]

Dressed in a tie and jacket with an image of Hussle on his lapel, Kameron recalled telling his mom about the dream. "After I told her I was thinking about it and I realized that Ermias told me what heaven was like. He told me it was paradise."

Kameron shared a memory of his stepfather standing at the window in the morning and saying "Respect" each day. "So on the count of three I want everybody to yell RESPECT," he told the auditorium, and then began counting down. "Three, two, one . . ." On his command, twenty-one thousand voices spoke as one. "Respect!"[3]

"In memory of Ermias Asghedom," Kameron said in closing. "August 15, 1985, to 2019 March 31st."[4]

"I was front row," says Killa Twan of the memorial service. "That was epic. That was amazing. That was something I will never forget. As many times as he talked about selling out the Staples Center, I didn't think it would be that way. That shit was sold out."[5]

"He packed out Staples Center at a funeral," said Wack 100, manager of Blueface and The Game, in a controversial No Jumper interview months later.[6] "But have you seen Nipsey Hussle headlining Staples Center and his fans bein' true fans, come out and pack it out for him? I seen Kendrick Lamar sell it out three nights in a row. We just talkin' numbers. We're not talkin' personal opinion." In Wack's opinion, Hussle was not worthy of "legend" status because his career had not yet reached that point at the time of his death. "Is it fucked up it happened?" Wack said. "*Definitely* fucked up it happened. Do I wish we could rewind life and he can re-do it again? Definitely. Did hip hop take a loss? Definitely." Still Wack insisted that Hussle did not deserve to be called a legend. "We didn't lose a *legend* at the time because the fans and the radio and things like that didn't support him to get him to where he shoulda been. Would he eventually got there? I believe so. Was he *that* what they say he is at the time of his demise? Definitely not. And we're just talking numbers." Hussle's bodyguard J Roc didn't appreciate Wack's opinion and later punched him in the face backstage at Rolling Loud.[7]

Smoke DZA and Jonny Shipes were among those who paid their respects at the Staples Center. "His service was so hard to articulate," says DZA. "It wasn't even a regular service. We were all mourning. It was a show, it was a nightclub, the NBA finals. It was everything as far as the people in there. I'm sure it's some shit that he's probably laughing about. You've got LeBron, you've got Kendrick Lamar. It was the Who's Who . . . All of these people honored him inside the Staples Center. The only other person who had a funeral in the Staples Center was Michael Jackson," DZA said with a laugh. "You feel me? So that's just the magnitude my man was on."[8]

Like his brother, Blacc Sam always preferred demonstration to conversation. Although he was never one for long speeches, the words flowed eloquently at his brother's memorial. Standing up in the Staples Center on national television in his black suit and black tie, Sam spoke about how he and his brother had molded themselves after the positive people, the hustlers. "They didn't even have to even say anything to us," he said. "They demonstrated with action. And you know that's what Nip was about . . . demonstrating and coming back [so] that people could walk up, touch, see."[9]

The words that Nip appreciated, his brother said, were the words of encouragement. "Whether he said it or not," Sam said, "the pats on the back, it meant a lot to him. 'Bro, keep doin' your thing.' 'We appreciate what you're doing.' 'You're making it look good.' 'You're putting us on the map.' That shit meant a lot to him. And that shit meant a lot to me from everybody who did that."

Quoting a lyric from Hussle's song "I Don't Stress," Sam said, "If I die today I made the set proud, nigga." Fighting to control his emotions, Sam spoke to his brother as the Staples Center filled with thunderous applause. "You made the world proud! You know? Look at this shit, bro!"[10]

There is no doubt that Hussle's legacy has made the world proud. His face, depicted in murals throughout the city, is now recognized all over the planet. His love of books—and the reading lists he would share with friends—inspired book clubs to form, gathering people together in his name to read and discuss Hussle's favorite works.

After gathering himself for a moment, Sam continued. "A lot of people thought, comin' up, and when he first got signed, he was gonna get some money and leave. Like he said, they didn't have a fuckin' clue. They had no clue of what he really was gon' do. I want everybody to know, Nip . . ." Sam paused for a long time "his heart and soul on Crenshaw and Slauson."

Samiel and Ermias Asghedom were as close as two brothers could be. They spoke to each other about everything, including death. "We used to talk." Sam said. "We gotta go. We don't know if we gonna go at eighty, sixty, thirty, or twenty. But the one thing is to make sure when you go, you go the right way. You stand up for what you believe in. You put your money where your mouth is. You *never* fold. Never let the pressure sway you from doin' what you wanna do. Never let anything, the politics, stop you from coming around and staying around. And I hope everybody knows that that's what bro did. Bro stayed and he died on Crenshaw and Slauson. And everybody who showed love, even the ones who didn't, Nip had nothin' but love. Nothin' but love and respect and humbleness."[11]

In his song "Ocean Views," Hussle asked for a Stevie Wonder song to be played at his funeral. At the Staples Center on April 11, 2019, Wonder came to sing in person. But first he had something to say. "I knew him from hearing his music," said the R&B icon, "hearing him rap, and had the pleasure through someone who's very close to my wife—Pastor P—who arranged a meeting for myself to have a meeting with him for us to talk. I was able to meet him as well as Lauren. We were celebrating Pastor P's birthday. But as well, celebrating the fact that we had a good conversation and looked forward to a wonderful life.

"It is a heartbreak to again lose a member of our family," Stevie continued. "It is a heartbreak because it's so unnecessary. We, to be a civilized nation, a civilized world . . . we still are living in a time where ego, anger, jealousy is controlling our lives. It is so painful to know that we don't have enough people taking a position that says, 'Listen, we must have stronger gun laws.'" The Staples Center cheered his words, too late to make a difference for Hussle. Still, they cheered.[12]

Even after Stevie's last song was sung, there were still more stories to be told, more tears to be shed. The faithful filed out of the Staples Center into late afternoon sunshine. Tens of thousands of mourners filled the streets of Los Angeles, on foot, on motorcycles and ATVs, on horseback, children on their mothers' shoulders. They climbed up lampposts and perched on rooftops to get a view as the king of L.A. passed by. Helicopters hovered overhead. Marching bands made a joyful noise, and everywhere, from every corner, the voice of Nip Hussle the Great rang out, echoing through his domain. Hussle's pallbearers—family and the closest of homies—wore white gloves as they lifted his casket into a silver hearse with an Eritrean flag on the roof and took him for one last ride through his city—every set, every hood. Everywhere they went, well-wishers turned out to pay their respects as his procession rolled through the streets of L.A., flanked by motorcycles and adoring crowds all along the twenty-five-mile route.[13]

"It was Bloods, Crips, Hispanic, Asian—I don't care what," said Cowboy. "Every hood we rolled through, the whole city showed love. We rolled all the way to Watts, came all the way back to Slauson and Crenshaw."[14]

"I want to salute the L.A. police," said Steve Lobel. "Throughout the parade and all of the stuff at his shop and everything, they didn't come in forcefully and tell people to leave and this and that. They fell back and let it go. I've seen things where riots start because the police get overprotective or say, 'Hey, get out of here.' And this was amazing, just to see the helicopters and the drones and all this stuff. It was crazy and he was going through all the enemy hoods and they were just loving him. He broke a lot of barriers. So, God might have needed him."[15]

Dexter Browne was in Trinidad with his family when the memorial took place, mourning the complex, charismatic young man he had raised like a son. "That really hurt us to lose him," he said. "It really took a toll on us. And it was hurtful not having an opportunity to attend the funeral given our history." The grand memorial reminded Dexter of all the funerals that Hussle paid for. "When he got on and he started making money, his allegiance to the hood never wavered," says Dexter. "For the homies who got shot and stuff like that, he would pay for the funerals and that obviously would give him some power over time. He became what he wanted to become. I don't think he wanted to lose his life for it, but oftentimes you don't get to pick exactly how it happens if you dream for it."[16]

After the memorial Atlantic Records approached Jorge Peniche about designing billboards in Hussle's honor. "Man, we gotta do this," they told him, "because the city and the people are hurting like they lost a family member." If the city was hurting, Hussle's actual family was heartbroken. "The people who knew him very well were completely devastated, broken into a million pieces," Peniche said. He hoped that the image might be part of the healing process. He got to work with the intention of "reinvigorating the spirit of resiliency and also celebrating the legacy and the greatness and the legend of Nip Hussle."[17]

"We had to do it," Peniche said. "We had to run a billboard that represented that." The design was finalized on the day his wife, the on-air personality Letty Peniche, was giving birth to the couple's second son. "We were in the delivery room," Peniche remembered. "My wife had just gotten there. We had just gotten settled in. The only creative is I got the photo and we were just trying to figure out how to design it."

The image was a shot from the "Higher" video set, taken by Roc Nation exec Lenny S. "Sam threw out the term 'Prolific,' which is something that was synonymous with Nipsey's name at this point," Peniche said. "Something that he took ownership and had license of. And I said, 'Okay, Prolific. This is great.'" So there he sat with his laptop, in the delivery room, still in mourning himself, and waiting for the birth of his son.[18]

"I *really* gotta dig deep and find inspiration to do this," he told himself. "I credit it to Nip, man," he said. "I think I had my antennas up and he helped direct it. Like he would with any other thing that we've done. A lot of the stuff was his genius that sparked it. And it's like, 'Okay, I know the execution part of it.' And 'How 'bout we do this?' or 'How 'bout we do that?'

So I think that series of billboards was no exception to that." He typed out the word "prolific," a word Hussle had tattooed on his face. A word Hussle used to describe himself in the first line of the song "Victory Lap." He positioned the word in capital letters from one side of the billboard to the other in the signature Marathon font, Franklin Gothic. "It seemed super fitting," he said. "And the photo, I put it as large as I could. I cut as carefully as I could around Nip with a pencil on Photoshop and positioned him, nestled him in between letters." In fifteen minutes the design was done. He sent it to the team and then his mother-in-law came to him and said, "Hey, your son's about to be born." They named the boy in Hussle's honor, Luis Ermias Peniche.

"I'm a man of faith and I believe that Nipsey's spirit lives with us," said the proud father. "And I see the many ways that he's pulling strings. Boy, man—this guy is doin' some phenomenal things for the people he loves and for his team. His impact will be forever remembered."

Peniche thinks of the billboards as a gift to the city. "People are healing and people are hurting," he said. "Nipsey represented more than a phenomenal artist but also a pillar of hope and, you know, like, an example that . . . 'I can do it too.'"[19]

"After Nipsey got killed, it feels like the love is gone from over here," says Ralo. "I know I'm probably biased because that's my nigga, but it's definitely never gonna ever be the same over here. There's a void. It feels like the love left and like the lights went out."[20]

Following Hussle's murder Ralo says he felt an anger come over him that he's never experienced before. "It was like the room would get still and quiet," he says. "I could've killed and like ate a sandwich right afterwards. I would have never mentioned it and it woulda never been . . . I had to pray to God that He remove that heat off me. I was demonically angry," he adds with a mirthless laugh.

Fortunately Ralo was able to get out of town, spend some time in Atlanta, and get his head together. He did a lot of thinking about the choices both he and Ermias had made in their teen years. "It made me realize what was missing when I came off the porch," he says. "It was the fact that I didn't feel like that in my adolescence. Now when you feel like that at 13, I can't fathom it. Imagine your friend is murdered. You can't leave. You just have to walk right past that spot where your friend's blood was in the concrete. You gotta keep lookin' over your shoulders, you don't even know why. It puts so much hate in your heart you'll never get all that hate out. You'll never be the same. It's gonna physiologically change who you are."[21]

Court proceedings for Eric Holder's murder trial have been delayed by the coronavirus. At a July 2020 pretrial hearing, he was brought into court shackled at the legs and wrist, and with chains around his waist. According to Alex Alonso, a gang expert and professor at California State University Long Beach, his yellow top and blue jumper pants indicated that he was in isolation and being held in a section known as High Power, where high-profile inmates are kept away from General Population. Holder was accompanied by defense attorney Lowynn Young, who has been representing him since Christopher Darden, famous for his role in prosecuting O.J. Simpson, resigned from this case due to death threats. There is a lot of hate out there for Eric Holder. Unconfirmed rumors circulate on the internet that several members of his family including his father have been killed or committed suicide, along with a plethora of conspiracy theories. At the hearing Holder's attorney told Judge Robert Perry that she had not been able to prepare a defense because she needed certain evidence in discovery but she had not been able to contact D.A. McKinney, who did not show up at court that day.[22]

It's possible that Holder, who was apprehended outside a mental hospital, will never stand trial. He may plead insanity or strike a deal with prosecutors. Although the case has officially been solved, there are so many theories swirling on the internet, from pharmaceutical companies to an Illuminati sacrifice, it's already clear that Hussle's murder will join those of Malcolm X, JFK, Biggie, and Tupac in the file of unsolved mysteries.

"I've heard all of the conspiracy theories," says one LAPD detective who asked that his name be withheld so that he could speak freely. "You know, the baby momma, the Muslims . . . but I just say keep it simple. Just like Tupac—Tupac jumped on a guy, the guy went over there and shot him. But people want to make it seem like it was the FBI and all this kind of stuff." Nevertheless the detective believes that someone had to sanction the killing within the Rollin' 60s. "In gangs you do have to have the okay to pull the trigger," he says. "You can't pull a trigger on somebody like that and not risk some repercussions to you and your family. I do know that. Sometimes you got to get the OK. 'Hey man I'm about to go do that.' And then handle your business or whatever."

Don't bother asking Ralo what happened to Nip. "I'm not willing to lose my life to answer that question," he says. Like Cuzzy and many of Hussle's closest friends, he doesn't buy the narrative that Hussle died in a random killing over a personal dispute with a member of the set.

"It just seemed like it's more than a fluke," says Cuzzy. "I'm not gonna say he was put up to it because I honestly don't know what the fuck happened. My mind thinks a million things. What I will say is this wasn't no fuckin' coincidence, man. That shit was heavily premeditated, I believe."[23]

"It's just street shit," says Killa Twan. "It ain't none of this government other extra bullshit they're trying to make it. It's the everyday struggle we all go through out here in L.A. Just being a young Black man trying to do something positive and show people another way. Somebody's gonna hate you for whatever you do. And that's the sad part." Twan says he never heard of Shitty Cuz until the day of the killing. "It's nothing to be spoke on. It's just an inner circle thing and folks know what's what and how it's gonna get handled. It's that type of shit. None of all this old, 'Oh, the government, Dr. Sebi . . .' No. It's real street shit."[24]

"Anybody that resembles a savior in the Black community is gunned the fuck down," says Ralo. "It's a narrative . . . It's like, we know how the movie ends. And the fact that we all can accept that that's not what happened because we want our normalcy is disgusting. We've become repulsive to me. We wouldn't have went for this in the '70s. We wouldn't have went for it in the '90s."[25]

One thing is for certain, Nipsey Hussle did not die in vain. The evidence of his impact is everywhere. Along with Tupac and Malcolm X, his image has become an emblem of liberation. Ralo wonders what Nipsey's thoughts might be on the nationwide uprising of 2020 and demands for racial reckoning. "I yearn to know what he would be doing right now—him and Kobe," he says. "Two of the most inspirational people in our city. Two of the role models. Do you know what it felt like being around individuals out of the Black community at that time? Everybody's head was down. It's like the wind was consistently getting knocked out of us. And then this Coronavirus. We can't even breathe."[26]

According to Ralo, Hussle's chains will end up in the Smithsonian. When he heard the news he was so overwhelmed he fell out laughing. "That's the second thing my homie did to impress me from the grave," says Ralo. The first was when he sent a cloud in the shape of his face over Crenshaw and Slauson on the day of the memorial. "Everybody saw it," Ralo insists. "Everybody was posting it. It was phenomenal. It's no way I would walk with a man and become a fanatic about him after he died. We weren't fully back on good terms. But it's just so miraculous that the whole story needs to be told from that level of mystique," he says with a laugh. "There is like glittering dust, like fairy dust in the room right now, just cause I'm popping this shit."

He marvels that Hussle "planned past his flesh" and kept his plans intact. "That's heavy duty business," Ralo says. "When you start talking about leaving a legacy—that word gets thrown around, but you gotta literally be talkin' from the grave in order to do that. And the only way to do that is if you were really focused while you were here. He outlined this shit."[27]

That example inspires people like Ralo to make sure The Marathon continues. "We gotta carry the torch," he says. "It's not even a Marathon no more. It's a relay. Nipsey definitely passed the baton to a lot of people. He empowered a lot of people."

"Yes, they are scared of what we can do,"[28] said Samantha Smith via Instagram Live shortly before the 2020 election. "And they want us to live below our power at all times. That's how they win. That's how they keep the power and that's how they keep the control, by making us stay at the lowest control level. So ascend and don't be scared, people. When you speak the truth you're gonna get a lot of backfire. Be a leader. Do not be a follower. If you feel in your heart that something needs to be done, don't let the people around you discourage that. Just do it. Please just vote. What do you got to lose?" Raising awareness of key issues and helping get out the vote is just one way of keeping the Marathon going. Sales of "FDT," her brother's protest anthem with YG, spiked 1,200 percent during the week of the election. Streamed a million times on election day, the song helped inspire record turnout, particularly among Black voters, who finally defeated Trump.

🏁🏁

"Racks in the Middle," featuring Roddy Ricch and Hit-Boy, the last song released during Hussle's lifetime, was nominated for two Grammy Awards after his death. It's become his highest-charting hit, entering the *Billboard* Hot 100 at number 44—buoyed by a 2,776 percent surge in the artist's music sales following his murder—but some of the lyrics hit different now. "I don't listen to that song," says Jonny Shipes. "It breaks my heart."[29]

In the song's second verse Hussle mourns the death of his childhood friend Fatts; in the song's music video, Nipsey visits his friend's grave site. "Damn, I wish my nigga Fatts was here," he raps. "How you die at thirty-somethin' after bangin' all them years?"

Hussle openly admitted shedding tears in the studio while recording that verse.[30] Every bit as painful as Hussle's words about Fatts is the top of the song's second verse, the part where he says, "Under no condition would you ever catch me slippin'." If only it were true, but the fact is people cannot stay hyper-vigilant all the time, especially in places where they feel most comfortable.

"I wish I woulda been there," says original Slauson Boy Hoodsta Rob. 'Cause it was different with me and bro. You know? I was a part of the group, but also too, I watched him. G Bob also watched him too. I loved everything, the music aspect and all that. But I knew that I'm supposed to watch my brother. So I never was too caught up in what was going on to where I'm not watching him. I wish I was there because I would jump in front of the gun. But everything happens for a reason. That was my brother and they know that about me. You gotta know when you a part of something bigger."

"There's a certain air of 'Oh, but I'm *here*,'" says Ralo. "And when you feel like that you're gonna let your guard down. And then you get got there. So that means whatever that means. You get comfortable and then you get rocked to sleep."[31]

"We always was aware of playing defense, and protecting ourselves," Hussle said while discussing "Racks in the Middle" with the lyrics website Genius.[32] "But then I got three full gun cases, so I don't play like that. I ain't out here playing with my daughter's well-being like that. I go to jail, it's all going to stop. And it's cheaper to hire the gunman than to pay the bail. Even if you do beat the case, the bail costs more than the salary, so we just had to start thinking on them levels."

Nevertheless, on March 31, 2019, Nipsey pulled up at his store—in the shopping plaza that he and his big brother and their business partner had recently purchased for $2.5 million—with no security. As surveillance footage clearly shows, the shooter was able to fire on Hussle, run away, return to fire again, retreat again, then return a third time to fire the final shots before making his escape from what should have been a suicidal attack.

"That shit hurt me the most," says Rick Ross, who recorded timeless collaborations with Hussle and tried to recruit him to join Maybach Music Group. "Homie was out there in a white T-shirt, basketball shorts. That's like when you're at home. That's when you're as comfortable as you can be. Because I'm sure with one phone call he could've had fifteen people, all black with machine guns standing out there. On my momma, last time I was with him I was there, and as the sun began to go down, and he's so at peace, so at home, I was thinking maybe it's time for me to leave before I bring a certain energy that's not here."

Ross fully understands the perils of elevating from a hometown hero to a nationally celebrated rap star. "When I move certain places, it's not a secret," he says. "I'm gonna have certain things in place. The same way he did, I wanna be as comfortable as he was in my basketball shorts. And I've had those same attempts on my life. Not just once, not just twice, maybe even more times than I could speak of. But before you stop coming home you're like, 'Fuck it.' You gotta do what you gotta do, as unfortunate as that may sound. I still ride the foreign cars through my neighborhood because I feel that's what my job is. That's how I inspire the youngsters because that's how I was inspired."[33]

"For him to lose his life in the place he gave so much to, it's a life lesson for everyone," says Master P, the New Orleans music mogul whose No Limit empire changed the game for independent rap labels, inspiring Hussle's All Money In movement, among others. "You still have to be able to understand the environment you are in because there are demons out there."[34]

Two days before Hussle's murder, P was in the studio with him recording their song "Street Millionaire" for the soundtrack to P's movie *I Got the Hook-Up 2*. "His mind was happy," P remembers. "He had just built a studio and he wanted everybody to see his studio. He was like, 'Man, I did it! I just bought this building over here, I'm doing business, I just got a shoe deal.' He's making moves. He and his girl had a great relationship. He had his kids. He had everything going for him. I think he was at his happiest time. He didn't hate on nobody. If I'd call him he'd say, 'What you need, big dog?' No one could've seen this coming. The devil just came."[35]

"Me and Nipsey got different mind frames," said Meek Mill in an interview with Charlamagne Tha God. "I think we was alike in certain ways, but we got two totally different mind frames. Me, you ain't never see me back in the hood without a pistol around, *close*—and I'm talking about in a legal way," said the Philly rapper, who wears a chain honoring Hussle and Lil Snupe, an artist signed to Meek's Dreamchasers imprint who was murdered in 2013. "No young kings should be gunned down in the hood. He's a legend just for that. You made it out, and you got gunned down by a *lowlife*. You a legend; you showed kids that you can make it out, and someone where you come from will pull you back and take your life. I guarantee you that Nipsey probably touched hundreds of millions of children from the ghetto. They know deep down that they will have their life took if they try to pursue their dreams to stay in the hood. Just that message alone." [36]

Cuzzy Capone isn't ready to give up on the hood, but he too has been shaken by the loss of his friend. "You've got to really handpick who you're fucking with, and make sure they're in control of their own life," he says. "Make sure it's nothing really tailing them because that shit . . . You see where it ends up at. You see what happened to bro in his life. We ain't never been the city where these producers and labels is quick to come fuck with us or grab a nigga. It's wild-ass shit everywhere, but something about L.A. is just like—it's not cool. You know what I'm saying? Niggas killed Biggie. Biggie died out here. Niggas killed Pac. Niggas killed Nip. All this shit stem back to L.A. niggas. The hatred and the evil in the street out here is like, that shit is overwhelming, bro." [37]

In the days following Hussle's passing, tributes would unfold in cities all over the planet. On Monday, April 1, Harlem rapper Dave East, who collaborated with Hussle on tracks like "Clarity" featuring Bino Rideaux, organized a candlelight vigil in New York City. With a blue rag on his head and a Mylar N balloon in his hand, Dave East wiped away tears while paying tribute to Hussle. "A sucka took out a fuckin' king," he said. "A real king for this era. I was a kid when Pac and Big so I couldn't feel that. I *feel* this shit." A crowd of mourners held candles as they yelled out, "Facts! Facts! Facts!" Dave East continued to say, "I'm not no revolutionary nigga. I'm not a preacher. I don't even do this. I'm used to fuckin' shows. I don't do this shit. That's my brother. You smell me? If nobody else in New York City gonna do this, I'm gonna do this."[38]

Nas, the legendary MC who signed East to Mass Appeal Records and was revered by Hussle, was one of countless luminaries to pay tribute to Hussle on Instagram. "We are at a great loss today," he wrote. "This hurts. Straight to the point. It's dangerous to be an MC. Dangerous to be a b-ball player. It's dangerous to have money. Dangerous To Be a Black Man. So much hatred. We live like our brothers and sisters in third world countries live. Right in America. Decisions we make about our own life be based on decisions cuz we might not live. It's so deep rooted. It's not a easy fix. Hard to fix anything when kids are still living in poverty. I ain't shutting up though. Nipsey is a True voice. He will never be silenced. He still is a stand-up General for the People who never left his people."[39]

"All the memorial services around the world are just a testament to how many people he touched," says Blacc Sam. "It's a testament to the message and what he represented and so many people that he inspired and touched. He was a true people's champ, man. The story, just making something out of nothing. And inspiring and never thinking he was bigger or more special or better than anybody. Just staying and showing people that if you believe and stay the course, you can always achieve. That's what everybody in every community and every area in the country loved and respected and valued about Nip. They're showing their love and it's humbling."[40]

"I feel like it's beautiful that so many people have been able to connect with such a special, chosen person," his younger sister, Samantha Smith, told me. "It just confirms the person that he is. I already knew he was this type of person, so I'm just grateful that the whole world knows he is."[41]

Iddris Sandu, the chief technical officer of All Money In, picks up the torch as he tries to find something positive in this staggering loss. "It's really interesting how everything is coming full circle now," he says. "When I use the word 'interesting' over 'tragic,' it's because I do not believe this is a tragedy. It's a breakthrough really. To say it's a tragedy would be to imply that his message won't be continued. It's a breakthrough because now you have so many people who were impacted by Nipsey—whether they met him or not—coming out and showing support. So to me it's a breakthrough."[42]

Could the end of such an amazing individual's life be considered some sort of breakthrough? Maybe, in a sense. But Samantha, for one, cannot overlook the tragic loss. "It also saddens me," she said, "because at the end of the day not only do I feel like I lost such a significant person in my personal life, in our family, but I also feel like the whole world lost such a significant person too."[43]

Entrepreneur and social media visionary Gary Vaynerchuk remembers how quickly he and Nipsey bonded over their passion for what Hussle called "creative destruction, the risky business of going against the grain." Although they came from very different worlds, Gary Vee recognized that he and Hussle both thought in fifty-year terms. "He wasn't as big as Pac and Biggie in the macro when this happened," said Vaynerchuk. "But a lot of people who never heard of him were like 'Whoah! Why are the biggest names in the game still posting so emotionally?' If you had the luxury to even know him a little bit, he impacted you immediately."[44]

"The meaning of Nip Hussle has taken on universal resonance and meaning now," said David Gross, the L.A.-born real estate investor and developer who backed the Asghedom brothers' acquisition of the plaza at Crenshaw and Slauson, carving out a foothold for them to lift up themselves and their community. "People around the world get what he was."[45]

His initiative "Our Opportunity" was designed to put the power of Opportunity Zones into the hands of people who cared about the well-being of folks in the neighborhoods in which they were investing. A year after Hussle's passing, Gross had not given up on their goals, but his vision had broadened over time. "I do want to get Tip, and I do want to get 2 Chainz and Meek and [Allen Iverson]," he said during a conversation with Van Lathan at Vector90. "I wanna get all these people who are the hometown heroes, and let's go and buy up their cities, 'cause they have the capital gains . . . But it would not be true to my initial concept that me and Nip had to always do things kind of shoulder-to-shoulder with the community."

Gross says he would like to see the Opportunity Zone legislation revised so that residents of the 8,700 designated areas can receive tax incentives for investing in their own neighborhoods, but until that happens, he's working with the tools available right now. With the aim of "awakening people who never invested before," Gross launched an Investor Challenge through Our Opportunity, offering to seed new accounts with $100 grants. Houston rapper and activist Trae the Truth, a close friend of Hussle's, was one of the first to reach out offering support. Others have since latched onto the idea, which continues rippling across the country. Meanwhile, Gross is teaching fundamental lessons on economics and finance on the ground floor of Vector90. Another initiative called Own Our Own allows people from the neighborhood to invest $1,000 into a real estate investment fund.

"The same diligence I'll put into something that me and Nip would do, I'm putting into those deals," Gross says. The ultimate goal is to "harness as much capital that is community-aligned, that's in the hands of people who care, who come from these neighborhoods, so we can retain the culture, so we don't displace. So we do make sure that this investment, the money gets recycled into businesses in our community."[46]

It's a former Wall Street guy's way of staying "ten toes down" and doing finance the Hussle way. If all goes as planned, the work Gross is doing may turn out to be one of Hussle's most enduring legacies. "I'm not doing this for the community," he says. "I'm doing this *with* the community.[47]

Nipsey's mother does not mourn her son. She would prefer to see those who loved him celebrate his memory and spirit. "I don't want you to be traumatized," she told a schoolteacher who said her students were saddened by Hussle's passing. "I want you to know that I am so happy and that Ermias is here with me right now. I feel him. Now my son knows the secret to the mystery of life . . . Death is not to be feared. Death is something to prepare yourself for. When you walk this earth and you do good deeds for people." Smith takes comfort in the look of peace on her son's face when he was laid in his casket. "I looked at him and I said 'That's my angel baby. Now he's a baby in the spirit world.'" With a smile on her face, Hussle's mother takes the time to comfort others in their grief. "Please do not stay down. Do not mourn. Because Nipsey is great and now he is even greater because he has no bounds and no limits . . . Ermias will never die. You have him in your heart. Every time you speak of Ermias, he lives."[48]

"As a father I wish my son was still here with me," said Dawit Asghedom, shortly after Ermias was laid to rest at Forest Lawn Cemetery in Hollywood Hills, the final resting place of Michael Jackson, Walt Disney, John Singleton, and Rodney King. "But also he's not died in vain. People recognize what he planned to do and what he has accomplished at a young age, at only thirty-three.

"Nobody imagined how much people loved him, the support they give him. There's no words to explain. Starting from the Marathon store to the Staples Center and when we marched through the streets. It was incredible."[49]

"We'll try to continue as much as we can," said Blacc Sam. His sister, Samantha, affirms that Nipsey's legacy will go on. "Definitely. Without a doubt. Without a doubt."[50]

Councilmember Marqueece Harris-Dawson foresees Nipsey's work growing as his example inspires others. "I expect the Marathon store to prosper—and more importantly, the Marathon store concept," he says. "I think others will begin to mimic his example, 'cause that's been a financial success. People will come to South L.A., to this neighborhood, to the Crenshaw District, to consume culture that's created here."

Nipsey understood the risks of remaining so accessible to his neighborhood. He accepted those risks as a self-made millionaire just the same as when he was a young Slauson Boy. "To be honest, that corner was known for robberies," he told me a year before his death. "People would get robbed a lot on that corner. It's none of that no more. We got an understanding in my whole community that anybody come over here, it's to support the overall well-being of the community."[51] Nipsey's reward for believing in his community was to lose his life in front of the place that he built. If his work does not continue, that sacrifice will have been in vain. And that would be an even greater tragedy. Hussle has passed the torch—actually many torches. For that reason alone the Marathon must never stop.

"Yeah, we're going to continue his legacy," says Iddris Sandu. "Everything he was working on. The STEM project. Vector90. Destination Crenshaw. The documentary. We're going to continue doing all of that. 'Cause he really understood, it's not about him. It's really for us."[52]

In a 2018 interview with *Billboard*, Hussle contemplated his legacy. "I just want to impact the next 12-year-old Nip Hussle," he said. "I want to impact the young dudes and young girls and give them the gems I've learned on my path. I'll let 'em know, and confirm their little gut feelings they got. I want to be one of the voices or one of the stories that say, 'Nah, you right. You are unbelievably powerful. Your potential is the illest . . . I want to be one of the people that not only say that, but live that as an example."[53]

"I'm a Black man first," says the Black LAPD officer. "If you want to know what the police department is thinking about Nipsey Hussle or what police officers feel, I'm working with these guys every day. They can't glorify a gang member. It doesn't matter that in the Black community they care about what he was doing and giving back and helping. But there's no way they can allow a gang member to have that kind of building over there representing him. And I suppress my feelings about that because I know where I am. I know where the hell I am. I'm not trying to come out here and carry a flag for Nipsey Hussle when I'm working for the police. They don't care about him giving back. To them he is a gang member and that's all he will ever be."[54]

On his final visit to *Big Boy's Neighborhood*, Hussle looked back over his journey to that point and summed up the indomitable spirit of the Marathon. "We got turned down," he said. "We failed. Had setbacks. Had to start over—a lot of times. You know, but we kept goin' at it. In anybody's case, that's always the distinguishing factor. The name of the brand, obviously, is the Marathon. It just stands for endurance. It stands for staying down."

Big Boy asked if he ever lost faith. "Did you ever feel like, 'Man, this ain't gonna work'?"

"That's why I call my thing the Marathon," Hussle said. "I

ain't gonna lie and portray this ultimate poise, like I been had it figured out. Nah. I just didn't quit. That's the only distinguishing quality. I went through every emotion. And I think that's what's gonna separate whoever is gonna try to go for something, is you ain't gonna quit. You gonna take the stance of 'I'm gonna die behind what I'm gettin' at right now.'"[55]

In that spirit, Blacc Sam has committed himself to the completion of the Nipsey Hussle Tower, a mixed-use residential building providing affordable housing as well as a revamped flagship store for The Marathon Clothing and a Nipsey Hussle museum.

> "Nipsey was a true inspiration for the have nots," Sam said in a statement responding to the Los Angeles city attorney's efforts to shut down The Marathon Clothing store. "He was the people's champ. He came from nothing and triumphed. He excelled in precarious situations. He had 100% respect from the streets. Because he [led] by example, his honor and his sense of duty was at all times his moral compass. . . .
>
> "Regardless of anyone's efforts to stop this from happening, Nipsey's dream will be seen through and passed down to his children. The Nipsey Hussle Tower will inspire and show the people that even though you come from nothing you can achieve greatness. History will tell the story of Nipsey Hussle. The Nipsey Hussle tower will be built and his legacy will be etched in stone and etched in the people['s] hearts forever."[56]

It's early afternoon on Slauson Avenue. Tourists are flocking to take selfies against the larger-than-life Nipsey Hussle murals in the alley by the Fatburger that connects Slauson Avenue to Fifty-Eighth Place. This is the same alley that the aptly nicknamed Shitty Cuz ran through with two guns in his hands and the hood on his chest on March 31, 2019. Whether Eric Holder was hired by police, put up to it by the hood, or acting alone out of jealous rage will likely be debated forever. And in the end, the loss is still the same. The murder of Neighborhood Nip was a crime against humanity.

"I'm praying for him too," says Hussle's grandmother. "I hope he does not get killed in custody. He has enough time to ask God for forgiveness. I'm a Catholic. I do believe in prayers, and I'm praying for him. He was a young, ignorant situation and I'm hoping he's sorry for what he did."[57]

Few people feel the loss as keenly as Slauson Bruce. He was down and out when Hussle first hired him to start cleaning the parking lot. Today Bruce is waiting for a business meeting, sitting on a short red concrete wall that stands just outside the locked chain-link fence that now surrounds the entire parking lot at 3420 West Slauson Ave, once the site of a bustling hub of commerce, the Marathon Clothing smart store. Next to Bruce is a shopping cart filled with odds and ends. Dressed in an Adidas tracksuit and a worn black fedora, Bruce spares a few minutes to talk.

"I did a lot," says Bruce. "I built this place, man. I'm tellin' you. I used to steam-clean this lot. All kinda shit. Wash windows. It's just me, really. Nipsey wouldn't be here. He'd be at the studio. He'd leave Sam, his brother, and Fatts and them in charge." Bruce coughs hard, then continues. "He said he wouldn't have time for that. He had to make songs."[58]

Bruce was riding his bike collecting cans when he first met Nipsey. "Fifteen long years ago," he says, recalling the life-changing moment vividly. "He backed his car out, and when he backed out he thought I was in the way."

Nipsey opened up the door.

"You all right?" he asked.

"I said, 'Yeah. I need a job.'"

"You keep this lot clean, you got one," Nipsey told him. That was 2004—when the name Nipsey Hussle was little known beyond the Crenshaw District. Slauson Bruce says he's been here ever since.

"You damn right," he says when asked if he could tell Hussle was someone special.

Hussle saw something in Bruce too, and they formed a bond.

"So we went on and on and talked," Bruce recalls. "And he said, 'Wait a minute, I'ma put you in a movie!'" True to his word, Nipsey cast Slauson Bruce to star in "The Midas Touch," a YouTube video posted on February 1, 2018, as part of the *Victory Lap* album rollout. In the ten-minute clip, Bruce leaves the shopping cart behind and hops into Nipsey's Maybach. Bruce gets a fresh cut at the Shave Parlor on Slauson and Seventh Avenue and a charcoal-gray suit from Tom Ford in Beverly Hills. He hits the jewelry store for a gold ring, watch, bracelet, and chain, then gets a mani-pedi and massage. Once he's properly swagged out, Bruce enjoys a lobster dinner with some of the All Money In team followed by a trip to a high-end strip club.[59]

Everything has changed since March 31. "Since then it's not too good," says Bruce. "I can't sleep at night." His dog Pet Bull looks at him and Bruce looks back.

"I break out cryin' every night," he says. "But I said ain't nothin' I can do about it. What he told me before he died—he was parkin' and leavin', and he said, 'The Marathon continues.' I said I'm gonna make sure of that. 'Cause he did so much for us."

Bruce had cleaned up the lot on the day Nipsey was killed. "I had just left," he says, his voice quieter than before. "I don't hang out here. At first I would hang around and stuff, but as it went on

I wouldn't do that. I'd come at six to clean the lot up. Then I was working at Woody's. Then at night I'd go clean up somewhere else. Three jobs a day—man!"

All of those jobs are gone now. Bruce's girlfriend died in her sleep two years ago. "I been goin' through all type of shit," he says. Since then he lost a little bit of that Marathon momentum. "I ain't doin' nothing," he says, turning his head to look up Slauson Ave toward Crenshaw. "I can't find nothing." But he believes that Blacc Sam is gonna rebuild this place. "That's why it's gated," Bruce says. "They're building it up, making apartments."

Just then, a lady from across the street approaches on foot. She says she's seen Nipsey's godbrother Adam a few blocks away.

"Where?"

"At the place."

"Talk to him?"

"Not this time." She hands Bruce some money without another word and walks back in the direction she came from. The hustle never ends.

"That was my sister just now," Bruce explains. "She brought some orders from Chicago. A friend of hers ordered some shirts. You can't even go online and get 'em. They backed up. You can't get none."

If Bruce could say one thing to Nipsey right now, it would be: "Hey, man, the Marathon continues. Believe it or not."

Yes, it really does continue. Even with the padlocked fence, the barbed wire, the sturdy green fabric blocking everything from view. The fence went up on August 1, 2019, to discourage uninvited guests from hanging around the lot where the Marathon Clothing store still stands. The police are always watching, waiting for someone to slip up and discredit Nipsey's team. Undeterred, Nipsey's fans continue to show up day after day. In the months since his passing, well-wishers from all over the world have converged on this place, snapping photos, saying prayers, and scrawling countless messages in his honor—*RIP Nip, TMC 4Ever, Hussle The Great!*—on every accessible square inch of wall and window space.

As special as it was to Nipsey and Sam and Adam and Fatts in life, this shopping plaza at 3420 West Slauson Ave is now hallowed ground. The blood of a prophet was spilled here, and there's no fence tall enough to hold back all the love. Nipsey Hussle is the people's champ and the whole world knows it, but somehow the Los Angeles City Attorney's Office doesn't see it that way.

"We bought the lot, man," Sam declared proudly during the April 11 memorial service for his brother at the Staples Center. "I don't know how we did it. And that was a big thing for bro, man, because he used to sell CDs out the trunk. He used to be in that parking lot, and they used to try to kick him out of the lot. And y'all know what we went through with the police in that lot."[60]

Bruce witnessed the conflict many times during his years of employment by the family business. "When police came and tore the place down, Sam told me—what'd he say? Oh, 'The big payback.' He built this sucker back in two days. 'They won't stop me!' That's what he said. And everything's legal. They wasn't selling no dope. They trying to look for guns and all that shit. Them boys didn't carry that shit. They was goin' legit."

Bruce has no patience for conspiracy theories. Ask him who killed Nipsey and he'll tell you straight up: "What you call a hater," he says. "Jealous motherfucker. That's what I think."

But what about the fact that he was supposedly someone Hussle knew?

"Your best friend could be a jealous motherfucker."[61]

Blacc Sam has continued to fight in court on behalf of his brother's legacy and to protect the interests of his family. On

May 16, less than two months after Hussle's death, the business entity Crips LLC filed trademark applications for his phrase "The Marathon Continues"—including one for the right to use it on clothing. Sam filed a similar trademark application on May 28. When Sam spoke out publicly, a spokesperson for Crips LLC issued a statement of apology in July 2019. "There will absolutely be no trademark legal battle between their organization and Blacc Sam, brother of the late Nipsey Hussle," the statement said, adding that the organization realized the filing may have been "offensive" and that they had reached out to the family. But actions speak louder than words. As Crips LLC did not abandon its application, Nipsey Hussle's estate filed suit in October 2020, seeking monetary damages and a court order forcing the company to destroy any unauthorized Marathon merchandise.[62]

Back in 2013, fresh off making one hundred racks in one night at the first Crenshaw pop-up shop, Hussle spoke with Complex about why Nipsey Hussle fans felt such a strong connection. "Because I'm *real*, my nigga," he said. "My story is real. There ain't no rap niggas in the game like me at all. Especially from my generation. There ain't no nigga that stood up to what I stood up to. Went through what I went through. Thought how I thought. Didn't give up. Stayed down, stayed in the shit. Built for his community. Stayed local and inspired his area. Came from a treacherous area like the Rollin' 60s. Went toe to toe and head up with killers. There ain't no nigga in the game like me. So that's what they're connecting to, and the fact that I express my truth via my music."[63]

Down the block from Slauson Bruce stands Reverend Abdullah, a clean-cut young brother in a crisp suit and tie selling copies of *The Final Call*, the newspaper published by the Nation of Islam. The paper's April 9, 2019, issue featured a cover story about "The

Life, Loss and Legacy of Nipsey Hussle." During the week of Hussle's funeral, the NOI distributed 100,000 copies of that issue all over Los Angeles.[64] When Minister Louis Farrakhan spoke at Hussle's nationally televised memorial at the Staples Center, he said Nipsey "is to hip-hop and rap what Bob Marley was to reggae; he is the prophetic voice of all in that community."[65] (When asked about Hussle's passing, Bob's son Stephen Marley said, "Although we didn't know him, it was a sad time for everyone. Everyone felt it.")[66]

"He never said no to the paper—him or his brother," says Reverend Abdullah. "Never said no."[67]

If there's anything positive that can come from the tragedy of March 31, 2019, Reverend Abdullah thinks it might be the spotlight it's put on the Crenshaw District and the work Hussle was doing here. "Unfortunate situation for sure. However, there is more awareness of what's happening in the community. Not that it's a positive thing that the brother passed away. But at least a lot of people are aware of what he was doing, what his message was, and what the problems are."

Reverend Abdullah has been selling the paper at the shopping plaza on Slauson and Crenshaw since long before Hussle passed. "One hundred percent," he says. "Familiar face to him. Had a few conversations. Seen each other in different places. That's why I wanted to do an interview, 'cause I really did love him. Heck yeah."

He can still remember the first time he met Hussle. "It was right over there," he says, pointing toward the parking lot. "It was just amazing how approachable he was, and that he's really in the streets doing what he's saying. He wasn't one of these rappers that's making stuff up, you know, making up a lifestyle. When I met him, he had a shoebox full of money. He stopped counting the shoebox to buy a paper, then he went back to counting. I don't know what the transaction was, but that's just what type of individual he was. So that's just what I want the world to know."

What lesson will people take from what happened to him? "I think people should keep giving back," says Reverend Abdullah. "I think people should just learn. I can't tell you my lesson. I got thousands of lessons from it. It's like certain books. I can't tell you what it means, you just gotta read it. But definitely invest in the community. Keep doing it. Pick up where he left off. He gave T.I. the book *Message to the Blackman in America*. Pick up where he left off."

If he could say one thing to Hussle, it would be this: "I love you. I love you, bro. That's it. One hundred percent. Thank you, Nipsey Hussle."[68]

ACKNOWLEDGMENTS

First and foremost, thank you Ermias Joseph Asghedom for loving hip-hop so much and for demonstrating its awesome power—as an art form, an economic engine, a tool for sociopolitical criticism, and a force for redemption—to the whole wide world. Your life stands as an example of what's possible if you believe in yourself and commit to that belief every single day. Your words kept me going through them lookin' for a reason nights, as fires blazed and a pandemic raged. I know I'm not the only person to have drawn tremendous inspiration from the way you ran your Marathon, and the motivational mantras you left for all of us. May your eternal soul Rest in Power.

While this is not an authorized biography, a portion of the proceeds from *The Marathon Don't Stop* will be donated to Nipsey's estate out of respect—and to the Neighborhood Nip Foundation as an investment in the aspiring hip-hop artists of tomorrow.

Love and respect goes out to Nip's entire family—his grandmother, his mother, his father, his sister Samantha, and especially his big brother Sam. Blessings, guidance, and protection to his children Mani Mon and Kross the Boss. Can't leave out the All Money In team—Fatts (RIP), Adam, Jorge—and Lady Hussle herself. Your grace and resilience have helped a lot of people keep on keepin' on.

Acknowledgment was important to Nipsey Hussle, whose artistry and intellect were severely underrated throughout most of his life. The fact that so few critics and gatekeepers recognized Hussle's importance only makes his story more important now. With that said, I'd like to acknowledge the people who made it possible for me to complete the most challenging and fulfilling project I've ever attempted.

Shout-out to Cuzzy Capone, who recognized my intention to tell the half that's never been told. Thanks for sharing so much knowledge with me and for introducing me to Young Goochaveli, Hoodsta Rob, and Wee Dogg, whose voices were essential to this book. Much respect to Infant J Stone, Killa Twan, BH, Pacman Da Gunman, and Cobby Supreme. Each of your lives is a movie in itself—keep flying that checkered flag like the whole world is watching, and listening.

Blessings to Dexter Browne, who reached out to me on the strength, trusting his own intuition, and opened the door to worlds within worlds. You and your family put everything on the line, then and now. The ButterVision story will be told in full one day. FTM! Thank you for introducing me to Ralo Stylez, co-creator of The Marathon sound. Shouts to DJ Felli Fel for setting shit off and to DJ VIP for keeping Hussle in rotation on the wheels of steel.

Big respect to Brittany Bell at Atlantic Records, who scheduled me as Nipsey's first interview during the New York press run for *Victory Lap*. Heartfelt thanks to Karen Civil, who spoke eloquently about Hussle's legacy while fighting back tears, and who connected me with Blacc Sam, Samantha Smith, David Gross, Iddris Sandu, and Marqueece Harris-Dawson. Shout-out to Steve Lobel who drove coast to coast with Nipsey on the LAX tour, and brought him up to the VIBE offices that day we first met. Thank you Jonny Shipes and Smoke DZA for keeping it 100 at all times.

Much respect to Snoop Dogg, Curren$y, Master P, and Ricky Rozay for sharing your personal testimonies about Nip Hussle the Great. Big up E.D.I. Mean for booking Hussle to headline his first ever festival, Welcome to the West, for honoring his memory a year later, and for sharing your unique perspective on the man who saw himself as "Tupac of my generation."

Shout-out to YG, Trae tha Truth, and ScHoolboy Q for meeting with me and chopping it up, even though we did not speak on the record for this book. In fact, shout-out to everyone who knew about this project but chose to hold your peace. Your reverence for Hussle speaks volumes and I heard every bit of it, loud and clear. Kudos to Kendrick Lamar for both of our conversations, for that verse on "Dedication," and for "The Heart" (all parts).

Shouts go out to all my peers and pioneers who put in work to lay the foundation this book was built upon. Big up every rap journalist, video blogger, and DVD hustler who took the time to preserve each and every precious tile of the Nipsey Hussle mosaic—you are appreciated.

To KevMac Videos for documenting so much of the early Nip Hussle come-up—your thoroughness and authenticity are an invaluable resource for anyone seeking to understand the L.A. streets. To Davey D for connecting with young Nip Hussle outside the Get Your Money Right seminar—your off-the-cuff convo for Hard Knock TV is a treasure. To Chuck Dizzle and DJ Hed of Home Grown Radio—your ongoing dialog with Nip was so real, thanks for sharing it with the world. To Vanessa Satten for giving Hussle that *XXL* Freshman cover, and for sharing your insights with me. Props to Will Welch and Mark Anthony Green for *GQ*'s "California Love." Shout-out to Toshi Kondo and Angel Diaz, whose Hussle interviews on *Complex* could stand as essential documents of a motherfuckin' rap phenomenon. Finally, shout-out to B-Dot, who challenged Nip to write a Rap Radar blog post about his Proud2Pay movement, and to my old friend Elliott "YN" Wilson, whose rapport with Jay-Z led directly to Hov purchasing 100 *Crenshaw* mixtapes for $10,000. As Hussle told me, "When Jay tapped into the wave, everybody became a believer."

Maximum respect to the living legend Quincy Delight Jones, Jr. for launching VIBE and sending me on the adventure of a lifetime. Your music will never stop playing as long as the earth turns and your blessing means the world, then and now. Thanks to Sacha Jenkins and the Mass Appeal massive—all my real ones, you know who you are. Shout-out to Pup Daddy even though you shitted on the conference room carpet.

To my agent, Robert Guinsler, a man with the patience of Job, thanks for never giving up.

To my editor, Michelle Herrera Mulligan, thanks for keeping the faith and fighting the good fight through every single lap of this marathon.

Many thanks to my tireless research assistant Nissim Hershkovits and to Semmi W. for invaluable insights on Eritrean culture.

To Reshma B, thanks for always keeping it real. As Hussle said, the highest human act is to inspire.

To Lisa, thanks for keeping everything in ConTextos. The world awaits your book.

To AI&M, you got next.

God bless my big sister Julie in heaven. "It takes as long as it takes."

BIBLIOGRAPHY

ABC News. "Watch Donald Trump's Grand Escalator Entrance to His Presidential Announcement." June 16, 2015. https://abcnews.go.com /Politics/video/watch-donald-trumps-grand-escalator-entrance -presidential-announcement-31802261.

ACLU National Prison Project. *Cruel and Unusual Punishment.* 2011. https://www.aclu.org/files/assets/78162_aclu_jails_r2_lr.pdf.

Alonso, Alex A. "Rapper Nipsey Hussle Linked to an Officer Involved Shooting in South LA." StreetGangs.com, March 18, 2011. http:// www.streetgangs.com/features/031811_ois_lapd.

Arnold, Paul. "Nipsey Hussle Talks Leaving Epic, Dissing Detox." *HipHopDX.* December 21, 2010. https://hiphopdx.com/news /id.13420/title.nipsey-hussle-talks-leaving-epic-records-dissing -detox#.

Associated Press. "Radio Stations in Several States Hacked with Anti-Trump Rap." January 31, 2017. https://apnews.com/article/416a 85c30dbc4e30981f813e5c034c31.

Australian Broadcasting Corporation (ABC). "Timeline: The Black Lives Matter Movement." Updated February 22, 2018. https://www.abc.net .au/news/2016-07-14/black-lives-matter-timeline/7585856?nw=0.

Bacher, Danielle. "YG Speaks Out for First Time Since Being Shot: 'I'm Hard to Kill.'" *Billboard* (website), June 24, 2015. https://www.bill board.com/articles/columns/the-juice/6605861/yg-speaks-out-since -being-shot.

Baker, Peter. "Alice Marie Johnson Is Granted Clemency by Trump after Push by Kim Kardashian West." *New York Times,* June 6, 2018. https://www.nytimes.com/2018/06/06/us/politics/trump-alice -johnson-sentence-commuted-kim-kardashian-west.html.

Barrett, Beth. "Rollin' 60s Give Unique Window into Gang Culture." *Los Angeles Daily News,* September 30, 2004. http://lang.dailybulletin .com/socal/gangs/articles/dnp5_culture.asp.

BBC. "Donald Trump Rally Police 'Ejected' Black Students." March 1, 2016. https://www.bbc.com/news/election-us-2016-35694006.

Bernanke, Ben. "Causes of the Recent Financial and Economic Crisis." Federal Reserve (website), September 2, 2010. https://www .federalreserve.gov/newsevents/testimony/bernanke20100902a .htm#:~:text=A%20too%2Dbig%2Dto%2D,would%20face%20 severe%20adverse%20consequences.&text=First%2C%20 too%2Dbig%2Dto,generates%20a%20severe%20moral%20hazard.

Berry, Peter A. "Nipsey Hussle and Lauren London Break Up." *XXL*, November 22, 2017. https://www.xxlmag.com/nipsey-hussle-lauren -london-break-up/.

Berry, Peter A. "Nipsey Hussle Says Artists Like 6ix9ine Are Bound to Self-Destruct." *XXL*, March 11, 2019. https://www.xxlmag.com /nipsey-hussle-artists-like-6ix9ine-self-destruct/.

BET. "BET Hip Hop Awards Nominees and Winners, 2014." BET.com.

Blistein, Jon. "Watch Eminem Demolish Donald Trump in BET Awards Freestyle." *Rolling Stone*, October 11, 2017. https://www.rollingstone .com/music/music-news/watch-eminem-demolish-donald-trump-in -bet-awards-freestyle-119122/.

Body Art Guru (website). "Nipsey Hussle's 31 Tattoos and Their Meaning." 2019. https://bodyartguru.com/nipsey-hussle-tattoos/.

Boffard, Rob. "Meet Nipsey Hussle, the Rapper Who Wants You to Pay $1,000 for His Album." *The Guardian*, January 20, 2015. https://www .theguardian.com/music/2015/jan/20/nipsey-hussle-rapper-mailbox -money-1000-dollars.

Box Office Mojo. *Straight Outta Compton*, https://www.boxofficemojo .com/release/rl292718081/.

Brown, August. "America's at a Breaking Point. So Is YG." *Los Angeles Times*, September 24, 2020. https://www.latimes.com/entertainment -arts/music/story/2020-09-24/yg-my-life-4hunnid-new-album-out -on-bail.

Brown, August. "'I Feel Good for Speaking Up': YG on His 2016 Protest Anthem That Goes After Donald Trump." *Los Angeles Times*, November 17, 2016. https://www.latimes.com/entertainment/music /la-et-ms-yg-trump-election-20161116-story.html.

Brown, Larry. "Floyd Mayweather Jr. and 50 Cent Allegedly in Middle of Vegas Strip Club Throwdown." Larry Brown Sports (website). August 5, 2011. https://larrybrownsports.com/boxing/floyd

-mayweather-jr-and-50-cent-allegedly-in-middle-of-vegas-strip
-club-throwdown/80799.

Burney, Lawrence. "What Freedom Feels Like to Nipsey Hussle." *The Fader*, Winter 2019.

Cárdenas, Vanessa, and Sophia Kerby. "Battleground States Go Blue Thanks to Multiracial Coalitions that Supported President Obama." Center for American Progress, November 15, 2012. https://www.americanprogress.org/issues/race/news/2012/11/15/45069/battleground-states-go-blue-thanks-to-multiracial-coalitions-that-supported-president-obama/.

Cardiga, Manuela. "Watch Nipsey Hussle's Ex Tanisha Detail Relationship with Rapper and Lauren London." AmoMama (website), May 30, 2019. https://news.amomama.com/153720-watch-nipsey-hussles-ex-tanisha-detail-r.html.

Carissimo, Justin. "Kendrick Lamar Asks Fox News: 'How Can You Take a Song about Hope and Turn It into Hatred?'" *Independent* (UK), February 4, 2016. https://www.independent.co.uk/news/people/kendrick-lamar-asks-fox-news-how-can-you-take-song-about-hope-and-turn-it-hatred-a6045726.html.

Carmichael, Rodney. "Nipsey Hussle Tells the Epic Stories Behind 'Victory Lap,' Track by Track." NPR, February 16, 2018. https://www.npr.org/sections/allsongs/2018/02/16/586361873/nipsey-hussle-tells-the-epic-stories-behind-victory-lap-track-by-track.

Carter, Terry. "Nipsey Hussle's Brother Battles the Crips for 'The Marathon Continues' Trademark." Revolt (website), June 5, 2019. https://www.revolt.tv/2019/6/5/20824807/nipsey-hussle-s-brother-battles-the-crips-for-the-marathon-continues-trademark.

Catanese, David. "The 10 Closest States in the 2016 Election." *US News & World Report*, November 14, 2016.

CBS Los Angeles. "Co-Working Space, Business Incubator Opens In Crenshaw District." February 15, 2018. https://losangeles.cbslocal.com/2018/02/15/vector90-coworking-crenshaw/.

Chang, Cindy, and Angel Jennings. "Nipsey Hussle Died in the Marathon Clothing Lot. Will His Legacy Die There Too?" *Los Angeles Times*, August 13, 2019. https://www.latimes.com/california/story/2019-08-12/nipsey-hussle-marathon-clothing-parking-lot-lapd.

Chazanov, Mathis, and Chuck Philips. "Rap Singer Faces Charge of

Murder, Violence." *Los Angeles Times*, September 4, 1993. https://www.latimes.com/archives/la-xpm-1993-09-04-me-31460-story.html.

Chesman, Donna-Claire. "How TDE's Albums Have Quietly Upheld the Concept of HiiiPower." Okayplayer, 2018.

CNN. "Trump Officially Joins Reform Party." October 25, 1999.

Coe, Kairi. "Nipsey Hussle Calls Out Radio Stations for Not Playing 'FDT.'" *XXL*, September 6, 2017.

Coe, Kairi. "Watch O.T. Genasis Crip Walk to YG's 'FDT' Outside of the White House." *XXL*, August 1, 2017.

Conway, Lindsey. "Valdosta State University Students Kicked Out of Trump Rally the Day before Georgia Primary." *Red and Black* (redandblack.com). March 1, 2016. https://www.redandblack .com/athensnews/valdosta-state-university-students-kicked-out -of-trump-rally-the-day-before-georgia-primary/article_2b3a3b58 -dfdb-11e5-978d-c3935b44f977.html.

Coscarelli, Joe. "6ix9ine's Testimony: The Rapper's Rise, Beefs and Crash, in His Own Words." *New York Times*, September 20, 2019. https://www.nytimes.com/2019/09/20/arts/music/tekashi-case -testimony.html.

Daniels, Tim. "LeBron James Talks Mental Health, Says He Lost 'Love for the Game' in 2011." Bleacher Report, December 10, 2019.

de Waal, Alex. *Evil Days: Thirty Years of War and Famine in Ethiopia* (Africa Watch Report). Human Rights Watch, 1991.

Destination Crenshaw (website). 2019. https://destinationcrenshaw.la/.

Diaz, Angel. "Interview: Nipsey Hussle Explains His Dispute with Complex, Going Indie, and 'Crenshaw.'" *Complex*, October 15, 2013.

Diaz, Angel. "Interview: Nipsey Hussle Talks Selling 'Mailbox Money' for $1,000, the Power of the Internet, and Squeezing Out the Middle Man." *Complex*, December 22, 2014.

Diep, Eric. "Dom Kennedy's 25 Favorite Albums." *Complex*, November 20, 2012.

Diep, Eric. "Karen Civil and Steve 'Steve-O' Carless Talk Consulting Firm Marathon Agency's 'Out-of-the-Box' Strategy." *Billboard*, October 28, 2016.

Dodson, Aaron. "Nipsey Hussle's Puma Partnership Was Strong and Authentic." The Undefeated (website), April 3, 2019.

Duck, Steve. "Nipsey Hussle on What Comes after the Victory Lap."
   Complex Australia, February 26, 2019.

Eisenberg, Jeff. "Inside the Special Bond between Late Rapper Nipsey
   Hussle and Texas Tech's Brandone Francis." Yahoo Sports (website),
   April 5, 2019.

Espinosa, Joshua. "Nipsey Hussle's Grade School Poetry, Short Stories
   Surface Online." *Complex*, April 5, 2019.

Final Call. "Spreading Light, Love and Honoring Nipsey Hussle." April 9,
   2019. https://www.finalcall.com/artman/publish/Perspectives_1
   /Spreading-light-love.shtml.

Fleming, Monya. "Days after Nipsey Hussle and Lauren London
   Announce Their Split, His First Baby Mama Has Tea to Spill." Dallas
   Black (website), December 2, 2017. http://dallasblack.com/entertain
   ment/nipsey-hussle-lauren-london-chyna-hussle.

Foshay, Karen. "I Was There: 'He Was Suggesting That Blacks Were Not
   Normal,' LA Doctor Recalls Bizarre Phone Call from Then LAPD
   Chief Daryl Gates." KCET-TV, 2020. https://www.kcet.org/shows
   /socal-connected/i-was-there-he-was-suggesting-that-blacks-were
   -not-normal-la-doctor-recalls.

Fresh, Mikey. "New Mixtape: Nipsey Hussle 'The Marathon.'" *Vibe*.
   December 21, 2010.

Fryer, Roland G., Jr., Paul S. Heaton, Steven D. Levitt, and Kevin M.
   Murphy. "Measuring Crack Cocaine and Its Impact." *Economic
   Inquiry* 51, no. 3 (2013): 1651–81. https://scholar.harvard.edu/fryer
   /publications/measuring-crack-cocaine-and-its-impact.

Gabbart, Adam. "Golden Escalator Ride: The Surreal Day Trump Kicked
   Off His Bid for President." *The Guardian* (UK), June 14, 2019.
   https://www.theguardian.com/us-news/2019/jun/13/donald-trump
   -presidential-campaign-speech-eyewitness -memories.

Gang Enforcement (website). "Gangs and Sports Attire." https://www
   .gangenforcement.com/gang-adopted-sports-attire-and-commercial
   -logos.html.

Gates, Daryl F. *Chief: My Life in the LAPD.* New York: Bantam, 1992.

Gaviria, Marcela (producer). *Frontline.* Season 2018, episode 5, "The Gang
   Crackdown." PBS. February 13, 2018. https://www.pbs.org/wgbh
   /frontline/film/the-gang-crackdown/.

Gray, Noah, Sara Murray, and Jim Acosta. "Valdosta State University Black Students Escorted out of Trump Rally." CNN, March 1, 2016. https://www.cnn.com/2016/03/01/politics/valdosta-state-university -students-escorted-out-of-trump-rally/index.html.

Green, Dennis. "Trump Tower Is Actually Not as Tall as Donald Trump Says." Business Insider (website), October 25, 2016. https://www .businessinsider.com/trump-tower-is-not-as-tall-as-trump-says -2016-10.

Green, Mark Anthony. "California Love with Nipsey Hussle and Lauren London." *GQ*, February 21, 2019.

Griffith, Janelle. "Nipsey Hussle's Planned Meeting with LA Police on Gang Violence to Go On in His Honor." NBC News, April 1, 2019. https://www.nbcnews.com/news/us-news/nipsey-hussle-s-planned -meeting-l-police-gang-violence-go-n989676.

Guardian (UK). "Trump: 'I Am the Least Racist Person There Is Anywhere in the World' video." July 30, 2019.

Hayden, Jen. "Nobody Is More Happy about Donald Trump's Presidential Campaign Announcement than Jon Stewart." Daily Kos (website), June 17, 2015. https://www.dailykos.com/stories/2015/6/17/1393954 /-Nobody-is-more-happy-about-Donald-Trump-s-presidential -campaign-announcement-than-Jon-Stewart.

Hochman, Steve. "Compton Rappers Versus the Letter of the Law: FBI Claims Song by N.W.A. Advocates Violence on Police." *Los Angeles Times*, October 5, 1989. https://www.latimes.com/archives/la-xpm -1989-10-05-ca-1046-story.html.

Hughes, Allen (dir.). *The Defiant Ones*. HBO. 2017.

Hundreds, Bobby. "Nipsey Hussle: At Conflict with the World." *The Hundreds* (blog), February 14, 2018. https://thehundreds.com/blogs /bobby-hundreds/nipsey-hussle-at-conflict-with-the-world.

Hussle, Nipsey. "For The Culture." *Players' Tribune*, October 25, 2018. https://www.theplayerstribune.com/articles/nipsey-hussle-for-the -culture.

Hussle, Nipsey. "'HUSSLE IN THE HOUSE' DEBUTS ON 106 & PARK TONITE!!" WordPress page. March 5, 2009. https:// nipseyhussle.wordpress.com/2009/03/05/hussle-in-the-house-debuts -on-106-park-tonite/.

Jasper, Jacky. "Big U Speaks on Nipsey Hussle's Impact, Developing Options Program and Crenshaw's Legacy." *Vibe*, April 2, 2020. https://www.vibe.com/2020/04/eugene-big-u-henley-interview.

Jennings, Angel. "Must Reads: Nipsey Hussle's Brother Found Him

Dying. These Are His Final Moments." *Los Angeles Times*, April 4, 2019. https://www.latimes.com/local/lanow/la-me-nipsey-hussle-final-moments-20190404-story.html.

Johnson, Louis. "Jorge Peniche: The *Badger Herald* Interview." *Badger Herald*, May 20, 2014.

Jones, Charisse. "Crack and Punishment: Is Race the Issue?" *New York Times*, October 28, 1995. https://www.nytimes.com/1995/10/28/us/crack-and-punishment-is-race-the-issue.html.

KABC-7. "Rapper Nipsey Hussle Released on Bail." August 30, 2014. https://abc7.com/nipsey-hussle-arrested-made-in-america/288013/.

Karnazes, Dean. "The Real Pheidippides Story." *Runner's World*, December 6, 2016.

Katz, Jesse. "An Ethic Dies with Gang Chief." *Los Angeles Times*, April 14, 1992. https://www.latimes.com/archives/la-xpm-1992-04-14-mn-109-story.html.

Kaufman, Gil. "YG and Nipsey Hussle's 'FDT (F—- Donald Trump)' Video Shoot Shut Down by Cops." *Billboard*, April 4, 2016.

Kelley, Sonaiya. "With a New STEM Center and a Revolutionary Marketing Strategy, Nipsey Hussle Is Music's Biggest Disruptor." *Los Angeles Times*, March 16, 2018. https://www.latimes.com/entertainment/movies/la-et-ms-nipsey-hussle-vector-90-victory-lap-2018 0228-story.html.

Kennedy, Gerrick D. "The Light of Los Angeles: The Legacy of Nipsey Hussle." *GQ*, December 2, 2019.

Kessler, Glenn. "Donald Trump and David Duke: For the Record." *Washington Post*, March 1, 2016. https://www.washingtonpost.com/news/fact-checker/wp/2016/03/01/donald-trump-and-david-duke-for-the-record/.

Khalifa, Wiz. "Wiz Khalifa Remembers Meeting Nipsey Hussle as a 2010 *XXL* Freshman/How Long Will They Mourn Me?" *XXL*, August 15, 2019.

Kirk, Michael. *Frontline*. Program #1915, "LAPD Blues," in "Race, Policing, and Rap." PBS, May 15, 2001. Transcript: https://www.pbs.org/wgbh/pages/frontline/shows/lapd/etc/script.html.

Klein, Patricia. "A Ram at Rest: These Are Quiet Times for LAPD's 'Battering' Vehicle." *Los Angeles Times*, February 10, 1986. https://www.latimes.com/archives/la-xpm-1986-02-10-me-27297-story.html.

Kohn, Daniel. "The Five Most Amazing Moments in VMA History." *LA*

Weekly, August 25, 2011. https://www.laweekly.com/the-five-most -amazing-moments-in-vma-history/.

Kondo, Toshitaka. "Nipsey Talks African Roots, Snoop Dogg Co-Sign, and Rappers Reppin' Gangs." *Complex*, March 31, 2010.

LAPD. "LAPD Police Veteran Arrested for Pirated DVD's; Arraignment to Be Held." LAPD website, December 19, 2003. http://www .lapdonline.org/hollywood_news/news_view/20801.

LAPD. "Officer-Involved Shooting Occurs as Police Disband Gang Fight NR11127rf." LAPD website, March 18, 2011. http://www.lapdonline .org/march_2011/news_view/47504.

Leland, John. "Public Enemy: Armageddon in Effect." *Spin*, September 1988.

Leovy, Jill. "New Job for an Old Gang." *Los Angeles Times*, May 3, 2008. https://www.latimes.com/archives/la-xpm-2008-may-03-me -businessmen3-story.html.

Levenson, Eric, and Tina Burnside. 2020. "Dylann Roof Believed He'd Be Freed from Prison after a Race War, Attorneys Say in Appeal." CNN, January 29, 2020.

Littleton, Cynthia. "Donald Trump, Univision Settle $500 Million Miss Universe Lawsuit." *Variety*, February 11, 2016.

Lockett, Dee. "YG on His Donald Trump Song Getting Censored." Vulture, June 16, 2016.

Lopez, German. "Donald Trump's Long History of Racism, from the 1970s to 2020." *Vox*, July 25, 2016.

Los Angeles Almanac (website). "Los Angeles County Population vs. State Populations." Accessed 2018. http://www.laalmanac.com /population/po04a.php.

Los Angeles Times. "Deaths during the LA Riots." April 25, 2012. https:// spreadsheets.latimes.com/la-riots-deaths/.

Los Angeles Times. "Read Volume 1 of the Nipsey Hussle Murder Case Grand Jury Transcripts." June 28, 2019. https://www.latimes.com/local/lanow/la -me-nipsey-hussle-grand-jury-transcripts-20190628-story.html.

Los Angeles Times. "Southwest Los Angeles: Reputed Crips Chief Gets 23 Years in Robbery Try." July 21, 1992. https://www.latimes.com /archives/la-xpm-1992-07-21-me-4224-story.html.

Lucey, Catherine. "Kanye West, in 'MAGA' Hat, Delivers Surreal Oval Office Show." Associated Press, October 11, 2018. https://apnews .com/article/bd17e63a655b4f73946dd95d83bb4dbe.

Lyle, Ashley. "Nipsey Hussle Brings Out Puff Daddy, YG, Marsha Ambrosius and More for *Victory Lap* Release Show." *Billboard*, February 16, 2018.

Mahadevan, Tara C. "Lauren London Shuts Down Speculation She and Diddy Are Dating: 'Forever and Even After Call Me Lady Hussle.'" *Complex*, February 20, 2020.

McBride, Jessica. "Eric Holder a.k.a. Shitty Cuz: 5 Fast Facts You Need to Know." Heavy (website). April 2, 2019.

McKinney, Debra. "Stone Mountain: A Monumental Problem." Southern Poverty Law Center *Intelligence Report*, Spring 2018.

Mitchell, Gail. "Nipsey Hussle's All Money In Label Teams with Atlantic Records for His *Victory Lap* Debut: Exclusive." *Billboard*, November 27, 2017.

Mlynar, Phillip. "Why Toddy Tee's Song 'Batterram' Is as Relevant Today as Ever." Track Record (website), September 21, 2016. https:// trackrecord.net/why-toddy-tees-song-batterram-is-as-relevant-today -as-1818668428.

Moore, Sam. "Hackers Break into US Radio Broadcast Signals and Force Stations to Play YG's 'Fuck Donald Trump.'" *NME*, February 2, 2017. https://www.nme.com/news/music/hackers-radio-stations-yg-fuck -donald-trump-1965837.

National Security Archive. *The Contras, Cocaine, and Covert Operations*. Electronic briefing book. George Washington University. https:// nsarchive2.gwu.edu//NSAEBB/NSAEBB2/index.html.

Nelson, Keith, Jr. "Tour Tales: DJ VIP Has Seen Nipsey Hussle's Evolution and the Rapper's Infamous Slap Altercation." Revolt (website), January 8, 2019.

Nelson, Louis. "Kanye West: 'If I Voted, I Would Have Voted for Trump.'" Politico, November 18, 2016.

New York Times. "California Proposition 64—Legalize Marijuana— Results: Approved." August 1, 2017. https://www.nytimes.com /elections/2016/results/california-ballot-measure-64-legalize-marijuana.

O'Connell, Michael. "*Crazy Ex-Girlfriend* Creators Remember Filming Rap Number with Nipsey Hussle: 'He Was Just Game.'" *Hollywood Reporter*, April 9, 2019. https://www.hollywoodreporter.com /rambling-reporter/crazy-girlfriend-creators-remember-filming-rap -number-nipsey-hussle-he-was-just-game-1200384.

Orcutt, KC. "Crips Issue Apology to Nipsey Hussle's Family over Trademark Debacles." Revolt (website), July 3, 2019. https://www .revolt.tv/2019/7/3/20825512/crips-issue-apology-to-nipsey-hussle -s-family-over-trademark-debacle.

Paine, Jake. "Ving Rhames Talks New Film, Nipsey Hussle, Gillie Da Kid." *HipHopDX*, June 18, 2009. https://hiphopdx.com/news/id.9324 /title.ving-rhames-talks-new-film-nipsey-hussle-gillie-da-kid.

Platon, Adelle. "Azealia Banks Endorses Donald Trump: 'He's 'Evil Like America Is Evil.'" *Billboard*, February 1, 2016. https://www.billboard .com/articles/columns/hip-hop/6859504/azealia-banks-donald-trump.

Platon, Adelle. "YG and Nipsey Hussle Discuss Their Anti–Donald Trump Track 'FDT' and Why 'Trump Is Not the Answer.'" *Billboard*, April 1, 2016. https://www.billboard.com/articles/columns/hip-hop/ 7318769/yg-nipsey-fdt-fuck-donald-trump-2016-election.

Platon, Adelle. "YG Says Secret Service Reached Out Following Release of Anti-Trump Song, May Try to Take His Album Off Shelves." *Billboard*, April 27, 2016. https://www.billboard.com/articles /columns/hip-hop/7348438/yg-secret-service-donald-trump-fdt.

Queally, James. "LAPD Gang Injunctions Deny Targets Due Process, ACLU Lawsuit Says." *Los Angeles Times*, October 24, 2016. https:// www.latimes.com/local/lanow/la-me-ln-aclu-gang-lawsuit-2016 1024-snap-story.html.

Raimoq (website). "9th National Youth Festival Sawa Will Be Conducted in July 2020." February 14, 2020. http://raimoq.com/9th-national -youth-festival-sawa-will-be-conducted-in-july-2020/.

Ransom, Jan. "Trump Will Not Apologize for Calling for Death Penalty over Central Park Five." *New York Times*, June 18, 2019. https://www .nytimes.com/2019/06/18/nyregion/central-park-five-trump.html.

Raspberry, William. "The Chief and the Choke Hold." *Washington Post*, May 17, 1982. https://www.washingtonpost.com/archive/politics /1982/05/17/the-chief-and-the-choke-hold/e17fa90f-c692-43c2 -935f-463da9cab500/.

Reed, Ryan. "YG Shot Three Times at Los Angeles Recording Studio." *Rolling Stone*, June 12, 2015.

Reyes-Velarde, Alejandra, Julia Wick, Alexa Díaz, Jaclyn Cosgrove, Cindy Chang, and Richard Winton. "Nipsey Hussle Procession: Thousands Line Streets of LA for Final Farewell to Slain Rapper." *Los Angeles Times*, April 11, 2019. https://www.latimes.com/local/lanow/la-me -ln-nipsey-hussle-funeral-procession-20190411-story.html.

Rhodan, Maya. "Accounts Differ on Why Black Students Ejected from Trump Rally." *Time*, March 1, 2016.

Ries, Al, and Laura Ries. *The 22 Immutable Laws of Branding*. New York: Harper Business, 2002.

Riotta, Chris. "Kendrick Lamar's 'DAMN' Slammed by Fox News' Geraldo Rivera, as per Usual." *Newsweek*, April 14, 2017.

Roberts, Randall. "YG Was Ready to Drop a New Album. Then His Friend Nipsey Hussle Died." *Los Angeles Times*, May 23, 2019. https:// www.latimes.com/entertainment/music/la-et-ms-yg-nipsey-hussle -4real4real-20190523-story.html.

Rogers, Katie. "Kanye West Visits Donald Trump." *New York Times*, December 13, 2016. https://www.nytimes.com/2016/12/13/us /politics/kanye-trump-tower-visit.html.

Santa Cruz, Nicole. "The Homicide Report: Stephen Donelson, 30." *Los Angeles Times*, October 12, 2017. https://homicide.latimes.com/post /stephen-donelson/.

Schwartz, Drew. "Now That You Can Trademark Swear Words, Here Are All the Wildest NSFW Requests." *Vice*, July 1, 2019.

Shakur, Mtulu. "Dare To Struggle." Archived web page. 2002. https://web .archive.org/web/20070331212952/http://www.daretostruggle.org/.

Sides, Josh. *LA City Limits: African American Los Angeles from the Great Depression to the Present*. Berkeley: University of California Press, 2003.

Simmons, Ted. "Nipsey Hussle Shows How Much Money He's Making as an Independent Artist." *XXL*, December 15, 2016.

Sisario, Ben. "Can Neil Young Block Donald Trump from Using His Songs? It's Complicated." *New York Times*, August 12, 2020. https:// www.nytimes.com/2020/08/12/arts/music/neil-young-donald-trump -lawsuit.html.

SlausonGirl. "The Assassination of Nipsey Hussle Becomes More Clear."

Slauson Girl (website), August 13, 2019. https://slausongirl.com/the
-assassination-of-nipsey-hussle-becomes-more-clear/.

Sloan, Cle. *Bastards of the Party*. Documentary. HBO, 2005.

Stanford News. "'You've Got to Find What You Love,' Jobs says."
Stanford.edu, June 12, 2005.

Stoltze, Frank. "Forget the LA Riots—Historic 1992 Watts Gang Truce
Was the Big News." KPCC Radio, April 28, 2012. https://www.scpr
.org/news/2012/04/28/32221/forget-la-riots-1992-gang-truce-was
-big-news/.

Stoltze, Frank. "LA Explained: The Police." *LAist*, June 27, 2018.

Stutz, Colin. "YG Invites Fans Onstage to Destroy a Donald Trump
Piñata." *Billboard*, September 19, 2016.

Sulaiman, Sahra. "Nipsey Hussle Understood Cities Better than You. Why
Didn't You Know Who He Was?" *Streetsblog LA*, August 15, 2019.

Tani, Maxwell. "How Rapper Pusha T Got Passionate about Politics and
Became a Fighter for Hillary Clinton." Business Insider (website),
August 18, 2016.

Taryor, Saye. "Zayd Malik, Rap Artist, Family Man, and Revolutionary."
Brother Saye's Official Site (blog), November 28, 2011. http://saye
.yolasite.com/official-blog/zayd-malik-rap-artist-family-man
-revolutionary.

Thompson, Sean. "Watch: Nipsey Hussle Discusses the N-Word on *Larry
King Now*." *Vibe*, June 3, 2014. https://www.vibe.com/2014/06/watch
-nipsey-hussle-larry-king-now.

TMZ. "Remembering Nipsey Hussle." March 31, 2019.

TMZ. "YG and Nipsey Hussle: Cops Shut Down 'F*** Trump' Video
Shoot." April 4, 2016.

Trammell, Kendall. "Barack Obama Pays Tribute to Nipsey Hussle."
CNN, April 11, 2019. https://www.cnn.com/2019/04/11
/entertainment/obama-letter-nipsey-hussle-trnd/index.html.

Tucker, Ken. "Enough Is Enough: Gangsta Rap." *Entertainment Weekly*,
May 27, 1994.

US Census Bureau. "Population Distribution and Change: 2000 to 2010."
census.gov.

Valdosta State University. "Integration: Our Early Days, 1963" web

page. https://www.valdosta.edu/academics/library/depts/archives
-and-special-collections/vsu-history/100-years/integration.php#:
~:text=Prior%20to%201963%2C%20the%20African,the%20
Christmas%20Festival%20in%201924.

Viebeck, Elise. "Why Rapper Killer Mike Endorsed Bernie Sanders."
Washington Post, November 24, 2015. https://www.washingtonpost
.com/news/powerpost/wp/2015/11/24/why-rapper-killer-mike
-endorsed-bernie-sanders/.

WABC-TV. "Remembering Kobe: A Look Back at Bryant's Astonishing
Final Game." January 26, 2020. https://abc7ny.com/kobe-bryant
-killed-kobes-last-game/5881130/.

Weingarten, Christopher R. "YG Talks Summer Protest Anthem 'FDT
(F–k Donald Trump).'" *Rolling Stone*, September 1, 2016.

Wick, Julia. "What Exactly Is Happening with the New LA County
Sheriff?" *Los Angeles Times*, July 23, 2019. https://www.latimes.com
/california/story/2019-07-23/what-exactly-is-happening-with-the
-new-l-a-county-sheriff.

Wilson, Merelean. "Congratulations to Our 2017 Men of Valor."
NAACPLA website, 2017. https://www.naacp-losangeles.org
/youthcouncil.html.

YellowPlace. Top Flight Collective listing, 2016. https://yellow.place/en
/top-flight-members-only-los-angeles-usa.

Zaru, Deena. "Donald Trump's Fall from Hip-Hop Grace: From Rap
Icon to Public Enemy No. 1." ABC News, October 11, 2018.

Zaru, Deena. "Russell Simmons Endorses Hillary Clinton, Says Bernie
Sanders 'Insensitive' to Black Voters." CNN, updated August 16,
2017. https://www.cnn.com/2016/03/04/politics/russell-simmons
-hillary-clinton-endorsement/index.html.

Zidel, Alex. "Tekashi 6ix9ine Survived NBA All-Star Weekend and
Continues to Taunt Rival Gang Members." HotNewHipHop
(website), February 19, 2018. https://www.hotnewhiphop.com
/tekashi-6ix9ine-survived-nba-all-star-weekend-and-continues-to
-taunt-rival-gang-members-news.44071.html.

Zirin, Dave. "Want to Understand the 1992 LA Riots? Start with the
1984 LA Olympics." *The Nation*, April 30, 2012.

Zisook, Brian "Z." "My Lost Interview with Nipsey Hussle from 2009."
DJ Booth (website), April 1, 2019.

NOTES

INTRO: TOP OF THE TOP

1. Tanika Ray, "Nipsey Hussle's Last *Extra* Interview before His Death" in ExtraTV, video, 2019, https://www.youtube.com/watch?v=3wrytaH_yac.
2. Tara C. Mahadevan, "Lauren London Shuts Down Speculation She and Diddy Are Dating: 'Forever and Even After Call Me Lady Hussle,'" *Complex*, February 20, 2020.
3. ETOnline, "Nipsey Hussle Memorial: Watch Lauren London's Emotional Tribute," video, 2019, https://www.youtube.com/watch?v=NNEpJGVWYfY.
4. Kendall Trammell, "Barack Obama Pays Tribute to Nipsey Hussle," CNN, April 11, 2019.
5. Keith Caulfield, "Nipsey Hussle's Music Sales Increase 2,776% after Death," *Billboard*, April 1, 2019.
6. Ralo Stylez, interviewed by the author, 2020.
7. Sway's Universe, "Nipsey Hussle Talks *Victory Lap*, Kendrick Lamar, Diddy, Cee-Lo and More | Sway's Universe," video, February 22, 2018, https://www.youtube.com/watch?v=8-RuYj7mlAo.
8. Dean Karnazes, "The Real Pheidippides Story," *Runner's World*, December 6, 2016.
9. Nipsey Hussle, "Nipsey Hussle's Journey of Opening a Store in the Middle of His Hood in Crenshaw (Documentary)," video, posted by WorldStarHipHop, June 14, 2017, https://youtu.be/2FnFUCgo7x8.
10. Nipsey Hussle, interviewed by the author, 2018.
11. Samiel Ashghedom, interviewed by the author, 2019.
12. Dan Charnas, interviewed by the author, 2020.
13. Dexter Browne, interviewed by the author, 2019.
14. Nipsey Hussle interview.
15. Ralo Stylez interview.
16. E.D.I. Mean, interviewed by the author, 2019.
17. MTV, "Tupac Shakur MTV Interview," video, 1994, https://www.capitalxtra.com/features/lists/tupac-career-highlights-facts/1994-mtv-interview/.

CHAPTER 1: TRUE STORY

1. Zack O'Malley Greenburg, "Inside Nipsey Hussle's Blueprint to Become a Real-Estate Mogul," *Forbes*, February 20, 2019.
2. Marathon Chris, "The Marathon Store Nipsey Hussle! (Grand Opening) First Smart Store!" video, June 20, 2017, https://www.youtube.com/watch?v=Y0VifTaIShU.
3. Iddris Sandu, interviewed by the author, 2019.
4. Homegrown Radio, "'Laps over Raps' with Nipsey Hussle," video, December 4, 2017, https://www.youtube.com/watch?v=Os_nxZtfcdg.
5. Nico Blitz, "Chuck Dizzle Interview: Founder of Homegrown Radio, On-Air at Real 92.3 | The Lunch Table," video, April 1, 2019, https://www.youtube.com/watch?v=VwB_i5Uddgc.

6. 4TheHype, "Nipsey Hussle's Grand Opening of 'The Marathon Store,'" video, June 18, 2017, https://www.youtube.com/watch?v=EoQo1fFNvQM.

7. Karen Civil, "Nipsey Hussle x Karen Civil | Revolt Unlocked," video, 2017, https://www.youtube.com/watch?v=24i8LxciaZA&feature=share.

8. 4TheHype, "Nipsey Hussle's Grand Opening . . ." video.

9. Nipsey Hussle, "Nipsey Hussle's Journey of Opening a Store in the Middle of His Hood in Crenshaw (Documentary)," video, posted by WorldStarHipHop, June 14, 2017, https://youtu.be/2FnFUCgo7x8.

10. Marathon Chris, "The Marathon Store" video.

11. BigBoyTV, "Nipsey Hussle on Cardi B Winning a Grammy, Album w/ Meek Mill and a Lot More!" video, March 11, 2019, https://youtu.be/3WCWPkceOc0.

12. Hussle, "Nipsey Hussle's Journey" video.

13. 4TheHype, "Nipsey Hussle's Grand Opening" video.

14. Iddris Sandu interview.

15. Gerrick D. Kennedy, "The Light of Los Angeles: The Legacy of Nipsey Hussle," *GQ*, December 2, 2019.

16. TMZ, "Remembering Nipsey Hussle," March 31, 2019.

17. Marqueece Harris-Dawson, interviewed by the author, 2019.

18. Sahra Sulaiman, "City Attorney Keeps Up Pressure to Evict Nipsey Hussle's Legacy from Crenshaw and Slauson," *StreetsblogLA*, August 4, 2019.

19. Nico Blitz, "Chuck Dizzle Interview" video.

20. HardKnockTV, "Nipsey Hussle (First Interview Ever???) from the Hard Knock TV Vaults," video, September 25, 2006, https://youtu.be/GwG4A_OrTmk.

21. *The Cruz Show* Power106, "Nipsey Hussle's New Store Will Blow Your Mind!" video, June 14, 2017, https://www.youtube.com/watch?v=RIFaDTMKTcY&lc=Ugj5JrGqb7_BVHgCoAEC

22. Sonaiya Kelley, "With a New STEM Center and a Revolutionary Marketing Strategy, Nipsey Hussle Is Music's Biggest Disruptor," *Los Angeles Times*, March 16, 2018.

23. David Gross, interviewed by the author, 2019.

24. Our Opportunity, "Dave Gross and Van Lathan in Conversation, Chapter 2," video, February 12, 2020, https://www.youtube.com/watch?v=k6ht2wOUxJo.

25. Nipsey Hussle, interviewed by the author, 2018.

26. Samantha Smith, interviewed by the author, 2019.

27. Our Opportunity, "Dave Gross and Van Lathan" video.

28. Jen DeLeon, "Nipsey Hussle Reveals What His Name Means! Talks Crenshaw," video, HotNewHipHop, October 8, 2013, https://youtu.be/g5FFb_3P2iw.

29. Nipsey Hussle interview.

30. David Gross interview.

31. Ibid.

32. KevMac, "Nipsey Hussle Remembered/Slauson Boys Part 3," video, March 31, 2020, https://www.youtube.com/watch?v=Hs_VcDvL_BU.

33. HER High End Radio, "Lauren London Accepts Nipsey's Grammy for Best Rap Performance," video, January 26, 2020, https://youtu.be/BeDoSx50xxQ.

34. Brittany Bell (@BrittanyBellPR), Instagram, November 20, 2019, . https://www.instagram.com/p/B5GLyFsgiYIPOeVjUTXUKJtbLQvfwxqFaDObgU0/?igshid=5ziiql0ws0s.

35. *The Cruz Show* Power106, "Nipsey Hussle: *Victory Lap* Release, 'I Gambled My Career,'

Signing to Atlantic, and More!" video, November 30, 2017, https://www.youtube.com /watch?v=dwO44bxu5s4&t=32s.

36. TMZ, "Nipsey Hussle's Family Granted Guardianship of Daughter; Lauren to Oversee Son," October 15, 2019, https://www.tmz.com/2019/10/15/lauren-london-nipsey -hussle-guardianship-son-estate/.

37. TMZ, "Nipsey Hussle Kids Don't Need Charity Handouts; He Set Them Up For Life," April 16, 2019, https://www.tmz.com/2019/04/16/nipsey-hussle-kids-children-no -handouts-donations-set-for-life.

CHAPTER 2: SLAUSON BOY

1. Luc Belaire, "Nipsey Hussle | Self Made Tastes Better, Episode 7," March 1, 2018, https://www.youtube.com/watch?v=dJ6pgb4O6wA.

2. *The Cruz Show* Power106, "Nipsey Hussle: *Victory Lap* Release, 'I Gambled My Career,' Signing to Atlantic, and More!" video, November 30, 2017, https://www.youtube.com /watch?v=dwO44bxu5s4&t=32s.

3. Damon Campbell, "Nipsey Hussle Interview with Damon Campbell," video, January 19, 2014, https://www.youtube.com/watch?v=xbt16U8dwwo.

4. BucciBoyDaDon TV, "Nipsey Hussle (My Block on Bucciboydadon TV) Part 9," video, March 2, 2010, https://www.youtube.com/watch?time_continue=2&v=F_2ZrA2rTsw.

5. Luc Belaire, "Nipsey Hussle | Self Made" video.

6. Damon Campbell, "Nipsey Hussle Interview" video.

7. *The Cruz Show* Power106, "Nipsey Hussle: *Victory Lap*" video.

8. DJ Nehpets, "Nipsey Hussle Advice for Chicago Gang Beefs, Dr. Sebi Movie and More | @Power92Chicago," video, March 3, 2018, https://www.youtube.com/watch ?v=ODqDHsoOdww.

9. Nipsey Hussle, "For the Culture," *Players' Tribune*, October 25, 2018.

10. BucciBoyDaDon TV, "Nipsey Hussle" video.

11. John Kent, "The Hidden History of Culver City Racism," *StreetsblogLA*, April 5, 2019.

12. Bridget Boakye, "You Probably Didn't Know That California Is Named after a Black Queen," Face2Face Africa (website), March 24, 2019.

13. Lynell George, "What It Is. (And What It Was.)," *Los Angeles Times*, October 22, 2006.

14. William D. Estrada, "The Life and Times of Pío Pico, Last Governor of Mexican California," KCET.org., October 10, 2017.

15. Marcelina Morfin, "The 10 Most Multicultural Cities In The World," Culture Trip (website), July 17, 2019.

16. Jane Wells, "American Diversity: Cities Where It Works," CNBC, May 21, 2015.

17. Kelley Simpson, "The Great Migration: Creating a New Black Identity in Los Angeles," KCET.org., February 15, 2012.

18. DJ Vlad, "Nipsey Hussle Details Decision to Join Rollin' 60s Crips," video, January 1, 2014, https://www.youtube.com/watch?v=Owc3oFyfaDs.

19. BucciBoyDaDon TV, "Nipsey Hussle" video.

20. Matthew Fleischer, "How White People Used Police to Make Los Angeles One of the Most Segregated Cities in America," *Los Angeles Times*, August 11, 2020.

21. Troy Campbell, "The Spook Hunters: LA's First Gang Targeted Black and Latino Community," Reel Urban News (website), July 12, 2020.

22. Tim Brennan and Robert Ladd, *Once Upon a Time in Compton* (Brown Girls Publishing, 2017).

23. Troy Campbell, "The Spook Hunters."

24. Cle Sloan, *Bastards of the Party*, documentary, HBO, 2005.

25. Ibid.

26. Darrell Dawsey, "To CHP Officer Who Sparked Riots, It Was Just Another Arrest," *Los Angeles Times*, August 19, 1990.

27. *Los Angeles Times*, "Chief Parker's Time Is Past," April 19, 2009.

28. History.com, "Watts Rebellion," September 28, 2017.

29. LBJ Presidential Library (website), On This Day in History segment, http://www .lbjlibrary.net/collections/on-this-day-in-history/july.html.

30. Sloan, *Bastards of the Party*.

31. Makeda Easter, "The Broad's 'Soul of a Nation': Art from the Rubble of Watts," *Los Angeles Times*, March 22, 2019.

32. Sloan, *Bastards of the Party*.

33. George Percy Barganier III, "Fanon's Children: The Black Panther Party and the Rise of the Crips and Bloods in Los Angeles" (dissertation, University of California Berkeley, 2011).

34. Eldridge Cleaver, *Target Zero: A Life in Writing* (New York: St. Martin's Griffin, 2006).

35. Sloan, *Bastards of the Party*.

36. Victoria Massie, "The Most Radical Thing the Black Panthers Did Was Give Kids Free Breakfast," *Vox*, October 15, 2016.

37. Mark Mazzetti, "Burglars Who Took on FBI Abandon Shadows," *New York Times*, January 7, 2014.

38. Malik Ismail, "They Called Him Bunchy, Like a Bunch of Greens," *San Francisco Bay View*, November 27, 2017.

39. Rob Kenner, "You Are Appreciated: Remembering Afeni Shakur," *Complex*, March 9, 2016.

40. Ashish Valentine, "Fifty Years after His Death, Fred Hampton's Legacy Looms Large in Chicago," NPR, December 5, 2019.

41. Nipsey Hussle (@NipseyHussle), Twitter, 2012, https://twitter.com/nipseyhussle/status /241676856145883136?lang=en.

42. Sloan, *Bastards of the Party*.

43. Melina Abdullah, interviewed by the author, 2019.

44. DJ Vlad, "Big U on His History with Nipsey Hussle (Full Interview)," video, April 9, 2019, https://www.youtube.com/watch?v=OyPi-_73HcU.

45. Jacky Jasper, "Big U Speaks on Nipsey Hussle's Impact, Developing Options Program and Crenshaw's Legacy," *Vibe*, April 2, 2020.

46. DJ Vlad, "Big U on His History" video.

47. Pat Harvey, "Pat Harvey Goes One-on-One with Rising Rapper Nipsey Hussle," video, CBS Los Angeles, February 11, 2019, https://youtu.be/uMM-ZsO0Eqo.

48. Genius, "Nipsey Hussle 'Racks in the Middle' Official Lyrics and Meaning," video, March 14, 2019, https://www.youtube.com/watch?v=pBV4tAAHiIM.

49. Alex de Waal, *Evil Days: 30 Years of War and Famine in Ethiopia* (Africa Watch Report) (Human Rights Watch, 1991).

50. ERi-TV, "Interview with Nipsey Hussle, Eritrean-American Recording Artist and Entrepreneur," video, May 3, 2018, https://youtu.be/LSjKr7nxiiQ.

51. William Raspberry, "The Chief and the Choke Hold," *Washington Post*, May 17, 1982.

52. Karen Foshay, "I Was There: 'He Was Suggesting That Blacks Were Not Normal,' LA Doctor Recalls Bizarre Phone Call from Then LAPD Chief Daryl Gates," KCET-TV,

2020, https://www.kcet.org/shows/socal-connected/i-was-there-he-was-suggesting -that-blacks-were-not-normal-la-doctor-recalls.

53. Michael Kirk, *Frontline*: "LAPD Blues," Daryl Gates interview segment, PBS, May 15, 2001.

54. Ryan Devereaux, "How the CIA Watched Over the Destruction of Gary Webb," *The Intercept*, September 25, 2014.

55. National Security Archive, *The Contras, Cocaine, and Covert Operations* (electronic briefing book), George Washington University, https://nsarchive2.gwu.edu//NSAEBB /NSAEBB2/index.html.

56. Sloan, *Bastards of the Party*.

57. Marcela Gaviria (producer), *Frontline*: "The Gang Crackdown" (season 2018, episode 5), PBS.

58. Sloan, *Bastards of the Party*.

59. DJ Vlad, "Big U on His History" video.

60. Roland G. Fryer Jr. et al., "Measuring Crack Cocaine and Its Impact," *Economic Inquiry* 51 no. 3 (2013).

61. Charisse Jones, "Crack and Punishment: Is Race the Issue?" *New York Times*, October 28, 1995.

62. US Census Bureau, "Population Distribution and Change: 2000 to 2010," census.gov.

63. Los Angeles Almanac (website), "Los Angeles County Population vs. State Populations," accessed 2018, http://www.laalmanac.com/population/po04a.php.

64. Julia Wick, "What Exactly Is Happening with the New LA County Sheriff?" *Los Angeles Times*, July 23, 2019.

65. Frank Stoltze, "LA Explained: The Police," *LAist*, June 27, 2018.

66. Daryl F. Gates, *Chief: My Life in the LAPD* (New York: Bantam, 1992).

67. Dave Zirin, "Want to Understand the 1992 LA Riots? Start with the 1984 LA Olympics," *The Nation*, April 30, 2012.

68. Patricia Klein, "A Ram at Rest: These Are Quiet Times for LAPD's 'Battering' Vehicle," *Los Angeles Times*, February 10, 1986.

69. Phillip Mlynar, "Why Toddy Tee's Song 'Batterram' Is as Relevant Today as Ever," Track Record (website), September 21, 2016.

70. Dawit Asghedom, "Nipsey Hussle's Mom and Dad Pay Tribute to Him During Memorial Service," video, posted to YouTube by 11Alive, April 11, 2019, https://www .youtube.com/watch?v=AZJx7Eg5xm0.

71. Nipsey Hussle, "Nipsey Hussle Fatherhood," video, April 25, 2019, https://www.youtube .com/watch?v=3wrytaH_yac.

72. Samiel Asghedom, "Nipsey Hussle's Brother Gives a Tribute," video, posted to YouTube by Ta&Co, April 11, 2019, https://youtu.be/RoDIOkTysKk.

73. Josh Sides, *LA City Limits: African American Los Angeles from the Great Depression to the Present* (Berkeley: University of California Press, 2003).

74. Jill Leovy, "New Job for an Old Gang," *Los Angeles Times*, May 3, 2008.

75. Jim Newton and Henry Weinstein, "On Tape, Fuhrman Describes Incident Similar to '78 Event," *Los Angeles Times*, August 18, 1995.

76. Samiel Asghedom, interviewed by the author, 2019.

77. Habtom Videos, "Nipsey Hussle's Family Shares Visuals of Nipsey's Childhood and Eritrea Trip," video, April 12, 2019, https://www.youtube.com/watch?v=wXQ_yu5l8y4.

78. Hussle, "For the Culture."

79. Hussle, "For the Culture."

80. Samiel Asghedom, "Nipsey Hussle's Brother" video.

81. DJ Vlad, "VladTV Full Interview with Nipsey Hussle (RIP)," April 11, 2019, https://www.youtube.com/watch?v=hSmjSPAdc40.

82. Joshua Espinosa, "Nipsey Hussle's Grade School Poetry, Short Stories Surface Online," *Complex*, April 5, 2019.

83. Espinosa, "Nipsey Hussle's Grade School Poetry."

84. DJ Vlad, "VladTV Full Interview" video.

85. Rap Radar, "Rap Radar: Nipsey Hussle," video, January 1, 2018, https://www.youtube.com/watch?v=GVCNREwfGuM.

86. Frank Stoltze, "Forget the LA Riots—Historic 1992 Watts Gang Truce Was the Big News," KPCC Radio, April 28, 2012.

87. Jesse Katz, "An Ethic Dies with Gang Chief," *Los Angeles Times*, April 14, 1992.

88. "Deaths During the LA Riots," *Los Angeles Times*, April 25, 2012.

89. Baby Gooch, interviewed by the author, 2019.

90. Hoodsta Rob, interviewed by the author, 2019.

91. Baby Gooch interview.

92. Hoodsta Rob interview.

93. John Leland, "Public Enemy: Armageddon in Effect," *Spin*, September 1988.

94. Allen Hughes, *The Defiant Ones*, HBO, 2017.

95. DJ Vlad, "Big U on His History" video.

96. Snoop Dogg, interviewed by the author, 2020.

97. Snoop Dogg interview.

98. Mathis Chazanov and Chuck Philips, "Rap Singer Faces Charge of Murder, Violence," *Los Angeles Times*, September 4, 1993.

99. Daniel Kohn, "The Five Most Amazing Moments in VMA History," *LA Weekly*, August 25, 2011.

100. Hot 97 *Ebro in the Morning*, "Nipsey Hussle Breaks Down Gang Culture and How Africa Changed Him," video, February 22, 2018, https://www.youtube.com/watch?v=XEgPVv_9_W8&feature=emb_title.

101. SnoopDoggTV, "Nipsey Hu$$le Takes a Victory Lap | GGN with Snoop Dogg," video July 2, 2013, https://www.youtube.com/watch?v=rui-Bjshh78.

102. Rap Radar, "Rap Radar: Nipsey Hussle" video.

103. HardBody Kiotti, "Nipsey Hussle Talks Gang Culture, Investing in Yourself and Making Sacrifices," video, March 11, 2018, https://www.youtube.com/watch?v=CgYJb6xgNMg.

104. Sonaiya Kelley, "With a New STEM Center and a Revolutionary Marketing Strategy, Nipsey Hussle Is Music's Biggest Disruptor," *Los Angeles Times*, March 16, 2018.

105. Angelique Smith, "Nipsey Hussle's Mom and Dad Pay Tribute to Him During Memorial Service," video, posted to YouTube by 11Alive, April 11, 2019, https://www.youtube.com/watch?v=AZJx7Eg5xm0.

106. Rap Radar, "Rap Radar: Nipsey Hussle 2," video, December 25, 2018, https://www.youtube.com/watch?v=5NndeiDIctM.

107. XXL, "Nipsey Hussle Outtakes from 2016 Interview," video, April 1, 2019, https://www.youtube.com/watch?v=D_WmzAFXCvY.

108. Hollywood Unlocked, "The Lost Episode: Yo-Yo Opens Up on the Effect of Tupac's Murder," video, May 7, 2019, https://www.youtube.com/watch?v=YMBdxjd13FE.

109. Gerrick D. Kennedy, "The Light of Los Angeles: The Legacy of Nipsey Hussle," *GQ*, December 2, 2019.

110. Hussle, "For the Culture."

111. Merelean Wilson, "Congratulations to Our 2017 Men of Valor," NAACPLA website, 2017.

112. Erin Burts, Facebook post, April 29, 2019, https://m.facebook.com/100000272985414 /posts/2448663261819416/.

113. Killa Twan, interviewed by the author, 2020.

114. Ibid.

115. Ibid.

116. Luc Belaire, "Nipsey Hussle | Self Made" video.

117. PyramidWest TV, "Nipsey Hussle Pt. 1," video, April 28, 2009, https://www.youtube .com/watch?v=5n7ZdaBogIs.

118. Samiel Asghedom, "Nipsey Hussle's Brother" video.

119. Ibid.

CHAPTER 3: ON HOOD

1. Sway's Universe, "Nipsey Hussle Talks *Victory Lap*, Kendrick Lamar, Diddy, Cee-Lo and More | Sway's Universe," video, February 22, 2018, https://www.youtube.com /watch?v=8-RuYj7mlAo.

2. Gerrick D. Kennedy, "The Light of Los Angeles: The Legacy of Nipsey Hussle," *GQ*, December 2, 2019.

3. Kev Mac, "Slauson Boys Nipsey Hussle Remembered by His Early Friends in Music," video, March 27, 2020, https://www.youtube.com/watch?v=Gpm9pudNXpY.

4. Ralo Stylez, interviewed by the author, 2020.

5. BucciBoyDaDon TV, "Nipsey Hussle (My Block on Bucciboydadon TV) Part 9," video, March 2, 2010, https://www.youtube.com/watch?time_continue=2&v=F_2 ZrA2rTsw.

6. Kev Mac, "Slauson Boys Nipsey Hussle" video.

7. Ibid.

8. Rimpau (@ami_rimpau), Instagram post, 2019.

9. BigBoyTV, "Nipsey Hussle on Cardi B Winning a Grammy, Album w/ Meek Mill and a Lot More!" video, March 11, 2019, https://youtu.be/3WCWPkceOc0.

10. Kev Mac, "Slauson Boys Nipsey Hussle" video.

11. Rimpau (@ami_rimpau), Instagram post, 2019.

12. Kev Mac, "Slauson Boys Nipsey Hussle" video.

13. Ibid.

14. Ibid.

15. Toshitaka Kondo, "Nipsey Talks African Roots, Snoop Dogg Co-sign, and Rappers Reppin' Gangs," *Complex*, March 31, 2010.

16. Nipsey Hussle, "Nipsey Hussle's Journey of Opening a Store in the Middle of His Hood in Crenshaw (Documentary)," video, posted by WorldStarHipHop, June 14, 2017, https://youtu.be/2FnFUCgo7x8.

17. Hussle, "Nipsey Hussle's Journey" video.

18. Ibid.

19. Brian "Z" Zisook, "My Lost Interview with Nipsey Hussle from 2009," DJ Booth (website), April 1, 2019.

20. DJ Vlad, "VladTV Full Interview with Nipsey Hussle (RIP)," April 11, 2019, https://www.youtube.com/watch?v=hSmjSPAdc40.

21. Ralo Stylez interview.

22. Nipsey Hussle, interviewed by the author, 2018.

23. Kondo, "Nipsey Talks African Roots."

24. DJ Vlad, "VladTV Full Interview" video.

25. Kondo, "Nipsey Talks African Roots."

26. DJ Vlad, "VladTV Full Interview" video.

27. Ibid.

28. Zisook, "My Lost Interview."

29. Genius, "Nipsey Hussle 'Racks in the Middle' Official Lyrics and Meaning," video, March 14, 2019, https://www.youtube.com/watch?v=pBV4tAAHiIM.

30. Zisook, "My Lost Interview."

31. Dexter Browne, interviewed by the author, 2019.

32. Dexter Browne interview.

33. Ibid.

34. Baby Gooch, interviewed by the author, 2019.

35. Cuzzy Capone, interviewed by the author, 2019.

36. Dexter Browne interview.

37. Cuzzy Capone interview.

38. Ibid.

39. Baby Gooch interview.

40. Ibid.

41. Dexter Browne interview.

42. Ibid.

43. Cuzzy Capone interview.

44. Kev Mac, "Slauson Boys Nipsey Hussle" video.

45. Cuzzy Capone interview.

46. Kev Mac, "Slauson Boys Nipsey Hussle" video.

47. Cuzzy Capone interview.

48. Dexter Browne interview.

49. Dexter Browne interview.

50. Kev Mac, "Slauson Boys Nipsey Hussle" video.

51. Ralo Stylez interview.

52. Dexter Browne interview.

53. Ibid.

54. Ibid.

55. Ralo Stylez interview.

56. Cuzzy Capone interview.

57. Dexter Browne interview.

58. Ibid.

59. Baby Gooch interview.

60. Hussle, "Nipsey Hussle's Journey" video.

61. Samiel Asghedom, "Nipsey Hussle's Brother Gives a Tribute," video, posted to YouTube by Ta&Co, April 11, 2019, https://youtu.be/RoDIOkTysKk.

62. Dexter Browne interview.

63. Baby Gooch interview.

64. Dexter Browne interview.

65. Dexter Browne, "ButterVision Video," 2006.

66. Dexter Browne interview.

67. Nipsey Hussle, *Fucc Tha Middleman* (mixtape), 2006.

68. Drew Schwartz, "Now That You Can Trademark Swear Words, Here Are All the Wildest NSFW Requests," *Vice*, July 1, 2019.

69. Dexter Browne interview.

70. Ibid.

71. Ibid.

72. Baby Gooch interview.

73. Ibid.

74. Kennedy, "The Light of Los Angeles."

75. Ibid.

76. Cam Capone, "Cobby Supreme on Doing Every Street Thing/Being Nipsey Hussle's Day One/Met Him at 14 (Part1)," video, March 2, 2020, https://youtu.be/OyMDXlscuzw.

77. Beth Barrett, "Rollin' 60s Give Unique Window into Gang Culture," *Los Angeles Daily News*, September 30, 2004.

78. Gang Enforcement (website), "Gangs and Sports Attire," https://www.gangenforcement .com/gang-adopted-sports-attire-and-commercial-logos.html.

79. DJ Vlad, "VladTV Full Interview" video.

80. Justin Lamarr, interviewed by the author, 2020.

81. Ralo Stylez interview.

82. Ibid.

83. Melina Abdullah, interviewed by the author, 2019.

84. Alex Alonso, 2009, "Nipsey Hussle Interview: Born in the 80s, Raised in the 60s," video, 2009, StreetGangs.com, https://www.youtube.com/watch?v=QYTYC9vBS Zg&feature=emb_title.

85. Rap Status, "Nipsey Hussle: Rap Status #BANGLIFEBIDNESS," video, December 5, 2014, https://youtu.be/h7KFsv-1sJA.

86. PyramidWest TV, "Nipsey Hussle Pt. 1," video, April 28, 2009, https://youtu.be /5n7ZdaBogIs.

87. PyramidWest TV, "Nipsey Hussle Pt. 1," video.

88. Ibid.

89. Dexter Browne interview.

90. Baby Gooch interview.

91. DJ Vlad, "VladTV Full Interview" video.

92. Baby Gooch interview.

93. Ibid.

94. Ibid.

95. Dexter Browne interview.

96. Manuela Cardiga, "Watch Nipsey Hussle's Ex Tanisha Detail Relationship with Rapper and Lauren London," AmoMama (website), May 30, 2019.

97. Baby Gooch interview.

98. Ibid.

99. Baby Gooch interview.

100. Dexter Browne interview.

101. Ralo Stylez interview.

102. Baby Gooch interview.

103. Ralo Stylez interview.

104. Doggie Diamonds, "Nipsey Hussle: Gangs Are Not the Problem, Gangs Terrorizing Your Own People Is," video, 2008, https://www.doggiediamondstv.com/nipsey-hussle-gangs-are-not-the-problem-gangs-terrorizing-your-own-people-is/.

105. Cuzzy Capone interview.

106. Rap Status, "Nipsey Hussle: Rap Status" video.

107. DJ Vlad, "VladTV Full Interview" video.

108. Ibid.

109. Kev Mac, "Slauson Boys Nipsey Hussle" video.

110. Dexter Browne interview.

111. Body Art Guru, "Nipsey Hussle's 31 Tattoos and Their Meaning," 2019, https://bodyartguru.com/nipsey-hussle-tattoos/.

112. Baby Gooch interview.

113. Kev Mac, "Slauson Boys Nipsey Hussle" video.

114. Ibid.

115. Dexter Browne interview.

116. Ralo Stylez interview.

117. Rimpau (@ami_rimpau), Instagram post, 2019.

118. Kev Mac, "Slauson Boys Nipsey Hussle" video.

119. Samiel Asghedom, "Nipsey Hussle's Brother" video.

CHAPTER 4: ERITREA

1. Dawit Asghedom, "Nipsey Hussle's Mom and Dad Pay Tribute to Him During Memorial Service," video, posted to YouTube by 11Alive, April 11, 2019, https://www.youtube.com/watch?v=AZJx7Eg5xm0.

2. Semmi W., interviewed by the author, 2019.

3. Alex de Waal, *Evil Days: 30 Years of War and Famine in Ethiopia* (Africa Watch Report) (Human Rights Watch, 1991).

4. Dexter Browne, interviewed by the author, 2019.

5. Toshitaka Kondo, "Nipsey Talks African Roots, Snoop Dogg Co-sign, and Rappers Reppin' Gangs," *Complex*, March 31, 2010.

6. Gerrick D. Kennedy, "The Light of Los Angeles: The Legacy of Nipsey Hussle," *GQ*, December 2, 2019.

7. Kennedy, "The Light of Los Angeles."

8. Dexter Browne interview.

9. Nipsey Hussle, interviewed by the author, 2018.

10. Kondo, "Nipsey Talks African Roots."

11. Hot 97 *Ebro in the Morning*, "Nipsey Hussle Breaks Down Gang Culture and How Africa Changed Him," video, February 22, 2018, https://www.youtube.com/watch?v=XEgPVv_9_W8&feature=emb_title.

12. The Breakfast Club, "Nipsey Hussle Talks New Album, West Side Protocols," video, February 21, 2018, https://www.youtube.com/watch?v=fGCMcu2iei0.

13. Nipsey Hussle interview.

14. *The Breakfast Club*, "Nipsey Hussle Talks New Album."

15. Tariq Nasheed, "Tariq Nasheed and Nipsey Hussle Chop It Up on IZM Radio," video, March 7, 2018, https://youtu.be/8yiWph2_G74.

16. Nipsey Hussle interview.

17. *The Breakfast Club*, "Nipsey Hussle Talks New Album."

18. Nipsey Hussle interview.

19. Habtom Videos, "Nipsey Hussle's Family Shares Visuals of Nipsey's Childhood and Eritrea Trip," video, April 12, 2019, https://www.youtube.com/watch?v=wXQ_yu5l8y4.

20. Nipsey Hussle interview.

21. ERi-TV, "Interview with Nipsey Hussle, Eritrean-American Recording Artist and Entrepreneur," video, May 3, 2018, https://youtu.be/LSjKr7nxiiQ.

22. Kev Mac, "Nipsey Hussle of Los Angeles Part 2 Africa, and New York Gangs 2008," video, January 19, 2017, https://www.youtube.com/watch?v=D1yXhJlkiyo.

23. Nipsey Hussle interview.

24. Ibid.

25. Ibid.

26. Dexter Browne interview.

27. HardKnockTV, "Nipsey Hussle (First Interview Ever???) from the Hard Knock TV Vaults," video, September 25, 2006, https://youtu.be/GwG4A_OrTmk.

28. Dexter Browne interview.

29. Nipsey Hussle interview.

30. The Breakfast Club, "Nipsey Hussle Talks New Album."

31. Nipsey Hussle, "Nipsey Hussle Fatherhood," video, April 25, 2019, https://www.youtube.com/watch?v=3wrytaH_yac.

32. Killa Twan, interviewed by the author, 2019.

33. Nasheed, "Tariq Nasheed and Nipsey Hussle" video.

34. Kennedy, "The Light of Los Angeles."

35. Nipsey Hussle (@nipseyhussle), Instagram post, April 6, 2017, https://www.instagram.com/p/BSjMP41BrDt/?igshid=12oo4t7y0bilb.

36. HardBody Kiotti, "Nipsey Hussle Talks Gang Culture, Investing in Yourself and Making Sacrifices," video, March 11, 2018, https://www.youtube.com/watch?v=CgYJb6xgNMg.

CHAPTER 5: HUSSLE IN THE HOUSE

1. Carl Chery, "XXL Pop the Trunk—Nipsey Hussle," video, September 6, 2009, https://www.youtube.com/watch?v=BI9IwbtOkrA.

2. Ibid.

3. Rap Radar, "Rap Radar: Nipsey Hussle," video, January 1, 2018, https://www.youtube.com/watch?v=GVCNREwfGuM.

4. Rap Radar, "Rap Radar: Nipsey Hussle" video.

5. Ralo Stylez, interviewed by the author, 2020.

6. Dexter Browne, interviewed by the author, 2019.

7. Ibid.

8. Rap Radar, "Rap Radar: Nipsey Hussle" video.

9. Ibid.

10. PyramidWest TV, "Nipsey Hussle Pt. 1," video, April 28, 2009, https://youtube
    /5n7ZdaBogIs.

11. J Stone, interviewed by the author, 2019.

12. Ibid.

13. Choc Watts, interviewed by the author, 2019.

14. Baby Gooch, interviewed by the author, 2019.

15. Gerrick D. Kennedy, "The Light of Los Angeles: The Legacy of Nipsey Hussle," *GQ*,
    December 2, 2019.

16. Kennedy, "The Light of Los Angeles."

17. Slauson Bruce, interviewed by the author, 2019.

18. Dexter Browne interview.

19. Ibid.

20. *Los Angeles Times*, "Southwest Los Angeles: Reputed Crips Chief Gets 23 Years in
    Robbery Try," July 21, 1992.

21. Kev Mac, "Big U Interview," in "Kev's Top Ten Favorite Interviews on KM Videos,"
    video, December 23, 2018, https://www.youtube.com/watch?v=n5NoxTeePc0.

22. Dexter Browne interview.

23. Ibid.

24. My AZ Lawyers (website), "Death Row Records Files for Bankruptcy," July 7, 2016,
    https://myazlawyers.com/death-row-records-files-for-bankruptcy/.

25. Dexter Browne interview.

26. Kev Mac, "Slauson Boys Nipsey Hussle Remembered by His Early Friends in Music,"
    video, March 27, 2020, https://www.youtube.com/watch?v=Gpm9pudNXpY.

27. Kev Mac, "Slauson Boys Nipsey Hussle" video.

28. Hoodsta Rob, interviewed by the author, 2019.

29. Kev Mac, "Slauson Boys Nipsey Hussle" video.

30. Hoodsta Rob interview.

31. Dexter Browne interview.

32. Kev Mac, "Slauson Boys Nipsey Hussle" video.

33. Toshitaka Kondo, "Nipsey Talks African Roots, Snoop Dogg Co-sign, and Rappers
    Reppin' Gangs," *Complex*, March 31, 2010.

34. Sahra Sulaiman, "Nipsey Hussle Understood Cities Better than You. Why Didn't You
    Know Who He Was?" *Streetsblog LA*, August 15, 2019.

35. Kev Mac, "Slauson Boys Nipsey Hussle" video.

36. Baby Gooch interview.

37. Ibid.

38. Ibid.

39. J Stone interview.

40. Ibid.

41. Ibid.

42. Rap Radar, "Rap Radar: Nipsey Hussle" video.

43. J Stone interview.

44. Hoodsta Rob interview.

45. Kev Mac, "Nipsey Hussle Slauson Boys Remembered Part Three," video, March 31,
    2020, https://www.youtube.com/watch?v=Hs_VcDvL_BU.

46. Ibid.

47. Dexter Browne interview.

48. Rap Radar, "Rap Radar: Nipsey Hussle" video.

49. Ibid.

50. LAPD website, "LAPD Police Veteran Arrested for Pirated DVD's; Arraignment to Be Held," December 19, 2003.

51. Dexter Browne interview.

52. PyramidWest TV, "Nipsey Hussle Pt. 1" video.

53. HardBody Kiotti, "Nipsey Hussle Talks Gang Culture, Investing in Yourself and Making Sacrifices," video, March 11, 2018, https://www.youtube.com/watch?v=CgYJb6xgNMg.

54. PyramidWest TV, "Nipsey Hussle Pt. 1" video.

55. TheNextLevelMag, "Nipsey Hussle Speaks about His Studio Being Raided by Police," video, July 7, 2018, https://www.youtube.com/watch?v=JXY9cqbbztg&trk=organization-update-content_share-video-embed_share-article_title.

56. Rap Radar, "Rap Radar: Nipsey Hussle" video.

57. Baby Gooch interview.

58. TheNextLevelMag, "Nipsey Hussle Speaks" video.

59. PyramidWest TV, "Nipsey Hussle Part 2," video, April 28, 2009, https://www.youtube.com/watch?v=UZ6lBVsnm8g.

60. The Breakfast Club, "Nipsey Hussle Talks New Album, West Side Protocols," video, February 21, 2018, https://www.youtube.com/watch?v=fGCMcu2iei0.

61. Nipsey Hussle, interviewed by the author, 2018.

62. Steve Lobel, interviewed by the author, 2019.

63. Ibid.

64. Ibid.

65. Kev Mac, "Slauson Boys Nipsey Hussle Remembered by His Early Friends in Music," video, March 27, 2020, https://www.youtube.com/watch?v=Gpm9pudNXpY.

66. Ibid.

67. Damon Campbell, "Nipsey Hussle Interview with Damon Campbell," video, January 19, 2014, https://www.youtube.com/watch?v=xbt16U8dwwo.

68. Rap Status, "Nipsey Hussle: Rap Status #BANGLIFEBIDNESS," video, December 5, 2014, https://youtu.be/h7KFsv-1sJA.

69. Kev Mac, "Nipsey Hussle of Los Angeles Part 2 Africa, and New York Gangs 2008," video, January 19, 2017, https://www.youtube.com/watch?v=D1yXhJlkiyo.

70. Nipsey Hussle, "Nipsey Hussle Fatherhood," video, April 25, 2019, https://www.youtube.com/watch?v=3wrytaH_yac.

71. Kev Mac, "Nipsey Hussle Slauson Boys Remembered Part Three" video.

72. Rap Status, "Nipsey Hussle: Rap Status" video.

73. Hussle, "Nipsey Hussle Fatherhood" video.

74. Luc Belaire, "Nipsey Hussle | Self Made Tastes Better, Episode 7," video, March 1, 2018, https://www.youtube.com/watch?v=dJ6pgb4O6wA.

75. DJ Drama, "Gangsta Grillz Radio—Nipsey Hussle Interview," video, September 28, 2014, https://www.youtube.com/watch?v=_yzY0-2agLw.

76. Ibid.

77. Ibid.

78. Toshitaka Kondo, "Nipsey Talks African Roots, Snoop Dogg Co-sign, and Rappers Reppin' Gangs," *Complex*, March 31, 2010.

79. Ralo Stylez interview.

80. Kev Mac, "Slauson Boys Nipsey Hussle" video.

81. Kondo, "Nipsey Talks African Roots."

82. Ibid.

CHAPTER 6: ALL MONEY IN

1. Wink$ Magazine, "Winks Magazine—Nipsey Hussle's Interview Pt.1," video, November 16, 2008, https://www.youtube.com/watch?v=8AUtx4YVQvw.

2. Baby Gooch, interview with the author, 2019.

3. Sahra Sulaiman, "Nipsey Hussle Understood Cities Better than You. Why Didn't You Know Who He Was?" *Streetsblog LA*, August 15, 2019.

4. Eric Diep, "Dom Kennedy's 25 Favorite Albums," *Complex*, November 20, 2012.

5. *Entertainment Tonight*, "Nipsey Hussle Memorial: Watch Snoop Dogg's Tearful Tribute," video, April 11, 2019, https://www.youtube.com/watch?v=mwNJJaDQfzM&list=LLE0mGp6YyRtsa1AM4nAyrWA&index=1005.

6. Desus & Mero, "Rapper Nipsey Hussle (Extended Cut)," video, February 26, 2018, https://www.youtube.com/watch?v=7SHYVJsOqes.

7. BigBoyTV, "The Game on His Last Album *Born 2 Rap*, Meeting Nipsey Hussle, Wack's Opinions + More!" video, December 5, 2019, https://www.youtube.com/watch?v=LkhyzQRktx0.

8. BigBoyTV, "The Game on His Last Album" video.

9. Ibid.

10. Uproxx, "Talib Kweli and The Game Talk Gang Life, 50 Cent, Meek Mill, Nipsey Hussle and LeBron | People's Party," video, December 9, 2019, https://www.youtube.com/watch?v=qoj4i8zdFRc.

11. Louis Johnson, "Jorge Peniche: The *Badger Herald* Interview," *Badger Herald*, May 20, 2014.

12. VIP Access, "Nipsey Hussle's Road Manager Jorge Peniche Details How He Got in the Game," video, March 3, 2018, https://www.youtube.com/watch?v=T3Nk8QFMTwY.

13. ItsTheReal, "#291: Jorge Peniche" in "A Waste of Time," video, December 18, 2019, https://www.youtube.com/watch?v=2hvemJyK5Uw.

14. ItsTheReal, "#291: Jorge Peniche" video.

15. Ibid.

16. AllHipHop, "Nipsey Hussle with Allhiphop.com and Mikey Fresh," video, January 21, 2009, https://www.youtube.com/watch?v=3EAiyJOfstc&feature=emb_title.

17. VladTV, "Exclusive: Nipsey Hussle—Top 5 He Would Smash," video, February 5, 2009, https://www.youtube.com/watch?v=sK9vAh3lM-g.

18. Desus & Mero, "Rapper Nipsey Hussle" video.

19. Steve Lobel, interviewed by the author, 2019.

20. BigBoyTV, "Nipsey Hussle Full Interview | BigBoyTV," video, June 4, 2015, https://www.youtube.com/watch?v=1E3rTJi-54k&t=53s.

21. TriniiityMedia, "Nipsey Hussle [On Stage Performance and Hussle Blog] LAX Tour," video, March 24, 2009, https://www.youtube.com/watch?v=x4bDmDKDI7s.

22. Uproxx, "Talib Kweli" video.

23. TriniiityMedia, "Nipsey Hussle" video.

24. Nipsey Hussle, "'HUSSLE IN THE HOUSE' DEBUTS ON 106 & PARK TONITE!!" WordPress page, March 5, 2009.

25. Nipsey Hussle, "Nipsey Hussle's Journey of Opening a Store in the Middle of His Hood in Crenshaw (Documentary)," video, posted by WorldStarHipHop, June 14, 2017, https://youtu.be/2FnFUCgo7x8.

26. Nipsey Hussle, "Nipsey Hussle's Journey" video.

27. Smacktube, "Nipsey Hussle Exclusive," video, June 16, 2009, https://www.youtube .com/watch?v=5LcuXvzofTQ&feature=emb_title.

28. Ibid.

29. Ibid.

30. Ibid.

31. Ibid.

32. Ibid.

33. Ibid.

34. Jake Paine, "Ving Rhames Talks New Film, Nipsey Hussle, Gillie Da Kid," *HipHopDX*, June 18, 2009.

35. Rap Status, "Nipsey Hussle: Rap Status #BANGLIFEBIDNESS," video, December 5, 2014, https://youtu.be/h7KFsv-1sJA.

36. Paine, "Ving Rhames Talks New Film."

37. Rap Status, "Nipsey Hussle: Rap Status" video.

38. Ibid.

39. Johnny Shipes, interviewed by the author, 2019.

40. Lawrence Burney, "What Freedom Feels Like to Nipsey Hussle," *The Fader*, Winter 2019.

41. Homegrown Radio, "'Laps over Raps' with Nipsey Hussle," video, December 4, 2017, https://www.youtube.com/watch?v=Os_nxZtfcdg.

42. Al Ries and Laura Ries, *The 22 Immutable Laws of Branding* (New York: Harper Business, 2002).

43. Alex Alonso, 2009, "Nipsey Hussle Interview: Born in the 80s, Raised in the 60s," video, 2009, StreetGangs.com, https://www.youtube.com/watch?v =QYTYC9vBSZg&feature=emb_title.

44. Smoke DZA, interviewed by the author, 2020.

45. BandwagonMobile, "Nipsey Hussle Interview w/ BandwagonMobile.com," video, September 2, 2009, https://www.youtube.com/watch?v=DvZSLSGl6iE.

46. Steve Lobel interview.

47. CinematicTV, "CinematicTV Ep. 7: Nipsey Hu$$le, Wiz Khalifa and Curren$y Studio Session," video, January 26, 2010, https://www.youtube.com/watch?v=w__W9Y_pwtA.

48. HardKnockTV, "Remembering Nipsey Hussle," video, March 31, 2020, https://www .youtube.com/watch?v=Ip_rDpe68jw.

49. CinematicTV, "CinematicTV Ep. 7" video.

50. Vanessa Satten, interviewed by the author, 2019.

51. Wiz Khalifa, "Wiz Khalifa Remembers Meeting Nipsey Hussle as a 2010 *XXL* Freshman/How Long Will They Mourn Me?" *XXL*, August 15, 2019.

52. Vanessa Satten interview.

53. Ibid.

CHAPTER 7: MARATHON MODE

1. SnoopDoggTV, "Nipsey Hu$$le Takes a Victory Lap | GGN with Snoop Dogg," video, July 2, 2013, https://www.youtube.com/watch?v=rui-Bjshh78.

2. Ibid.

3. *Saturday Night Live*, "We Are the World 3" (season 35, 2010), https://www.youtube.com/watch?v=nUkBhVnFxdM.

4. VIP Access, "Nipsey Hussle's Road Manager Jorge Peniche Details How He Got in the Game," video, March 3, 2018, https://www.youtube.com/watch?v=T3Nk8QFMTwY.

5. BandwagonMobile, "Nipsey Hussle Interview w/ BandwagonMobile.com," video, September 2, 2009, https://www.youtube.com/watch?v=DvZSLSGl6iE.

6. Ibid.

7. ItsTheReal, "#291: Jorge Peniche" in "A Waste of Time," video, December 18, 2019, https://www.youtube.com/watch?v=2hvemJyK5Uw.

8. ShiftaMedia, "Nipsey Hussle 'I LOVE ERI TOUR' London Journal Pt1," video, October 19, 2010, https://www.youtube.com/watch?v=wxwx9nkqxPs.

9. A Team Media, "Nipsey Interview London England," video, 2010, https://vimeo.com/17013772.

10. Diesel, "Diesel Presents: Only the Brave Part 2 (Success and Style)," video, April 16, 2011, https://www.youtube.com/watch?v=6lh0izU-0Oo.

11. J Stone, interviewed by the author, 2019.

12. Pacman da Gunman, interviewed by the author, 2019.

13. Ibid.

14. Ibid.

15. Ibid.

16. ItsTheReal, "#291: Jorge Peniche" video.

17. @contacthigh, Instagram post, March 31, 2020.

18. ItsTheReal, "#291: Jorge Peniche" video.

19. Nico Blitz, "Chuck Dizzle Interview: Founder of Homegrown Radio, On-Air at Real 92.3 | The Lunch Table," video, April 1, 2019, https://www.youtube.com/watch?v=VwB_i5Uddgc.

20. Blitz, "Chuck Dizzle Interview" video.

21. Curren$y, interviewed by the author, 2020.

22. Curren$y interview.

23. Curren$y interview.

24. Mikey Fresh, "New Mixtape: Nipsey Hussle 'The Marathon,'" *Vibe*, December 21, 2010.

25. Ralo Stylez, interviewed by the author, 2020.

26. VIP Access, "Nipsey Hussle's Road Manager" video.

27. TuneIn Music, "Nipsey Hussle on Spirituality, Telling the Truth, Creating Timeless Music," February 5, 2018, video posted to YouTube by VladTV July 16, 2019, https://www.youtube.com/watch?v=rET1h_Y5ONc.

28. Ralo Stylez interview.

29. Nipsey Hussle, *The Marathon* liner notes, 2010.

30. Paul Arnold, "Nipsey Hussle Talks Leaving Epic, Dissing 'Detox,'" *HipHopDX*, December 21, 2010.

31. Toshitaka Kondo, "Nipsey Talks African Roots, Snoop Dogg Co-sign, and Rappers Reppin' Gangs," *Complex*, March 31, 2010.

32. BigBoyTV, "Nipsey Hussle Full Interview | BigBoyTV," video, June 4, 2015, https://www.youtube.com/watch?v=1E3rTJi-54k&t=53s.

33. Nipsey Hussle, interviewed by the author, 2018.

34. Nipsey Hussle, "Nipsey Hussle's Journey of Opening a Store in the Middle of His Hood in Crenshaw (Documentary)," video, posted by WorldStarHipHop, June 14, 2017, https://youtu.be/2FnFUCgo7x8.

35. Nipsey Hussle, "Nipsey Hussle's Journey" video.

36. Diesel, "Diesel Presents: Only the Brave" video.

37. Ralo Stylez interview.

38. LAPD website, "Officer-Involved Shooting Occurs as Police Disband Gang Fight NR11127rf," March 18, 2011.

39. Nipsey Hussle, "Nipsey Hussle's Journey" video.

40. Nipsey Hussle (@nipseyHussle), "I ain't dead . . . I ain't in jail . . . and I ain't on tha run. TMC," Twitter post, 2011.

41. Nipsey Hussle, "Nipsey Hussle's Journey" video.

42. DJ Vlad, "Big U on His History with Nipsey Hussle (Full Interview)," video, April 9, 2019, https://www.youtube.com/watch?v=OyPi-_73HcU.

43. Enlightened Prophets, "Deeper Than Rap: The Assassination of Nipsey Hussle Vol 1," video, March 30, 2020, https://www.youtube.com/watch?v=uhnLNhSFcEU.

44. Enlightened Prophets, "Deeper Than Rap" video.

45. Ibid.

46. Rollin' 60s, interview with the author, 2019.

47. Dexter Browne, interviewed by the author, 2019.

48. TK7Live, "Lebron James Locker Room Game 6 NBA Finals 2011," video, July 12, 2011, https://www.youtube.com/watch?v=hJ5kqZnRh6E.

49. Tim Daniels, "LeBron James Talks Mental Health, Says He Lost 'Love for the Game' in 2011," Bleacher Report, December 10, 2019.

50. Starting Blocks, "LeBron James: 'Not 2, not 3, not 4, not 5, not 6, not 7' titles . . . None?" video, 2019, Cleveland.com, https://www.miaminewtimes.com/news/lebron-james-was-right-to-predict-he-could-win-seven-titles-in-miami-10416100.

51. TK7Live, "Lebron James Locker Room" video.

52. Rap Radar, "Rap Radar: Nipsey Hussle," video, January 1, 2018, https://www.youtube.com/watch?v=GVCNREwfGuM.

53. Rap Radar, "Rap Radar: Nipsey Hussle," video.

54. HardKnockTV, "Remembering Nipsey Hussle," video, March 31, 2020, https://www.youtube.com/watch?v=Ip_rDpe68jw.

55. Andrew Chery, "Nipsey Hussle and Drew Chery at Palms Las Vegas (Clinton Sparks' Awesome Weekend)," video, July 20, 2011, https://www.youtube.com/watch?v=qVRqyDNYzkc&list=RDq3jVGrUXp6s&index=2.

56. Larry Brown, "Floyd Mayweather Jr. and 50 Cent Allegedly in Middle of Vegas Strip Club Throwdown," Larry Brown Sports (website), August 5, 2011.

57. Cam Capone, "Cobby Supreme on Crazy Tour Story with Nipsey Hussle from 'Grinding All My Life' Video (Part 2)," video, March 6, 2020, https://www.youtube.com/watch?v=ZF5TN6ry-gE.

58. Cam Capone, "Cobby Supreme on Crazy Tour Story" video.

59. The Breakfast Club, "Nipsey Hussle Talks New Album, West Side Protocols," video, February 21, 2018, https://www.youtube.com/watch?v=fGCMcu2iei0.

60. WTNH news report via Lipstick Alley website, thread begun August 4, 2011, https://www.lipstickalley.com/threads/club-ignorant-negros-fuckery.321448/

61. Ralo Stylez interview.

62. SkeeTV, "Nipsey Hussle—TMC (The Marathon Continues) Mixtape Trailer," video, October 29, 2011, https://www.youtube.com/watch?v=TB1r3ql6ERI.

63. Ibid.

64. Fly Times Daily, "Nipsey Hussle Interview 11/6/2011 (FlyTimesDaily.com Exclusive)," video, November 8, 2011, https://www.youtube.com/watch?v=m3zxNQRl46g.

65. Stanford News, "'You've got to find what you love,' Jobs says," Stanford.edu, June 12, 2005. "Steve Jobs' 2005 Commencement Address," video, https://www.youtube.com/watch?v=UF8uR6Z6KLc&feature=emb_title.

66. DJ V.I.P., interviewed by the author, 2019.

67. 1500 or Nothin', Instagram live discussion, March 21, 2020.

68. Fly Times Daily, "Nipsey Hussle Interview" video.

CHAPTER 8: PROUD 2 PAY

1. All Def, "Nipsey Hussle Live in Concert #Proud2Pay | All Def," video, May 26, 2014, https://www.youtube.com/watch?v=yaKQ0WPU5so.

2. Sway's Universe, "Nipsey Hussle Freestyles, Speaks on *Crenshaw* Profit, and Reveals Single off *Victory Lap*," video, October 25, 2013, https://www.youtube.com/watch?v=W1vHVOYm4wQ.

3. Nipsey Hussle, interviewed by the author, 2018.

4. All Def, "Nipsey Hussle Live in Concert" video.

5. Ibid.

6. Nipsey Hussle interview.

7. Ralo Stylez, interviewed by the author, 2020.

8. Ibid.

9. Hot 97, "Lauren London Opens Up on Her Relationship with Lil Wayne and Kissing Terrence J," video, March 28, 2013, https://www.youtube.com/watch?v=Gi2HKW16Hfc.

10. HipHopUncensored, "ATL Actor Jackie Long Tells Never Heard Before Story about Nipsey Hussle and Lauren London!" video, April 23, 2020, https://www.youtube.com/watch?v=63bVvwhNC-Y.

11. Ibid.

12. Ibid.

13. DJ Clue, "Nipsey Hussle Stop By to Talk #victorylap," video, February 27, 2018, https://www.youtube.com/watch?v=w1MURVsCyQk.

14. DJ Clue, "Nipsey Hussle Stop By" video.

15. Gerrick D. Kennedy, "The Light of Los Angeles: The Legacy of Nipsey Hussle," *GQ*, December 2, 2019.

16. Kennedy, "The Light of Los Angeles."

17. BigBoyTV, "Lauren London and Cassie Ventura on New Movie *The Perfect Match* (Full Interview) | BigBoyTV," video, March 8, 2016, https://www.youtube.com/watch?v=IfbNZ2g00HM.

18. BigBoyTV, "Nipsey Hussle on Cardi B Winning a Grammy, Album w/ Meek Mill and a Lot More!" video, March 11, 2019, https://youtu.be/3WCWPkceOc0.

19. Sean Thompson, "Watch: Nipsey Hussle Discusses the N-Word on *Larry King Now*," *Vibe*, June 3, 2014.

20. Ibid.

21. DJ Drama, "Nipsey Hussle Rates His Music '*Victory Lap* Is My Best Album," video, 2018, https://www.youtube.com/watch?v=_yzY0-2agLw.

22. Sahra Sulaiman, "Nipsey Hussle Understood Cities Better than You. Why Didn't You Know Who He Was?" *Streetsblog LA*, August 15, 2019.

23. 4TheHype, "Nipsey Hussle Arrested During a Store Raid in Los Angeles," video, January 29, 2017, https://www.youtube.com/watch?v=Woq7nsA3Fko.

24. KABC 7, "Rapper Nipsey Hussle Released on Bail," August 30, 2014.

25. Nipsey Hussle (@nipseyHussle), Instagram post, December 14, 2017.

26. BET, "BET Hip Hop Awards Nominees and Winners," 2014.

27. DJ Drama, "Gangsta Grillz Radio—Nipsey Hussle Interview," video, September 28, 2014, https://www.youtube.com/watch?v=_yzY0-2agLw.

28. Ibid.

29. Ibid.

30. Ibid.

31. BH, interviewed by the author, 2019.

32. Angel Diaz, "Interview: Nipsey Hussle Talks Selling *Mailbox Money* for $1,000, the Power of the Internet, and Squeezing Out the Middle Man," *Complex*, December 22, 2014.

33. Rob Boffard, "Meet Nipsey Hussle, the Rapper Who Wants You to Pay $1,000 for His Album," *The Guardian*, January 20, 2015.

34. BigBoyTV, "Nipsey Hussle Full Interview | BigBoyTV," video, June 4, 2015, https://www.youtube.com/watch?v=1E3rTJi-54k&t=53s.

35. Diaz, "Interview: Nipsey Hussle."

36. Ibid.

37. BigBoyTV, "Nipsey Hussle Full Interview."

38. TMZ, "Remembering Nipsey Hussle," March 31, 2019.

39. Ibid.

CHAPTER 9: FDT

1. Danielle Bacher, "YG Speaks Out for First Time Since Being Shot: 'I'm Hard to Kill,'" *Billboard*, June 24, 2015.

2. Ryan Reed, "YG Shot Three Times at Los Angeles Recording Studio," *Rolling Stone*, June 12, 2015.

3. Reed, "YG Shot Three Times."

4. Bacher, "YG Speaks Out."

5. Dennis Green, "Trump Tower Is Actually Not as Tall as Donald Trump Says," Business Insider (website), October 25, 2016.

6. Adam Gabbart, "Golden Escalator Ride: The Surreal Day Trump Kicked Off His Bid for President," *The Guardian* (UK), June 14, 2019.

7. ABC News, "Watch Donald Trump's Grand Escalator Entrance to His Presidential Announcement," June 16, 2015.

8. Ben Sisario, "Can Neil Young Block Donald Trump from Using His Songs? It's Complicated," *New York Times*, August 12, 2020.

9. Gabbart, "Golden Escalator Ride."

10. Ibid.

11. Cynthia Littleton, "Donald Trump, Univision Settle $500 Million Miss Universe Lawsuit," *Variety*, February 11, 2016.

12. German Lopez, "Donald Trump's Long History of Racism, from the 1970s to 2020," *Vox*, July 26, 2015.

13. Jan Ransom, "Trump Will Not Apologize for Calling for Death Penalty over Central Park Five," *New York Times*, June 18, 2019.

14. Lopez, "Donald Trump's Long History."

15. CNN, "Trump Officially Joins Reform Party," October 25, 1999.

16. Australian Broadcasting Corporation (ABC), "Timeline: The Black Lives Matter Movement," updated February 22, 2018.

17. Australian Broadcasting Corporation, "Timeline."

18. Eric Levenson and Tina Burnside, "Dylann Roof Believed He'd Be Freed from Prison after a Race War, Attorneys Say in Appeal," CNN, January 29, 2020.

19. BET, "Kendrick Lamar—BET Awards 2015," video, posted to YouTube by Kassan Williams, August 17, 2015, https://www.youtube.com/watch?v=ILjHYMAGDuI.

20. Chris Riotta, "Kendrick Lamar's 'DAMN' Slammed by Fox News' Geraldo Rivera, as per Usual," *Newsweek*, April 14, 2017.

21. Justin Carissimo, "Kendrick Lamar Asks Fox News: 'How Can You Take a Song about Hope and Turn It into Hatred?'," *Independent* (UK), February 4, 2016.

22. Nipsey Hussle, interviewed by the author, 2018.

23. BigBoyTV, "YG on BigBoyTV," video, July 16, 2015, https://www.youtube.com/watch?v=pu9CfjVl4Os.

24. Ibid.

25. BigBoyTV, "Nipsey Hussle on Cardi B Winning a Grammy, Album w/ Meek Mill and a Lot More!" video, March 11, 2019, https://youtu.be/3WCWPkceOc0.

26. Randall Roberts, "YG Was Ready to Drop a New Album. Then His Friend Nipsey Hussle Died," *Los Angeles Times*, May 23, 2019.

27. Valdosta State University, "Integration: Our Early Days," Valdosta.edu website.

28. Glenn Kessler, "Donald Trump and David Duke: For the Record," *Washington Post*, March 1, 2016.

29. Lindsey Conway, "Valdosta State University Students Kicked Out of Trump Rally the Day before Georgia Primary," *Red and Black* (redandblack.com), March 1, 2016.

30. Conway, "Valdosta State University Students."

31. BBC, "Donald Trump Rally Police 'Ejected' Black Students," March 1, 2016.

32. Maya Rhodan, "Accounts Differ on Why Black Students Ejected from Trump Rally," *Time*, March 1, 2016.

33. Lynn Hatter, "Valdosta PD Responds to Claims Protestors Kicked Out of Trump Rally Based on Race," WFSU.org, March 2, 2016.

34. Noah Gray, Sara Murray, and Jim Acosta, "Valdosta State University Black Students Escorted Out of Trump Rally," CNN, March 1, 2016.

35. *Guardian* (UK), "Trump: 'I Am the Least Racist Person There Is Anywhere in the World,'" July 30, 2019.

36. Jen Hayden, "Nobody Is More Happy about Donald Trump's Presidential Campaign Announcement than Jon Stewart," Daily Kos (website), June 17, 2015.

37. Deena Zaru, "Donald Trump's Fall from Hip-Hop Grace: From Rap Icon to Public Enemy No. 1," ABC News, October 11, 2018.

38. G-Unit Radio, "President Trump on G-Unit Radio w/ 50 Cent, DJ Whoo Kid and Tony Yayo (2005)," video, May 26, 2017, https://www.youtube.com/watch?v=MjVW0iw3uLY.

39. ComedyCentral, "*The Nightly Show*—Mac Miller Unloads on Donald Trump," video, March 10, 2016, https://www.youtube.com/watch?v=Zm8ISls_TBA.

40. Maxwell Tani, "How Rapper Pusha T Got Passionate about Politics and Became a Fighter for Hillary Clinton," Business Insider (website), August 18, 2016.

41. Deena Zaru, "Russell Simmons Endorses Hillary Clinton, Says Bernie Sanders 'Insensitive' to Black Voters," CNN, March 4, 2016, updated August 16, 2017.

42. Elise Viebeck, "Why Rapper Killer Mike Endorsed Bernie Sanders," *Washington Post*, November 24, 2015.

43. Katie Rogers, "Kanye West Visits Donald Trump," *New York Times*, December 13, 2016.

44. Catherine Lucey, "Kanye West, in 'MAGA' Hat, Delivers Surreal Oval Office Show," Associated Press, October 11, 2018.

45. Adelle Platon, "Azealia Banks Endorses Donald Trump: 'He's 'Evil Like America Is Evil,'" *Billboard*, February 1, 2016.

46. Vanessa Cárdenas and Sophia Kerby, "Battleground States Go Blue Thanks to Multiracial Coalitions that Supported President Obama," Center for American Progress, November 15, 2012.

47. Adelle Platon, "YG and Nipsey Hussle Discuss Their Anti–Donald Trump Track 'FDT' and Why 'Trump Is Not the Answer,'" *Billboard*, April 1, 2016.

48. Platon, "YG and Nipsey Hussle."

49. BigBoyTV, "YG on BigBoyTV" video.

50. HardKnockTV, "Nipsey Hussle (First Interview Ever???) from the Hard Knock TV Vaults," video, September 25, 2006, https://youtu.be/GwG4A_OrTmk.

51. Hot 97 *Ebro in the Morning*, "Nipsey Hussle Breaks Down Gang Culture and How Africa Changed Him," video, February 22, 2018, https://www.youtube.com/watch?v=XEgPVv_9_W8&feature=emb_title.

52. Platon, "YG and Nipsey Hussle."

53. BigBoyTV, "YG on BigBoyTV" video.

54. DJ Swish, artist page on Genius, 2016, https://genius.com/artists/Dj-swish.

55. BigBoyTV, "YG on BigBoyTV" video.

56. Hot 97 *Ebro in the Morning*, "Nipsey Hussle Breaks Down."

57. Christopher Weingarten, "YG Talks Summer Protest Anthem 'FDT (F–k Donald Trump),'" *Rolling Stone*, September 1, 2016.

58. BigBoyTV, "YG on BigBoyTV" video.

59. August Brown, "America's at a Breaking Point. So Is YG," *Los Angeles Times*, September 24, 2020.

60. Adelle Platon, "YG Says Secret Service Reached Out Following Release of Anti-Trump Song, May Try to Take His Album Off Shelves," *Billboard*, April 27, 2016.

61. Cle Sloan, *Bastards of the Party*, documentary, HBO, 2005.

62. Nessa, Hot 97, "Nipsey Hussle on *Victory Lap*, FDT + Kanye, and Ownership," video, June 8, 2018, https://www.youtube.com/watch?v=Ec0uxHUDG8A.

63. Gil Kaufman, "YG and Nipsey Hussle's 'FDT (F— Donald Trump)' Video Shoot Shut Down by Cops," *Billboard*, April 4, 2016.

64. TMZ, "YG and Nipsey Hussle: Cops Shut Down 'F*** Trump' Video Shoot," April 4, 2016.

65. Kaufman, "YG and Nipsey Hussle's 'FDT.'"

66. BigBoyTV, "YG on BigBoyTV" video.

67. Platon, "YG Says Secret Service."

68. Steve Hochman, "Compton Rappers Versus the Letter of the Law: FBI Claims Song by N.W.A. Advocates Violence on Police," *Los Angeles Times*, October 5, 1989.

69. BigBoyTV, "YG on BigBoyTV" video.

70. Roberts, "YG Was Ready to Drop."

71. Nessa, Hot 97, "Nipsey Hussle" video.

72. BigBoyTV, "YG on BigBoyTV" video.

73. Steve "Steve-O" Carless, artist page on Genius, 2020, https://genius.com/artists/Steve-steve-o-carless.

74. Dee Lockett, "YG on His Donald Trump Song Getting Censored," Vulture, June 16, 2016.

75. Weingarten, "YG Talks Summer Protest Anthem."

76. BigBoyTV, "YG on BigBoyTV" video.

77. Ibid.

78. Weingarten, "YG Talks Summer Protest Anthem."

79. Lockett, "YG on His Donald Trump Song."

80. Colin Stutz, "YG Invites Fans Onstage to Destroy a Donald Trump Piñata," *Billboard*, September 19, 2016.

81. Weingarten, "YG Talks Summer Protest Anthem."

82. Nessa, Hot 97, "Nipsey Hussle" video.

83. Ibid.

84. August Brown, "'I Feel Good for Speaking Up': YG on His 2016 Protest Anthem that Goes After Donald Trump," *Los Angeles Times*, November 17, 2016.

85. Brown, "'I Feel Good for Speaking Up.'"

86. Nessa, Hot 97, "Nipsey Hussle" video.

87. Nipsey Hussle (@nipseyhussle), Instagram post, January 30, 2017.

88. Associated Press, "Radio Stations in Several States Hacked with Anti-Trump Rap," January 31, 2017.

89. Sam Moore, "Hackers Break into US Radio Broadcast Signals and Force Stations to Play YG's 'Fuck Donald Trump,'" *NME*, February 2, 2017.

90. Kairi Coe, "Watch O.T. Genasis Crip Walk to YG's 'FDT' Outside of the White House," *XXL*, August 1, 2017.

91. Kairi Coe, "Nipsey Hussle Calls Out Radio Stations for Not Playing 'FDT,'" *XXL*, September 6, 2017.

92. BET, "Nipsey Hussle Says All Radio Stations Should Be Playing 'FDT,'" September 7, 2017.

93. Jon Blistein, "Watch Eminem Demolish Donald Trump in BET Awards Freestyle," *Rolling Stone*, October 11, 2017.

94. David Catanese, "The 10 Closest States in the 2016 Election," *US News & World Report*, November 14, 2016.

95. Louis Nelson, "Kanye West: 'If I Voted, I Would Have Voted for Trump,'" Politico, November 18, 2016.

96. Nessa, Hot 97, "Nipsey Hussle" video.

97. Ibid.

98. Peter Baker, "Alice Marie Johnson Is Granted Clemency by Trump after Push by Kim Kardashian West," *New York Times*, June 6, 2018.

99. Nessa, Hot 97, "Nipsey Hussle" video.

100. Nessa, Hot 97, "Nipsey Hussle" video.

101. Keith Nelson Jr., "Tour Tales: DJ VIP Has Seen Nipsey Hussle's Evolution and the Rapper's Famous Slap Altercation," Revolt (website), January 8, 2019.

102. Nessa, Hot 97, "Nipsey Hussle" video.

103. Ibid.

CHAPTER 10: VICTORY LAP

1. Sway's Universe, "Nipsey Hussle Freestyles, Speaks on *Crenshaw* Profit, and Reveals Single off *Victory Lap*," video, October 25, 2013, https://www.youtube.com/watch?v=W1vHVOYm4wQ.

2. 1500 or Nothin', Instagram live discussion, March 31, 2020.

3. Sway's Universe, "Nipsey Hussle Freestyles."

4. SnoopDoggTV, "Nipsey Hu$$le Takes a Victory Lap | GGN with Snoop Dogg," video, July 2, 2013, https://www.youtube.com/watch?v=rui-Bjshh78.

5. Ibid.

6. XXL interview by Carl Chery, "XXL Pop the Trunk—Nipsey Hussle," video, September 6, 2009, https://www.youtube.com/watch?v=BI9IwbtOkrA.

7. Rap Status, "Nipsey Hussle: Rap Status #BANGLIFEBIDNESS," video, December 5, 2009, https://youtu.be/h7KFsv-1sJA.

8. Rap Status, "Nipsey Hussle: Rap Status" video.

9. Brian "Z" Zisook, "My Lost Interview with Nipsey Hussle from 2009," DJ Booth (website), April 1, 2019.

10. Rap Status, "Nipsey Hussle: Rap Status" video.

11. Melina Abdullah, interviewed by the author, 2019.

12. Nipsey Hussle, interviewed by the author, 2018.

13. Sway's Universe, "Nipsey Hussle Talks *Victory Lap*, Kendrick Lamar, Diddy, Cee-Lo and More | Sway's Universe," video, February 22, 2018, https://www.youtube.com/watch?v=8-RuYj7mlAo.

14. Nipsey Hussle interview.

15. Ibid.

16. Gail Mitchell, "Nipsey Hussle's All Money In Label Teams with Atlantic Records for His *Victory Lap* Debut: Exclusive," *Billboard*, November 27, 2017.

17. Angel Diaz, "Interview: Nipsey Hussle Explains His Dispute with Complex, Going Indie, and *Crenshaw*," *Complex*, October 15, 2013.

18. Diaz, "Interview: Nipsey Hussle."

19. The Breakfast Club, "Nipsey Hussle Talks New Album, West Side Protocols," video, February 21, 2018, https://www.youtube.com/watch?v=fGCMcu2iei0.

20. Ralo Stylez, interviewed by the author, 2020.

21. Ibid.

22. TuneIn Music, "Nipsey Hussle on Spirituality, Telling the Truth, Creating Timeless Music," February 5, 2018, video posted to YouTube by VladTV July 16, 2019, https://www.youtube.com/watch?v=rET1h_Y5ONc.

23. BigBoyTV, "Nipsey Hussle Full Interview | BigBoyTV," video, June 4, 2015, https://www.youtube.com/watch?v=1E3rTJi-54k&t=53s.

24. GaryVee, "Are You Happy? | DailyVee 278," video, August 7, 2017, https://www.youtube.com/watch?v=iC3txVRbP9E.

25. Adelle Platon, "Side Hustle: Nipsey Hussle," Tidal, video, September 10, 2018, https://www.youtube.com/watch?v=OR09Hq8JEyo.

26. 1500 or Nothin', Instagram live discussion, March 31, 2020.

27. 247HH, "Nipsey Hussle—Evicted from Studio and Recording 'Young Niggas' and 'Real Big' (247HH Exclusive)," video, April 23, 2018, https://www.youtube.com/watch?v=-Mn0i8jEaTs.

28. Ibid.

29. 1500 or Nothin', Instagram live discussion, March 31, 2020.

30. Rap Radar, "Rap Radar: Nipsey Hussle 2," video, December 25, 2018, https://www.youtube.com/watch?v=5NndeiDIctM.

31. Rap Radar, "Rap Radar: Nipsey Hussle 2" video.

32. TuneIn Music, "Nipsey Hussle on Spirituality" video.

33. Rap Radar, "Rap Radar: Nipsey Hussle 2" video.

34. Ibid.

35. Ibid.

36. TuneIn Music, "Nipsey Hussle on Spirituality" video.

37. Nation of Billions, "Nipsey Hussle Arrival Live in London, Performs Tracks from *Crenshaw* and *Mailbox Money*," video, February 26, 2015, https://www.youtube.com/watch?v=LBqcZYCTPBI.

38. 247HH, "Nipsey Hussle—Evicted" video.

39. GaryVee, "Are You Happy?" video.

40. 247HH, "Nipsey Hussle—Evicted" video.

41. Ibid.

42. GaryVee, "Are You Happy?" video.

43. Box Office Mojo, *Straight Outta Compton*, https://www.boxofficemojo.com/release/rl1292718081/.

44. BigBoyTV, "Nipsey Hussle Full Interview" video.

45. Ibid.

46. Ibid.

47. Rachel Bloom, "The Sexy Getting Ready Song (Explicit)—*Crazy Ex-Girlfriend*," video from TV show, posted October 5, 2015, https://www.youtube.com/watch?v=ky-BYK-f154.

48. Michael O'Connell, "*Crazy Ex-Girlfriend* Creators Remember Filming Rap Number with Nipsey Hussle: 'He Was Just Game,'" *Hollywood Reporter*, April 9, 2019.

49. Rachel Bloom, "The Sexy Getting Ready Song" video.

50. Mark Anthony Green, "California Love with Nipsey Hussle and Lauren London," *GQ*, February 21, 2019.

51. DJ Drama, "Nipsey Hussle Rates His Music '*Victory Lap* Is My Best Album,'" video, 2018, https://www.youtube.com/watch?v=wdc3CPu1psw.

52. Sway's Universe, "Nipsey Hussle Talks *Victory Lap*" video.

53. The Breakfast Club, "Nipsey Hussle Talks New Album" video.

54. Ibid.

55. DJ Drama, "Nipsey Hussle Rates His Music" video.

56. Ibid.

57. Ibid.

58. Ibid.

59. Ibid.

60. HardBody Kiotti, "Nipsey Hussle Talks Gang Culture, Investing in Yourself and Making Sacrifices," video, March 11, 2018, https://www.youtube.com/watch?v=CgYJb6xgNMg.

61. HardBody Kiotti, "Nipsey Hussle Talks Gang Culture" video.

62. Rap Radar, "Rap Radar: Nipsey Hussle 2" video.

63. 1500 or Nothin', Instagram live discussion.

64. *The Cruz Show* Power106, "Nipsey Hussle's New Store Will Blow Your Mind!" video, June 14, 2017, https://www.youtube.com/watch?v=RIFaDTMKTcY&lc=Ugj5JrGqb7_BVHgCoAEC

65. Zane Lowe, "Nipsey Hussle on 'Dedication' and working with Kendrick Lamar," posted to iTunes, February 13, 2018, https://itunes.apple.com/us/post/sa.5d2d2ef0-10d9-11e8-ae82-88b135a87e74.

66. Rap Radar, "Rap Radar: Nipsey Hussle 2" video.

67. Hot 97 *Ebro in the Morning*, "Nipsey Hussle Breaks Down Gang Culture and How Africa Changed Him," video, February 22, 2018, https://www.youtube.com/watch?v=XEgPVv_9_W8&feature=emb_title.

68. Hot 97 *Ebro in the Morning*, "Nipsey Hussle Breaks Down" video.

69. Donna-Claire Chesman, "How TDE's Albums Have Quietly Upheld the Concept of HiiiPower," Okayplayer, 2018.

70. Zane Lowe, "Nipsey Hussle on 'Dedication.'"

71. Rap Radar, "Rap Radar: Nipsey Hussle 2" video.

72. Ibid.

73. 1500 or Nothin', Instagram live discussion.

74. HardKnockTV, "Remembering Nipsey Hussle," video, March 31, 2020, https://www.youtube.com/watch?v=Ip_rDpe68jw.

75. 1500 or Nothin', Instagram live discussion.

76. Steve Duck, "Nipsey Hussle on What Comes after the Victory Lap," *Complex Australia*, February 26, 2019.

77. Rodney Carmichael, "Nipsey Hussle Tells the Epic Stories Behind *Victory Lap*, Track by Track," NPR, February 16, 2018.

78. 1500 or Nothin', Instagram live discussion.

79. Ibid.

80. Carmichael, "Nipsey Hussle Tells."

81. DJYoungSammTV, "Mr.Lee—The Making of Nipsey Hussle 'Blue Laces 2,'" video, February 20, 2018, https://www.youtube.com/watch?v=mBudydK4njU.

82. WhoSampled (app), "Nipsey Hussle 'Blue Laces 2,'" 2018, https://www.whosampled

.com/sample/559190/Nipsey-Hussle-Blue-Laces-2-Willie-Hutch-Hospital-Prelude
-of-Love-Theme/.

83. Carmichael, "Nipsey Hussle Tells."

84. Letty Set Go, "Nipsey Hussle on Standing Up to Critics, Business Tips, Dr. Sebi Doc + More!" video, March 12, 2019, https://www.youtube.com/watch?v=50i_dqQfqTY.

85. Tariq Nasheed, "Tariq Nasheed and Nipsey Hussle Chop It Up on IZM Radio," video, March 7, 2018, https://youtu.be/8yiWph2_G74.

86. *Sway in the Morning*, "Dr. Sebi's Family," video, July 25, 2019, https://www.youtube.com/watch?v=qTrc5_-052c&list=PLwo5MhGfuZN6cjUJASY3X_eEes-fwUCSE&index=549.

87. Carmichael, "Nipsey Hussle Tells."

88. HardKnockTV, "Remembering Nipsey Hussle" video.

89. Carmichael, "Nipsey Hussle Tells."

90. Genius, "Nipsey Hussle 'Racks in the Middle' Official Lyrics and Meaning," video, March 14, 2019, https://www.youtube.com/watch?v=pBV4tAAHiIM.

91. Homegrown Radio, "'Laps over Raps' with Nipsey Hussle," video, December 4, 2017, https://www.youtube.com/watch?v=Os_nxZtfcdg.

92. *The Cruz Show* Power106, "Nipsey Hussle: *Victory Lap* Release, 'I Gambled My Career,' Signing to Atlantic, and More!" video, November 30, 2017, https://www.youtube.com/watch?v=dwO44bxu5s4&t=32s.

93. Homegrown Radio, "'Laps Over Raps'" video.

94. *The Cruz Show* Power106, "Nipsey Hussle: *Victory Lap*" video.

95. TheMovieReport, "13th Documentary Film Discussion with Ava DuVernay and Nipsey Hussle," video, February 5, 2017, https://www.youtube.com/watch?v=N1Z-z_6GeU8.

96. TheMovieReport, "13th Documentary Film Discussion" video.

97. Jonny Shipes, interviewed by the author, 2019.

98. Ibid.

99. Ted Simmons, "Nipsey Hussle Shows How Much Money He's Making as an Independent Artist," *XXL*, December 15, 2016.

100. Eric Diep, "Karen Civil and Steve 'Steve-O' Carless Talk Consulting Firm Marathon Agency's 'Out-of-the-Box' Strategy," *Billboard*, October 28, 2016.

101. ItsTheReal, "#291: Jorge Peniche" in "A Waste of Time," video, December 18, 2019, https://www.youtube.com/watch?v=2hvemJyK5Uw.

102. Karen Civil, interviewed by the author, 2019.

103. Ibid.

104. James Queally, "LAPD Gang Injunctions Deny Targets Due Process, ACLU Lawsuit Says," *Los Angeles Times*, October 24, 2016.

105. XXL, "Nipsey Hussle Outtakes from 2016 Interview," video, April 1, 2019, https://www.youtube.com/watch?v=D_WmzAFXCvY.

106. XXL, "Nipsey Hussle Outtakes" video.

107. Genius, "Nipsey Hussle 'Racks in the Middle.'"

108. Nico Blitz, "Chuck Dizzle Interview: Founder of Homegrown Radio, On-Air at Real 92.3 | The Lunch Table," video, April 1, 2019, https://www.youtube.com/watch?v=VwB_i5Uddgc.

109. Blitz, "Chuck Dizzle Interview" video.

110. HardBody Kiotti, "Nipsey Hussle Talks Gang Culture" video.

111. Ibid.

112. *New York Times*, "California Proposition 64—Legalize Marijuana—Results: Approved," August 1, 2017.

113. Nipsey Hussle interview.

114. Rap Radar, "Rap Radar: Nipsey Hussle 2" video.

115. Ralo Stylez interview.

116. Nipsey Hussle interview.

117. YellowPlace (website), "Top Flight Collective," 2016, https://yellow.place/en/top-flight -members-only-los-angeles-usa.

118. Rollin' 60s member #1, interviewed by the author, 2020.

119. Nicole Santa Cruz, "The Homicide Report: Stephen Donelson, 30," *Los Angeles Times*, October 12, 2017.

120. Rollin' 60s member #2, interviewed by the author, 2020.

121. Masonite333, "A Million Hits/Crenshaw/RIP FATTS/Western/Homicides 2017," in "A Million Hits," video, October 13, 2017, https://www.youtube.com/watch?v =7XrYj9ikaNY.

122. Masonite333, "A Million Hits" video.

123. @nipseyhussle, Oct 16, 2017, https://www.instagram.com/p/BaUlDcphqLQ/?igshid =1f9qkytwgyn6t.

124. Santa Cruz, "The Homicide Report."

125. Genius, "Nipsey Hussle 'Racks in the Middle.'"

126. Rap Radar, "Rap Radar: Nipsey Hussle," video, January 1, 2018, https://www.youtube .com/watch?v=GVCNREwfGuM.

127. Gerrick D. Kennedy, "The Light of Los Angeles: The Legacy of Nipsey Hussle," *GQ*, December 2, 2019.

128. *The Cruz Show* Power106, "Nipsey Hussle: *Victory Lap*" video.

129. The Breakfast Club, "Nipsey Hussle Talks New Album" video.

130. DJ Drama, "Nipsey Hussle Rates His Music" video.

131. Tidal, "10 Rings: Nipsey Hussle Documentary," 2018, https://tidal.com/browse/video /82083394.

132. Tidal, "10 Rings."

133. Ibid.

134. DJ V.I.P., interviewed by the author, 2019.

135. Keith Nelson Jr., "Tour Tales: DJ VIP Has Seen Nipsey Hussle's Evolution and the Rapper's Famous Slap Altercation," Revolt (website), January 8, 2019.

136. DJ V.I.P. interview.

137. Aaron Dodson, "Nipsey Hussle's Puma Partnership Was Strong and Authentic," The Undefeated (website), April 3, 2019.

138. Peter A. Berry, "Nipsey Hussle and Lauren London Break Up," *XXL*, November 22, 2017.

139. Monya Fleming, "Days after Nipsey Hussle and Lauren London Announce Their Split, His First Baby Mama Has Tea to Spill," Dallas Black (website), December 2, 2017.

140. Nipsey Hussle, "For the Culture," *Players' Tribune*, October 25, 2018.

141. Alex Zidel, "Tekashi 6ix9ine Survived NBA All-Star Weekend and Continues to Taunt Rival Gang Members," HotNewHipHop (website), February 19, 2018.

142. Joe Coscarelli, "6ix9ine's Testimony: The Rapper's Rise, Beefs and Crash, in His Own

Words," *New York Times*, September 20, 2019, https://pitchfork.com/news/tekashi
-6ix9ine-testifies-at-trial-about-alleged-kidnapping-brutal-assault-by-former-fellow
-gang-members/.

143. Peter A. Berry, "Nipsey Hussle Says Artists Like 6ix9ine Are Bound to Self- Destruct," *XXL*, March 11, 2019.

144. DJ Drama, "Nipsey Hussle Rates His Music" video.

145. Ibid.

146. HardBody Kiotti, "Nipsey Hussle Talks Gang Culture" video.

147. TMZ, "Remembering Nipsey Hussle," March 31, 2019.

148. DJ Drama, "Nipsey Hussle Rates His Music" video.

149. Receptionist at Pepe's Towing, interviewed by the author, 2020.

150. DJ Drama, "Nipsey Hussle Rates His Music" video.

151. TMZ, "Remembering Nipsey Hussle."

152. Ralo Stylez interview.

153. David Gross, interviewed by the author, 2019.

154. Nipsey Hussle interview.

155. Sonaiya Kelley, "With a New STEM Center and a Revolutionary Marketing Strategy, Nipsey Hussle Is Music's Biggest Disruptor," *Los Angeles Times*, March 16, 2018.

156. CBS Los Angeles, "Co-Working Space, Business Incubator Opens in Crenshaw District," February 15, 2018.

157. Ashley Lyle, "Nipsey Hussle Brings Out Puff Daddy, YG, Marsha Ambrosius and More for *Victory Lap* Release Show," *Billboard*, February 16, 2018.

158. Sway's Universe, "Nipsey Hussle Talks *Victory Lap*" video.

159. Cindy Chang and Angel Jennings, "Nipsey Hussle Died in the Marathon Clothing Lot. Will His Legacy Die There Too?" *Los Angeles Times*, August 13, 2019.

160. Rap Radar, "Rap Radar: Nipsey Hussle 2" video.

161. Hot 97 *Ebro in the Morning*, "Nipsey Hussle Breaks Down" video.

CHAPTER 11: EXIT STRATEGY

1. Homegrown Radio, "'Laps over Raps' with Nipsey Hussle," video, December 4, 2017, https://www.youtube.com/watch?v=Os_nxZtfcdg.

2. TheMovieReport, "13th Documentary Film Discussion with Ava DuVernay and Nipsey Hussle," video, February 5, 2017, https://www.youtube.com/watch?v=N1Z-z_6 GeU8.

3. Ibid.

4. Ibid.

5. Ibid.

6. Ibid.

7. Ibid.

8. Ibid.

9. Ibid.

10. Ibid.

11. Ibid.

12. Ibid.

13. Marqueece Harris-Dawson, interviewed by the author, 2019.

14. Complex News, "Nipsey Hussle's Business Partner David Gross on Ownership and

Buying Back Blocks," video, October 25, 2019, https://www.youtube.com/watch?v
=K-czYvcShW4.

15. Complex News, "Nipsey Hussle's Business Partner" video.

16. Lawrence Burney, "What Freedom Feels Like to Nipsey Hussle," *The Fader*, Winter 2019.

17. Tariq Nasheed, "Tariq Nasheed and Nipsey Hussle Chop It Up on IZM Radio," video, March 7, 2018, https://youtu.be/8yiWph2_G74.

18. HardKnockTV, "Remembering Nipsey Hussle," video, March 31, 2020, https://www
.youtube.com/watch?v=Ip_rDpe68jw.

19. HardKnockTV, "Remembering Nipsey Hussle" video.

20. Luc Belaire, "Nipsey Hussle | Self Made Tastes Better, Episode 7," March 1, 2018, https://www.youtube.com/watch?v=dJ6pgb4O6wA.

21. Rap Radar, "Rap Radar: Nipsey Hussle 2," video, December 25, 2018, https://www
.youtube.com/watch?v=5NndeiDIctM.

22. Vanessa Satten, XXL, "Nipsey Hussle Talks LA Hip-Hop," in "Boost Mobile/Where You At?" video, December 9, 2016, https://www.youtube.com/watch?v=tqiaKf
H8J-s.

23. Ralo Stylez, interviewed by the author, 2020.

24. Rap Radar, "Rap Radar: Nipsey Hussle 2" video.

25. DJ Drama, "Nipsey Hussle Rates His Music '*Victory Lap* Is My Best Album,'" video, 2018, https://www.youtube.com/watch?v=wdc3CPu1psw.

26. Steve Duck, "Nipsey Hussle on What Comes after the Victory Lap," *Complex Australia*, February 26, 2019.

27. DJ Drama, "Nipsey Hussle Rates His Music" video.

28. Ibid.

29. The Breakfast Club, "Nipsey Hussle Talks New Album, West Side Protocols," video, February 21, 2018, https://www.youtube.com/watch?v=fGCMcu2iei0.

30. The Breakfast Club, "Nipsey Hussle Talks New Album" video.

31. BigBoyTV, "Nipsey Hussle on Cardi B Winning a Grammy, Album w/ Meek Mill and a Lot More!" video, March 11, 2019, https://youtu.be/3WCWPkceOc0.

32. Cindy Chang and Angel Jennings, "Nipsey Hussle Died in the Marathon Clothing Lot. Will His Legacy Die There Too?" *Los Angeles Times*, August 13, 2019.

33. Rap Radar, "Rap Radar: Nipsey Hussle 2" video.

34. Chang and Jennings, "Nipsey Hussle Died."

35. Slauson Girl (website), "The Assassination of Nipsey Hussle Becomes More Clear," August 13, 2019.

36. Nipsey Hussle (@nipseyHussle), "Sam bailed Himself Out #Putsomerespectonhisname," 2018 post.

37. BH, interviewed by the author, 2019.

38. Ibid.

39. Ibid.

CHAPTER 12: TOO BIG TO FAIL

1. *GQ*, "Nipsey Hussle Gets Asked 30 Questions by Lauren London | GQ," video, March 28, 2019, https://www.youtube.com/watch?v=ou8FAbw4YTs&list=RDB
0Ybkw4Kq_Q&index=12.

2. Ibid.

3. Vanessa Satten, interviewed by the author, 2019.

4. *GQ*, "Nipsey Hussle Gets Asked" video.

5. Mark Anthony Green, "California Love with Nipsey Hussle and Lauren London," *GQ*, February 21, 2019.

6. Ben Bernanke, "Causes of the Recent Financial and Economic Crisis," Federal Reserve website, September 2, 2010.

7. Homegrown Radio, "'Laps over Raps' with Nipsey Hussle," video, December 4, 2017, https://www.youtube.com/watch?v=Os_nxZtfcdg.

8. Stephen Curry, "Nipsey Hussle and Stephen Curry on Hip Hop and Fatherhood," video, July 10, 2018, https://www.youtube.com/watch?v=x7i52u__Nro.

9. Curry, "Nipsey Hussle" video.

10. TheTexas Plug, "Full Interview | Firebugg Talks Nipsey Hussle, LA Peace Treaty," video, April 2, 2020, https://www.youtube.com/watch?v=6l1S4W_LoD0.

11. Killa Twan, interviewed by the author, 2020.

12. TheTexas Plug, "Full Interview | Firebugg" video.

13. @firebugg68, "Nips Last Tweet ? 💀 ???, but Satan at work early, woke up to this. Black People Beware These Agent Provacatuers are amongst us, slithering and whispering to the hearts of the week and misguided. 'Burdens of Betrayals weigh heavy on my my Soul', 'Where Life Has No Value Death Has It's Price' that's tatted in my flesh. Malcolm X in my flesh when you see what Me And Nip Seen at the Table. You Move Different, Think Different, Stop PLAYING WITH YA Life, Pray More Tweet Less. Rebuke you Satan??" posted 2019.

14. TheTexas Plug, "Full Interview | Firebugg" video.

15. Ibid.

16. Killa Twan interview.

17. BETNetworks, "Lauren London, Angelique Smith and Family Accept Nipsey Hussle's Humanitarian Award | BET Awards 2019," video, June 24, 2019, https://www.youtube.com/watch?v=ehlvFTSLk-4.

18. *Los Angeles Times*, "Read Volume 1 of the Nipsey Hussle Murder Case Grand Jury Transcripts," June 28, 2019.

19. DJ V.I.P., interviewed by the author, 2019.

20. ItsTheReal, "#291: Jorge Peniche" in "A Waste of Time," video, December 18, 2019, https://www.youtube.com/watch?v=2hvemJyK5Uw.

21. Nipsey Hussle (@nipseyHussle), Instagram post, March 30, 2019.

22. Jeff Eisenberg, "Inside the Special Bond between Late Rapper Nipsey Hussle and Texas Tech's Brandone Francis," Yahoo Sports (website), April 5, 2019.

23. Janelle Griffith, "Nipsey Hussle's Planned Meeting with LA Police on Gang Violence to Go On in His Honor," NBC News, April 1. 2019.

24. Marqueece Harris-Dawson, interviewed by the author, 2019.

25. Destination Crenshaw (website), 2019, https://destinationcrenshaw.la/.

26. Marqueece Harris-Dawson interview.

27. DJ E Dubble, "The Meaning behind the Last Tweet from Nipsey Hussle," April 8, 2019, https://jamn945.iheart.com/featured/dj-e-dubble/content/2019-04-08-the-meaning-behind-the-last-tweet-from-nipsey-hussle/.

28. DJ V.I.P. interview.

29. DJ Vlad, "Kerry Lathan on Getting Shot Next to Nipsey Hussle, Police Violating Parole and Facing Life," video, April 15, 2019, https://www.youtube.com/watch?v=m2li0VU5Uzs.

30. *Los Angeles Times*, "Volume 1 / Nipsey Hussle transcripts."

31. Ibid.

32. Cuzzy Capone, interviewed by the author, 2019.

33. Baby Gooch, interviewed by the author, 2019.

34. Jessica McBride, "Eric Holder a.k.a. Shitty Cuz: 5 Fast Facts You Need to Know," Heavy (website), April 2, 2019.

35. *Los Angeles Times*, "Volume 1 / Nipsey Hussle transcripts."

36. Ibid.

37. Ibid.

38. Ibid.

39. Ibid.

40. Ibid.

41. Ibid.

42. Ibid.

43. Ralo Stylez, interviewed by the author, 2020.

44. LA Show, "Nipsey Hussle Series: Joshua Baerga AKA #KidFlashy Interview Pt.1," video, September 26, 2019, https://www.youtube.com/watch?v=1lCIsNU3yA0.

45. LA Show, "Nipsey Hussle Series: Joshua Baerga" video.

46. *Los Angeles Times*, "Volume 1 / Nipsey Hussle transcripts."

47. Ibid.

48. DJ Vlad, "Kerry Lathan" video.

49. *Los Angeles Times*, "Volume 1 / Nipsey Hussle transcripts."

50. Ibid.

51. Ibid.

52. ExtraTV, "Nipsey Hussle's Friend Recalls Rapper's Last Moments," video, April 12, 2019, https://www.youtube.com/watch?v=87fzCeOt_78&list=RDYrhA171D0as&index=12.

53. Rimpau (@ami_rimpau), Instagram post, April 4, 2019.

54. *Los Angeles Times*, "Volume 1 / Nipsey Hussle transcripts."

55. Ibid.

56. Ibid.

57. Ibid.

58. Ibid.

59. Ibid.

60. Ibid.

61. Ibid.

62. Ibid.

63. Ibid.

64. CBS Los Angeles, "CBS2 Exclusive | Nipsey Hussle's Grandmother Prays for Accused Killer, Thanks Community for Support," video, April 5, 2019, https://www.youtube.com/watch?v=0ztwRcjAw-E.

65. Angel Jennings, "Must Reads: Nipsey Hussle's Brother Found Him Dying. These Are His Final Moments," *Los Angeles Times*, April 4, 2019.

66. ExtraTV, "Nipsey Hussle's Friend" video.

67. Jennings, "Nipsey Hussle's Brother."

68. Ibid.

69. Killa Twan interview.

70. Ibid.

71. BETNetworks, "Humanitarian Award" video.

72. Ibid.

73. BigBoyTV, "YG on BigBoyTV," video, July 16, 2015, https://www.youtube.com/watch?v=pu9CfjVl4Os.

CHAPTER 13: HIGHER AND HIGHER

1. Gerrick D. Kennedy, "The Light of Los Angeles: The Legacy of Nipsey Hussle," *GQ*, December 2, 2019.

2. Fox11 Los Angeles, "Kameron Carter at Nipsey Memorial," video, April 11, 2019, https://www.foxla.com/video/553079.

3. Ibid.

4. Ibid.

5. Killa Twan, interviewed by the author, 2019.

6. Wack 100 and Blueface No Jumper interview, https://www.youtube.com/watch?v=FVXG5B6g_bs.

7. J Roc punches Nipsey Hussle, https://ambrosiaforheads.com/2019/12/nipsey-hussle-bodyguard-wack-100-video/.

8. Smoke DZA, interviewed by the author, 2019.

9. Samiel Asghedom, "Nipsey Hussle's Brother Gives a Tribute," video, posted to YouTube by Ta&Co, April 11, 2019, https://youtu.be/RoDIOkTysKk.

10. Samiel Asghedom, "Nipsey Hussle's Brother" video.

11. Ibid.

12. 11Alive, "Stevie Wonder Pays Tribute to Nipsey Hussle," video, April 11, 2019, https://www.youtube.com/watch?v=bVTX2SXc6j0.

13. Alejandra Reyes-Velarde, et al., "Nipsey Hussle Procession: Thousands Line Streets of LA for Final Farewell to Slain Rapper," *Los Angeles Times*, April 11, 2019.

14. Spotlight Digital Magazine, "Cowboy Breaks His Silence," video, May 20, 2019, https://www.youtube.com/watch?v=xCPxTPSlvMs.

15. Steve Lobel, interviewed by the author, 2019.

16. Hoodsta Rob, interviewed by the author, 2019.

17. Dexter Browne, interviewed by the author, 2019.

18. ItsTheReal, "#291: Jorge Peniche" in "A Waste of Time," video, December 18, 2019, https://www.youtube.com/watch?v=2hvemJyK5Uw.

19. Ibid.

20. Ibid.

21. Ralo Stylez, interviewed by the author, 2020.

22. Ibid.

23. Alex Alonso, "Alex Alonso Speaks on Eric Holder Trial," video, July 19, 2020, https://www.youtube.com/watch?v=hsQumkjhDSQ.

24. Cuzzy Capone, interviewed by the author, 2019.

25. Killa Twan, interviewed by the author, 2019.

26. Ralo Stylez interview.

27. Ibid.

28. Samantha Smith, Instagram live, October 12, 2020.

29. Jonny Shipes, interviewed by the author, 2019.

30. Rodney Carmichael, "Nipsey Hussle Tells the Epic Stories Behind *Victory Lap*, Track by Track," NPR, February 16, 2018.

31. Ralo Stylez interview.

32. Genius, "Nipsey Hussle 'Racks in the Middle' Official Lyrics and Meaning," video, March 14, 2019, https://www.youtube.com/watch?v=pBV4tAAHiIM.

33. Rick Ross, interviewed by the author, 2019.

34. Master P, interviewed by the author, 2019.

35. Master P interview.

36. Meek Mill explains how Nipsey taught him to stay away from the hood, https://ambrosiaforheads.com/2019/12/meek-mill-nipsey-hussle-hood-video/.

37. Cuzzy Capone interview.

38. Dave East Memorial Service, "50 Cent Finally Breaks Silence on Nipsey Hussle Death," video, April 4, 2019, https://www.youtube.com/watch?v=QdEvXUXMiNs.

39. Nas, Instagram post, April 1, 2019.

40. Samiel Asghedom, interviewed by the author, 2019.

41. Samantha Smith, interviewed by the author, 2019.

42. Iddris Sandu, interviewed by the author, 2019.

43. Gary Vee Speaks on Nipsey Hussle, https://www.youtube.com/watch?v=nvfAj8z8IL0.

44. Samantha Smith interview.

45. David Gross, interviewed by the author, 2019.

46. Our Opportunity, "Dave Gross and Van Lathan in Conversation, Chapter 2," video, February 12, 2020, https://www.youtube.com/watch?v=k6ht2wOUxJo.

47. Ibid.

48. *Inside Edition*, https://www.youtube.com/watch?v=qASuGxe1E1U.

49. Dawit Asghedom, "Nipsey Hussle's Father Gives a Tribute," video, April 11, 2019, need URL.

50. Samiel Asghedom interview.

51. Nipsey Hussle, interview with the author, 2018.

52. Iddris Sandu interview.

53. Rachel George, "Nipsey Hussle Brings YG Out for Hometown Halftime Performance," *Billboard*, March 12, 2018.

54. LAPD officer, interviewed by the author, November 25, 2019.

55. BigBoyTV, "Nipsey Hussle on Cardi B Winning a Grammy, Album w/ Meek Mill and a Lot More!" video, March 11, 2019, https://youtu.be/3WCWPkceOc0.

56. Samiel Asghedom Statement Regarding Nipsey Hussle Tower, August 5, 2019, https://catimes.brightspotcdn.com/59/30/2d40aa914951bddd74d4f54a1603/samiel-asghedoms-statement.pdf.

57. CBS Los Angeles, "CBS2 Exclusive | Nipsey Hussle's Grandmother Prays for Accused Killer, Thanks Community for Support," video, April 5, 2019, https://www.youtube.com/watch?v=0ztwRcjAw-E.

58. Slauson Bruce, interviewed by the author, 2019.

59. Nipsey Hussle, "Nipsey Hussle 'The Midas Touch' with Slauson Bruce," video, February 1, 2018, https://www.youtube.com/watch?v=8Ak7peG-Xxo.

60. Samiel Asghedom, "Nipsey Hussle's Brother" video.

61. Slauson Bruce interview.

62. Claudia Rosenbaum, "Nipsey Hussle Estate Sues the Crips LLC for Trademark Infringement," *Billboard*, October 13, 2020.

63. Angel Diaz, "Interview: Nipsey Hussle Explains His Dispute with Complex, Going Indie, and *Crenshaw*," *Complex*, October 15, 2013.

64. *Final Call*, "Spreading Light, Love and Honoring Nipsey Hussle," April 9, 2019.

65. Global News, "Nipsey Hussle Funeral: Louis Farrakhan Full Eulogy," video, April, 2019, https://www.youtube.com/watch?v=fsCKPwOyyh8.

66. Stephen Marley, interviewed by B Reshma, 2019.

67. Reverend Abdullah, interviewed by the author, 2019.

68. Ibid.

INDEX

ABOUT THE AUTHOR

Rob Kenner is one of the most prolific and influential voices in hip-hop publishing. A founding editor of *Vibe*, Kenner joined the start-up team of Quincy Jones's groundbreaking hip-hop monthly in 1992. During a nineteen-year run at *Vibe*, he edited and wrote cover and feature stories on iconic cultural figures, ranging from Tupac Shakur to Barack Obama, as well as writing the acclaimed column "Boomshots." Kenner's writing has appeared in *Complex, Genius, Mass Appeal, Pigeons & Planes, Ego Trip, Poetry* magazine, the *New York Times,* and *Billboard.* He has also produced and directed documentary shorts on the likes of De La Soul, Nas, and Post Malone. As an editor at Vibe Books, Kenner worked on the *New York Times* bestseller *Tupac Shakur* and contributed to *The Vibe History of Hip Hop.* He went on to coauthor *VX: 10 Years of Vibe Photography* and produced the book *Unbelievable,* a biography of The Notorious B.I.G. by Cheo Hodari Coker.

Follow Rob Kenner on Instagram and Twitter @RobertJKenner